The History of Belle Meade

The History of

Belle Meade

Mansion, Plantation,
and Stud

By Ridley Wills II

VANDERBILT UNIVERSITY PRESS • 1991

Copyright © 1991 by Ridley Wills II
Published in 1991 by Vanderbilt University Press
Printed in the United States
First paperback edition 1993
Fourth printing 2008

Library of Congress Cataloging-in-Publication Data

Wills, Ridley, 1934–
    The history of Belle Meade : mansion, plantation, and stud /
    by Ridley Wills II.
        p.   cm.
    Includes bibliographical references and index.
    ISBN 0-8265-1244-5 (cl.)
    ISBN 0-8265-1245-3 (pbk.)
        1. Bell Meade Plantation (Tenn.)—History.   I. Title
    F444.B43W54   1991   91-30353
    976.8'55—dc20   CIP

Contents

Preface   ix

1   Dunham's Station   1
2   From Middletown to McSpadden's Bend   13
3   Stones River Years   26
4   John Harding: Land and Spirit   36
5   A New Role   43
6   Alpha to Omega   55
7   A Spacious and Elegant Home   65
8   Life in the Fifties   75
9   War Arrives   83
10   Imprisonment   96
11   The Long Ordeal   109
12   Surrender, Loss, and Endurance   123
13   The Old Order Changes   132
14   The Hardings and the Jacksons   148
15   Home of the Racehorse   163
16   Family and Friends   181
17   Palmy Days   196
18   New South, Old South   214
19   Tennessee Day   225
20   Cracks in the Foundation   235
21   The Last Hurrah   252
22   End of an Era   274

Epilogue   287
Abbreviations   299
Notes   301
Bibliography   343
Index   361

Illustrations

(The following list cites illustrations as they appear in the text.)

Genealogies of the Harding and Jackson families   xiv-xv
John Harding's cabin   7
Servants' quarters   7
John Harding   12
Susannah Harding   12
William Giles Harding, student years   18
Col. Alden C. Partridge   18
American Literary, Scientific and Military Academy   18
William Giles Harding, ca. 1846   29
Mary Selena McNairy Harding   29
Elizabeth McGavock Harding   47
Priam   60
Gamma   60
Epsilon   60
Belle Meade Mansion, showing open breezeway   73
View in the Deer Park   73
Ft. Mackinac   101
Tennessee State Capitol, ca. 1863   101
William Giles Harding, ca. 1865   114
Elizabeth McGavock Harding, 1850s   114
Selene Harding, ca. 1866   118
Mary Elizabeth Harding, ca. 1866   118
Farm workers   135
Susanna Carter   137
Lizzie Hoover   137
William Giles Harding family, ca. 1867   137
Gen. William Hicks Jackson   155
Selene Harding Jackson   155
Howell E. Jackson   155
Mary Harding Jackson   155
Uncle Bob Green   172
Bonnie Scotland   178

Jack Malone   178
Bramble   178
Entrance Hall   188
Harding Light Artillery reunion   188
Picnic at Belle Meade   191
Assembled for a hunt   192
Enquirer   202
Luke Blackburn   202
Iroquois   202
President Cleveland and the deer   217
Selene and William Harding Jackson, 1880s   224
View of Belle Meade from the paddocks   240
Carriage house/stable   240
Belle Meade dining room   256
Judge Howell E. Jackson   259
Jackson Building   259
Annie D. Richardson Jackson   266
William Harding Jackson   266
Dispersal sale catalog   277
General Jackson and Gen. Fitzhugh Lee   277
Jacob McGavock Dickinson and William Howard Taft   291
1984 Nashville map showing the acreage of the 1884 Belle Meade
    Plantation   294

Preface

In 1927, Douglas Anderson, a well-known Sumner County, Tennessee, historian, wrote a three-part sketch of the "Belle Meade Farm and its Founders" for the *Nashville Banner*. He concluded part one by saying,

> It is apparent that some of the family connection would render a public service by preparing a comprehensive sketch for future use. As the years come and go, public interest in Belle Meade will increase and the story of its founding and growth ought to be available. The most important features of such a sketch would be the details showing how Belle Meade made itself out of itself. A feat of that sort cannot be accomplished now; nor will such a feat ever be possible again in this country.

When I read Mr. Anderson's article twenty-five years ago, the thought crossed my mind that I might write such a history. My grandmother, Elizabeth Jackson Buckner, was born at Belle Meade, the home of her grandfather, Gen. William Giles Harding. In the 1930s, she gave a large collection of Harding family letters, which her mother had found tied together with a pink ribbon in an attic trunk at Belle Meade, to the University of North Carolina's Southern Historical Collection. Throughout the 1960s and 1970s, I read, transcribed, and footnoted copies of those letters, which my grandmother had left to my mother. As it turned out, that was the first work on what would become this book.

The availability of the letters and a love for Belle Meade's history that I had acquired as a child from Harrison Vernon, a fine and gentle black man who worked for my parents, encouraged my continued interest in the project. Mr. Vernon, whom I always called Bud, grew up at Belle Meade. As a little boy, I listened to wonderful stories of his childhood there, how he herded cattle in Jocelyn Hollow, grappled for fish under the banks of Richland Creek, and saw the first automobile that came to Belle Meade. Over the years, the older members of my family, especially my mother, Ellen Buckner Wills, and my aunt, Mary Harding Ragland, have shared family stories with me that stirred both wonder and curiosity.

Their recollections form a valuable kind of history and are the foundation of my enthusiasm.

When I retired, I decided to write the story of the Hardings and the Jacksons: how pioneer John Harding began Tennessee's most famous and profitable plantation; and how his son, Gen. William Giles Harding, and his wife, Elizabeth McGavock Harding, built the mansion that stands today and saved it and the plantation from destruction during the Civil War; and how General Harding and his son-in-law, Gen. William Hicks Jackson, rebuilt the farm and brought recognition to Belle Meade as one of the world's greatest Thoroughbred studs.

Almost from the outset it was clear that the book would embrace more than the history of a family circle. The story of Belle Meade—of the Harding and Jackson families that called it home—necessarily involves the countless lives of neighbors and houseguests, soldiers and civilians, statesmen and common citizens, prewar slaves and postwar workers. The events at Belle Meade reflected the larger events of Southern history taking place simultaneously. In telling the smaller story of one family, their home, and their plantation way of life, this book also tells the larger story, placing planter, mansion, plantation, and stud in a cultural-historical context of which Belle Meade was a highly reflective part.

When John Harding, born during the American Revolution, came to Tennessee from Virginia in 1798, his family's move was part of the larger push westward from the early colonies into the Northwest Territory, Kentucky and Tennessee, and the deep South. The land he bought and cleared had seen, only a generation earlier, the unhindered traffic of buffalo and Indian. Establishing the community of industry and agriculture called a plantation on that land was part of the rapid development of the central South's commercial linkage with Natchez and New Orleans.

When John's son, William Giles Harding, assumed control of Belle Meade, its strength as a plantation grew, and so did its dependence on the economic, social, and political forces shaping the larger community. When war came to Belle Meade, it came with a destructive force poorly imagined by the planter class, which stood to lose so much. But viewed from Belle Meade, the Civil War and its wake are as much a story of survival as of destruction and loss, of rebuilding as of ruin. When Harding and his son-in-law William Hicks Jackson reconstructed their plantation, the Belle Meade Stud proudly stood, for a time, as a model of the reconstructed South. And when decline came with the new century and the passing of the agrarian society, it came because Belle Meade and other Southern plantations were never in control of the economic forces that encouraged their flourishing, but dependent on them. Belle Meade passed from the scene because the world it so well reflected was pushed from the stage by a new order of historical, cultural, and economic reality.

Within the smaller story of Belle Meade and its owners are three separate contributing themes. First, there was the land, its purchase, its clearing, and its development into a complex agricultural organism—a plantation. That story evolves and refines into the history of the Belle Meade Stud, perhaps the most successful and certainly one of the two most famous horse nurseries in the Southern United States in the last third of the nineteenth century. Finally comes the story of the mansion, its origins as a relatively modest, Federal-style house John Harding built to replace his dogtrot-cabin residence. Each succeeding generation added to, renovated, or altered the house to suit and reflect its own tastes and times. And it is the house as remaining historical artifact that still offers direct contact with the history of Belle Meade and with the history in which Belle Meade played a part.

No one will be surprised to find that the view of a century's events by four generations of Hardings and Jacksons from the porch of Belle Meade Mansion is an oblique view—one informed or misinformed by feelings, ideas, triumphs, and mistakes peculiar to another time and another mode of living. What is instructive is that there are so many surprises among the commonplaces—how absolute the control of white over black, but at Belle Meade, at least, how mutual the respect; how influential the planter class in the agrarian setting, but how relatively powerless in the larger political or economic arenas; how intense the bitterness between institutionalized North and South, but how civil the day-to-day relations between enemies; how devastating the war to this region, but how adaptive the post-war Southern Americans, indeed, how quickly they were Americans once again. From pioneer settlement to grand plantation and stud, Belle Meade represents a history of agricultural and Thoroughbred-breeding success without equal in the mid-South. Its rise and eventual fall encompass a full century of Southern history and myth.

Because of the wonderful availability of materials at the Tennessee State Library and Archives and other local sources, much of the necessary research was done here in Nashville. Over a period of years, Ann

Alley, Ann Bomar, Ruth Clements, Robert DePriest, Marylin Hughes, Vincent J. McGrath, Chadra Moore, Dr. Wayne Moore, Genella Olker, Wayne Jervis, and others at the Library and Archives were especially helpful in facilitating my research there. Fellow historian Paul Clements, while conducting his own research at the State Library, enthusiastically shared with me many bits and pieces of Belle Meade history that he found in microfilm copies of old Nashville newspapers. I will always be grateful for the assistance I received from Margaret Lindsley Warden, a former chairman of the Belle Meade Mansion Board of Governors. Margaret gave me much of the material she has collected over many years on Belle Meade, including copies of the *Spirit of the Times* and *Turf, Field and Farm*. Donna Russell, Director of the Belle Meade Plantation, Nashville Chapter of the Association for the Preservation of Tennessee Antiquities, was generous in making available to me material and information from the archives at Belle Meade. Similarly, Mary Glenn Hearne, director of the Nashville Room of the Ben West Public Library, graciously helped whenever I called on her.

Others who helped include my friends Joan Chappell, Martha Jean Dorris, and Joan Nave; my aunt, Elizabeth Buckner Maddin of Nashville; my niece, Carter Wills McKenzie of Richmond, California; Jacqueline S. Painter, Norwich University archivist; and cousins Emmie Jackson McDonald of Nashville, Elizabeth Ragland Perkins of Charlottesville, and Evelyn Ragland Zink of Baltimore. I would also like to thank Charlotte Grider of Memphis. Early in my research efforts, three Harding descendants—Ann Curd Balch of Murfreesboro, Tennessee; Ellen Snell Coleman of Nashville; and Jeanne Harding Leach of Gadsden, Alabama—and Page family descendant Thomas E. Page of Lebanon, Tennessee, furnished me with much helpful information. I am also indebted to Dr. Bobby Lovett, James Radford, Ann Harwell Wells, and my sons, Ridley Wills III and Morgan J. Wills, all of whom read portions or all of my manuscript and made many useful suggestions. I am equally appreciative of Ann McGinley, who typed multiple versions of many chapters.

I wish to thank my editors, Kendall Cram, Dimples Kellog, John Poindexter, and Bard Young. They all afforded me their impressive editorial talents, which have greatly improved the quality of the finished product.

Finally, I am grateful to my wife, Irene. Over the long period required by this project, she has provided consistent encouragement and sound advice.

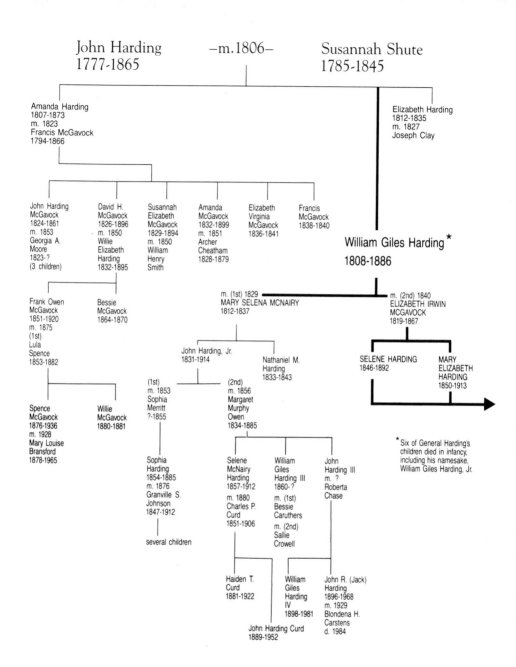

John Harding
1777-1865

— m.1806 —

Susannah Shute
1785-1845

Amanda Harding
1807-1873
m. 1823
Francis McGavock
1794-1866

Elizabeth Harding
1812-1835
m. 1827
Joseph Clay

John Harding
McGavock
1824-1861
m. 1853
Georgia A.
Moore
1823-?
(3 children)

David H.
McGavock
1826-1896
m. 1850
Willie
Elizabeth
Harding
1832-1895

Susannah
Elizabeth
McGavock
1829-1894
m. 1850
William
Henry
Smith

Amanda
McGavock
1832-1899
m. 1851
Archer
Cheatham
1828-1879

Elizabeth
Virginia
McGavock
1836-1841

Francis
McGavock
1838-1840

William Giles Harding *
1808-1886

Frank Owen
McGavock
1851-1920
m. 1875
(1st)
Lula
Spence
1853-1882

Bessie
McGavock
1864-1870

m. (1st) 1829
MARY SELENA MCNAIRY
1812-1837

m. (2nd) 1840
ELIZABETH IRWIN
MCGAVOCK
1819-1867

John Harding, Jr.
1831-1914

Nathaniel M.
Harding
1833-1843

SELENE HARDING
1846-1892

MARY
ELIZABETH
HARDING
1850-1913

Spence
McGavock
1876-1936
m. 1928
Mary Louise
Bransford
1878-1965

Willie
McGavock
1880-1881

(1st)
m. 1853
Sophia
Merritt
?-1855

(2nd)
m. 1856
Margaret
Murphy
Owen
1834-1885

* Six of General Harding's
children died in infancy,
including his namesake,
William Giles Harding, Jr.

Sophia
Harding
1854-1885
m. 1876
Granville S.
Johnson
1847-1912

Selene
McNairy
Harding
1857-1912
m. 1880
Charles P.
Curd
1851-1906

William
Giles
Harding III
1860-?
m. (1st)
Bessie
Caruthers
m. (2nd)
Sallie
Crowell

John
Harding III
m. ?
Roberta
Chase

several children

Haiden T.
Curd
1881-1922

William
Giles
Harding
IV
1898-1981

John R. (Jack)
Harding
1896-1968
m. 1929
Blondena H.
Carstens
d. 1984

John Harding Curd
1889-1952

The Harding Family

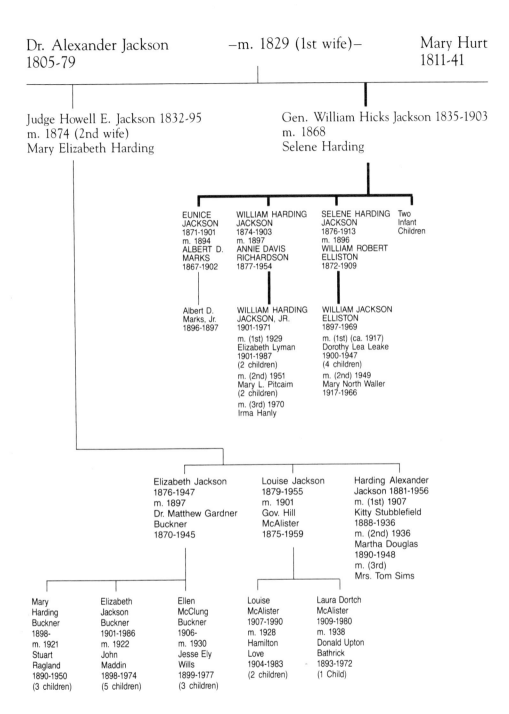

The Jackson Family

1/   Dunham's Station

L IKE SO MANY OTHER SETTLERS WHO CAME TO Tennessee in the late eighteenth century, John Harding, founder of the Belle Meade Plantation, was a native Virginian. He was born November 2, 1777, in Goochland County, where his family had lived since the county was created fifty years earlier. Three generations of Hardings before John were tobacco farmers and members of the Church of England. His father and grandfather, Giles and William Harding, each owned a few slaves, with whom they toiled on their land.[1]

John Harding's formal education was as limited as his father's means. His spelling would always be atrocious. When the English overran Goochland County in 1781, his father's property was plundered. Giles never recovered from that setback and, until 1798 when the family moved to Tennessee, his financial situation was bleak. Nine children, six of whom were younger than John, put additional strains on the family's finances and on their mother's health. John's mother, Amidia ("Amy"), died a middle-aged woman before 1800.[2]

Giles's financial difficulties, which seem to have precipitated his move to Tennessee, became public when the executors of the estate of Robert Baine, also of Goochland County, filed a claim against him for ninety-seven pounds, twelve shillings, and six pence. After paying off that debt in 1797, Giles decided to leave Virginia.[3] With the death of his mother, Sarah LaForce Harding, during the winter of 1796-97, he no longer had parental responsibilities because his father, William, had been dead for nearly thirty years. The very day that Sarah's will was probated, Giles sold his tract of 167 acres on Genito Creek. When he did so, he knew that whatever future he had lay in the West.[4]

When Giles Harding and his family moved to the West in the summer of 1798, they did not follow their many neighbors who went to

Kentucky or to the tiny settlements scattered along the north bank of the Ohio in the Northwest Territory. Instead, Harding decided to locate in Davidson County in the new state of Tennessee. He and his older sons had heard stories of the fertile soil in the Cumberland country. It was said that with no more effort than was required to produce three hogsheads of tobacco in Virginia or in the Carolinas, six hogsheads could be produced along the Cumberland River. It was also common knowledge to Virginians who had visited the west country across the mountains that a hundred bushels of Indian corn were frequently gathered from an acre of the best land there. Men like Giles and his son John, then twenty-one years old, were also attracted by the possibility that they could acquire more land in the Cumberland country than they could ever own in Virginia.

Most likely, the Hardings travelled via the Three Notched Road to the Shenandoah Valley, and from there down the Great Wagon Road to Fort Chiswell, Virginia, where James McGavock, Jr., ran a well-known tavern that catered to immigrants on their way to the Southwest.[5] At that point, settlers bound for Tennessee took the Island Road, considered the oldest and best wagon road in southwest Virginia. It led to the Long Island of the Holston and from there to Knoxville, the capital of Tennessee.[6] The distance from Knoxville to the fort at Southwest Point, the jumping-off place for the Cumberland country, was forty-five miles. From the fort, garrisoned by Federal troops under Col. Thomas Butler, Avery's Trace ran west over the Cumberland Plateau to Nashville, a frontier town of less than three hundred people. The village's unimposing log cabins, many with dirt and stick chimneys, were scattered over twenty-five or thirty acres of rocky land on a high limestone bluff overlooking the Cumberland River.[7] John Harding and his family were in a new country that looked toward Natchez and New Orleans rather than Richmond, Baltimore, and Philadelphia.

By 1798, most of the land close to Nashville was in the hands of men who knew its value: North Carolina Revolutionary War veterans, settlers, and speculators. Less expensive land was more easily obtained farther from town. The Harpeth River Valley, lying about twelve miles to the south and southwest of town, particularly appealed to Giles Harding and his brother Thomas, who came along to see if he wanted to bring his family to Tennessee. Only thinly populated, the valley was both beautiful and fertile, covered over by tall stands of wild cane growing throughout its bottomlands.

In November, Giles and Thomas selected land they wanted to live on. Giles bought, for three dollars an acre, a hundred-acre tract lying a short distance north of the confluence of the Little and Big Harpeth Rivers. Most of his purchase was bottomland ideal for farming. Only in the northern portion did the tract include what he termed "knob land." The same day and for the same price per acre, Thomas purchased a two-hundred-acre tract immediately to the west. It, too, included good farmland.[8]

During his earliest years in the Cumberland country, John Harding, who was unmarried, helped his father clear and farm his land on the Harpeth. Two days before Christmas in 1799, John's father and his uncle Thomas, who had brought his family to Tennessee from Virginia earlier that year, entered into an agreement to rent a tract of cleared land from John Gordon, a well-known Indian fighter and pioneer. The Harding brothers planned to raise crops on the land and share the profits. In a separate agreement, the older Hardings employed young John to "look over the whole lands" and serve as overseer.[9]

The property that Giles Harding bought to live on did not include a suitable dwelling for his family. Consequently, an early priority must have been to build a cabin large enough to accommodate himself and his unmarried children. His sons John and Giles, Jr., then twenty-one and fourteen years old respectively, and his son-in-law, Robert Page, were available to help. The house they built was the original part of the home now known as Devon Farm on State Highway 100 in Davidson County near the Williamson County line. It stands near the southeast corner of the land that Giles Harding bought in 1798.[10] Giles Harding deeded the farm, which he named Oak Hill, to John Harding in 1807 for ten dollars an acre. John bought the land with the understanding that, as soon as his youngest brother, David Morris, reached his twenty-first birthday, he would deed the property to David and another brother, Thomas. The fact that he paid his father triple what Giles paid for the land eight and a half years earlier was probably due to the construction of the house and outbuildings.[11]

John's father, Giles, remarried on July 31, 1804. His second wife was Martha Donnelly, daughter of Davidson County pioneers James and

Isabel Donnelly. During their few years together, Giles and Martha had two sons—James Donnelly and Peter Perkins—both a generation younger than Giles's children by his first marriage. The Donnellys lived nearby, and John Harding knew them well. He later served with Martha's father, James, and her brother, John, in Captain Mullen's Militia Company.[12]

John Harding married two years after his father's second marriage. John and Susannah ("Susan") Shute, a daughter of Philip and Elizabeth Waller Shute, married on August 6, 1806. Her parents, of German and English ancestry, were both born in New Jersey.[13] After the birth of their second child in March 1767, the Shutes and about 150 other pioneer families crossed the Alleghenies and settled in the Indian country watered by the Monongahela and Youghiogheny Rivers and their tributaries.[14] In an effort to dislodge the squatters, Pennsylvania passed an act stating that if they did not leave the Indians' land within thirty days they would suffer death "without benefit of clergy." In February 1768, Deputy Governor John Penn commissioned the Reverend John Steele, a Presbyterian minister, and three other men to visit the settlements to distribute the proclamation and warn the settlers to move out. Steele later reported to the governor that Phil Sute (Shute) was one of the settlers to whom he read the act at the Redstone Creek settlement. The inhabitants felt that there would be no Indian war and that the act was contrived by "gentlemen and merchants of Philadelphia" who wanted to take away the settlers' improvement rights when the land was purchased. Consequently, Phil Shute and most of the others refused to leave.[15]

After the English acquired Western Pennsylvania from the Indians the following November, Philip Shute legitimized his claim to the 263¼ acres he occupied by purchasing the tract, then known as Thorn Bottom.[16] He lived there near a community called Laurel Hill from about 1767 until shortly after his wife's death late in 1790. There, twelve of their fourteen children were born, including Susan, who was born on August 22, 1785.[17]

Leaving Pennsylvania in 1790 or 1791, Philip Shute took his children, who ranged in age from a few months to twenty-three years, to an even newer frontier—the Mero District of North Carolina (now in Middle Tennessee). They reached the Mero District by floating down the Ohio River and either poling up the Cumberland River or coming overland from the falls of the Ohio. In the Cumberland country, Shute rented land on Mansker's Creek in Sumner County for a little more than a year before moving to Davidson County, where he bought a 540-acre tract several miles southwest of Nashville on the road to Fletcher's Lick. There, in a wild country with few neighbors, the Shutes lived in a fort for protection against the Indians.[18]

Even before his marriage, John Harding was looking for a piece of land that he and Susan could call home. He purchased a well-watered 250-acre tract on the east side of Richland Creek, six miles from Nashville.[19] He had seen it countless times as he passed back and forth to town from his father's home on the Harpeth. The road along Richland Creek was an old buffalo trail known as the Natchez Road. The property was part of a 640-acre preemption grant made by the state of North Carolina to Daniel Dunham in 1786.[20]

Dunham had arrived in the Cumberland country in 1780 in the large party of settlers who came by river with Col. John Donelson. After exploring the wilderness that surrounded French Lick, Dunham concluded that the fertile creek valley six miles or so southwest of Fort Nashborough was an ideal spot to build a cabin for his family. There, possibly on the same knoll where the log cabin at Belle Meade stands today, Dunham built a station or small fort.[21]

Soon, Indians forced the Dunham family to seek the relative safety of Fort Nashborough. During one of the intervals between Indian raids, the Dunhams decided the time was right to return to their cabin on Richland Creek. Their timing was bad. In May 1788, Daniel Dunham was killed, scalped, and "chopped." Despite the harrowing loss of her husband, Mrs. Dunham, her children, and perhaps one or more slaves, continued to live there until March 6, 1792, when Indians burned her home.[22] Her son, Daniel A. Dunham, apparently rebuilt the station soon after it was burned. By that time, Indian traders, preachers, mail carriers, highwaymen, soldiers, and boisterous "Kaintuck" boatmen were using the Natchez Road. The boatmen walked or rode horses back up the trace from Natchez after dismantling and selling the rafts on which they floated their flour, tobacco, pork, hemp, and corn down the Mississippi.[23]

Scholars think Daniel A. Dunham built the east section of the cabin still standing at Belle Meade. The use of a half dovetail in log cabin construction was characteristically found in upper East Tennessee and North Carolina, the areas from which the Dunhams had come. "The large fireplace of limestone with the central keystone and radiating voussoirs was again in keeping with the characteristics of the region from which the Dunhams emigrated."[24] The deed to the land John Harding purchased from Daniel A. Dunham in February 1807 indicated that the tract included "Dunham's Old Station." The fact that the station was described in the deed as being old raises the possibility that the cabin standing on the property when Harding bought it was the original one. If this is true, the cabin survived the Indians' attempts to destroy it in 1792.[25]

Soon after John and Susannah Harding moved to Dunham's Station, John's younger brother, Giles, Jr., bought a hundred-acre tract between his father's place and John's land. It lay at the headwaters of Richland Creek on the Nashville side of the Harpeth Ridge. Giles, Jr., and his wife, Charlotte, became John and Susan's closest neighbors. They reared twelve children in a large brick house that stood on a knoll just north of a fine spring.[26]

John and Susan Harding had six children, three of whom—Amanda P., William Giles, and Elizabeth Virginia—lived to maturity. They were born on October 23, 1807, September 15, 1808, and April 5, 1812, respectively.[27] By the time of Elizabeth's birth, it seems almost certain that her father had more than doubled the size of their house by adding a second cabin, not quite square and one-and-a-half stories high. The two sections were connected by a dogtrot, also thought to have been built by Harding. The other significant feature of Harding's addition was the diamond notched corner timbering technique John probably learned in Virginia, where that method was prevalent. As was the case with the older cabin, the new one included a limestone fireplace and external chimney.[28]

For some years before the Hardings moved to the area, a public road had run from Nashville, by way of Cockrill's Spring and Dunham's Station, to a spring on the land Giles Harding bought in 1798. Before 1800, neighborhood men extended the road over the Harpeth Ridge to the mouth of Flat Creek and from there across the Big Harpeth to John Dillahunty's place.[29] The extension of the public road was a great convenience to Dillahunty. Traffic increased, other settlers moved in, and the Richland Creek area soon needed a church. By 1795 or 1796, Dillahunty had established on the east bank of the creek, near John Harding's north property line, the first church in Tennessee west of Nashville.[30]

DOGTROT CABIN enlarged by John Harding and birthplace of William Giles Harding. Photo by Jesse F. Foreman, collection of Belle Meade Plantation, Nashville Chapter of the Association for the Preservation of Tennessee Antiquities

SERVANTS' QUARTERS built before the Civil War and surviving into this century. Belle Meade collection

John and Susan Harding were constantly busy during the years they lived at "Dunham's Old Station." Harding, known for his "energy, industry and good habits," had land to clear; a cabin addition, outbuildings, and fences to build; and crops to grow, harvest, and haul to market.[31] The slaves who helped him turn his woods and fields into a working farm included Ben, whom he purchased in Richmond in 1806; Dicey, bought from his father; and Patrick, inherited when Giles Harding died in 1810.[32]

When death came, Giles Harding was nearing his sixty-first birthday, relatively old for someone who lived his last dozen years on the western frontier. He had not realized, in material terms, all he had dreamed as an immigrant to Tennessee in 1798. At his death, he did not even own any land, having deeded his farm to John three years earlier. His four slaves, his household furniture, horses, livestock, crops, and farm equipment were divided among his widow, Martha, his children, and his grandchildren.[33] No one got much. Nevertheless, he successfully reared a family of strong, independent sons and daughters. His sons, John, Giles, Jr., William, Thomas, and David Morris, all became successful farmers, known for their hospitality and fondness of field sports. They were considered men of "the strictest integrity, truth-tellers, and fair in their dealings, but firm in contending for their rights."[34]

After providing housing for his family and slaves, John built a blacksmith shop on the west bank of the creek, fifty yards or so upstream from his house. It would soon produce valuable farm implements and additional income. His slave Ben became his blacksmith. The shop, strategically located at a ford where the Natchez Road crossed the creek, was mentioned in the Davidson County Court Minutes for the January 1810 session. Later, in October 1814, troops under Gen. John Coffee stopped at Harding's shop to have their horses shod on their way to the Gulf Coast to aid Andrew Jackson in the War of 1812.[35]

John Harding did not fight the British. When Coffee's troops stopped at his blacksmith shop, Harding was approaching his thirty-seventh birthday. Several family members did fight, however. Harding's nephews, Giles Harding Page and Robert Thomas Page, Jr., sons of Robert and Sallie Harding Page, both enlisted in Captain Robert Evans's company of mounted gunmen.[36] John's younger brother Thomas also was in the army; in January 1881 his widow, Elizabeth W. Harding, received a pension because of his service.[37] Matthew Locke Johnston, Harding's brother-in-law, was a captain in the sixty-day mounted infantry volun-teers who were on the Natchez campaign. Johnston later fought at New Orleans.[38] Though John Harding was never a soldier, he, like all adult males, was also obligated to perform other public services, such as clearing and maintaining roads and serving on juries.[39]

The same Natchez Road that carried boatmen, mail carriers, and soldiers by John Harding's blacksmith shop also had traditionally been used by the Chickasaw, Choctaw, and Cherokee Indians. In particular, the Chickasaw made their trading visits to Nashville by that road, bringing with them furs, pelts, and other trading goods, and John Har-ding welcomed them. As soon as young William Giles was big enough to ride, Harding gave him a pony purchased from a band of Indians.[40]

During his childhood, William Giles played with his sisters, black children from the slave quarters, and a few other neighborhood children. He was usually barefoot; during warm weather in those days, children seldom wore shoes until they were twelve years old. He began, at an early age, working on the farm because his father believed that a valuable part of a boy's education was to learn how to work. When William Giles was growing up, amusements for boys included logrollings, house-raisings, and harvesting.[41] His most memorable childhood recollection, however, was that of sitting on the hill in front of his log cabin home watching General Andrew Jackson ride by, leading his troops back from the Battle of New Orleans. The impression Jackson made on the six-year-old boy's mind was "never effaced." Although Harding and Jackson later became close friends, Harding never saw "Old Hickory" without thinking of the day in 1815 when he "got a good look at the general" at the head of his victorious soldiers.[42]

In March of 1816, John's youngest full brother, David Morris, became twenty-one, which meant that it was time for John to honor the confi-dence placed in him by his father to turn over to Thomas and David Morris the hundred-acre family farm on the Big Harpeth. John did that on May 25.[43] He may have waited until then to surrender his title to the land because of the illness of his stepmother, Martha Harding, who presumably was still living there with Thomas, David, and their younger half brothers, James and Peter. Martha must have died late that spring; her administrator, Ellis Maddox, turned in to court an inventory of her estate at the July 1816 session.

During the years he lived at Dunham Station, John Harding significantly increased his real estate holdings. Between 1809 and 1813, he purchased in six separate transactions an additional 498 acres along Richland Creek, including all the remaining portion of Daniel Dunham's preemption grant. He bought none of the old Dunham lands directly from the Dunham family, however, because they had already passed into other hands. Harding's largest purchase was from John Shute, his brother-in-law. In the deed an "acre of land dedicated for the use of a meeting house" was carefully excluded. That was the meeting house for the Richland Creek Baptist Church.[44]

In 1817, after several years out of the real estate market, Harding bought a fifty-acre section of a three-hundred-acre tract that separated his lands from those of his brother Giles, Jr. Over the next decade, John acquired the five remaining sections. He also made a small but significant purchase in 1818 when he bought a tract along Richland Creek from James Maxwell. That parcel, coupled with an earlier purchase from Maxwell, was the land Harding's daughter, Amanda, would live on following her marriage, in 1823, to Francis ("Frank") McGavock.[45]

To maximize the return on his expanded plantation, Harding needed more help. Consequently, he bought Ned, a stout twenty-one- or twenty-two-year-old black man, in February 1818. Ned escaped a short time later, taking with him a handsome bay horse. When Ned ran away, according to a newspaper account, he was wearing a white hat, a dark brown coat with a large cape, heavily worn black velvet pantaloons, a homespun blue coat, and a calico spotted waistcoat. Harding offered a forty dollar reward for his return.[46] Four months earlier, Ben, Harding's blacksmith, escaped. Harding suspected that he would try to work his way back to Virginia, where Harding had bought him, or to Ohio.[47] The accounts of the two black men escaping from Harding within four months of each other give silent testimony to the harsh conditions under which slaves lived.

John Harding must have been incredibly tough, both mentally and physically, to accomplish what he did during his Dunham Station years. Of all the recorded instances of his life, none demonstrated those qualities more clearly than a story Memucan Hunt Howard told in an article he wrote in 1884 for the Tennessee Historical Society. Although Howard did not say when the story took place, it was likely sometime before steamboats ran flatboats off the Western rivers. Despite being far advanced in years when he recorded the story, Howard's manuscript was neatly and clearly written with "hardly an imperfect letter":

> Mr. John Harding told me that in descending the Mississippi River, on his way to Natchez with some negroes for sale he stopped at New Madrid, where there was a settlement of white people, and a negro man made his escape and he had to proceed without him; after having been awhile at Natchez he learned that the negro had been captured and was in confinement. He started alone in a skiff up the river, and paddled against the current to New Madrid, a distance of some six or seven hundred miles; got his man, started down the river, stopped at Judge Foy's [sic] opposite Memphis and sold him the negro; was paid for him in silver, which he poured into the bow of his skiff, and covered it over with earth on which he did his cooking, and proceeded to Natchez. At that time there was no settlement between New Madrid and Memphis, I believe, and none from there to Natchez, unless at Vicksburg, or Warrenton, ten miles farther down.[48]

The story that John Harding told M. H. Howard, a man "of great virtue and uprightness" and the person for whom Nashville's Howard School was named, is important.[49] Not only does it demonstrate Harding's powers of will and body but, if accurate, indicates the strength of the economic force binding slaveholder to slave.

John Harding could not help comparing the elegant homes he saw in Natchez with his own modest cabin. Having decided to build a more appropriate home for his family, he made significant purchases of building materials in 1819. One was for twenty-one loads of brick from Samuel Marshall. Then, in December, he ordered 9,201 shingles from William Bell. The next year, he bought fifteen pairs of linen and five pairs of homespun sheets, twelve tablecloths (four were imported), eighteen counterpanes, six coverlets, seventeen blankets, forty-three bottles of wine, and thirty-two empty ones.[50] The most logical explanation for these purchases is that he was building a new home. Although no plans for the house have survived, we have some idea of what it looked like. It was a simple two-story brick house, probably of Federal style, which still exists at the core of the present-day Belle Meade Mansion. A careful look beneath the first floor of today's mansion reveals two abutting stone foundations. The rear section is the foundation of the house built by John Harding. The foundation closer to Richland Creek supports the large addition made in 1853 by William Giles Harding. The house must have reminded John of similar brick homes he had known in his youth in

Virginia. When Harding moved Susan and the children from their log
cabin to their new home on the gentle slope of the hill, he had every
reason to be proud of his achievements. At some point, possibly even
then, he named his plantation Belle Meade, the name his father-in-law
had used for his Davidson County property near Fletcher's Lick.

JOHN HARDING (1777–1865).
Engraving by Samuel Sartain,
Belle Meade collection

SUSANNAH SHUTE HARDING
(1785–1845). Painting by
Washington Cooper, Belle Meade
collection

2/ From Middletown to McSpadden's Bend

I N 1820, JOHN HARDING INVESTED CAPITAL IN HIS Richland Creek plantation and in experiences for his son. He built a house, completed a gristmill that cost $150 and a load of hay, and began work on a stone mill dam and millrace.[1] He also gave his twelve-year-old son, William Giles, $60 to go to Virginia by stagecoach over the Christmas holidays. Young William Giles would never forget the hospitality of his Uncle George, Aunt Betsy, and his first cousins in Powhatan County.[2]

What schooling William Giles missed while on his trip to Virginia was most likely made up at the Richland Creek Meeting House only a short distance down Richland Creek from his home. His sisters, Amanda and Elizabeth, attended the same "old field" school before they enrolled at the Nashville Female Academy, said to be the first school in the United States to appreciate "the separateness and the importance of female education." When the academy was established in 1816, John Harding was included among its stockholders.[3] Eighteen years later, he served one term on the school's board as treasurer. Both girls were there for the school's ninth term, which lasted from July until well into December 1821. The previous summer, John Harding gave Rhoda Boyd a hundred dollars credit on her account at his gristmill for boarding his two daughters for the fall term.[4]

In 1822, at age fourteen, William Giles enrolled in the preparatory department of Nashville's struggling Cumberland College. When he arrived, the school was in a deplorable state. After the death of its president, Dr. James Priestley, in 1821, no one had taken his place. The students were bright but, because of the lack of leadership, unmotivated and unruly. Some of them, led by a fun-loving group from Alabama and Mississippi, were particularly adept at playing pranks. One night a few of the boys took a calf to the third-floor room of an eccentric teacher named Hamilton, leaving him the task of getting it down again. Other students broke school rules by going off campus to attend the theater.[5]

Unlike many of his classmates, William Giles took school seriously. His course work at Cumberland apparently emphasized the classics. One of his classes was a Greek course that had as its text Xenophon's *Education of Cyrus* [*Cyropaedia*], an idealization of education's role in the lives of great men, and, clearly, William Giles saw education through the eyes of the classical humanist.[6] After putting up with the disruptive antics of his classmates for two years, he told his father that he wanted to attend another school. Harding encouraged his son to return to class and resist the temptations about him. William Giles answered, "These boys are my friends. I will not offend them. My only way is to leave the school and seek another." After receiving his father's permission to attend a school of his choice, young Harding set out to learn for himself how discipline was maintained at the College of New Jersey, now Princeton, and at Harvard. While in New England, he also visited the American Literary, Scientific and Military Academy, founded in 1819 by Capt. Alden Partridge.[7] A scholar and disciplinarian, Partridge had been superintendent of the United States Military Academy from 1815 to 1817. When Harding examined the school's academic program, which focused on the training of soldiers and engineers, he liked what he saw and enrolled. He was then sixteen years old.[8]

At Partridge's academy, Harding deliberately refrained from forming friendships until he became acquainted with "the characters of his fellows." Although he entered as a "total stranger to professors and students alike," an unusually large number of Southern cadets was there at the time, including sizable contingents from Charleston, Natchez, and New Orleans.[9]

Although cadets received only one vacation each year, normally in December, Harding did not make it home for Christmas in 1826. On the day that school let out, eighty-two cadets, including Harding and fellow Tennessean Thomas Harden Perkins, left Middletown on the steamboat *Oliver Ellsworth* for a twenty-two-day tour of New York City, Philadelphia, Baltimore, and Washington. The students traveled by steamboat, stages, railroad, and foot. While in Philadelphia, they visited the U.S. Mint, the Academy of Fine Arts, the Navy Yard, and a museum, and they inspected the Water Works. In Baltimore they marched from their hotel, the Indian Queen, to Fort McHenry, where they examined the fortifications. They also met Charles Carroll, then the only surviving signer of the Declaration of Independence.[10]

In Washington the cadets continued their fast-paced tour. They visited the Capitol, where they met President John Quincy Adams and Vice-President John C. Calhoun. They next traveled to Mount Vernon, where they fired three volleys over George Washington's grave.[11] Harding also visited his congressmen, Sam Houston and James K. Polk. Six weeks later, Houston wrote William Giles thanking him for some pamphlets and a music catalog and expressing pleasure that "I was instrumental in rendering you and your young friends facilities in reaching your destination."[12] After the corps was dismissed on December 26 in Washington, Harding may have visited his brother in nearby Virginia. In a day when stagecoaches averaged about four miles an hour, however, he did not have time to visit Tennessee before school reconvened on January 15.

Academy athletics consisted of drills, fencing, hiking, rowing, skating, and swimming. On a hike with some fellow cadets, Harding learned something about Yankee parsimoniousness. As his group was passing a farm, Harding noticed a woman about to pour out a pail full of buttermilk for her pigs. Being thirsty, he asked her for a drink. She gave him some of the buttermilk, then charged him for it.[13] Having grown up in a home where his mother fed "all comers or goers without stint or care" and in a section of the country famous for its open-handed hospitality, Harding was taken aback.[14]

At Middletown, Harding kept up an active correspondence with friends and kinsmen at home. In 1826, he received a letter from Charles H. Dickinson, a former academy cadet from Plaquemine, Louisiana, who was then enrolled at the University of Nashville. Dickinson wrote that he had spent the previous night with Harding's parents and that Mrs. Harding could not talk about her only son without tears welling up in her eyes. Dickinson said that Harding's parents' "whole affections" were centered on him.[15] Twice in 1827, Harding wrote Francis "Frank" McGavock, his brother-in-law. In a responding letter, Frank told William Giles that "our country is perhaps laboring under greater pecuniary embarrassments at this time than it ever has." He also reported that William Giles's sister Amanda was well, that their boys, John and David, were in perfect health, and that he had been working on his "little farm near your father's."[16] That was the beginning of McGavock's extensive farm on both sides of what would later become the Harding Turnpike. Another of Harding's correspondents was Albert W. Dunbar of Dunbarton Plantation, Adams County, Mississippi. Dunbar had been at the academy, but because of a medical condition had transferred to the University of Nashville in 1827. He wrote William Giles that October to thank him for writing letters of introduction to Harding's family and friends. Albert was pleased to learn that Mr. Harding and Albert's father, William, were old friends from flatboat days.[17]

Agustín Jerome de Itúrbide, son of Mexico's first president, Agustín de Itúrbide, was another academy schoolmate.[18] On March 2, 1822, William Giles's father and fifty-seven other prominent Middle Tennesseans signed a document addressed to President Itúrbide congratulating Mexico on having won its independence and asking for permission "to settle in the jurisdiction of that part of your dominions contiguous to the United States, for the purpose of supporting and maintaining our families by the cultivation of the soil." Although in 1826 a group of the Tennesseans went as far southwest as Texas, John Harding chose to remain in Tennessee. Nevertheless, his outlook, like that of William Giles, was always Southern and Western.[19]

A much less renowned academy schoolmate was George Norris of Alabama. Fifty years after his graduation, Norris wrote William Giles's son-in-law, General William H. Jackson, about his relationship with Harding when they were students together at Middletown. In Norris's letter offering condolences on the death of William Giles, he praised his college friend in this manner:

> While at the Academy I was frequently in company with General Harding but not on intimate terms as I was with Horatio Seymour, Charles D. Drake, John R. Davidson, A. B. Huntington and others, for I was small of stature and not near to the Gen'l while in ranks and he was so far in advance in his classes that we did not often meet. His college name was "Monsieur Tonson" [a favorite stage character of the day] as he was the best imitator of the character, in our stage plays, we boys had ever seen, and for that and for his manhood, generosity, and nobleness of mind and body he became our idol, and we fairly worshipped him; he was to me too lofty a boy to approach, but not for his inaccessibility for he was the reverse, but from a certain awe of his high standing and my own insignificance.[20]

There is an inclination to discount Norris's flowery tributes to Harding as those of a seventy-nine-year-old man trying to bring comfort to the family of an old friend. However, a characteristic of all the letters written to Harding by his academy friends during the 1826-30 period was the high degree of esteem and respect they had for him. In Harding's biography in Clayton's *History of Davidson County, Tennessee,* his record at the academy was described as follows: "His course was marked by studious ways and high military habits and bearing, holding every office in his company from corporal to captain. He was also inspector of the corps of cadets, the highest military office of the institution."[21]

Because there were no formal commencement exercises at the academy, it is not known when Harding graduated. Degrees may have been conferred at the close of the public examinations in August 1828.[22] At any rate, he did not immediately go home but remained in the East for some weeks. On July 30, his father sent him a five-hundred-dollar check drawn on the United States Bank of Providence, Rhode Island. The check represented a great deal of money and suggests John Harding's growing trust in and plans for his increasingly mature, educated, and experienced son.[23]

In August 1828, Washington J. Bennett of Charleston, South Carolina, an 1827 graduate of the academy, wrote Harding at Hartford to ask whether he was still as strong an advocate of Andrew Jackson as when he used to debate "on the merits of the illustrious champion of New Orleans." He urged Harding to desert Jackson's "bloody standard" before it was too late. On a more conciliatory note, Bennett also asked to be remembered to some of his old friends and "especially to the family of my charming Selena."[24] That was a reference to Harding's girl friend at home, Mary Selena McNairy. By October, some of Harding's former schoolmates had heard that William Giles was studying law, presumably at the Litchfield, Connecticut, law school. One correspondent, R. T. Rodgers of Washington, expressed the hope that Harding's law studies would not prevent him from coming to the capital for the presidential inauguration the following March should "Hickory win the race."[25]

William Giles decided to drop his law studies and return home rather than stay in the East over the winter and attend the presidential inauguration. In October, he came South in the company of Captain Partridge, who had recently retired from the active management of the academy.[26] They arrived in Nashville by October 21 because on that date John

WILLIAM GILES HARDING during
his student years. Painting by an
unknown artist, collection of
Tennessee State Library and
Archives, cited hereafter as TSLA

COL. ALDEN C. PARTRIDGE.
Engraving by H. W. Smith after a
portrait by John Vanderlyn, 1818,
collection of Norwich University
Archives, Northfield, Vermont

AMERICAN LITERARY, SCIENTIFIC AND MILITARY ACADEMY, from an engraving in
John Holbrook's *Military Tactics*, 1826, collection of Norwich University Archives,
Northfield, Vermont

Harding made an entry in his ledger that William Giles "had returned home from the North." John and Susannah Harding felt enormous pride when they read their son's graduation certificate, which closed with these words: "I hereby recommend William G. Harding, a graduate of this institution, as a scholar, a gentleman, and a soldier, to whom it may concern." It was said to have been the only graduation certificate ever given in Captain Partridge's own handwriting.[27]

While William Giles was in school at Cumberland College and at Middletown, his father kept him posted on farm matters at his Richland Creek plantation. During those years, John Harding steadily built a clientele for his farm products. By the early 1820s, two hundred or more customers were buying clover, corn, flour, fodder, hay, meal, oats, pumpkins, sweet potatoes, and straw from Harding. He also traded in cattle and sold quarters of beef, cowhides, scrap iron, and whiskey. Other activities were the boarding of horses and the standing of stallions, both of which were significant sources of income. With the addition of a sawmill, Harding not only sold lumber but used it in constructing an assortment of buildings for his growing plantation. That same year he also finished the mill dam begun in 1819.[28]

Among the buildings Harding erected were decent houses for his slaves. The quarters were perched on the hill to the left of the mansion. The group was still standing nearly seventy years later when the October 17, 1887, *Daily American* described the Belle Meade slave quarters as "neatly white-washed cabins." A 1989 archaeological dig in the area uncovered handmade nails, glass, a percussion cap, and ceramics of the kinds used in the 1820-60 period. The last of the old cabins was still standing and occupied by a black family as recently as the early 1970s.[29]

By 1823, Harding's blacksmith shop was producing harrows, plows, and wagon wheels for sale. William Gray, Ben's successor as Harding's blacksmith, made the implements from iron purchased from early Tennessee ironmasters Richard C. Napier and Anthony Wayne Vanleer. In 1820, Harding bought 2,720 pounds of iron at ten cents a pound from Napier's Laurel Furnace in Dickson County. The following year, Harding traded Vanleer flour, hay, and meal for a load of iron. At the same time, Vanleer sold Harding an additional 322 pounds.[30] The iron came from an ironworks at Cumberland Furnace, which Anthony and Bernard Vanleer had purchased from Montgomery Bell in 1820.[31]

John Harding built a smokehouse by 1828 when he was acquiring large quantities of salt as partial payment on accounts due him. The implication is that he was curing pork and beef to feed the increasing number of people living on the plantation. The original smokehouse was a one-and-a-half-story red brick building with a gabled, shingled roof and diamond-shaped vents in each wall. Though the smokehouse still stands at Belle Meade, the second story was probably added during the 1850s.[32]

The gardener's house at Belle Meade also dates from John Harding's days. Later, William Giles brought his own gardener to Belle Meade from Switzerland.[33] By then the building was probably used as the gardener's house. Carrie Eliza Ewing, a cousin who visited Belle Meade frequently in the post-Civil War years, said that during her lifetime "it was called the dairy but [was] never used for anything but a general storeroom."[34] Clyde Seale identified the building, which still stands as a springhouse in his drawing of Belle Meade in *History of Homes and Gardens of Tennessee,* published in 1936.

In Tennessee—and throughout the West and the South—President Andrew Jackson was extremely popular. Not only was he a dominating figure in the military and political arenas, but also in the world of the "blood horse." His Thoroughbreds Truxton and Pacolet were among the best in the country. In Jackson's era, Tennessee's racehorses were as well known as the famous preachers and politicians of the day. There were several reasons. Jackson's prominence as a turfman was one. Additionally, the altitude, climate, limestone soil, and bluegrass of the Middle Tennessee basin were ideally suited to breeding Thoroughbreds. Nashville's geographic position on a navigable river leading to New Orleans was also a factor. Many Middle Tennessee planters and businessmen, such as Isaac Franklin of Fairvue Plantation, grew wealthy as owners of great sugar or cotton plantations in Louisiana or as partners in New Orleans mercantile houses. They spent some of that wealth on blood horses.[35] It is not surprising, therefore, that John Harding was passionately interested in the Thoroughbred and that he gained a local reputation as a stud manager. Harding's reputation had grown considerably since Montgomery Bell's imported (imp.) stallion Boaster stood the 1816 season at Harding's stable. This marked Belle Meade's beginning as a stud farm.[36]

The following season, Boaster again stood at Harding's farm. In an advertisement in the *Nashville Whig* on May 12, 1817, Harding said that

Boaster "will be let to mares at $25 in cash, or cotton at cash price delivered at any gin in Davidson County on or before the first day of January next." Harding went on to say that he had excellent pasturage with good fences and that, although he could not assume liability for injury or escapes, "those who send their mares may rest assured that the best care will be taken to prevent either."

Two of the early entries in John Harding's ledgers indicate that the firm of Crockett & Adams and Robert Faugherson boarded horses with him in 1818. Harding's 1819 ledger lists accounts for a small but influential group of customers, including William Carroll, Ralph E. W. Earl, Felix Grundy, and Sam Houston. Collectively, they bought Harding's hay, boarded horses and ponies at his establishment, and patronized his blacksmith shop. Harding normally requested cash payment for his services, which in Houston's case consisted of boarding ponies in March and a bay horse for three weeks in December. For those services, Houston paid Harding $7.75.[37]

Gradually John Harding's plantation was gaining prominence as one of the more important studs of the region. Dr. Robert B. Sappington, a Nashville physician, brought his stallion Messina to stand at John Harding's for the 1819 season.[38] The next sire there was Eagle, a bay stallion bred in England in 1796 by Sir Francis Standish. Eagle, who had placed a disappointing third in the 1799 English Derby but was considered one of the best racehorses of his day, was imported into Virginia in 1811.[39] The horse was brought to Tennessee to stand the 1821 season at the stable of Henry Wade, one of Harding's neighbors.[40] Montgomery Bell bought the horse and boarded him at Harding's stud where he stood for the 1822 and 1823 seasons. Bell advertised his Thoroughbred as combining "more power and beauty than any horse on earth—more even than the human mind can imagine." Eagle was so popular during the 1822 season that Harding and Bell refused more mares than they accepted for service by him. The stallion died in Kentucky in 1826 at the age of thirty.[41]

Bagdad, a brown Arabian sired in Tripoli, was the next noted stallion known to stand at John Harding's stud. Harding purchased him for a syndicate of eight Davidson County men in November 1823 for eight thousand dollars, which they paid in four annual installments. Bagdad stood at Harding's stable from 1824 until 1829.[42] During those years, he serviced mares owned by some of Middle Tennessee's most prominent men. An 1826 entry in Harding's ledger provides evidence that Bagdad sired several good horses despite a preference by horsemen of that day for the get of Sir Archy and Pacolet. In 1835 the Mississippi Association for the Improvement of the Breed of Horses awarded the premium for yearlings to Col. Philip Hoggatt for his filly Arab, by Bagdad.[43]

Sir Archy and Glencoe were two of the most important sires of the nineteenth century. Col. W. R. Johnson of Petersburg, Virginia, owned Sir Archy. His challenge to race him against any horse in the world was not accepted, and under Johnson's management, Sir Archy was undefeated.[44] As a sire, Sir Archy had many distinguished get. Some of his colts were promoted in their own right. On February 17, 1827, Lewis Shearly advertised in the *Nashville Republican* that "Sir Archie—A son of the unequalled horse, Old Sir Archie, will stand the ensuing season on John Harding's farm where D. A. Dunham Esq. lived six miles southwest from Nashville."

John Harding occasionally took some of his horses to Burns's stable and racetrack near Ashland in Wayne County, Tennessee, to be trained by a well-known horse trainer and saddle and harness maker named Mark Fletcher Edwards. The early Wayne County settler, who had come to the Buffalo River country in 1815 from North Carolina, represented the fifth generation in his family to train horses. His great-great-grandfather had done so for the king of England. Fifty years later, Frank Burns of Waynesboro, a descendant of the original settler, bought a Bonnie Scotland colt at a Belle Meade yearling sale.[45]

Sometime during the 1820s, a Nashville racecourse was established on land owned by M. Burns in the river bottom below town. The track was carefully described in the May 1831 edition of the *Turf Register* by "a Western subscriber":

The half of the track, next to the river, is alluvial, and, of course, deep sand; the other half is a sweetgum flat, and from the nature of such soil, very hard when dry, and very tough when wet; and the whole nearly level and is considered unfavorable to good time. The same horses run quicker at Gallatin, and other Tennessee courses by two or three seconds in the mile. The buildings on the course are a mansion house large enough to accommodate the gentlemen of the turf, a dining room about 100 feet long, a stage of the same length, a stage for the judges and stables with about forty stalls, painted white.

The track, which was under the jurisdiction of the Nashville Jockey Club, was open for the fall 1827 season. John Harding was a judge of the races that year and served as club president for many years.[46]

Harding continued to board horses and sell blacksmith services, farm products, and dressed lumber throughout the 1820s. In 1828, Dr. John Newman, a physician, accepted a load of hay from Harding as partial payment on his medical statement. The next January, Presbyterian Parson William Hume paid for a load of hay he bought from Harding "by preaching." During 1828, Harding also sold twenty-three plows for ten to twelve dollars each, depending on their size. He often deposited proceeds from his various enterprises in the Nashville bank owned by Thomas Yeatman and Joseph and Robert Woods. Harding's clients that year included such prominent men as Felix Grundy, William Hume, Governor Sam Houston, and John Overton. The next spring, Governor Houston sent his gray horse to Harding's stable to be pastured only twelve days before he resigned as governor of Tennessee, and less than three weeks before he boarded the steamboat *Red Rover* for the destiny that awaited him in the West. Throughout the decade, Harding also had a scattering of clients from Alabama, Mississippi, North Carolina, Pennsylvania, and Virginia.[47]

Harding nearly tripled the amount of land he owned in Davidson County during the decade. To the approximately 1,000 acres he owned at the end of 1819, he added nearly 3,000 during the 1820s, bringing his total holdings in the county to more than 3,800. James Maxwell's death in the middle of the decade presented Harding with an opportunity to add to the several small neighboring tracts he purchased from Maxwell while alive. Three years later, Harding bought from Maxwell's children their interests in the 291½-acre farm their father formerly lived on. Not included was a one-acre piece of land beside Richland Creek that Maxwell had sold earlier to John Nichols, another neighbor.[48]

John Harding made other Richland Creek purchases during the 1820s from his brother Giles, Daniel A. Dunham, and other neighbors. He also bought land on Flat Creek, Sams Creek, Whites Creek, Mill Creek, and the south side of the Cumberland River in McSpadden's Bend. For a short time he also owned an unimproved lot in Nashville.[49]

The eastern section of Davidson County, including McSpadden's Bend, was well suited for the cultivation of cotton. Farmers there, including Andrew Jackson, grew cotton generally shorter and lighter than that grown in the southern half of West Tennessee, but it often brought good prices in New Orleans. In 1825, from fifteen to twenty steamboats ran from Nashville to New Orleans, Louisville, and Pittsburgh.[50] That same year, nearly $1 million worth of cotton was shipped from the port of Nashville.[51]

John Harding became a cotton factor during the decade. He bought cotton from local growers, ginned and baled it, and either sold it to Nashville merchants or shipped it himself to New Orleans. In 1824, twenty-four farmers sold cotton to Harding. Business was so good that he built a warehouse in time to store his next season's crop, which consisted of 183 number-two-weight bales averaging approximately 440 pounds each. Harding sold his 1825 crop to Josiah Nichol, a prominent Nashville merchant. Often, Harding's contracts called for planters to deliver their "good dry merchantable cotton" to his gin by the first of January. Following the 1826 season, he baled and sold 38,096 pounds of cotton for a single planter.[52] Harding did not grow cotton himself until 1827 because his bottomland along Richland Creek was better suited for raising corn, hay, oats, and wheat. That spring, however, he was on the lookout for good cotton-producing land. Because of the suitability of the soil in the eastern portion of the county, he focused on that area. Two of his brothers, William and Thomas, lived there, and John had bought cotton from planters in the section.

Harding's interest in acquiring more land in 1827 was also motivated by family considerations. On April 26, his youngest child, Elizabeth, married Joseph W. Clay, a racehorse man whose horses had run at the Nashville meetings for the previous two seasons. As had been the case when Harding's daughter Amanda married four years earlier, the ceremony was performed by the Reverend William Hume.[53] Joseph and Elizabeth wanted a place of their own where Joseph could operate a stud and farm. Harding decided to help. On May 18, he bought a 441-acre tract lying primarily on the north side of Lebanon Road near the bridge over Mill Creek.[54] The land included the hilltop site where, about 1832 or 1833, he built for Elizabeth and Joseph a brick home named Belair.[55] By then, Clay owned an adjoining 170-acre tract that included the house where early settler James Mulherin, Sr., formerly lived.[56] The Clays probably lived in Mulherin's house, or in a two-story brick dwelling adjacent to Belair, until their new house was completed. The same year,

John Harding lent additional help by building a cotton gin for Clay at a cost of $225.[57]

Harding knew that William Giles would want land as soon as he returned from school in the North. So, at a July 1827 sale held by the sheriff, he bought for his son two large tracts immediately north of his brother William Harding's land. The combined tract of 579 acres extended all the way across McSpadden's Bend and included a portion of today's Opryland U.S.A. complex. In 1827, its southwest corner was anchored on the Cumberland near Priestley's Springs.[58]

John's younger brother, William, was the first Harding to own land and live in McSpadden's Bend. In 1819, while living in Powhatan County, Virginia, he bought from Willie Barrow 476 acres at the confluence of the Cumberland and Stones Rivers with the idea of rejoining his brothers and sisters in Tennessee. William moved to Davidson County by 1823 when he expanded his holdings on Stones River by purchasing an additional 150 acres. His cotton plantation, which he named Two Rivers, stretched all the way from the Stones River on the east to the Cumberland River, west of today's Briley Parkway, on the west.[59] William, still a bachelor, probably lived in the two-and-a-half-story brick house that still stands today beside Two Rivers Mansion. In 1830, he married Elizabeth Clopton, an eighteen-year-old neighbor. When William died two years later, his plantation had grown to 1,081 acres.[60]

Another younger brother, Thomas, also lived in the eastern section of the county. He was married to Elizabeth Bosley, a daughter of Beal and Margery Shute Bosley and a niece of John Harding's wife, Susan.[61] By 1827, Thomas and Elizabeth had four children, including Rachel, who would grow up to marry Col. John Overton. Their family would not be complete, however, until they had ten children, four of whom were named for presidents Washington, Jefferson, Monroe, and Jackson. By 1832, Thomas had accumulated 900 acres along McCrory's Creek and Stones River.[62]

John Harding and his brothers were, by the late 1820s, major landowners in two of the most prosperous sections of Davidson County. John alone owned almost 2,500 acres along Richland Creek in the southwest portion of the county and another 1,293 acres in the McSpadden's Bend/ Mill Creek area. In an era when wealth was often measured by how much land a man owned, he had done extremely well.

3 / Stones River Years

S OON AFTER THE TWENTY-YEAR-OLD WILLIAM GILES
Harding and Captain Partridge arrived in Nashville from
Louisville in October 1828, they visited Gen. Andrew Jackson at the
Hermitage.[1] It must have been a satisfying part of his homecoming for
William Giles to be received by his childhood hero. For Partridge, the
meeting was a renewal of acquaintance. A dozen years earlier, when
Partridge was superintendent of West Point, Jackson had written him a
letter introducing Andrew Jackson Donelson, Rachel Jackson's nephew.[2]
Donelson graduated from the military academy in 1820 and was a confi-
dant to the general.[3]

Although there had been speculation that William Giles would accompany Captain Partridge to North Carolina following the educator's
visit to Tennessee, he did not do so.[4] He stayed at home and courted
Mary Selena McNairy, the sixteen-year-old daughter of Nathaniel and
Kitty Hobson McNairy. Selena lived at the corner of Cherry and Spring
Streets, only a block away from Nashville's Presbyterian Church, which
her family attended. Since about 1820, Selena's father had been clerk of
the Federal Court of Tennessee.[5] Her uncle, John McNairy, was judge of
the Western District Court and the man responsible for Andrew Jackson's
coming to Tennessee. Selena's mother was a homemaker and hostess,
who gave a ball at Clayton Talbot's tavern in 1815 to celebrate the return
of Major General Jackson from his victory at New Orleans.[6]

On Selena's seventeenth birthday, November 19, 1829, she and
William Giles were married by the Reverend Mr. Hume. They began life
together at John Harding's plantation on Stones River "with forty-five
dollars in money."[7] That farm was the 579-acre tract John Harding had
bought two years earlier. Among the presents given Selena were a black
couple named Green and their small son, Bob. "Uncle" Bob Green

would one day be recognized nationally as a spokesman for Belle Meade's tradition of horse-breeding excellence. Another present was a large family Bible, published in Philadelphia in 1829. It is now an important source of Harding family history.[8]

William Giles Harding and his family probably lived in a log cabin for the entire decade they resided in McSpadden's Bend. In 1987, Charles P. Curd III, a great-great-grandson, gave to the Association for the Preservation of Tennessee Antiquities, Nashville Chapter, photographs of a log cabin and a sawmill thought to have been the ones there during the 1830s. Although William Giles and Selena lived a half day's ride away from his parents' home on Richland Creek and eight or nine miles from town, they did not lack for company. Elizabeth and Joseph Clay lived only a few miles away, while William and Elizabeth Harding were close neighbors. Soon, several babies were added to the Harding households. In January 1831, Selena gave birth to her first child, whom she and William Giles named John for his Harding grandfather. The same year, Elizabeth and Joseph Clay had a son, Henry.[9] A few miles to the south, Uncle Thomas had a house full of children.

The year 1832 brought sadness to the Harding clan on Stones River. One morning that spring, William Giles's uncle, William Harding, became violently ill with "bilious colic" and died the next day, leaving a pregnant widow not yet twenty-one years old.[10] Masking her grief as well as she could, Elizabeth Clopton Harding attended her husband's funeral service and the dinner for all the mourners. Jane Thomas recalled, years later, that Parson Hume preached at the service held a month after Harding's death. In those days, Miss Thomas said, funeral services were never held on the day of burial.[11] During the same period, William Giles helped his uncle's widow, Elizabeth Harding, and her infant daughter, Willie Elizabeth. Although Elizabeth and her brother-in-law, David Morris Harding, had been appointed administratrix and administrator of William Harding's estate, William Giles took Morris's place in October 1833. He was also named Elizabeth's guardian for a short time.[12] One of his first acts as administrator was to sell seven of her slaves to his Uncle Morris.[13]

On September 9, 1832, Selena and William Giles's second son was born, Nathaniel Adams McNairy Harding, named for his maternal grandfather. Less than three weeks later, the widowed Elizabeth Harding gave birth to a baby daughter, Willie Elizabeth, at Spring Place, the home of Mrs. Harding's uncle, John Clopton. Although Nathaniel lived only two months, Willie Elizabeth lived a long and fruitful life.[14]

For William Giles and Selene (her nickname, passed on in later generations of Hardings and Jacksons as a given name), life at the Stones River plantation was busy from the outset, as they made the most of the opportunity John Harding had provided. William Giles had profitable cotton crops in the early thirties. In April 1833, he had enough capital or borrowing power to make the first of his many land purchases in Davidson County. That month he bought for two thousand dollars a one-sixth interest in an adjoining 500-acre plantation that an old settler, Leonard Keeling, had lived on. Three months later, Harding acquired another one-sixth interest in the same farm.[15] Since some of Harding's expanded Stones River plantation was in woods, game abounded. Occasionally, he picked up orphaned fawns and raised them by hand. In 1833 or 1834, he and his father took five of the deer to Belle Meade and established a deer park so that they would be safe and could multiply. In time, the herd grew to several hundred, and the deer park became a landmark and an unofficial park for Davidson County.[16]

Two births, a marriage, and three deaths were significant milestones for the Stones River Hardings during the mid-1830s. William Giles and Selena's third child, a son, was born the day after Christmas, 1833. They named him Nathaniel McNairy Harding for her father.[17] By the time Nathaniel was born, William Giles had expanded his Stones River plantation with the purchase, a few days before Christmas, of one-fifth of the tract formerly owned by James Priestley.[18] The marriage came next. Late in 1834, when Willie Elizabeth Harding was two years old, her mother remarried. Elizabeth's second husband was Francis ("Frank") Owen, a Methodist minister from northern Alabama who had been preaching in Memphis since 1831.[19] Although Elizabeth and her daughter lived in Memphis with Frank, she held on to the dower land she inherited from her first husband.[20] The first death was that of Elizabeth Virginia Harding Clay, William Giles's younger sister. When she died in 1835, she left a young husband and a four-year-old son, Henry. Her remains were buried in the family burying ground at Belair.[21]

Christmas festivities in 1835 were somewhat subdued because Selena was expecting her fourth child at any time. Accordingly, she could not devote her usual attention to her little boys, John and Nathaniel. On

WILLIAM GILES HARDING, ca. 1846.
Painting by Washington Cooper, Belle
Meade collection

MARY SELENA MCNAIRY HARDING
(1812-37), W. G. Harding's first wife.
Painting by an unknown artist, Belle
Meade collection

Christmas Day, Selena gave birth to her last child, William Giles Harding, Jr.[22] Evidence suggests there were serious complications. In March of 1836, Harding withdrew as a candidate for brigadier general of the militia from Davidson and Dickson counties, citing circumstances beyond his control.[23] Proof of Selena's serious illness came a few months later when her uncle, Dr. Boyd McNairy, wrote his friend, Henry Clay of Lexington, Kentucky, on her behalf. McNairy informed Clay that "my relation Mr. William G. Harding visits your state for the benefit of his lady's health." After expressing his personal esteem for the "Great Pacificator" and his wife, McNairy asked that a Dr. Dooley "examine Mrs. Harding's case."[24]

Despite Selena's worsening illness, Harding soon changed his mind and accepted an appointment in the militia. One week before McNairy wrote Clay on behalf of Selena, William Giles was appointed brigade major of the Tennessee Militia by Gen. Joel A. Battle. The following January, Major Harding was named to a committee appointed to welcome the Tennessee Brigade of Volunteers on their return from their Florida campaign against the Seminoles.[25]

By the winter of 1836-37, Selena had a strong premonition of her death. Sometime during her final illness, she wrote a close relative who was also ill and in need of spiritual support. Selena was so fatigued by the ordeal of writing the letter, in which she eloquently expressed her Christian faith, that William Giles had to finish it for her. A portion of the letter, a copy of which is preserved at the Belle Meade Mansion, follows:

> I cannot refrain saying something appertaining to our eternal destiny; a subject so interesting to me, that I am oftentimes so delighted and absorbed in the contemplation as to forget my pains and afflictions, which are very great—often as much as weak human nature can bear. But thanks to God this is not to endure. My Saviour has suffered before me—even more than I. . . . If it is our lot to go first, let us depart rejoicing—Surely, B., if I can bid adieu to all earthly ties, it will not be a severe trial to you should it please God to remove you from this vale of tears. True you have a fond husband and affectionate mother, from whom you would not wish to be separated. I have father, mother, sisters and brothers, and a father and mother-in-law, to all of whom I am devotedly attached;—I have also a fond husband, who has not obtained the great promise of salvation, and from whom I may be eternally separated. I pray God it may not be so, and that he may yet learn to know

the truth, and feel its consoling and comforting influence in life, and its support in death. I would wish to live for his sake, that I might advise and admonish him to make preparation for the future. I, too, have three dear little babies; for them I would wish to live.[26]

Selena's willingness just before her death on March 29, 1837, to express in a letter her concern for William Giles's spiritual state said a great deal about the depth and intensity of her faith. Selena was a member of the Disciples movement, also known as the Reform movement, for several years. She probably joined that group as a result of Alexander Campbell's visit to Nashville in December 1830. That month, Campbell debated Dr. Obediah Jennings, the McNairys' pastor. Immediately after the debate, Campbell baptized by immersion in the Cumberland River a number of people, including Selena's father-in-law, John Harding.[27]

William Giles, who probably attended the Campbell-Jennings debate with his father and Selena, read the text of the celebrated debate between Campbell and Robert Owen, and he considered it to be the finest triumph of Campbell's life. Despite this favorable impression of Campbell, the encouraging influence of his father and his wife, and his own "burning desire" for the better life he believed that a full and free embrace of Christianity would bring, Harding resisted. He would not become a Christian until he professed his faith in Jesus Christ at a Sam Jones revival in Nashville nearly fifty-five years later.[28]

William Giles, Jr., Harding's infant son, died just six days after his mother. In spite of such crushing loss, Harding found the emotional stamina needed to face reality. His ledger shows he promptly paid his wife's and son's medical and burial bills—from the physician, an apothecary, the undertakers, the gravediggers, and the sexton—amounting to $450. He then dealt with recent tragedies in a more rewarding way: he had portraits made of Selena and his sister, Elizabeth, who died in 1835.[29]

By the second quarter of 1837, the national economy was near rock bottom. The price of cotton on the New Orleans market fell by nearly half, and there was a collapse in real estate. The effects of the panic, which lasted until 1842 or 1843, were particularly devastating in the South and West.[30] Nevertheless, William Giles managed fairly well. In 1837, he built a corn crib, bought two flatboats to take his plantation

produce to market, spent money on clothes for his slaves and for himself, purchased four young mules and some sheep, bought one thousand
gunny sacks, paid his taxes, and had enough cash left to lend Thomas
Harding $90, contribute to the Baptist Church, and subscribe to a
newspaper. Harding also purchased stock in a turnpike concern, most
likely the Nashville and Lebanon Turnpike Company, in which
Thomas Harding and Joseph W. Clay were shareholders. William Giles's
income that year came from various sources: property rental, the marketing of crops, and the sale of plantation animals, including his bay
colt Alpha for $1,240.[31]

Though William Giles's judgment was normally sound, a notable
lapse occurred in 1838. One day early that year, Harding saw his friend
John Nichols in Nashville. Nichols mentioned having heard of an
argument between William Giles's father and George C. Childress, a
lawyer and former editor of Nashville's *National Banner* newspaper. The
argument took place in Arkansas where the two men owned adjoining
plantations and where John Harding was visiting. William Giles wrote
his father to ask what happened. Mr. Harding replied that "it was a
matter of little consequence" and would discuss it when he came home.
Unsatisfied, William Giles made "a most thorough examination" to
ascertain the facts. He concluded that "the insult [to his father] was
unprovoked and most unjustifiable," and he resolved to avenge it unless
Childress "made the retraction which as a gentleman I conceived him
bound to do."[32]

In April, William Giles and Childress chanced to meet in Nashville.
When Childress offered to shake hands, Harding "folded his arms and
said: 'Mr. Childress, my father has written that he had an unpleasant
altercation with you which he would recount upon his return. Until I
hear from him, I must decline to accept your hand.'" Childress lost his
temper and said, " 'Do you mean to insult me?' Harding replied: 'I have
nothing to add to what I have said, and you are at liberty to construe it as
you please.' A little later, Childress sent Harding a challenge which was
promptly accepted." William Giles promptly sent Frank McNairy, his
former brother-in-law, to borrow dueling pistols from U.S. Senator
Ephraim H. Foster.[33]

Foster and Dr. Boyd McNairy, Frank's uncle, tried to resolve the
matter through "an amicable and honorable adjustment." They appealed
to Childress and Harding to "agree to submit the whole difference to the

decision of two or three friends to be designated by us." After Childress and Harding agreed to do so, Foster and McNairy chose Generals Robert Armstrong and Washington Barrow to serve as mediators.[34]

After reading statements from Childress and Harding, Armstrong and Barrow decided that "the whole difficulty arose out of a misapprehension" on the part of William Giles as to the existing relation between Mr. Childress and Harding's father. They also realized that, being unaware of a reconciliation between Childress and John Harding in New Orleans the previous winter, "Mr. Harding was only yielding to the feelings of a son and a man, and ought not to be blamed, in refusing the hand of a person, who, he believed, had abused his father." Their third conclusion was "that it was natural for Mr. Childress, being ignorant of any cause of complaint or offense on the part of Mr. Harding, to be irritated and excited by the refusal of Mr. Harding to receive his professed [*sic*] hand." Since the confrontation between Childress and William Giles Harding had taken place "by an ignorance of facts on both sides," and since neither man's honor had been impugned, the mediators recommended that the matter be dropped and "the intercourse ordinarily existing among gentlemen . . . be revived between them."[35]

Despite having promised to abide by the decision of the mediators, Harding appeared at the dueling site with his second and his surgeon at the appointed time. Childress, however, did not appear and left Nashville "without explanation." According to Frank McNairy, Harding and Childress soon thereafter met at the St. Charles Hotel in New Orleans where Childress told Harding that "the affair in Nashville had not gone off satisfactorily and he was not in a position to explain but wanted to send another invitation." Harding is supposed to have answered that Childress had disappointed him once, and that he had forfeited his right to meet him on a field of honor, but Harding was ready to meet any attack Childress might make.[36] McNairy's version of the story was that Childress committed suicide that night. Although McNairy was mistaken about the date and place of the suicide, George Childress did take his own life in Galveston, Texas, on October 6, 1841. "A melancholy man who was a tragic failure in almost every venture he touched," he died penniless and was buried in an unmarked grave on Galveston Island.[37] His one notably successful venture took him to Washington-on-the-Brazos, Texas, where on March 2, 1836, he drafted the Texas Declaration of Independence.[38]

William Giles's disagreement with Childress was an anomaly. While Harding lived in McSpadden's Bend, he enjoyed visiting with his neighbors, with whom he had congenial relationships. He admired one neighbor—Andrew Jackson—above all others. Once when Harding went to the Hermitage following the president's return from the White House in 1837, he asked Old Hickory whether a brave man could experience fear. Jackson's reply was, "I do not know, sir, that I am competent to answer that question." Harding pressed him to say more. Jackson responded by saying that "I have been as badly frightened as any man ought to be." Harding then asked about the occasion, thinking Jackson would mention some incident in the Indian wars. Jackson said,

> It was, sir, when I fought the duel with Mr. Dickinson. . . . I knew that he could shoot quicker and truer than I could. I therefore went upon the ground expecting to be killed, and I owe the preservation of my life to the fashions of the day, for I wore a coat with rolling collar and very full breasted: but fortunately for me, sir, I was organized with a very narrow chest. Dickinson's ball struck very near the center of my coat, and, while it scraped the breast bone, it did not enter. In an instant, under the impression that I was perhaps mortally wounded, and upon the impulses of the moment, I fired, and my antagonist fell, and no event of my life, sir, have I regretted so much.

Jackson went on to tell Harding that "Dickinson stood in his position and received my fire like a brave man as he was."[39]

Like Jackson, John and William Giles Harding had established themselves as serious horsemen by the close of the 1830s. John Harding had a racetrack in McSpadden's Bend near where Two Rivers Baptist Church stands today. The level land was an ideal spot for a track and stables, and William Giles probably stabled his horses there. Among the Thoroughbreds William Giles owned or partially owned during the 1830s were Juliet by Kosciusko, bred by a Colonel Singleton of South Carolina, and foaled in 1822; Alpha, a bay colt foaled in 1836 by Leviathan out of Juliet; Beta, a chestnut filly by Leviathan out of Juliet; Gamma, a gray filly by Pacific; and Florestine, Nannie Kilham, and Equity, three horses he acquired from Hugh and John Kirkman's stud on the Murfreesboro Turnpike.[40] Alpha, Beta, and Gamma all won premiums for Harding at the Tennessee Agricultural and Horticultural Society Stock Fair in October 1838.[41]

During his Stones River sojourn, William Giles was active in the Nashville Jockey Club. On several occasions, he served as judge for race meetings at the Nashville course. In June 1838, he was a judge for the celebrated horse race between Sara Bladen, representing the House of Leviathan, and Leila, representing the House of Luzborough. Sara Bladen won on a cold, rainy day before a huge crowd.[42] Harding also continued to enter his horses in area meets, including one sponsored by the Franklin Jockey Club.[43]

On May 9, 1838, Nashville's *Republican Banner* ran a notice that Edward Troye, the animal painter, would be in Nashville for a few days. The article encouraged the "proprietors of our fine horses" to avail themselves of his skills. Although neither William Giles nor his father commissioned Troye on that visit, Troye would return to Nashville twice in later years to paint horse portraits for William Giles.

As 1838 drew to a close, John Harding felt that the time had come to give responsibility for the management of Belle Meade to his son. At McSpadden's Bend, William Giles had proved himself to be a good businessman and planter. By turning Belle Meade over to him, John could direct his energies to his plantation in Arkansas. William Giles and his two boys, John Harding, Jr., and Nathaniel McNairy Harding, probably moved to Belle Meade that winter. Proof that they were there the following March was provided by an advertisement in the *Republican Banner* of March 18, 1839. The notice said that the celebrated imported Durham bull Sam Patch would stand the season alternately at Belle Meade, the residence of W. G. Harding, and at Belair, the plantation of J. W. Clay.

Having lost a wife and two babies during the decade he lived at the Stones River plantation, William Giles was emotionally ready to go home and begin a new chapter in his life. He knew how to manage a plantation and felt prepared for whatever challenges lay ahead.

4/ John Harding: Land and Spirit

F OLLOWING HIS BAPTISM BY ALEXANDER CAMPBELL IN 1830, John Harding became "notorious" for his liberality toward the church. He was, in the eyes of friends and acquaintances, a man "who could not do too much to aid those of like faith with himself."[1] The first evidence of Harding's fidelity to the church comes from a history of the Franklin, Tennessee, Church of Christ.[2] Harding's role in the founding of the Franklin church was that of a trustee. In January 1836, he and his fellow trustees, Andrew Craig and Thomas Hardeman, both of Williamson County, accepted on behalf of the Christian congregation a sixty foot by eighty foot lot on the west side of Indigo Street. The property was a gift of Thomas Harden Perkins, Sr. Fifteen years later, John Harding and Andrew Craig purchased an adjoining lot for the congregation.[3]

Throughout the 1830s, John Harding kept a relatively high profile in Middle Tennessee aside from his religious activities. He frequently entertained guests at Belle Meade. In the fall of 1833, a half dozen gentlemen bagged 920 partridges while on a hunt there.[4] Sometime before David Crockett left Tennessee for Texas and his eventual stand at the Alamo, John and Susan Harding entertained the famous bear hunter and congressman. At dinner, a dessert of a particularly light consistency was served. When Crockett asked his host what it was, Harding said, "The ladies call it syllabub, I believe, Mr. Crockett. Do you like it?" Crockett, whose reputation as a witty man was legendary, replied, "Well, I don't know. I took a snap or two at it but I reckon I missed it."[5]

In 1840, Harding was nominated by Governor James K. Polk to serve as a director for the newly established Bank of Tennessee at Nashville. Among the others nominated and appointed were Nicholas Perkins of

Williamson County, fomer Gov. William Carroll, William Nichol, and Dr. Felix Robertson, all of Davidson County.[6]

John Harding's position as a conspicuous player in the Davidson County real estate market was coming to a close in 1840. By that fall, after he acquired a 460-acre tract of ridge land south of Belle Meade, his total holdings in the county amounted to more than 8,500 acres, the most acreage he would ever own there. Harding and other family members always referred to the ridge land he purchased that year as the "High Pasture." With William Giles having assumed responsibility for Belle Meade, John Harding was free to split his time between his Stones River plantation, where he probably employed an overseer to supervise his slaves, and his recently acquired plantation in Mississippi County, Arkansas.[7]

In 1838, John Harding purchased a plantation in Louisiana, which he soon sold for a sizable profit. That enabled him to concentrate his out-of-state holdings in Arkansas, which was closer to home. Lands there were first surveyed by the United States government from 1824 to 1826 and put on sale in the land office at Helena at $1.25 per acre. Pioneers did not take long to find the sections best suited for cultivation, the majority of which were near the Mississippi River. David and Thomas B. Craighead; Felix Grundy and his sons-in-law, Jacob McGavock and John M. Bass; and John, Giles, Jr., and Thomas Harding, all of Davidson County, went to Mississippi County and cleared lands for plantations between 1833 and 1840. Arkansas' admission to the Union as a slave state in 1836 encouraged such men to buy land in the wonderfully fertile cotton-growing area between the Mississippi River and Crowley's Ridge.[8]

John Harding first visited Mississippi County when he went down the Cumberland, Ohio, and Mississippi Rivers in a skiff and made large land purchases there.[9] The land he chose was about fifty miles north of Memphis, bordered on three sides by a horseshoe bend of the Mississippi. Having already cleared three plantations in Tennessee, Harding was undaunted by the job of clearing another in Arkansas. There was big money in cotton in those days; so, with the labor of "eight hands" from Belle Meade, Harding cleared and put into successful operation a ten-thousand-acre cotton plantation near Plum Point Bend, for which he once refused an offer of $150,000 in gold.[10]

Despite being about sixty when he went to Arkansas, John Harding was exceptionally strong and healthy. He possessed an indomitable will and an iron constitution. At the age of seventy, at one end of a cross-cut saw and his best black man of 250 pounds at the other, "he would go through the toughest tree of five feet in diameter without stopping to blow." Standing six feet tall, he was "of very gentle presence, mild in expression, careful of speech, never going above the mark in assertion. His motto was, 'If you had tried a little harder, don't you think you could have got a little further?'"[11]

When William Giles remarried in January 1840, John Harding felt that his son's and grandsons' adjustment to having a new wife and stepmother would go more smoothly if he and Mrs. Harding lived elsewhere. Consequently, he bought a two-story red-brick town house near the Nashville Christian Church, where he and Susan worshiped. The house was situated on a half-acre lot at 85 Spring Street in Nashville's most fashionable and affluent residential section.[12]

If William Giles and his new bride, the former Elizabeth Irwin McGavock, thought they would see considerably less of his father after he moved to town, they were mistaken. The story was told that John Harding would rise early and ride out to Belle Meade, often arriving before William Giles and his family had finished breakfast. Susan Harding probably did not go nearly as often. Although considered kind and charitable, she was also known to be of high character, strong-willed, and straight to the point. It was said that "she would not, out of mere formal courtesy, invite anyone to visit her whom she did not want to see again, so great was her devotion to truth."[13] If Susan Harding did not want to go to Belle Meade with or without her husband, she did not go.

A year or two after his move to town, John Harding gave responsibility for a married slave couple, Norris and Rachel, to friends. The fact that he transferred rather than freeing them suggests several possible motives. The most likely is that he was insensitive to their aspirations for freedom. He also may have been unwilling for them to leave the state, which emancipated blacks were then required to do. Or he may have feared that they might become a charge to the public if freed. Regardless of his motives, he was interested in their welfare. Harding wrote William McGavock and another McGavock a letter indicating how he wanted the slaves treated. The letter reveals Harding's limited education while supporting his reputation as a kind and paternal master.

I make this request of you boath that Norris and Rachel his wife may be well taken cheare of as long as theay live out of my estate. should theay conclude to come heir to live give them a hundred dollars a yeare and a good place to live on doring their natarel lives or more should it be nessery and should theay wish to live aney whare else give them five hundred Dollars and let them go whare theay please for it is my wish and desier he shall never serve aney one after my death but should be well taken cheare of as one of the famley as long as theay live and have the hundred dollars greater anualley should theay continieu to behave themseves well which I have no fears but theay will.[14]

The name *Rachel,* this time spelled *Rachael,* reappeared in the 1860 census. That June, the census taker recorded that a free mulatto named Rachael Noris (*sic*) was the sole occupant of the household immediately beyond the one occupied by William Giles Harding and his family. The woman was listed as being sixty years old, and her state of birth as Louisiana.[15] She likely was the same Rachel whom John Harding took such an interest in eighteen years earlier. Rachael may have taken her husband's first name as her last name, possibly when she gained her freedom. The fact that she was a mulatto living next door to the Hardings suggests that she may have been kin to John Harding, even his daughter. In 1800, when Rachael was born, Harding was a twenty-three-year-old bachelor. The best evidence that he was not her father is that John Harding is not known to have been in Louisiana in 1800. However, he could have conceived Rachael while in Louisiana on a flatboat trip or taken her mother there to have his baby. Rachael also could have lied about her state of birth to protect her father. Though John Harding and all the subsequent owners of Belle Meade were relatively humane masters of their slaves and paid workers, the unusual attention John Harding accorded Rachael Norris suggests a familial tie.

When their grandchildren were out of school, John and Susan Harding sometimes invited them to spend nights with them in town. City life was exciting to the children. In June 1843, while Nathaniel McNairy Harding was visiting his grandparents, he went horseback riding. While galloping down Church Street, the little boy, not yet ten years old, was thrown and instantly killed.[16] William Giles Harding was devastated. So, too, must have been the grandparents who were so conscious that all but one of William Giles and Selena's four children were now dead, and that the tragic accident occurred while Nathaniel was staying with them. Nearly seventy years later, Nathaniel's half sister, Mary Elizabeth Harding Jackson, would not allow her grandchildren to use stirrups when they rode horses at her home, West Meade. Mrs. Jackson remembered hearing from her parents that if Nathaniel had ridden without stirrups, he would have been able to dismount before crashing into a tree and being thrown to his death.[17]

During the summer of 1845, "one of the most sickly seasons" that people could remember, Susan Harding became dangerously ill, having been "taken with a carbuncle." John Harding hurried home from Arkansas to be with her. Two or three operations were performed in desperate efforts to save her life. They were to no avail, however. On September 12, she died in her sixty-first year, leaving a husband, a son, a daughter, and five grandchildren. Mrs. Harding was buried the next day in the family vault at Belle Meade.[18]

John Harding asked Washington Cooper, Nashville's best-known artist of the time, to paint his wife's portrait posthumously. Cooper, whose training included making death masks, came to Belle Meade and made a mask of Mrs. Harding's face, which he then used for her portrait. He also painted portraits of John and William Giles. Those of Susan and John were signed by the artist and dated 1846.[19]

Harding probably stayed in Nashville long enough for his children and grandchildren to help him celebrate his sixty-eighth birthday on November 2. Then, two months after Susan's death, John returned to Arkansas. His nephew, Giles Harding Page, and Page's wife, Henrietta, said in a letter written to their children the following winter that Harding returned to Arkansas in early November and that, when they saw him, his health was "about as usual."[20]

During the 1840s and early 1850s, John Harding alternately divided his time between Nashville and Arkansas. His presence in Mississippi County in the winter of 1850-51 was confirmed by Henry W. Poynor, a horse trainer, friend, and sometime land agent for William Giles. Writing to the younger Harding from Pecan Point, Arkansas, Poynor mentioned that, while on his way there, he passed Mr. Harding "in the night."[21] A year later, John H. McGavock wrote his uncle William Giles from Mississippi County, Arkansas, where he was busy buying and clearing land and building levees to protect it. The twenty-seven-year-old bachelor expressed excitement about the possibility of amassing a princely fortune through land acquisition and looked forward to his grandfather Harding's coming down to spend the winter with him.[22]

John Harding's relationship with his grandson, John McGavock, was extremely close. When McGavock married Georgia Moore of Columbus, Mississippi, on December 1, 1853, Harding gave him his ten-thousand-acre Mississippi County, Arkansas, plantation as a wedding present.[23] Although Sans Souci, the home John and Georgia built there, burned in 1921, approximately a thousand acres remain in the hands of descendants of John H. McGavock today.[24]

Earlier the same year, John Harding invited another grandson, John Harding, Jr., to assume responsibility for the twelve-hundred-acre plantation on the Stones River, which John Harding, Jr., named Bellevue. Young Harding, who had just graduated from the University of North Carolina, accepted. That March, after he married Sophia ("Sophie") Merritt, of Lawrenceville, Virginia, they moved to McSpadden's Bend, where a daughter, Sophie, was born the following year.[25] On September 28, 1855, Sophie Merritt Harding died at her family home in Virginia, leaving the twenty-four-year-old widower to rear the little girl. John and his daughter remained at the Stones River plantation where he farmed and raised horses.[26]

Meanwhile, John Harding sold all his holdings in Davidson County except those plantations where his children and grandchildren lived.[27] He still owned nearly sixty-eight hundred acres in the county, including Belle Meade, adjoining land on which his daughter Amanda and Frank McGavock, her husband, resided, and Bellevue, the Stones River plantation. In 1856, Montgomery Bell's extensive landholdings, the largest in Davidson County, became part of the newly created Cheatham County. That meant John Harding was probably the largest landowner in Davidson County. His holdings would remain intact until his death in 1865, when they were left to his two surviving children, William Giles and Amanda.[28]

Harding's decisions to give his Arkansas plantation to one grandson, responsibility for another plantation to another grandson, and to quit buying land reflected his growing preoccupation with his spiritual well-being. When the minister James Challen visited the First Christian Church in Nashville in February 1860, he reported on the affairs of the congregation to Alexander Campbell, the man who had done so much to shape the Reform movement in Tennessee. In his letter, Challen said about Harding:

Brother Harding whom you immersed with fifteen others, on December 28, 1830—immediately after your debate with Dr. Jennings—is still a constant attendant at the church. He sits before the pulpit; and, although he cannot hear a word, he watches intently the countenance of the speaker, and catches his spirit as he proceeds. He is now 83 years old; and a more grave, dignified, venerable or lovely disciple of Christ I have not seen. On last Lord's night, when three confessed the Lord, he was overwhelmed with joy, and tears ran freely down his furrowed cheeks. [29]

5/ A New Role

I N ADDITION TO THE EXCITEMENT OF COMING HOME to Belle Meade, William Giles Harding had another reason for celebration. In February 1839, he was elected brigadier general of the Sixteenth Brigade, Tennessee Militia.[1] As a general, Harding had the honor of mustering into service Tennessee troops called to active duty for the Seminole War.[2] In order to be properly attired for such duties, he purchased a sword and epaulets the following September. The same month, he underwrote the cost of music and dinner at a county-wide militia drill.[3] From the day of his election as brigadier general until his death, William Giles Harding would be known as General Harding.

A priority for William Giles in the years immediately following the deaths of Selena and their infant son was to build a vault at Belle Meade to house their remains and those of other deceased family members. In 1838, he sold Adolphus Heiman, the early Nashville architect, twenty loads of stone for a vault for Nathaniel McNairy, Harding's father-in-law. Harding also had a number of other customers for stone from the three limestone quarries at Belle Meade.[4] The ready availability of stone, Harding's employment of a stonemason, and his father's ownership of a 50 percent interest in a water-powered mill for sawing stone made building the Belle Meade vault feasible.[5] Several 1839 entries in General Harding's account book seem to have been related to the construction of the mausoleum. One was payment for "cement for vault," another for "white cut stone."[6]

Belle Meade's stone mausoleum was ready to receive the remains of General Harding's mother, Susan Harding, when she died in September 1845. Sometime after its completion, probably in 1839, General Harding moved his wife's and son's remains to the vault. Similarly, the remains of

Harding's sister, Elizabeth Clay, and her son, Henry, were moved from the graveyard at Belair to the Belle Meade mausoleum, possibly about the time Clay sold his place in 1842.[7]

With full responsibility for the Belle Meade Plantation on his shoulders, General Harding asked a McNairy brother-in-law to take his grain to New Orleans to sell. McNairy also agreed to buy a farm bell for Harding, using some of the sale proceeds. Harding figured that a good bell would cost him a hundred dollars or so. Apparently McNairy did not fully appreciate the value of money because he came back with a bell that cost a thousand dollars, consuming most of the profits. McNairy was captivated by the tone of a Mississippi River steamboat bell he heard and could not resist buying it. Made of fine metal, the bell had been imported from France, where it once hung in a church belfry. Harding was astonished; nevertheless, he installed the bell on a tall tower in the slave quarters beside the building where the slaves held church meetings. It was used three times daily: to awaken the slaves, to announce lunch, and to signal quitting time.[8]

In June 1839, Gen. Sam Houston, after serving as the first president of the Republic of Texas, visited Nashville on the third leg of a trip to the southern United States to raise money for his Texas enterprises and to buy blooded horses. While in Davidson County, he called on William Giles Harding, from whom he borrowed five hundred dollars.[9] Before moving on to East Tennessee, Houston was entertained by his Middle Tennessee friends, including Harding, at Nashville's Vauxhall Gardens, a popular resort in the southern part of town.[10]

In 1841 Houston wrote Harding from Cedar Point, Texas, to apologize for not having repaid the loan. Houston explained that the only money in Texas was the republic's depreciation notes and that, of the $25,000 owed him, he could not "collect as much as will pay one-fourth of my law tax." Houston also lamented the fact that two black boys "for which I had paid in cash $2100 previous to my visit to Nashville ran away last spring to Mexico." Rather than remain in debt to Harding, Houston offered to let his friend "have [Texas] property (warranted) at any price."[11] Despite Houston's difficulty in repaying him, William Giles remained a firm supporter of him and Texas. Three years later, when the South was so strong for the annexation of Texas, Harding presided over a "large and enthusiastic meeting of the friends of Texas" at the Davidson County Courthouse.[12]

A complete record of General Harding's financial dealings and accounts from 1837 through 1842 has been preserved, providing thorough documentation of his income and expenses. His farm operation included expenses for a wide variety of seed, such as bluegrass, clover, millet, oats, timothy, and seed potatoes; kegs of powder; "blowing a well"; equipment repairs; twenty-five mules for twenty-five dollars each and hiring a boy to bring them from Carthage, Tennessee; the services of one J. T. Hill on board Harding's flatboats; and an assortment of buckets, cups, pails, and a hamper.[13]

General Harding's accounts covered personal as well as household expenses. In 1839, Dr. Dorris was his physician; a Mr. Beck was his druggist; Will Purdy, his tailor; Kay, Thomas & Co., Wholesale and Retail Grocers, his purveyor of brandy, wine, and sugar; Vanleer, Hicks & Co., his iron suppliers; and William and Uriah Jones, his overseers. Samuel B. Davidson, a neighbor, sold Harding whiskey that year. Harding also spent about two hundred dollars during the summer of 1839 on renovations to the Belle Meade residence, including carpentry work, painting, and papering.[14]

In spite of the general's religious doubts, his records reveal an interest in institutionalized religion. Twice during 1839, William Giles made gifts to the Baptist Church. He also gave money to the Episcopal Church and to Tolbert Fanning, an evangelist for the Reform movement and a member of the Nashville Church of the Disciples of Christ.[15] When asked why an agnostic like himself would be so supportive of Christian churches, Harding answered, "I am not willing to hinder or shadow any life with my doubts, therefore, I never mention them where they might do harm. I want everyone who can believe to give their adherence to Christianity; for this world it is the best possible aid."[16]

Harding's account book indicates that he never left Middle Tennessee in 1839. Expenses were recorded, however, for short trips to nearby spas, and for two trips to Charlotte, Tennessee. Harding's 175 accounts show an amazing variety of products and customers, indicating the extent to which his activities at Belle Meade involved him in the community at large. They include bills for hay for the City Hotel, the Union Hall, and the city of Nashville. In the spring, Harding sold thirty-four loads of rock and one load of walnut planking to the state penitentiary on Church Street. He also sold planking, considerable amounts of wool and flour, and sheep and lambs. Harding had, by 1839, a herd of Durham cattle.

During the summer, neighbors brought their heifers and cows to Belle Meade to be serviced by his bull, Sam Patch. Harding also received income from blood horse stud fees. Among those who brought their mares to be serviced were John Chickering and Gen. William Carroll.[17]

General Harding worked hard to justify his father's confidence in his ability to manage Belle Meade. He allocated enough time, however, for trips to Williamson County to court Elizabeth Irwin McGavock, the nineteen-year-old daughter of Randal and Sarah Rodgers McGavock. Harding had known the McGavocks all his life. As a matter of fact, nearly everyone in Davidson and Williamson counties knew of that politically and socially prominent family. After holding minor judicial offices in Nashville, Randal McGavock had been elected Nashville's mayor in 1824. Following one term in office, he moved to Williamson County where he had extensive landholdings along the Harpeth River near Franklin. There, around 1826, he completed his magnificent home, Carnton, which he named after the McGavock family's ancestral home in County Antrim, Ireland.[18]

Elizabeth grew up at Carnton accustomed to seeing and helping entertain distinguished guests such as Andrew Jackson, John Eaton, John Overton, Sam Houston, James K. Polk, and her mother's brother-in-law, Felix Grundy.[19] On special occasions, she sang and played the piano, which had been brought to Tennessee from Philadelphia. Years later, General Harding said that Elizabeth's singing voice was the loveliest he had ever heard except for Jenny Lind's.

Elizabeth McGavock and William Giles Harding married at Carnton on a bitterly cold night in January 1840.[20] Frozen snow covered the ground. To warm their wedding guests, Mr. and Mrs. McGavock served a "full bushel of steaming hot apple brandy toddy." General Harding made quite an impression when he arrived from Belle Meade in a sleigh pulled by a span of blooded horses.[21] Edward Troye painted matching portraits of William Giles and Elizabeth at the time of their wedding. Elizabeth posed for her portrait in her wedding dress.[22]

Randal McGavock is thought to have given Elizabeth a slave, Susanna, to assist in establishing and managing her new Belle Meade household. Susanna's descendants believe that she and her four sisters were freeborn and that they were illegally enslaved by McGavock when their father, an English adventurer, died of cholera in New Orleans. Family oral history indicates that Susanna's grandmother was a full-

Elizabeth McGavock Harding (1818-67), Harding's second wife. Painting by Edward Troye, collection of Mr. and Mrs. John H. Zink III, Baltimore

blooded Creek Indian named Grandma Jonah, who lived on Cedar Knob where the Tennessee State Capitol stands today. Grandma Jonah's husband was a black man whose name is unknown. Their daughter married the English adventurer and was Susanna's mother.[23]

Susanna's mixed racial features are prominent in a photograph made of her in later years. She married "Big" Ike Carter, another Belle Meade slave, raised three children, and remained as a trusted and beloved housekeeper and servant there until near the end of her long life, which spanned most of the nineteenth century. Susanna's sister Ann was once owned by David H. and Willie Harding McGavock and lived at their farm, Two Rivers.[24]

With a new wife to support, General Harding was eager to collect money owed him by several parties, some local and some in the Deep South. Three times during the first half of the 1840s, he was a successful plaintiff in the Davidson County Circuit Court for debts owed him. The tables were turned on Harding in May 1845, however, when he and two co-defendants were ordered by the circuit court to pay the Bank of Tennessee a debt of $850 plus damages.[25] Ironically, Harding's father and his brother-in-law, Joseph Clay, were, or had been, directors of the bank. Nevertheless, General Harding eventually moved his account to the Union Bank of Tennessee where his friend John M. Bass was president.[26]

To deal with his more distant debtors, Harding employed William Claiborne to go to New Orleans and other river towns to collect outstanding amounts. On March 18, 1842, Claiborne wrote Harding from aboard the steamboat *Red Rover* at New Orleans to report that, in his opinion, nothing could then be done about the claim against Sam Houston. He enclosed with his letter "all the accounts except that against [Thomas] Wells," which he promised to "endeavor to collect." He also commented on the impressive residence of a Mr. Thomas Duncan.[27] Those comments imply that Harding had charged Claiborne to observe the architectural features of some of the handsome houses along the river.

Perhaps stirred and encouraged by Claiborne's reports of the magnificent plantation houses of the Deep South, Harding launched a major remodeling of his own home. He added a nursery on the second floor over the office and built a two-story kitchen wing, which he connected to the house by an open two-story breezeway. Though no drawings or other records exist to certify that both structures were added as part of the same project, the type of roof construction used for the nursery and kitchen house indicates that both were built during the same period. The common bond pattern and the type of mortar used to lay the brick additions were similar but of a lesser quality than those of the original house. In addition, the baseboards in the nursery and kitchen match each other but differ from those in the original house, suggesting a common plan.[28]

To allow access from the master bedroom of the main house to the nursery, a door was cut through the southwest wall of the main structure. Since the nursery was on a slightly lower level, some steps had to be built to connect the two rooms. A doorway was also added leading from the nursery onto the second floor of the breezeway, allowing access to servants who may have slept on the second floor of the kitchen house.[29] With two small stepsons to care for, Elizabeth could use the additional rooms. And because she and General Harding wanted more children, they were pleased when Elizabeth soon became pregnant. Sadly, some years would pass before William Giles and Elizabeth had children of their own. A baby daughter was born dead in 1841. Another pregnancy in 1844 resulted in another stillbirth. Between those events came nine-year-old Nathaniel's horseback-riding accident and tragic death in 1843. Then, in 1845, came the death of General Harding's mother, Susan.[30]

Personal tragedy did not lessen the general's spirit of innovative building, however. By the mid-1840s, it is likely that Harding had built a greenhouse attached to the south wall of his garden house. Constructed partially below ground to take advantage of the earth's heat, the pit-style greenhouse is thought to be one of the earliest of its type in the South. The mortar in its brick walls contains large granules of lime characteristic of the mortar used in the first half of the nineteenth century. Harding's innovativeness also demonstrated itself when he devised a rain gauge in the early 1840s. Apparently tired of having his hands return from the fields to say that it was too wet to plow, he needed a way to tell how much rain had fallen, particularly at night. Consequently, he had his slaves set in the ground a post seven feet long and six or eight inches in diameter. He chose an open space where neither house nor trees would obstruct the rainfall. They then nailed a tin cup to the post. For the rest of his working life, Harding used a rain cup to measure and record rainfall. Later, he substituted a quart cup, then a glass jar. He even had a glazier cut off the jar at a desired height and graduated it in inches to save the trouble of measuring. In 1873, Harding said that he had used his rain cup for thirty years and that it had profited nobody but himself.[31]

One of the most exciting developments of the 1840s was the macadamized road connecting the Richland Creek area with the Harpeth
River. On January 30, 1844, the Richland Turnpike Company was
incorporated. When the turnpike was completed a few years later at a
cost about thirty-five thousand dollars, it ran out the valley and over the
Harpeth Ridge to terminate at Providence Baptist Church.[32] The turnpike had been in the planning stage a long time. Alternative plans had
been drawn in 1838 for a macadamized road to lead from Belle Meade to
Forehand's Lane beyond the Harpeth River. One alternative was for the
road to go by Giles Harding's and Vaughn's Gap to the Harpeth River.
The other was to follow the old road through Giles Harding's land and up
the "big hill" before descending the hill's west side and proceeding by
Abram Demoss's house to the Harpeth. At that point, the new road
would cross the river and proceed through Forehand's pasture to the
ending point south of his gin.[33] The new turnpike, which followed the
latter route, was constructed largely by General Harding, Demoss, Daniel
Graham, and Frank McGavock. Harding owned stock and was active in
the affairs of the turnpike company for the rest of his life.[34]

Throughout the 1840s, Belle Meade grew increasingly important as a
place of welcome and hospitality for visitors. In earlier years, the plantation had been visited by distinguished Tennesseans such as Generals John
Coffee and Sam Houston and Presidents James K. Polk and, of course,
Andrew Jackson. When Jackson died in 1845 at age seventy-eight, Harding commanded a company of Nashville Blues, a local military company of volunteers, at the funeral. After the solemn ceremony ended, the
company discharged three volleys over the grave.[35] Harding remained a
"dyed in the wool" Democrat of the Andrew Jackson school the rest of his
life. Among the portraits at Belle Meade was one that William S. Speer
described forty-three years later, in *Sketches of Prominent Tennesseans*, as
the most lifelike of Jackson in existence.[36]

One of the first of many visits to Belle Meade by famous Americans
from outside Tennessee occurred in May 1843 when Gen. Edmund
Pendleton Gaines, U.S. Army, and Gen. Robert Patterson of Philadelphia spent a day there. The *Nashville Whig* reported that they were
"highly pleased" with the discipline of the Blues and Guards, another
volunteer company.[37] Gaines may have told General Harding the story of
the roles he and Harding's kinsman, Nicholas ("Bigbee") Perkins of
Williamson County, played in the capture of Aaron Burr in the Mis-

sissippi Territory in 1807. Although that took place the year before Harding was born, he had grown up hearing the story.[38]

The growing prominence of the Harding family and farm paralleled the Hardings' growing real estate holdings. After Elizabeth's father, Randal McGavock, passed away in 1844, his will recorded generous settlements for all his children.[39] Elizabeth received much of his Nashville property, including several lots in town—one on College Hill adjoining the college square, and a number of others in Southfield.[40] General and Mrs. Harding quickly sold their interest in one of the lots to her first cousin, Jacob McGavock, for $3,180. They decided to hold the rest of the property for the time being.[41]

Twice in 1842, General Harding added to his McSpadden's Bend holdings.[42] Six years later, he bought from John W. Pennington, a McSpadden's Bend farmer, 30 acres on the bend's east side at the north end of an island that was separated from the main portion of the bend by a slough.[43] Harding also purchased 471 acres from his Belle Meade neighbor John Johns in 1846.[44] The following year, he and Mrs. Harding sold one of her town lots to the University of Nashville for the handsome sum of eleven thousand dollars.[45] Finally, between 1849 and 1851, the Hardings purchased from Mary McGavock and Joseph J. B. Southall several pieces of property, including a significant portion of Rosemont, the Southall farm on Mill Creek.[46] General and Mrs. Harding may have done so because of Southall's failing health.[47]

William Giles was also a landowner in Arkansas in the 1840s. In January 1844, his agent, Stephen Cantrell, notified Harding that he had successfully acquired 960 acres of Arkansas River bottomland near Pine Bluff and had registered the deed in the Jefferson County Court Clerk's Office. Cantrell described the land as "good" and added that "one or two quarter sections were not flooded during the last high rise." Cantrell also told Harding that he had spent five dollars to persuade a potential competitor not to bid on it.[48]

The second half of the decade brought its own share of good times and troubles. When his cousin William M. Harding became engaged in 1846, General and Mrs. Harding offered Belle Meade as the wedding site. William and his fiancée, Marion Roberts, accepted and were married there on November 26, 1846.[49] Belle Meade was also the scene of rejoicing earlier that year. On April 5, Elizabeth gave birth to a healthy baby girl, whom she and General Harding named Selene in memory of

Harding's first wife, Selena.[50] That was a generous concession on Elizabeth's part. Her decision to do so may have been influenced by the fact that she already had a namesake, Elizabeth Harding McGavock, the nearly ten-month-old daughter of her brother, James Randal McGavock, and his wife, Louisa C. McGavock.[51]

Early in 1847, Elizabeth became pregnant again. Her next child, the Hardings' fourth daughter, was born on October 15, 1847.[52] Her name was Sarah Susan in honor of her two grandmothers. The rate of infant mortality was high in the 1840s, however, and less than nine months later little Susan died.[53] The Hardings were also saddened when William M. Harding, General Harding's first cousin, who had so recently married at Belle Meade, died in 1848. William was buried in the Belle Meade family cemetery beside the graves of his parents. He left a young widow and a baby.[54]

In the spring and early summer of 1849, cholera struck Davidson County, and General Harding was among those stricken. Many of Harding's friends expressed concern, including James K. Polk. Harding recovered, but a few weeks later just after returning to Nashville from the White House, the former president died of the dread disease.[55] General Harding, who had supported Polk politically, joined the many mourners shocked by the president's death and saddened because their friend had no chance to enjoy his retirement.

During the late 1840s and well into the 1850s, General Harding regularly went to one of the best "tonsorial establishments" in Nashville. There, he had his hair cut and was shaved by James Thomas, an intelligent young mulatto, who ran the shop. Thomas was the son of a slave named Sally and John Catron, chief justice of the Tennessee Supreme Court and an Andrew Jackson appointee to the United States Supreme Court. In 1851, when Thomas was about twenty-four years old, he became the first black in Davidson County to gain both residency and freedom. Until then, there was a state law that required freed blacks to emigrate from Tennessee. From 1841 until about 1846, Thomas worked as an apprentice barber. Having gained a reputation for industriousness, he opened his own shop on Deaderick Street. The location proved to be convenient for Nashville bankers, merchants, editors, lawyers, politicians, and planters. Among Thomas's clients were former Gov. William Carroll, Parson William G. Brownlow, lawyer Francis Fogg, and General

Harding. Thomas later recalled that the "old time barber shop was the best of all places to learn the ways and peculiarities of the old time gentlemen."[56] It was also a place to hear discussed the controversial topics of the day.

In his autobiography, *From Tennessee Slave to St. Louis Entrepreneur,* Thomas recalled instances when General Harding talked about a runaway slave and Northern abolitionists. Once Harding said to Thomas, "You have a brother in Buffalo, I believe." Thomas, whose brother Henry K. Thomas was a barber in Buffalo, answered that he did. Harding then said, "Well he treated me in a gruff manner. I went to ask him if he knew anything about a boy who ran off from me. I told him I only wanted to see him. I had come to Buffalo for that purpose."[57] By that time, everyone in the shop was listening to Harding, who continued:

> I received a very cold and indifferent reply which made me feel bad. I went to others and met the same cool treatment. I felt mortified. After two days' search I concluded to leave. While on the street, however, I suddenly found myself in the arms of a strapping Negro. He was the fellow I had been looking for. I believe he was the happiest Negro I ever saw on finding me. He said that he had just heard that I was in town and he started in search of me.[58]

Among the favorite topics discussed by the men who frequented Thomas's barbershop during the 1840s and 1850s were the price of cotton on the Liverpool market, horse racing, the value of land along the Mississippi River, politics, and especially the growing tensions between North and South. All of Thomas's customers condemned the abolitionists' apparent insincerity and duplicity. Thomas once heard General Harding remark, "After stealing the Negroes, they try to starve them. Do you know that when they want to frighten their children into submission, they tell them black Nigger will catch you. They only spirit away our Negroes to provoke us, then laugh at us. They have no use for the Negroes."[59] The Nashvillians' concern over Northern animosity toward Southern rights was common among similar groups all across the South. For over two decades, attacks on slavery and the whole structure of Southern society had been growing, with the most outspoken criticism coming from New England moral and intellectual leaders.[60]

Newspapers urged that a convention of Southern states be called to devise and adopt a platform to "present an unbroken front toward the

North." Nashville was chosen as the site of the convention to be held in May 1850. The selection of Tennessee's capital and largest city showed its increasing importance in the South and Southwest. The purposes of the convention were to protect Southern rights, including the right to extend slavery to the territories recently won from Mexico, and to develop a Southern sectional party to counter the aggressions of the North. Tennessee had the largest delegation. Most delegates were from Middle Tennessee, and almost a third were from Davidson County. One man reported that Tennessee "sent up a mass of yeomanry" who "were honest in the main."[61]

William Giles Harding was, according to the 1850 census, the wealthiest of all the Tennessee delegates, having property valued at $170,000. Harding, Daniel Graham, Gideon J. Pillow of Maury County, and former Gov. Aaron V. Brown were among the better known of the Volunteer State representatives. For the most part, the Tennesseans weighed the merits of secession but continued in their devotion to the Union. The fire-eaters from the Deep South were outvoted. Although the convention could claim little in the way of concrete accomplishments, it probably delayed secession.[62]

6/ Alpha to Omega

O N JUNE 1, 1839, WILLIAM GILES HARDING WROTE A letter to the editor of the *American Turf Register* that Thoroughbred expert James Douglas Anderson said pinpointed "the beginning of the Belle Meade breeding establishment." Though the letter identifies how and why William Giles got started as a horse breeder, it does not announce Belle Meade's beginning as a stud. That occurred at least as early as 1816, when Montgomery Bell's imported stallion Boaster stood the season at John Harding's stable on the "old Natchez Road."[1] Nevertheless, the 1839 letter provides valuable insight into the breeding environment in Middle Tennessee at that time and names the first blood horses that General Harding owned.

Sir—This is, I suppose, the acknowledged centre of the racehorse region. Blood stock here is all the go. To be without it is to be out of fashion, and destitute of taste. So I too have procured a little bit of the real grit, which by-and-by I hope to increase. . . . I began with old Juliet, by Kosciusko; bred by Col. Singleton of South Carolina, foaled in 1822. . . . Since it is a custom to bespeak names in your valuable Journal I will claim for all mine at once, the Greek Alphabet from Alpha to Omega, inclusive. Alpha, bay, by imp Leviathan, out of Juliet; the first colt bred by me; foaled 10th March, 1836. Sold to John C. Beasley for $1,240, and taken to Louisiana last Fall. Beta, ch. f. by imp Leviathan, out of Juliet; of good size and beautiful proportions. She is entered in the Criterion Stake, 4-mile heats, subscription $1,000 each. Gamma, gr. f. by Pacific, out of Melsare's dam by Sir Richard [Tonson], grandam by imp Eagle, g. grandam by Wilkes' Wonder—Chanticleer—imp Sterling—Clodium—imp Silver-Eye—Jolly Roger—Partner, etc. Gamma is a promising filly and has two engagements for next Fall. I hope ere long I shall be able to send you a more interesting account of this Greek Alphabet.[2]

At the second fall meeting of the Nashville Jockey Club in 1839, General Harding was a judge, just as his father had been a decade earlier.[3] He also entered his filly Gamma in a race for three-year-olds. Gamma won both heats and was also a winner at a meet held that fall by the Franklin, Tennessee, Jockey Club.[4]

In the fall of 1840, Wagner, a celebrated and thoroughly tested stallion bred in Brunswick County, Virginia, came to Nashville to test Gamma. Although Wagner had spent the summer at stud in Kentucky and was inadequately prepared for the race, his owner was overconfident. He offered to bet Harding ten thousand to one thousand dollars that Wagner would win. Harding had never bet on a horse in his life, but he was tempted. According to a story told by Jacob McGavock Dickinson many years later, the general felt confident of victory, had the thousand, and needed the ten thousand.

> Feeling the force of the temptation, under excitement, to violate a purpose I had deliberately formed to guide my life, I turned away, walked a short distance, leaned against the fence, turned the question of gain and principle over in my mind, and turned back and declined the bet. Gamma won as I believed she would do, but I was then and ever after more gratified at my victory over the temptation to bet than of my favorite's triumph over the most celebrated racer of the day.[5]

Thoroughbred horse races at that time were usually run in heats of one to four miles. The winner's purse went to the horse with the best record. Sometimes the race was determined in a single heat. More often, races were determined by the best overall finisher in multiple heats, usually the best two out of three or the best three out of five. Some races were open to horses of all ages, and in those cases the older horses normally carried heavier weights than the younger ones. Races were more often restricted to horses of a certain age, such as three- or four-year-olds; fillies normally were allowed to carry a little less weight than colts. For example, in the 1841 Nashville fall races, colts carried eighty-six pounds and fillies eighty-three pounds in a sweepstake for three-year-olds. Entry fees for that stake were three hundred dollars while forfeit charges were one hundred.[6]

In the 1841 spring races at Nashville, Harding and Joseph W. Clay entered Beta and a gray filly by Leonard Cheatham's imp. Merman. In the Proprietor's Purse on May 22, Beta placed third, sixth, first, and first in mile heats.[7] Some weeks later, a traveling correspondent for the *Spirit of the Times* visited eight studs in the Middle Tennessee area. The first on his list was "Harding's and Clay's" where he found six horses in training: Beta and Gamma; Flaxinalla, a four-year-old gray filly by imp. Autocrat, dam by Virginian; Blalock, a six-year-old bay horse by Bertrand, dam by Eclipse; a three-year-old chestnut filly by Priam, out of Isabella, Picton's dam; and a bay colt, a two-year-old by Anvil, out of Harry Hill's dam.[8]

At the fall races at the Nashville Course, Flaxinalla placed second, third, and second in the Jockey Club's five-hundred-dollar purse on the third day. Gamma won both heats in two four-mile races on the fifth day; her times in the eight-hundred-dollar purse were 8:00 and 8:04, respectively.[9] Sometime that year Harding, Charlie Bosley, Henry M. Clay, and William Wynne were equal partners "in the entry of a gray filly by imp. Philip, out of Gamma's dam, in a stake called the Alabama Stake, three mile heats, two thousand entrance [fee] to come off the fall of forty-three over the Nashville Course."[10]

In addition to being a member of the Nashville Jockey Club, Harding held memberships in the Ashland Jockey Club in Columbia, Tennessee, organized in 1839, and in the Huntsville, Alabama, Jockey Club. It seems likely that he and Joseph W. Clay, also a member of those clubs, raced horses in those towns during the early forties.[11]

By 1843, Belle Meade's reputation as a stud farm had spread beyond the state. During that season, John Lamar of Macon, Georgia, had a couple of mares at Belle Meade. In April, he wrote Harding asking that they be put to Priam, an imported sire famous for having won the English Derby in 1830 and for having been the leading American horse in 1842.[12] Joseph T. Harrison was another out-of-state breeder who did business with Harding. Though he knew Harding only by reputation, he wrote him from his Diamond Grove Plantation in Brunswick, Virginia, about the pedigree of some Virginia horses he thought might be of interest.[13]

That Nashville was becoming a major center of horse breeding and racing was clear in 1843. Racehorse talk in the United States during that summer focused on the great Peyton Stake, to be held in Nashville the tenth of October. The stake, worth an estimated thirty-five thousand dollars, was the richest of its day.[14] The *Spirit of the Times* heralded it as "by far the most splendid [event] that was ever gotten up in the country." When the bugle sounded the call at one o'clock on that wet autumn afternoon, only four of the thirty horses nominated for the race came to the post. The two colts carried one hundred pounds each, while the two fillies carried ninety-seven pounds each. On a heavy and muddy Nashville Course track, Col. Thomas Watson's chestnut filly, the get of Giantess and imp. Glencoe, won the heralded event.[15] After the race, the filly was named Peytona in honor of Balie Peyton, the founder of the stake. Peyton was a distinguished Tennessee lawyer, diplomat, and soldier, whose "strongest passion [was] love of country; next to that, love of a race horse; and next to that, love of a horse race."[16]

Among the enormous gathering of racing enthusiasts for the Peyton Stake was Edward Troye, the leading American painter of horses. When Troye stopped in Nashville apparently on his way from Lexington, Kentucky, to Col. John Crowell's stud farm at Fort Mitchell, Alabama, General Harding commissioned him to paint Gamma, one of the first and best of his mares.[17] In his later years, tears were said to well up in Harding's eyes when he pointed out the portrait of Gamma to visitors at Belle Meade.

As the decade reached its middle years, Harding found himself an increasingly major player in American horse breeding, even though the immediate financial prospects were not especially bright. The stallion Epsilon, a brother of Gamma, was in service at Belle Meade from 1844 until 1856. He was advertised to stand the 1844 season at General Harding's at the reduced rate of fifteen dollars. In the same advertisement, Harding solicited the owners of mares to bring them to his residence "six miles southwest of Nashville," where he would keep them at fifty cents per week or twenty-five dollars for the season.[18]

The owner of the celebrated Priam moved the stallion to Belle Meade for the 1844 season, and prospects brightened temporarily. That March, General Harding signed an agreement with his friend Henry W. Poynor that required Harding to take Priam for the season and pay all expenses "attending said season, for one-third of the horse's earnings." The owner was to receive two-thirds of the earnings.[19] Since Poynor signed the agreement, he either owned the horse or, more likely, acted as an agent. Priam earned $2,505 in 1844 from twenty-five horsemen, including Mark R. Cockrill and Balie Peyton. Harding considered only four of the accounts, totaling $260, "uncollectible."[20] Priam's popularity that season was due to the fact that his get east of the mountains won "a larger number of purses than the get of any horse in America and nearly as many as any two."[21] The following season, the number of clients whose

mares were serviced by Priam dropped to twelve, and the stud fees to
$726.66, a substantial decrease. Worse than that, seven of the twelve
accounts in 1845 were deemed uncollectible, including one of $50 owed
by Montgomery Bell.[22]

The reduced fees Harding charged for Epsilon in 1844, the sharp drop
in Priam's stud fees in 1845, and the alarming escalation in uncollectible
debts were all caused by a slump in the blood horse business that lasted
until 1848. The slump, brought about by an economic depression, was so
great in Tennessee that many Thoroughbred foals were not reported in
stud books but were diverted to common use on farms.[23] That depression
may also explain why Harding did not enter any horses in the 1845 spring
races at the Nashville Course. To make matters worse, Priam died at
Belle Meade in 1847. The horse, after slipping to second among American sires in 1843, had regained his title in 1844 and held it through
1846.[24] Priam was considered one of the best English Derby winners of
the nineteenth century. His portrait by Ben Marshall hangs in England's
National Horseracing Museum in Newmarket, and one by John Ferneley
is in the collection of the National Museum of Racing in Saratoga
Springs, New York.

To supplement the stud and pasturage fees Harding received during
the forties, he sold farm products such as corn in New Orleans and fine
mules and hogs at home. Unfortunately, someone stole a number of his
mules in 1844. Harding offered a fifty-dollar reward for the capture of the
thief described as being "about 30 years old, stoutly built, about 5 foot 8
or 9 inches in height and weighing about 150 pounds."[25] In 1849,
Harding sold a mammoth hog weighing one thousand pounds. A local
reporter said it "resembled a small elephant with its snout drove up."[26]

In 1848, the effects of the four-year-long depression started to wane.
Because of the economic upturn, Samuel J. Carter, a friend of General
Harding and a man well known to most Western turfmen, decided to
open a new track in Nashville.[27] He built it on a 250-acre tract owned by
Dr. David T. McGavock. The course, named Walnut Grove, was just east
of the place where General Harding's uncle and aunt, Thomas and
Elizabeth Harding, lived on land given them in 1837 by Elizabeth's father,
Beal Bosley.[28] Walnut Grove had a springy, if uneven, surface that was
"deep and heavy" in wet weather but fast under ideal conditions. Exten-
sive stabling was built at the track, located only a short distance from the
Nashville Race Course.[29]

PRIAM. Engraving by R. G. Reeve, 1830, of
original painting by J. F. Herring, collection of
Mr. and Mrs. Ridley Wills II, Franklin, Tenn.

GAMMA. Painting by Edward Troye, 1843.
Belle Meade collection

EPSILON. Painting by Henri De Lattre, 1855.
Belle Meade collection

With jockey clubs and races at the Nashville and Walnut Grove courses, prospects for racing in Nashville in 1848 were considered the brightest in twenty years.[30] That spring, General Harding entered horses at both courses. On the second day of racing at the Nashville course, Harding's Priora, by Priam, won both mile heats. On the next day, Wednesday, his Corsett by Epsilon won both heats, and Priora finished first in both heats on Saturday. Although her times were impressive enough—at 1:51 and 1:50—the *Spirit of the Times* erroneously published the time for the first heat as 1:41. Two weeks later, the periodical's retraction stated that the time should have been 1:51, adding, "No such time as 1:41 was ever made in this country."[31]

For the fall races at the Nashville course, Harding had two entries. A two-year-old bay colt by Priam came in second in a one-hundred-dollar sweepstakes on September 26. The next day, his bay filly Priora placed third and second in the two heats of a two-hundred-dollar sweepstakes.[32] At the Walnut Grove Course, Harding's bay colt by Priam placed second in the sweepstakes for two-year-olds on September 25. In the day's second race, Priora placed third and second in the two-mile heats. The following day, Harding's brown filly by Epsilon placed second, third, first, and first in the four heats of the two-hundred-dollar Proprietor's Purse.[33]

At the Walnut Grove races the next spring, the betting sentiment was for Harding's chestnut colt Lamar against the field. Winning both heats, he did not disappoint his backers.[34] Just as Harding's celebrated filly Gamma had begun the decade of the forties by upsetting Wagner on the Nashville Course, other Harding colts and fillies, such as Lamar and Priora, excelled on two Nashville tracks during the last two years of the decade.

By the middle of the 1850s, Belle Meade had reached a new height of national recognition. In 1854, a *Union and American* correspondent wrote that there were too many Thoroughbreds at Belle Meade to put all their names in his article, but he cited fourteen mares "whose performances upon the turf, in days gone by, have made them famous": Beta, Bude Light, Corsett, Delta, Diamond, imp. Florestine, Gamma, Kate King, Linnet, Nannie Kilham, Seabird, Tinnet, Velvet, and Volante. The reporter commented that most of the mares had sucklings, yearlings, or two-year-olds. He also mentioned the fine stallion Epsilon, describing him as one of the best sons of Pacific. The correspondent praised Belle

Meade as "one of the best stock farms in Tennessee" and said that Harding's breeding stud comprised "the greatest number of Thoroughbred horses of any, perhaps, in the Union."[35]

With an increasingly large number of blood horses, Harding was engaged in all sorts of horse-related activities during the fifties. In addition to operating a nationally recognized horse nursery, he was involved with racing, showing his Thoroughbreds at state and county fairs, and providing leadership to two jockey clubs.

In the fall of 1851, Harding was president of a new racing association known as the Walnut Association Jockey Club. Stock was sold to members at twenty-five dollars a share. One of his first official acts was to lease from Dr. McGavock, on October 15, 1851, the one-mile-long Walnut Race Course with all its buildings, stables, and fixtures. The agreement called for a three-year lease, with the jockey club having the option to renew it for an additional three-year term. The consideration was five hundred dollars to be paid McGavock semiannually.[36] When the lease expired in 1854, the jockey club chose not to renew it and disbanded. A year later, the track was used for the biennial State Fair of Tennessee.[37] In December 1856, General Harding and Dr. McGavock moved on to become president and vice-president, respectively, of the newly formed Nashville Jockey Club.[38]

During the 1840s and 1850s, General Harding accumulated a large collection of silver cups, pitchers, and trophies won on the turf and at stock exhibitions at state and county fairs across the South. To display his collection, estimated in 1856 to number "as many as one hundred," he purchased three handsome mahogany cases.[39] In February 1927, Jacob McGavock Dickinson recalled, in an article in *Outdoor America* about Belle Meade, that in General Harding's sitting room were "three large mahogany cases containing hundreds of pitchers, goblets and vases worth many thousands of dollars."

In 1855, General Harding, realizing that Epsilon was nearing the end of his career, wanted a painting of his stallion. He knew that the French artist Henri De Lattre had painted Thoroughbreds belonging to his friends Col. William R. Johnson of Oaklands, Chesterfield County, Virginia, and Col. Wade Hampton II of Millwood, Columbia, South Carolina.[40] Fortunately, he persuaded De Lattre, then living in Philadelphia, to come to Nashville in 1855 and paint Epsilon shortly before the famous blood horse died.[41]

Epsilon's successor at Belle Meade arrived in time to stand the 1856 season at the stud. On February 21, the Union and American announced that Childe Harold, "one of the most distinguished horses in America," had arrived by rail from Virginia the previous Saturday and proceeded immediately to the stables of General Harding, who purchased the sire "to improve the blood of Tennessee." The beautiful dark brown horse standing sixteen hands high had been bred by Colonel Hampton, one of the principal figures in the Thoroughbred world.[42]

Harding entered Childe Harold at the 1856 Tennessee State Fair. The Thoroughbred lived up to his reputation by winning the premium for blood stallions. General Harding also won either premiums or certificates at the fair for the best two-year-old stallion, the best one-year-old stallion, the best suckling stallion, the best brood mare, the best one-year-old filly, and the sweepstake for blood horses.[43] Harding's winnings that year included a julep cup at the Maury County Fair and two more at Kentucky county fairs.[44] Childe Harold picked up in 1857 where he left off the previous year by winning the sweepstakes for blood horses at the Davidson County Spring Fair in May and at the State Fair in October. On both occasions, General Harding came away with the lion's share of the premiums and certificates.[45]

In the years just before the Civil War, Harding's breeding and racing activities produced for Belle Meade a reputation that survived the cataclysm. The most outstanding racehorse bred at Belle Meade before the Civil War was Allandorf, foaled in 1855 by George Elliott out of Miss Peyton. In April 1860, the chestnut gelding won two jockey club purses at New Orleans. In one of those victories, Allendorf lowered the American mile record to 1:44.5.[46] Two years later, Loyalty was foaled at Belle Meade, by Childe Harold out of Delta. Loyalty, a gray like his dam and grandam, stood at Belle Meade through the remaining years of the war.[47] He was extremely fast in the mile, and Harding once described him as "one of the most perfectly formed horses ever seen."[48] Jack Malone, a chestnut colt that stood at Belle Meade in the early 1870s, was a foal of 1858. Bred by Harding's friend Jo C. Guild of Gallatin, he was a son of the great Lexington out of Gloriana by American Eclipse. After the Civil War, Jack Malone mares were excellent producers for General Harding.[49] At the Nashville spring races in 1858, Harding's bay filly by Epsilon, dam by Priam, won the sweepstakes for untried three-year-olds.[50] In the fall races at Nashville, his chestnut filly by imp. Albion, out of Delta by

Priam, won both two-mile heats of the sweepstakes for three-year-olds. That same fall, a five-year-old horse named Belle Meade placed second in a jockey club race at Independence, Missouri.[51] By then, the Belle Meade name was familiar to horsemen across the country.

In 1860, the fall meeting of the Nashville Blood Horse Association opened on October 15. Harding intended to enter Loyalty; Caroline, a filly by imp. Sythian; and Chivalry and Louden, two more Childe Harold colts. Unfortunately, he paid forfeits for at least two of them.[52] He had better luck at the Maury County Fair a week earlier; during the blood horse competition, his Corsair, Labrador, Delta, Meteor, and Gem won premiums or certificates.[53] A small coin silver pitcher in the trophy collection at Belle Meade has the following inscription: "To Delta Columbia, Tenn. 1860 W. G. Harding." It was one of the last premiums Harding won in the prewar era.

7/ A Spacious and Elegant Home

THE SPRING OF 1850 WAS AN EXCITING TIME IN THE Harding household for a variety of reasons. First, Elizabeth McGavock Harding had given birth to a baby girl named Mary Elizabeth on February 5.[1] By the early spring it was clear that, unlike Elizabeth's two preceding babies, Mary was healthy and would live. The joy of a healthy baby was tempered in April by a damaging spring storm that unleashed "awful hail" and high waters. The cost of damage to the plantation was "at least $1.50 per acre."[2] Then, in May, came a wedding. Because Mrs. Harding was not up to par following Mary's birth, she and General Harding did not go to Memphis for the engagement party for David H. McGavock, Harding's nephew, and Willie Elizabeth Harding, the general's first cousin. David had met and fallen in love with Willie soon after she graduated from the Nashville Female Academy. The young couple were temporarily separated when Willie returned to Memphis to live with her mother and stepfather, Elizabeth and Frank A. Owen. Following their marriage on May 23, 1850, David and Willie set up housekeeping at Two Rivers, the thousand-acre farm her father, William Harding, had owned prior to his death in 1832.[3]

Following the birth of their new daughter, the Hardings likely began making plans for further remodeling their house. But before launching that project, General Harding's attention was focused on a vacation he had been planning for Elizabeth and himself for some months. Traditionally, Harding's friends and other Southern gentry traveled to one or more of the regional mountain springs, such as Beersheba Springs, Tennessee, or the Warm and Hot Springs in Virginia, to take the waters for their supposed medicinal benefits and to escape the summer heat. Harding had something more ambitious in mind. He wanted his wife to see the Eastern cities and New England countryside he had known when he was a student at Captain Partridge's academy. As preparation for the trip, Harding asked four Nashville friends to write letters of introduction to acquaintances in Philadelphia, Boston, Burlington, Vermont, and New York City.

In late June, General and Mrs. Harding, his son John, and "the Misses Bass" left for the Eastern seaboard.[4] The party stopped briefly at Richmond, where Harding enjoyed seeing his first cousin, George M. Harding.[5] They then pushed on by stage to Cape May, New Jersey, a posh resort at the tip of Delaware Bay, where reservations had been made for them at the Columbia House by a young McGavock kinsman, possibly Randal W. McGavock, who was traveling in the North at the time.[6]

An unfortunate incident occurred at the Columbia House, culminating a series of unpleasant quarrels and fights in almost every city young McGavock and his friends passed through.[7] Here is General Harding's version of what happened:

> We arrived about 9 P.M., Saturday night [August 2] in a storm—our trunks arrived about two hours afterwards—and, in the meantime, the ladies had to sit in their wet clothes. As soon as the trunks were placed upon the gallery, the gentleman referred to (Mr. McGavock) requested the porter . . . to take the baggage to the ladies' room, as speedily as possible. He replied that he understood his business, and did not intend to be hurried. Mr. McGavock then told him to let them alone, and he would get someone else to take them up immediately. The negro said that it was his business, and that he would do it in his own time. Mr. McGavock then said if he touched one of the trunks, he would knock him down. The negro rose immediately, in a threatening manner, saying, that was a two-handed game. McGavock turned to a youth standing near, to take an umbrella from his hand, but failed in getting it. At this instant . . . the negro seized McGavock's collar, and tore it open; a half dozen blows were rapidly exchanged, when McGavock having staggered the negro, gained time to seize two tumblers. With the first he missed—with the second he gave the negro a blow between the eyes, which stunned him though it did not knock him down. During the fight, the youth referred to did break the umbrella by a blow upon the negro's head; but I presume he did very little injury. An instant after, the room was filled with infuriated negroes, swearing vengeance, . . . and defying the authority of the landlord. At this time, McGavock certainly was in danger of assassination, when a sister of his rushed through the crowd, seized him, and induced him to go to the parlor, as cool as a man ever was under the circumstances. . . . The gentleman

kept assuring us the whole matter should be settled. About this time, some of the boarders . . . volunteered their assistance to the landlord in quelling the riot. McGavock was not secreted, nor did he take the New York boat next morning. He with the rest of the party went the next day to the table and other public places. We could not get the attention we required, many of the negro waiters refusing when requested by the landlord to attend to us, and we met with insolent and threatening looks on every side. . . . Having borne the insolent looks and manners of the blacks all day, after 10 P.M., we consulted with a few friends, and concluded for the sake of the peace and quiet of the house, and particularly on account of the ladies, . . . also, to avoid the annoyance of a suit, with none but infuriated and prejudiced negro witnesses, the two young gentlemen had better leave. This they did in the regular Philadelphia boat on Monday morning. Since that time we have been well waited upon and provided for.[8]

A few days after the fight at Cape May, a *Philadelphia Public Ledger* correspondent wrote an article giving, according to General Harding, an incorrect account of the affair. Because of the article's unfairness and the "unmerited and vulgar reflections on the character of a gentleman [McGavock]," the Tennesseans were outraged. Accordingly, General Harding mailed the newspaper his version of what took place. Though the correspondent wrote a new version, correcting his former errors and "giving the facts as they occurred," the *Public Ledger* never retracted the original story, which was carried in a number of newspapers.[9]

After writing the editor a final letter, General Harding and his party left for Philadelphia. From there they continued north to Boston and Cambridge, where John Harding, Jr., would soon enroll at Harvard College.[10] While in New England, the Tennesseans undoubtedly stopped by the American Literary, Scientific and Military Academy campus in Middletown, Connecticut, even though the school was no longer there.[11] General Harding wanted his family to see the campus and buildings where he spent his college years. The northernmost point on their tour was Vermont. After visiting sites in that state, the party returned to Nashville by way of New York City.[12]

A year or so after the marred vacation, a fire damaged Belle Meade. Family lore holds that about 1851 General and Mrs. Harding's daughters were dropped from an upstairs window to a feather bed to escape it. When Henry A. Judd, chief of the Branch of Restorations in the Office of Archaeology and Historic Preservation in Washington, D.C., made an architectural survey of Belle Meade in 1968, he found no physical evidence of a fire inside the mansion. However, he discovered a charred wood lintel above the side basement entrance to the house. A few years later, in 1977, an archaeological probe revealed an eleven-foot foundation at the northeast side of the house. Although excavation for a cistern system and the construction of a sidewalk, both after the fire supposedly took place, have destroyed most of the evidence of the foundation, enough remained in 1977 to indicate that some sort of structure adjoined the 1820 house at that end. One theory is that the structure burned in the early 1850s and debris from the fire fell into the open basement entrance catching the lintel on fire. Smoke from the fire could have been reason enough to drop the two little girls from the upstairs window.[13]

The fire may have been the reason for General Harding's construction projects in 1853 and 1854. He made a two-story twenty-four- by fifty-five-foot addition with a full basement, raised the ceilings, created an attic, added a second—or front—parlor and a library on the main floor, and built a portico and two enclosed gable-end chimneys, corresponding to the chimneys of the earlier structure.[14] In effect, the renovation produced a whole new front half of the house. A structural seam on the northeast side of the house reveals that the new section was "butted against, but not necessarily tied into, the earlier house." Probably because the brick did not match, General Harding finished the exterior with a natural gray stucco. The roof was of wood shingles.[15]

In the 1854 addition, an outside door to the central hall, perhaps the original front door, was lowered to allow the construction of the cantilevered, circular stairway. Three sets of sliding doors were built at that time. One set, probably removed early in the twentieth century, separated the double parlors on the first floor.[16] The doors were rebuilt in 1987.[17] A second set separated the library on the west side of the house from the room behind it, thought to have been a sitting room. Upstairs, the third set separated the two bedrooms on the east side of the house. The rear set downstairs does not date to 1854. Those doors are considerably thicker than the two other sets that survive and operate on a different track system.

In keeping with the Greek Revival style of the mid-nineteenth century, the new Belle Meade was "bold in silhouette, broad in proportions, and simplified in detail."[18] The baseboards, cornices, and interior door and window trim were also consistent with the Greek Revival period. The walls of the downstairs hall were painted a buff color above a chair rail and burgundy between the rail and the baseboard, while the plaster niches in the hall and on the stairway were originally painted a rich tan. The earliest paint found on the parlor walls is a brown that was common in American interiors in the 1840s and 1850s. The existing parlor floors of tongue and groove, heart of pine boards, one inch thick and of random width, probably date to 1854. The expensive ruby glass installed in the transoms above the entrances to the front porch and the balcony above the porch also dates to 1854. The color was achieved by adding gold to the molten glass during its manufacture.[19]

Ronald W. Miller, an architectural consultant with the Historic Natchez Foundation, concluded in 1987 that the mantels in place in each of the two parlors when the remodeling was complete stayed in place until a much later date, when they were replaced by Colonial Revival mantels. Two original mantels of the 1854 period remain, one in the office and one in the nursery. In 1987, wood mantels, patterned after the one in the office, were built and installed in the parlors. The primary sources of lighting after the 1853-54 addition were gas chandeliers and wall fixtures.[20]

A correspondent for the *Union and American* (Nashville), who visited Belle Meade in October 1854, offered a description and personal impression of the grand house:

> The mansion of this estate is located on a slight but beautiful eminence, some hundred paces from a well macadamized road that leads immediately to the city of Nashville, and, though not entirely complete at this time, is one of the most spacious and elegantly constructed buildings of which the country can boast. It is true that the massive towering stone pillars that are seen in front, impress one more with the idea of extravagance than utility, yet they so agree in architectural beauty with the whole, that economy would even not seem to require their removal.[21]

The six columns are twenty-two feet tall. Each consists of two sections of limestone cut by Harding's slaves from one of the three quarries on the plantation.[22]

Harding was proud of his new house. On the entablature of the portico, he had his stonemason carve a rectangular inset with the painted inscription "W. G. HARDING. 1853."[23] Mrs. Harding's nephew, Randal McGavock Southall, also wrote his name and the year 1855 on a foundation wall in the basement.

The identity of the designer of Belle Meade is a mystery. Middle Tennessee's two outstanding architects of the period were William Strickland, the architect of the state capitol and Nashville's First Presbyterian Church, and Adolphus Heiman, another of the region's finest antebellum architects. Although Belle Meade's design has been attributed to Strickland by local tradition, no significant evidence supports this theory. For example, the "carefully detailed stone porch at Belle Meade does not quite show the finesse Strickland displayed at Hugh Kirkman's house five years earlier."[24] Also, Strickland always signed his finished work in some obvious but unobtrusive place. His signature has never been found at Belle Meade. Finally, when Belle Meade was under construction, Strickland was in poor health. He died on April 6, 1854, before Harding's great plantation house was finished.[25] The evidence favoring Adolphus Heiman as the designer is similarly inconclusive. He and Harding certainly knew each other and had business dealings in 1838 and 1839. Belle Meade's open pedimented porch of six square columns crowned by anthemions was a detail that Heiman used in his design of the medical department of the University of Nashville in 1851 and the Nashville Masonic Lodge in 1860. The anthemions, however, were not added at Belle Meade until 1883.[26]

The most likely explanation of the mystery is that Harding himself worked out the plan for the mansion with the help and ideas of skilled carpenters and bricklayers. He had studied civil engineering at the American Literary, Scientific and Military Academy and possessed drawing skills. He also had access to practical builders' guides then available in Nashville, such as the *American Architect* by Janis and Newman. His granddaughter, Louise Jackson McAlister, believed that he was his own architect. Handwritten notes found with her obituary notice in 1955 indicate that Harding directed the construction of the house, using "selected workmen assisted by slaves." He also could have given the contract to a single skilled builder, who then acted as superintendent.[27] Whether General Harding, a house carpenter, or an architect designed Belle Meade, the work was that of a well-trained and talented man. The result was one of Middle Tennessee's great antebellum plantation homes.

Soon after their new home was completed, the Hardings had a house-warming.[28] Apparently, the garden drew as much attention as the house. Roses, clematis, coral honeysuckle, and jasmine grew along and over a white paling fence that separated the rear of the house from the garden, two ten-foot-wide beds edged with a mat of white spiced pinks. A wide gravel walk separated the beds and extended all the way from the smoke-house to the family vault where blue periwinkle grew on either side of the entrance. In the middle of the walk was the pit greenhouse, causing a break in the garden's border of nearly twenty-five feet. In the center of the pit was a large box surrounding a mar rosebush (*Roses des Maures*), its trunk almost as large as a tree. Roses grew "to the top of the pit, twining in and out of a wire netting." Their blossoms "hung down overhead like a shower of gold."[29]

The Hardings' Swiss gardener is given credit for the rare and beautiful plants in the garden, including almost every kind of perennial imagin-able. There were lavender, bergamot, thyme, heliotrope, rose geranium, musk cluster roses, peonies, tuberoses, lilies, ferns, hyacinths, jonquils, and tulips. Lilies of the valley were not in the garden but could be found in a bed running the entire length of the house. Virtually all the shrubs known at that time, including box plants, old-fashioned Sweet Betsy, burning bush, and snowball, were also in the garden.[30]

Beyond the flower beds, planted in rows running in the opposite direction, was the vegetable garden, divided down the middle by a grape arbor. Although tomatoes, then called "love apples," were grown, they were used for decorative purposes only because they were considered poisonous. Beyond the arbor and garden was the orchard planted with apple, cherry, peach, and pear trees.[31] Some of the herbs and plants in the garden came from Carnton. Elizabeth Harding's mother, Sarah McGavock, was said to have planted her garden with the help of her friend, Rachel Jackson, who furnished slips and seedlings for it from her garden at the Hermitage. Consequently, many of the flowers and herbs at Belle Meade probably came originally from the Hermitage.[32]

The men who visited Belle Meade were less interested in seeing the garden than the Thoroughbred horses and especially the deer park. The park held a fascination for Nashvillians that would last for decades. It contained fourteen buffalo and "as many as two hundred deer," according to one of the earliest accounts of the park published in 1854 by a local newspaper.[33] Harding later introduced elk, brought from the Northwest, and eventually imported Indian water-oxen for his menagerie.[34] In 1858, an article on a picnic at "Belle Meade Park" appeared in the *Republican Banner and Nashville Whig*. Observing that "everybody knows something of this delightful spot," the reporter boasted that the park's natural beauties were unrivaled, particularly to "one who spends his days and nights in a dusty city." Sometimes groups brought a complete band to the park, but more frequently only a violin or banjo. The typical picnic supper "consisted of ham, sandwiches of various kinds and shapes, pickles, cold chicken, cold broiled pigeons, salad, crackers, and usually a bottle of claret or Scotch ale."[35]

While enjoying the surroundings, picnickers kept their eyes open for animals. Many of them knew that, some years earlier, General Harding had almost been killed in the park by charging buffalo. The near calamity occurred when the general, having brought a stag to the ground, knelt over the animal to cut its throat with his hunting knife. When the stag managed a plaintive bleat, some nearby buffalo apparently mistook it for one of their calves in distress. Startled by a thunderous commotion and the vibration of the earth, Harding looked up to see the buffalo bearing down on him. Escape being impossible, the terrified Harding jumped to his feet, brandished the bloody knife over his head, and ran full tilt toward the charging herd, which parted around him, leaving him unharmed.[36]

Belle Meade guests often had the opportunity to hunt deer. The hunts were usually held outside the park, which was separated from the rest of the plantation by a fence fourteen rails high. Once when Jacob McGavock Dickinson joined the general on a deer hunt, he wanted to take the stand and let Harding drive the deer, but the general insisted that his wife's young kinsman do the driving. Soon, Mac and some others got behind a fine buck and drove him toward Harding's stand near the east end of the farm. Harding was ready, armed with a double-barreled flintlock gun made to order in England for his Uncle Morris. When the deer approached the stand, Dickinson heard the gun "belch forth" and ran up to see what had happened. Dickinson asked General Harding if he had gotten one. Harding proudly pointed to a thicket and said that he rarely missed a shot. Pressing into the thicket, Mac gleefully discovered that General Harding had killed a cow belonging to his neighbor, John H. Williams. Harding paid for the slain cow, but nobody in the family dared mention the hunt in the general's presence for some time to come.[37]

BELLE MEADE MANSION, showing the open breezeway that W. G. Harding added to his father's house around 1843 and the front addition completed in 1854. TSLA

VIEW IN THE DEER PARK (note a deer in left background). From *Art Work of Nashville*

Although the deer park, deer hunts, and Harding's blood horses attracted many to Belle Meade during the 1850s, there was yet another attraction for summer visitors. About a mile beyond the house, on the west fork of Richland Creek close to the new turnpike, was the Red House Spring. The "favorite resort of pleasure seekers" took its name from a "large, red-tinted structure" near the spring where visitors gathered in the years before the Civil War.[38] The spring was also a secondary source of water for Belle Meade. Years later, Harding's son-in-law, William Hicks Jackson, installed a pump, built a pump house, and from there laid pipe more than a mile to the hill east of the mansion. On the crest of the hill, he built a reservoir used to irrigate portions of the farm. Though the deer park and the Red House are gone, the spring house and pump house still stand.[39]

8/ Life in the Fifties

F OR ELIZABETH HARDING THE DECADE OF THE FIFTIES was a time of struggle against declining health. In a letter to General Harding, written early in 1852, Henry Poynor inquired about his "dear friend" Mrs. Harding and expressed the hope that she was well.[1] That remark, coupled with Harding's comment seventeen months earlier about several ladies in his party at Cape May being "in delicate health," suggests that Elizabeth Harding was not well. Between 1854 and 1860, she lost three infants and suffered a serious illness. Her six-month-old baby, William, died of croup early in 1855; an infant daughter, Louise Stephenson, lived less than two months after her birth in 1856.[2] Apparently, there were complications at Louise's birth, because Mrs. Harding spent the next three months in bed suffering from "palpitations of the heart" and a weakness that caused her hand to tremble so much she could hardly write.[3] General Harding took Elizabeth to Kentucky in August to consult with physicians there.[4] Gradually, her health improved. Less than four years later, she was again pregnant, but her last child, born in 1860, lived only briefly.[5] Only two of Elizabeth and General Harding's children, Selene and Mary, survived infancy.

When Elizabeth's brother-in-law, Joseph J. J. B. Southall, died in 1853, his widow, Mary McGavock Southall, and children, Josephine and Randal McGavock Southall, found solace at Belle Meade. Although the Southalls continued to live at Rosemont, they frequently spent nights with General and Mrs. Harding. Soon after Josephine died of consumption in 1859, Mrs. Southall, who was burdened with rheumatism, and her son Randal moved to Belle Meade.[6] Although Elizabeth was glad to offer the hospitality of her home to her sister and nephew, their presence placed an additional burden on her shoulders.[7]

Another death that grieved the Hardings during the decade was that of Elizabeth Harding's mother, Sarah Dougherty Rodgers McGavock, in October 1854. Mrs. McGavock, who was called "good aunt Sally" by her young female relatives and friends, spent a great part of her last years at Belle Meade. She was fondly remembered as a sincere, unostentatious Christian and friend of the poor and hungry.[8]

The haven that General and Elizabeth Harding, in spite of her poor health, provided their family members in the 1850s made Belle Meade a symbolic home for the extended Harding family, particularly for the children of General Harding's deceased uncle, Giles Harding, Jr. One first cousin, Giles Scales Harding, and his wife, Mary Blackman Harding, frequently visited Belle Meade from their home in Rutherford County, where Giles Scales hoped to build a home to rival Belle Meade.[9]

General Harding's hospitality extended far beyond family members. One recipient was a maverick and fascinating physician-turned-farmer and Whig politician named Alexander Jackson. Born in Virginia, Jackson had moved to Tennessee as a youth, studied medicine at the University of Pennsylvania, and practiced for a time in his adopted home of Paris, Tennessee, before moving to Jackson, Tennessee, in 1840. Married three times and twice a widower, Dr. Jackson had twelve children. Harding probably met Jackson when the latter came to Nashville as a member of the Tennessee state legislature in 1849. Among the legislators, Jackson was a prominent figure, admired for his intelligence and skill as a conversationalist.[10]

The Hardings and Jacksons were friends by 1851. In November of that year, Jackson's wife, Eunice, asked her husband to thank Mrs. Harding for the stone slab Elizabeth had sent her for their kitchen table. The following winter, Dr. Jackson spent a weekend at Belle Meade where he was treated to a dinner that included "nice fresh venison." Good food was a weakness of Jackson's, who enjoyed nothing more than a barbecue or a squirrel stew, a "sweetened toddy," and a good cigar. It is easy to visualize the two men in the sitting room at Belle Meade discussing agriculture, politics, and the general's growing interest in better turnpikes and railroads.[11]

While on a trip to South Carolina, Harding became convinced of the importance of linking Nashville with Charleston by railroad. When he returned, he presented the idea to Dr. James Overton, whose initial reaction was that Harding was "wild and visionary."[12] Nevertheless,

Harding's suggestion is said to have led to the building of the Nashville & Chattanooga Railroad. It was appropriate that, early in 1854, General Harding shipped five hundred sacks of corn to Charleston, by some accounts the first such shipment ever to reach that city from Nashville by rail.[13] Harding was also reputedly the first man from the Middle Tennessee area to ship a load of hay to New Orleans by rail.[14]

Despite having proposed the construction of a railroad to the South Atlantic coast, William Giles was considered by some Nashvillians to be a non-progressive thinker, "a man who held to the old for the old's sake." Harding got this reputation because he canvassed Davidson County against the issue of bonds to build railroads to the North. General Harding explained his position this way:

> The interests of our country lie in the direction of easy transportation to our markets. We have all we are able to do in opening railroads to the South, where we find sale for our produce. Let the North seek us by lines which will bring their products to their best market.[15]

In January 1853, General Harding debated R. N. Williamson on the bond question at the Davidson County Courthouse.[16] A month later, John H. McGavock wrote his uncle from Arkansas praising him for "demolishing Humphreys, annihilating Underwood and clashing with the 'Juice locomotive'" Vernon K. Stevenson, president of the Nashville & Chattanooga Railroad and a forceful advocate of railroads in all directions.[17]

General Harding's debating ability, his interest in public matters, and his prominence encouraged others to approach him with the idea of running for public office. In 1855, he was on the Democratic ticket for the state senate. The party's other standard bearers in the election were Andrew Johnson of Greene County for governor, Granville Torbett of Davidson County for Congress, and Randal W. McGavock for joint representative from Davidson, Robertson, and Montgomery counties. Harding and McGavock, who stumped the county together, were beaten badly. Harding received 1,846 votes while his Know-Nothing party opponent, A. W. Johnson, received 3,052. In Harding's home district, he lost by an even more lopsided margin—14 to 48. McGavock came in third in his race, behind Neill S. Brown, the winner, and L. M. Temple.[18] Despite losing the gubernatorial race, the Know-Nothings, who were also known as the American party, elected six congressmen and gained control of the General Assembly. The party, spawned by an angry response to an influx of mostly Irish-Catholic and German immigrants in the 1840s and 1850s, protested against the election of Catholics and foreign-born persons to official positions. After his humbling defeat, Harding never again sought public office.

The following year, Governor Johnson nominated his Democratic ticket-mate and friend General Harding to serve on the three-man state prison board, but the Know-Nothing party, having gained control of the Senate, was strong enough to reject him.[19] Several years later, Democratic Governor Isham Harris, Johnson's successor, had better luck. His nomination of Harding for the nonpaying prison position was successful.[20]

During the election campaign of 1855, Charles Sumner, the Boston abolitionist, made a swing through Kentucky and Tennessee to gain his first real acquaintance with the South's "peculiar institution" of slavery. Sumner visited Belle Meade where General Harding showed him the slave quarters and allowed him to talk freely with the slaves. Before leaving, Sumner said to Harding, "General, if this is a fair type of Southern slavery, I shall have greatly to modify many of my preconceived views of it." Harding, though he had read many of Sumner's attacks on slavery and the morality of Southerners, replied, "I fear that this cannot be taken as an average specimen."[21]

At the time of Sumner's visit, there were well over one hundred slaves at Belle Meade. Census records from five years earlier indicate that fifty-two male slaves, whose average age was 18.4, and forty-one female slaves, whose average age was just under 16, were living there. By 1860, the Belle Meade slave population had grown to seventy-one male slaves with an average age of nearly 20, and sixty-five female slaves, whose average age had risen to 16. Of the slaves there in 1860, fifty-eight had been born since 1850, suggesting that the slave increase during the decade came about through natural means.[22]

With more slaves, Harding could work more land. Ever since the death of Giles Harding Page in 1850, General Harding had been systematically buying from his cousin's widow and children their interests in the 180-acre Page farm bordering Belle Meade on the north and west.[23] Harding further expanded Belle Meade by buying from Samuel B. Davidson, his neighbor to the west, and Lewis Joslin's heirs substantial tracts of largely ridge land.[24] Without an increasing slave population, it is unlikely that Harding would have purchased those tracts.[25]

Though Harding's regard and provisions for his slaves were relatively humane, he was insensitive to the plight of free blacks and lacked any sense of civil rights generally. In December 1856 he chaired a county committee charged with enforcing the rule that all free blacks within each civil district of Davidson County must leave the state unless authorized to be there. At that time across the South, groups of agitated citizens were worried about supposed plots for black insurrections. The many free blacks who had moved to Davidson County from other areas were considered a threat to the slaveholding society. The effort to force them to leave was largely a failure; blacks born free were not required to leave, and many manumitted blacks successfully petitioned county courts to remain.[26]

In January 1860, several free blacks and slaves were convicted of stealing between three and four hundred dollars worth of dry goods subsequently discovered in a slave cabin at Belle Meade. General Harding learned that Henry Hardin, a slave whom he did not own but who was married to one of his slaves, admitted taking the goods to his wife's cabin. Although Hardin argued that he did not know they had been stolen, he was convicted of possessing stolen goods and sentenced to eighty lashes.[27]

Though the reception he gave Abolitionist Charles Sumner in 1855 was lukewarm at best, General Harding loved nothing better than welcoming guests to his home, especially good friends like Alex Jackson. Harding was delighted when Jackson's two boys, Howell and William Hicks, visited Belle Meade a year later. They stopped by following Howell's graduation from Cumberland Law School and Billy's graduation from the United States Military Academy.[28] The most frequent visitor to Belle Meade during the decade was probably Randal W. McGavock, the son of Jacob McGavock, Elizabeth's first cousin. Although Randal was eighteen years Harding's junior, the two men were great friends. Once when General Harding invited Randal and his wife Seraphine for a stay at Belle Meade, the two men talked late into the night and spent the greater part of the next day discussing railroads and their effects on the country. Another topic they discussed was the tense situation in Kansas, where "Free Soilers and Border Ruffians as the Missourians are termed had a desperate battle."[29] As Nashville's mayor in 1858-59, McGavock regularly accompanied out-of-town visitors to the plantation and stock farm.[30]

Randal also attended the party General and Mrs. Harding gave at Belle Meade in February 1857 for John Harding, Jr., and John's second wife, Margaret ("Mag") Murphy Owen. McGavock described it as the largest party he ever attended in Tennessee.[31] John and Mag, the widow of a brother of Frank Owen, had married the previous December. Since both had had previous marriages, their wedding was a quiet affair with only close family members present.[32]

A much less sophisticated or educated man than Charles Sumner or Randal W. McGavock came to Belle Meade around 1852 "to stay for a few days." His name was William Hague, a midwestern stonecutter with "quakerish ways." Hague enjoyed working for General Harding so much that he remained there off and on for a decade or more. Soon after arriving, Hague wrote his brother in Galesburg, Illinois, that he was "at the best place that I ever were at in all my travels" and bragged that he was "doing the best job of stone cutting in the State of Tennessee." Hague added, "The man I am with [General Harding] has 200 mules of the first class."[33]

Hague gained Harding's complete confidence and on several occasions served as Harding's agent for the purchase or sale of livestock, particularly sheep and goats.[34] In a letter to his Illinois family in 1859, Hague predicted that "we will have [at Belle Meade] about three hundred lames [sic] in the spring." He also anticipated that he would go to Texas soon to sell some cashmere goats for General Harding, who was one of the first Tennessee farmers to breed them.[35] Starting with about fifty common ewe goats acquired several years earlier, Harding had, by 1860, goats worth "some 10 to 15 thousand dollars."[36] In November 1860, Harding shipped nine thousand dollars worth of full-blooded cashmere goats to New Orleans on the steamer *James Johnson*. A month later, Hague went to Bell County, Texas, probably in connection with Harding's sale of two pairs of full-blooded goats to Messrs. Black and Hendricks. For the goats, Harding was paid four thousand dollars worth of land in the Peters Colony of Texas.[37]

One of the most interesting men General Harding was associated with during the decade of the 1850s was Matthew F. Maury—naval commander, adventurer, agronomist, and political theoretician. One of their several meetings occurred at the 1859 Tennessee State Fair. General and Mrs. Harding looked forward to attending the two major fairs held annually at Nashville's State Fairgrounds—the Davidson County Agricultural and Mechanical Association Fair in the spring and the Tennessee State Fair in the fall. At the Davidson County Spring Fair in 1858, Mrs. Harding won premiums for a lamp stand map and a colored photograph by John Wood Dodge, as well as a certificate for her entry in the artificial flower category.[38] During Spring Fair in 1859, General Harding won a premium for his horse, Little Trick. He was even more pleased when Belle Meade was selected as the most outstanding farm "of no less than 500 acres." Harding also delivered the fair's concluding address.[39] Commander Maury delivered the annual address at the Tennessee State Fair in the fall. He spoke on the cultivation of the soil and the manufacture of its products. General Harding was undoubtedly in the audience, and he may have reflected on the possibility that Maury, with all his connections, might be able to help him and Mark Cockrill with a scheme to import llamas or vicuñas into Middle Tennessee from South America.[40]

A month after Maury's Nashville speech, Harding wrote "the Pathfinder of the Seas" in Washington, soliciting his assistance. Maury did his best to help his two "pastoral" friends from back home. On their behalf, he enlisted the assistance of George Hobson, a New Yorker who had spent thirty years in Peru and Chile; John Randolph Clay, the American minister in Lima; and Governor Dana, the former U.S. minister to Bolivia. They tried with little success to intercede with the Peruvian and Bolivian governments on behalf of Harding and Cockrill.[41] Correspondence between Harding and Maury on the exotic animal venture dragged on through 1860 with a variety of obstacles preventing it from ever becoming a reality. The illegality of exporting llamas, vicuñas, or alpacas from Peru, a threatened war between Peru and Bolivia, the possible overthrow of Bolivian President José María Linares, and the break in relations between the United States and Peru finally caused Harding to drop the idea.[42]

By 1860, Harding and Maury were both preoccupied with a much more serious matter—the possibility that Tennessee would soon be drawn into a civil war. Maury outlined to Harding a plan he had formulated for a people-to-people type of mediation to prevent war. The idea was for commissioners from New Jersey to meet with political leaders from

Alabama and Mississippi to "ask for a statement of the terms and conditions on which they will be content to remain in the Union." After getting a statement from the aggrieved states, New Jersey would then "lay the ultimatum of the South before her sister states of the North" in the hope that those states would instruct their senators and representatives to support a bill incorporating the terms of the ultimatum as amendments to the Constitution. [43]

Maury wanted Harding to "let the plan be known in Nashville and get up a meeting there to express the pleasure with which the people of the South would regard such a move by New Jersey." He suggested that Harding get the support of the Nashville newspapers and send copies of all proceedings there to the "Governor of New Jersey, to Commo[dore] Stockton at Princeton, Alexander & etc." Maury closed with a plea couched in seaman's language: "Rely on it [;] things have gone beyond the reach of politicians, and if quiet men like yourself will not bestir yourself and lead the people on in the right direction, then the ship is going to continue the drift which for so many years has been constantly & steadily setting it toward the breakers." [44]

When Harding read Maury's letter, he knew that South Carolina had just passed without a dissenting vote an ordinance declaring that the union existing between that state and the United States of America had been dissolved. He also knew that Mississippi and Alabama could secede any day, and that Tennessee would soon have to make its choice. The rift between North and South was perhaps already so wide that no compromise could bridge it. Harding had many troubling thoughts. Would the plantation economy and the world he loved and helped to build be blown to bits forever? Would Belle Meade, the home of his heart, be destroyed? Would Carnton and Bellevue, John and Mag's new home in McSpadden's Bend, also be sacrificed? And what about his extended family? What would the new decade bring?

9/ War Arrives

DURING THE WINTER OF 1860-61, ISHAM HARRIS, Tennessee's governor, was a vocal and powerful advocate of secession. On January 7, 1861, he called the Tennessee legislature into special session, and at his urging the legislators authorized a referendum of the people to determine whether Tennessee should call for a state convention to decide the issue. The referendum date was set for February 9. General Harding followed the proceedings with keen interest. He agreed with Harris that the slave-holding states had suffered many grievances resulting from the "systematic, wanton, and long continued agitation of the slavery question."[1]

By the time Mississippi, Florida, and Alabama withdrew from the Union on three successive days early in January, Harding had made up his mind that nothing Commander Maury or anyone else could say or do would prevent war. It was coming, and Tennessee could not escape it. Accordingly, on the twelfth, he organized and armed the Harding Light Artillery for military service in defense of the South.[2] It was one of the first Civil War companies organized in the state. Had Governor Harris been a Unionist, Harding would have been arrested.

In the middle of January, Harding made what was to be his last purchase of land until 1867. The fifteen acres he bought on the headwaters of Fletcher's Creek completed his ownership of the old Giles Harding Page place.[3]

On February 9, referendum day, Tennesseans rejected by a substantial majority the call for a convention, in effect a rejection of secession. Although they loved the South, they loved their country more and felt that somehow an honorable and peaceful settlement could be reached. In East Tennessee, there was a strong vote against calling the convention. The Middle Tennessee vote was close, with a small majority opposing it.

In West Tennessee, where sentiment was strongest for secession, a majority favored the convention.

Elsewhere, the situation between North and South was deteriorating rapidly. A Washington Peace Conference, to which Tennessee sent delegates, floundered on February 4.[4] On the same day, delegates from six of the seven seceding states met in Montgomery, Alabama, and set up a temporary government.

In March, the Hardings held a Monday afternoon reception for Mrs. James K. Polk. Aware of the possibility that the forthcoming war would preclude such pleasant events for a long time to come, Mrs. Harding made sure the reception would be remembered. She served no less than six cakes—angel, chocolate, devil, Italian, lady, and ribbon. At the head of the table where the cakes were placed, a large crystal bowl held syllabub, a delicacy Susanna, Mrs. Harding's servant, made from pure cream delicately flavored and whipped with madeira.[5] Mrs. Polk's presence at Belle Meade was a compliment to the Hardings because the nation's former first lady seldom left Polk Place, her downtown residence, except to attend church or visit her family in Murfreesboro.

Meanwhile, more pro-rebel militia companies were being organized across the state. Tennesseans in the United States Army were reevaluating their feelings and loyalties. One of them was Lt. Billy Jackson of the U.S. Regiment of Mounted Rifles stationed at Fort Union, New Mexico. On March 10, he was poised to start out on an expedition against the Apaches, but before doing so he wrote his father, Dr. Alexander Jackson, General Harding's old friend from Madison County. Dr. Jackson stated that Billy "shared his anxiety about the political status of Tennessee, and his determination to resign whenever Tennessee dissolved her connection with the old Union, or sooner" if his father advised it.[6]

About the same time, General Harding's stock manager, William Hague, returned from Texas where he had been all winter. On April 14, Hague wrote his relatives in Ohio: "Texas is a hard place and ruff place to live. Everything is high and scarce and they all give the North fits. They all want to fite." Then he added, "They have got into it at Charleston. What will be done it's hard to say."[7] The next day, President Abraham Lincoln called for seventy-five thousand volunteers, including three thousand Tennesseans, to put down the insurrection in South Carolina.

When Governor Harris received Lincoln's request, his response was defiant: "Tennessee will not furnish a single man for purposes of coercion, but 50,000 if necessary for the defense of our rights and those of our southern brothers."[8] As soon as Dr. Jackson heard about Lincoln's call for troops, he wrote Billy to resign knowing that "Tennessee would be out of the union before my letter could reach him."[9]

At Belle Meade, General Harding learned of the South's attack on Fort Sumter the same day John H. McGavock died at Cliff Lawn, the home of his parents, Frank and Amanda Harding McGavock. Young McGavock died of lung complications developed from a deep chest cold caught while fighting a break in a levee at Sans Souci, his Arkansas plantation home, in the spring of 1859.[10] The death of a favorite grandson and namesake must have especially saddened the eighty-three-year-old John Harding. He no doubt recalled happy days spent with John and his young family at Sans Souci.

General Harding also grieved over his nephew's death, but the prospect of war preoccupied him. Sentiment in Nashville had suddenly changed. Confederate flags and secession parades were commonplace. Many men who had been strong for the Union the day before Lincoln issued his call were "among the first to raise the standard of resistance."[11] Harding joined a vigilance committee along with some other prominent Davidson County citizens. The Davidson County Committee of Vigilance and Safety, meeting as frequently as twice a week, assisted legal authorities in locating and removing subversive elements from the community.[12]

In response to the president's call for troops, the legislature quickly convened and passed an act providing for a state military organization. Under the act, Governor Harris appointed former Gov. Neill S. Brown, General Harding, and James E. Bailey of Clarksville to the Military and Financial Board of Tennessee. The board's charge was to spend up to $5 million to equip an army to take the field for the South. Harding was named the board's president.[13] The *St. Louis Daily Missouri Democrat* of May 25 described the three men as "the rankest description of fire-eating rebels," who intended to detain any steamer on the Mississippi going north. Fire-eater or not, Harding virtually had a new full-time job, meaning he would have to rely more than ever on his wife, William Hague, and James A. Beasley, his farm manager, to oversee his plantation. Although somewhat concerned about Elizabeth's health, he was confident that she would handle her role well.

Harding's commitment to the South was absolute. On April 28, the *Union and American* reported that prominent Nashvillians Byrd Douglas, John Overton, William Giles Harding, John M. Lea, and Mark R. Cockrill had "unreservedly tendered" to Governor Harris "their credit and cash, whenever he calls on them, to any amount they can command, to sustain the independence and sovereignty of their state." According to rumors, Harding gave $500,000 in cash to aid the South's cause. [14] The *Nashville Daily Union* reported that "he offered his whole estate, worth several hundred thousand, to Governor Harris." [15]

Between April 27 and the end of 1861, the Military and Financial Board sent at least 108 telegrams and more than 500 letters in support of the Confederate war effort in Tennessee. The first telegram sent was signed by General Harding and Felix Zollicoffer, a newly appointed brigadier general in Tennessee's military establishment. It instructed A. Anderson, Esq., to "immediately examine the Tennessee and Cumberland Rivers with the object of [determining] what are the proper military defenses on those streams north of Nashville and . . . south . . . to the Tennessee line, and report to us." [16] During May, General Harding signed as many as a half-dozen letters or telegrams a day, involving such matters as buying gunpowder in Chattanooga, New Orleans, and St. Louis; authorizing the acquisition of mill property at Allisona, Tennessee, for a troop camp; and asking Gov. John Letcher of Virginia for the loan of "two sets of machinery from that taken from Harper's Ferry." [17]

With the approach of June 8, the date set for another referendum on secession, it became increasingly clear that Middle Tennessee would vote heavily to secede. Two weeks before the vote, General Harding's daughter-in-law, Margaret "Mag" Harding, voiced her sentiments unequivocally in a letter to her grandmother in Mississippi: "Tennessee will cast her vote on the 8th of June for or against entering the Southern Confederacy, & I believe she will withdraw from the rotten dynasty of the North by an overwhelming vote. Our country is in a blaze & all are bidding Abraham an eternal farewell without a thought of reconstruction except upon the Montgomery constitution." [18] Mag was correct. Tennesseans voted for separation by a substantial majority. The vote statewide was 104,913 for separation and 47,238 against. In Middle Tennessee, the vote for separation was 58,265 for and 8,198 against. [19]

Following Tennessee's decision to cast its lot with the other ten Confederate states, Harding, Bailey, and Brown felt growing frustration as members of the Military and Financial Board. Not nearly enough guns were available for all the Tennesseans volunteering their services to the South. To remedy the situation, they asked each gunsmith in the state to "go to work with all his force" and modify or build rifles "for delivery at the armory in Nashville."[20] A bright spot was that Nashvillian Samuel D. Morgan's factory was turning out one hundred thousand percussion caps a day, most of them being shipped "express" to Virginia.[21] For a short period, probably during the summer, Harding was in charge of a Nashville factory that manufactured percussion caps for the army.[22]

Harding learned in late June that he, Bailey, and Brown would interview young Billy Jackson, who had just returned home from New Mexico. The month before, Governor Harris had appointed Jackson a captain in the Artillery Corps of Tennessee. After Jackson talked with the board about "cavalry and artillery equipment, etc," he took the train to Memphis where he reported to Maj. Gen. Gideon Pillow, commander of Confederate forces there.[23] To assist Captain Jackson in reaching his post, an order was issued on July 5 to the railroad conductors in Middle and West Tennessee to pass Captain Jackson "over your roads & charge to public account."[24]

Frustrations only increased for the members of the Military and Financial Board when, during July, the Confederate government became responsible for protecting Tennessee from Northern invasion. On July 2, Governor Harris transferred authority for twenty-four regiments of infantry and calvary, ten artillery companies along with an ordnance bureau, and an engineering corps to Confederate President Jefferson Davis. Davis accepted the troops and replaced General Pillow with Leonidas Polk. Following the change, there was periodic correspondence between the Military and Financial Board and either Polk or his subordinates. Friction immediately developed over an unauthorized attempt by one of Polk's officers to establish an armory at Memphis.[25] A few days after, Harding and Bailey informed the governor of that officer's resignation and his demand for a court of inquiry. They then wired General Polk to request that he "suggest to [his] subalterns to be a little more respectful in their communications."[26]

The transition from state to Confederate government control took its largest step on July 31 when the Provisional Army of Tennessee was transferred to the Confederate states and became part of the army of Major General Polk, commanding Department #1, with its headquarters at Memphis. [27] By September 23, the state had transferred to the Confederate government all its ordnance, ordnance stores, arms, and equipment of every kind. [28] At that point, Harding, Bailey, and Brown reported to the General Assembly on their charge and activities. They expressed the opinion that "as the Provisional Army has been turned over to the Confederate Government, together with all the supplies on hand, there is no longer any necessity for a Military and Financial Board, and that it can and ought to be dispensed with for the future." A detailed statement accompanying the report indicated that the board had spent $4,637,198.77. [29] Though Governor Harris praised the work of the board, he did not disband it.

During the fall of 1861, B. F. Terry's Texas Rangers roared into Nashville. The 1,170-man regiment of Texas college students and graduates, cowboys, and professional men was headed for Virginia when Gen. Albert Sidney Johnston interceded with the secretary of war to have the Rangers sent to his headquarters at Bowling Green. Johnston delivered on his promise to give them horses and munitions while they were camped on the "old fair grounds in South Nashville." There, the Rangers were a great attraction to the populace as they "put their spurs" to their newly acquired horses, mostly wild and unbroken. An even more popular event for the spectators was watching the Texans ride "in full gallop or fast run and pick up from the ground anything they wished to." [30]

A violent epidemic of measles broke out in the Texas Rangers' camp in November. Hospitals and homes in Nashville were soon filled with sick and dying soldiers. That was probably why one Texan, T. L. Ritter, spent some time under General and Mrs. Harding's "hospitable roof" at Belle Meade. One night, presumably while Ritter was recuperating there, some soldiers slipped out of the Texans' camp and went to town. They ended up at a play about Pocahontas and John Smith, and just at the moment Pocahontas threw her body across Smith's bound body to save his life, a drunken Texan fired his six-shooter at the actor playing the part of the executioner. Although the shot missed, two policemen were killed in the ensuing brawl. Governor Harris heard about the tragedy and immediately telegraphed General Johnston at Bowling Green. By daylight the next morning, by order of the general, Terry's regiment was on a train to southern Kentucky. [31]

The Rangers' departure was so sudden that Ritter did not have time to thank General Harding for his hospitality. On January 7, Ritter wrote Harding to apologize for not having done so, and he spoke of Harding's "most interesting family," which may have meant that Ritter was smitten by Harding's attractive and patriotic daughter Selene, whose nickname was Lena. He also gallantly said that "should it be my good fortune to return to my Southern sunny home, I will teach 'others' to praise, admire, and love them [ladies of Tennessee], and Mrs. Harding, your devoted lady, will come in for no small share of it."[32]

Early in December, Harding and Brown, the two remaining members of the Military and Financial Board, wrote Gen. Albert S. Johnston suggesting that a gunboat be constructed on the Cumberland River. Both General Johnston and Governor Harris endorsed the idea, which Mayor Cheatham of Nashville presented to the secretary of war. Possibly in response, Confederate Secretary of the Navy Stephen R. Mallory on Christmas Day authorized Navy Lt. Isaac N. Brown, then stationed at Nashville, to purchase four well-known Cumberland River packets for conversion to gunboats.[33]

When 1862 rang in, General and Mrs. Harding were grateful that no one in their immediate family had been killed or wounded and that Albert Sidney Johnston's soldiers were holding firm to their position extending from the Mississippi on the west to Cumberland Gap on the east. As their thoughts focused on the new year, they were no doubt apprehensive because the war was so close and because Johnston's line was stretched so thin. It was just as well that they did not know how soon war would engulf them.

On January 17, the Tennessee legislature praised the members of the Military and Financial Board and its secretary, F. G. Roche, "for having faithfully and efficiently discharged their duties in accounting for all the monies entrusted to them." The board, under Harding's leadership, had expended a total of $5,034,819.04 over a hectic and trying eight and a half months.[34] General Harding and Governor Brown, the board's two remaining members, had finally closed the books on the Military and Financial Board of Tennessee.

Only a day after a vote of confidence from the legislature, Harding and Brown received the news of the defeat and death at Mill Springs of Brig. Gen. Felix Zollicoffer, commander of the right wing of Johnston's Confederate army. On the heels of that loss came two more stunning defeats—the fall of Forts Henry and Donelson commanding the lower Tennessee and Cumberland Rivers. Dispatches from Fort Donelson, published by the *Union and American* early on Sunday morning, February 16, gave Nashvillians a false feeling of security and hope, which changed when a rumor was circulated at midmorning that Fort Donelson had surrendered and that the entire Confederate force was captured.

When General and Mrs. Harding learned of Fort Donelson's fall, their thoughts turned immediately to kinsmen and friends there. First to come to mind was Elizabeth Harding's twenty-four-year-old nephew, Randal McGavock Southall, who had been appointed an adjutant of the Tenth Tennessee by his kinsman Lt. Col. Randal W. McGavock shortly before the fall of Fort Henry. Mary Southall, Randal's mother, was still living at Belle Meade when the surrender occurred. If Randal was captured, she and Elizabeth hoped that his black servant, Henry Southall, who was with him, would be allowed to accompany him to prison. When the Hardings and Mrs. Southall heard that the Tenth Tennessee was in the thick of the fighting, their concerns for the safety of the two Randals intensified. General Harding worried also about the safety of such old friends as Adolphus Heiman and James E. Bailey, commanding the Forty-second and Forty-ninth Tennessee. [35]

Soon, news reached Belle Meade that Randal Southall, Henry Southall, McGavock, Bailey, and Heiman were all captured and sent by steamboats to St. Louis. There, on February 22, Randal Southall and Randal McGavock met. Shortly afterward, Southall, being sick, was sent to a St. Louis hospital and was later transferred to a prison on Johnson's Island off Sandusky, Ohio. McGavock, Bailey, Heiman, and a large group of other Confederate prisoners were sent by train to Camp Chase at Columbus, Ohio, for a brief stay before being shipped to Fort Warren, a prison on a small island outside Boston's harbor. [36]

For more than two weeks after the morning of February 16, no mail entered Nashville from the south. At Belle Meade, the Hardings were at least able to keep up with local events because General Harding spent some time in town. The news from Nashville in those weeks following the Union victories was of panic, the looting of government stores, and the destruction of the suspension and railroad bridges over the Cumberland River. [37]

On Tuesday, February 18, Col. Nathan Bedford Forrest took command of the city and began to restore order. By the weekend, the Yankees were still not on the scene, so Forrest had his men remove supplies from the quartermaster's department. Because high water had washed out two bridges on the Nashville & Chattanooga Railroad on Saturday evening, he hauled a large amount of meat south over the Tennessee & Alabama Railroad the next morning. The same day Forrest found "a large amount of fixed ammunition in the shape of cartridges and ammunition for light artillery in the magazine." With General Harding's help, the colonel conveyed thirty-odd wagonloads of ammunition over seven miles on the Tennessee & Alabama Railroad. Concurrently, Federal pickets made their appearance at Edgefield on the opposite bank of the river. Later, in a report on the panic at Nashville made to the Confederate House of Representatives, Forrest testified that the chaos was unjustified and that the government stores might all have been saved had the quartermaster and commissary remained at their posts. He went on to state that "General Harding and the Mayor of the city, with Mr. Williams, deserve special mention for assistance rendered in removing the public property." [38]

On Monday, Gen. Washington Barrow, one of the two men who had been mediators in the controversy between Harding and George Childress in 1838, tried to cross the Cumberland by boat from his home, Fatherland, in Edgefield. To do so he needed Federal permission. The officer with whom Barrow spoke about the matter "put his hand in his pocket and took out a photograph & compared the faces and said I believe you are one of the gentlemen we want and would not allow him to pass." [39] The fact that Union officers had a picture of Barrow one day before Nashville officially surrendered indicates that they also had pictures and intelligence files on other known or suspected traitors in Davidson County.

Barrow and Harding must have been aware of the seriousness of their respective situations. Nearly a half century later, Harding's son, John Harding, Jr., said that his father fled Nashville sometime after the fall of Fort Donelson only to return when Federal Gen. Carlos Buell announced a general amnesty to all political offenders. [40] Harding must have left shortly after helping Colonel Forrest move the ammunition on February 23. He was probably gone only a few days since Buell's proclamation was made on the twenty-sixth. [41] In any event, Harding was definitely back by early April.

From the time of the fall of Nashville, rumors circulated that former Gov. Andrew Johnson would be dispatched there to "assist in organizing a provisional government." Harding heard the stories and pondered the implications. Perhaps Johnson would consider their friendship should he assume control of the state government. Johnson arrived in Nashville at night in a boxcar pulled by an engine "patched up from odds and ends" at Bowling Green. [42] It was an inauspicious debut for President Lincoln's newly appointed brigadier general and military governor of Tennessee. Harding and Barrow may have been among those who heard Johnson's speech delivered from the balcony of the St. Cloud Hotel on March 13. In it, Johnson cried out for traitors to be punished and treason crushed. [43] Everyone in the audience assumed that Johnson was speaking in a broader context than Jefferson Davis and Robert L. Toombs of Georgia when he mentioned traitors. As Harding considered Johnson's speech and the fact that a volunteer infantry company, the Tenth Indiana, was at that very time camped in tents next to his deer park, he realized that his plantation was in jeopardy and his arrest likely. He was at least glad that he had asked his trusted servants, Susanna Carter and Bob Green, to hide the family silver. He was not concerned that he did not know where they hid it. [44]

While Harding and Barrow were waiting and worrying, Governor Johnson was busy taking over the machinery of government, appointing loyalists to positions of authority, responding to requests of all sorts, corresponding with the secretary of war and others on the progress of the war, and receiving advice. Prominent Unionist Return J. Meigs and others identified secessionist ringleaders who had been influential and instrumental in Tennessee's secession. Among those discussed were Barrow, Josephus Guild of Gallatin, and Harding, whose alleged contribution of $500,000 undoubtedly drew much attention.

Washington Barrow was the first of Harding's friends to be arrested. On the last day of March, Johnson ordered Provost Marshal Stanley Matthews to arrest Barrow on charges of "offering treasonable language and exerting his influence against and expressing himself as inimical to the Government of the United States." The next day, Matthews was instructed to arrest John Overton, whose first wife, Rachel Harding, was Harding's first cousin. Matthews was unsuccessful, however: Overton, supposedly the richest man in Tennessee, had gone farther south, not to return until shortly before the Battle of Nashville. [45]

The order for Harding's arrest was issued on April 2. Henry R. Meyer was likely the major who arrested Harding. Meyer was a Californian on

Governor Johnson's staff and apparently led the governor's guard, the Tenth Tennessee Infantry, out to Belle Meade to arrest Johnson's old friend. [46] When the detail arrived, a group of Harding's slaves, armed with hoes, axes, guns, and staves, surrounded the soldiers. They asked the general if he wanted them to protect him. Harding told them "of the futility of such an attempt, its evil consequences to him as well as to themselves and with the authority habitual to him ordered them to disperse." He was taken to the State Prison on Church Street where he and James Overton had been inspectors two years earlier. [47]

Governor Johnson wanted to make examples of Barrow and Harding by sending them to some prison "beyond the limits of the state." Accordingly, he appealed to both Edwin M. Stanton, secretary of war, and President Abraham Lincoln for guidance. Stanton wired the governor to "send them to Detroit under guard with directions to take them over to Captain [Alfred] Gibbs," commanding. "They will be sent from there to Fort Mackinaw [*sic*] on Lake Huron." The day after getting that message, Johnson ordered the arrest of a third prominent rebel, Josephus Conn Guild, a Gallatin attorney who had been particularly vocal in his support of the rebellion. [48]

With Barrow, Harding, and Guild safely in jail, Governor Johnson informed them that they would be sent North to an island none of them had ever heard of. The three men located Mackinac Island on a map and discussed the situation. Guild said, "There is one consolation. It is at the top of the map and, when we get there, they cannot send us a damned foot farther." Harding was more serious. "Gentlemen," he said, "we are all old men unused to that severe climate and will never come back alive." [49]

Provost Marshal Stanley Matthews received orders on Saturday, April 16, 1862, to send Washington Barrow, Josephus Guild, and William Giles Harding to Detroit for transfer to Fort Mackinac. [50] Three days later, the secessionist leaders were on their way. When they stopped in Louisville, Harding wrote his wife, assuring her that he was well and bearing his trip into forced exile as well as he could. [51]

Elizabeth immediately responded, telling him how many servants, family members, and friends had offered their help. She also gave some plantation news; among other things, a buffalo had been struck and killed by lightning. Much of her letter expressed anxiety born of concern and uncertainty.

I write as though you had been absent a month, instead of a week, and indeed you have been away a month nearly, from home, though a week and a day from my vision; oh me, how much more like a month does it seem and my very state of uncertainty, as to where you were taken to, makes the time drag heavily. If I only knew you were well, and your spirits as good as your companions, that you would or could bear this enforced separation from your home, with cheerful fortitude, I would be content. I fear the cold climate of Mackinaw [sic], will not agree with your constitution, as I know it will not with your feelings; and hope you will provide additional underwear, particularly drawers, as none you have are heavy; you will find warm undershirts in the top of your trunk. . . . How I wish I had insisted more on your taking a servant; Manuel would have been so faithful, and waited on you so closely, if you were ailing. He was greatly disappointed. That God may protect and have you in his Holy keeping is the unceasing prayer of your loving wife, E. [52]

On April 24, Randal W. McGavock and James E. Bailey at Fort Warren, Massachusetts, heard a rumor that Barrow, Guild, and Harding were coming there and that General Harding was losing his mind. Bailey made preparations to have Harding share his room and mess. [53] Only three days later, McGavock read in a Nashville paper that the three men "had been sent to Ft. Wayne." He noted in his diary, "I wanted them to come here." [54]

Instead of causing Nashville secessionists to have a change of heart about pledging their loyalty to the Union, as Johnson had hoped, there was great sympathy for the plight of Barrow, Guild, and Harding. [55] The *Nashville Daily Union*, though strongly supportive of the Unionist cause, hinted at that sentiment on May 2. The paper ran an article noting the removal of Generals Barrow and Harding as a most melancholy spectacle but putting forward the newspaper's sympathies that went out "in search of the poor bereaved wives and helpless little children of the common soldier." In the paper's view, Southern men had been "induced to forsake their families by such men as Gens. Barrow and Harding."

Andrew Johnson was furious when he learned from a Detroit newspaper that Barrow, Guild, and Harding had received an outpouring of hospitality there. The *Nashville Union* quoted the *Detroit Advertiser*: "They have been feasted at one of our first hotels, have paraded our streets with an officer of the United States service as their lackey, and . . . have visited places of amusement, and have been in communication with prominent secessionists in our midst. . . . Why are they not thrown into fetid dungeons? Why are they not confined?" In contrast, another Detroit paper, the *Free Press*, published a report, picked up by the *Boston Post*, saying that Barrow, Guild, and Harding had "professed repentance for their treason." The military governor wanted to know what was going on. [56]

Johnson fired off a letter to the secretary of war, complaining that the "manner in which these prisoners have been treated by the gov't has increased rather than diminished secession sentiments" in Middle Tennessee. Stanton responded by ordering the commanding officer at Detroit not to allow the prisoners "to go at large." Concurrently, he assured Johnson that he had ordered them "into close custody." Capt. C. H. Wood, the officer who had them in custody, explained that inclement weather on Lake Huron and the incompleteness of facilities at Fort Mackinac, closed since the end of the War of 1812, were the reasons the prisoners stayed in Detroit at the Michigan House as long as they did. [57] The prisoners were reported to have said that

> so far from relenting, they held to the same opinions and purposes they had held from the beginning—that it was an insult to their intelligence, and the intelligence of their Tennessee friends to claim that they did not know as much about Northern sentiment before being brought here as prisoners as afterwards; that their Tennessee friends know that they had all repeatedly traveled over the North, and that they did not like to have the story about them go back to Nashville and their intimate friends, that they had changed or repented, as the *Free Press* reported. [58]

These bold statements made good reading in the local papers, but matters at Belle Meade would soon test the will and strength of Elizabeth Harding as she tried to hold together family and farm during the worst ordeal of her life.

10/ Imprisonment

WITH GENERAL HARDING IN PRISON, ELIZABETH Harding faced daily decisions he formerly had made. Each evening she would sit at the secretary in the farm office and go over plantation records with James Beasley, the farm manager.[1] One uncertainty was how to answer a letter from W. E. Million of Louisville. He wanted Harding to pay a $525 forfeit for failing to enter several colts and fillies in the Galt House Stakes the pevious fall.[2] Elizabeth asked John Harding, Jr., for advice. John said that he did not feel his father owed the forfeit since "you could not have gotten your horses there while two armies were between you and Louisville.[3]

Because of the slowness of mail between Nashville and Detroit, Harding had received only one letter from Elizabeth when he left there for Fort Mackinac on the steamer *Illinois*.[4] Once at the fort, probably by May 15, Barrow, Guild, and Harding were put up at the Mission House until their quarters at the fort were ready.[5] On May 17, William Giles wrote Elizabeth on her forty-third birthday. He described the island and spoke of the congeniality of the two daughters of the hotel's proprietor, a Mr. Edward A. Franks. He also told her that he was sending some photographs taken of himself at Fort Mackinac. Captain Wood, who was on his way back to Nashville after handing over his charges to Captain Gibbs, would deliver them.[6]

Although Harding was being sent the *Nashville Union* and the *Dispatch*, Elizabeth warned him not to trust their accounts of events. Sometime later he learned from her and from various other family members and friends about events at home. Among those of interest were the arrests of Neill S. Brown, James W. Childress, and David H. McGavock; Brown's and McGavock's subsequent releases; Andrew Johnson's refusal to allow John Overton to return to Nashville without taking an oath of allegiance; Lena and Mary's visit with their Ewing cousins at Riverside near Franklin; an order that goods could no longer be taken from Nashville to "any place in the interior without a permit from the Provost Marshal"; praise for a Delta colt; concern for Harding's stallion Childe Harold being "down in his loins"; and the death of elderly servants on the place—Alex and Isabel. Elizabeth mentioned that Isabel died despite being well nursed and attended by Dr. Charles K. Winston, a leading Nashville physician. Dr. Winston had also treated another servant, Manuel, who had been kicked in the ribs by a colt.[7]

With time on his hands for the first time in his life, General Harding composed long letters. In addition to writing his wife weekly, he wrote his daughter Selene ("Lena");[8] "Uncle Bob" Green, his favorite servant; William Hague, his stock manager;[9] and Elizabeth's nephew, Randal Southall.[10] He also asked his Nashville banker, John Porterfield, to write Thomas Eakin, a Nashvillian then living in New York, about the possibility of making drafts on Eakin's account for funds he would need during his confinement. Such advances would be charged to Harding's bank account in Nashville. Eakin was glad to help.[11]

Life at Belle Meade went on, if not smoothly then at least with regularity and in no small measure because Messrs. Hague and Beasley were determined to run their departments as efficiently as possible during their employer's absence. Beasley reported, in a letter to Harding, on the varying conditions of the oat, wheat, and corn crops. He also spoke of the attitude of the slaves whom he described as "vary ancherous to know when you will return to them." Beasley said that the hands were working well, and that they thought everything would "come out right a gain and be as it was fore the war."[12] Lena and Mary went into town every other day to take French and music lessons. Their grandfather Harding often came out to have Elizabeth read him the latest letter from his son. Neighbors and friends visited regularly.[13] Rarely did two days pass that Mrs. Harding did not have a visit from Maj. Daniel Graham, their elderly neighbor.[14]

A minor annoyance was the number of people coming to the deer park on Sundays. Although Mrs. Harding had Bob Green put up a sign at the gate pointing out that the park was closed on Sundays, visitors still came to the house and begged permission to go in, saying that Sunday was the only time they could visit. Mrs. Harding usually relented.[15]

After a month at Fort Mackinac, Barrow, Guild, and Harding were "getting on quite well." Harding, however, was already concerned about freezing to death in the winter. One man told him that the winter temperature on Mackinac Island "was sixty or seventy degrees below Cairo."[16] His spirits were lifted, though, by letters he received from Colonel Bailey, Randal W. McGavock, Randal Southall, and other friends. In a letter dated May 23, Randal Southall, still a prisoner in a Union camp, expressed relief on hearing that Harding was fine. He told his uncle that there were 1,100 of them at the prison on Johnson's Island and that he read newspapers regularly.[17] Randal McGavock, writing two weeks later, expressed delight in receiving Harding's letter, which put to rest rumors circulating at Fort Warren that Harding had died at Detroit.[18] Bailey commented, in a letter written May 28, on the irony of all three members of the Military and Financial Board—Harding, Bailey, and Brown—being "within the control of Federal power," and he spoke of embarrassment over the lateness of Neill Brown's arrest, his capitulation, and immediate release.[19] Both Bailey and McGavock had read a newspaper report that Brown and Governor Johnson had shared a rostrum at Columbia, Tennessee, where Brown denounced secession and the war and advocated Tennessee's return to the Union. Brown's brother, also a prisoner at Fort Warren, felt "very much mortified," according to McGavock.[20]

Elizabeth Harding finally received, on June 6, seven photographs of her husband that Captain Wood brought from Detroit. When Wood handed them to her, tears came to her eyes and she had to excuse herself until she could regain her composure. Wood had earlier told Mrs. Harding that the general's likeness was better than the John Wood Dodge portrait of him hanging over the mantel. But Elizabeth thought that her husband's complexion looked pale "and not as healthful as I hoped." Although Mrs. Harding did not mention it, the photographs must also have showed her husband with a beard because earlier he had vowed not to shave until the South won the war. At Wood's request, Mrs. Harding gave him one of the photographs. Within a few weeks, all the others but one had been given to various family members and friends.[21]

As spring turned into summer, life at Belle Meade seemed more or less normal, but conditions were gradually deteriorating at home and among other family and friends. Mary Southall, Mrs. Harding's sister, who was suffering intensely from attacks of rheumatism in the back of her neck and head, rarely left her bedroom. On June 17, Mary roused herself enough to ride with Elizabeth to Rosemont, her home on the Murfreesboro Turnpike. At Rosemont, only recently vacated by occupying Federal soldiers, the ladies found the house a wreck. Fruit trees, shrubbery, and some of the hardwoods had been cut down and left to rot on the front lawn.[22] A week later, news reached Belle Meade that Mary Bostick McGavock, Felix Grundy McGavock's wife, had died in Memphis during the gunboat battle on the river there. Elizabeth also heard from Federal sources that Joseph A. S. Acklen had not behaved well in Louisiana and had spoken "in a manner unbecoming a southern man." In a letter to Harding, Elizabeth referred to this incident saying Adelicia, Acklen's wife, did not believe the account and that, for her sake, she hoped the story was not true. Elizabeth added, however, that she had "always thought him without any stability of character." The incident, shrouded in mystery, may have been connected to Acklen's equally mysterious murder a year later.[23] In town, eighty-four-year-old John Harding could not understand why his son was in prison. Mrs. Harding wished "to God" that she could answer his predictable question, "When is he coming home, daughter?"[24]

To give her teenage daughter some pleasure, Mrs. Harding invited two of Lena's closest friends, Ida Hamilton and Felicia Bass, to spend a few days at Belle Meade. After Ida returned home, her mother, Louise Hamilton, wrote General Harding enthusiastically about her daughter's visit. Food was still plentiful, she reported, even though one thousand Federal troops had recently descended on Belle Meade "to eat up his substance." Mrs. Hamilton said that her daughter was also impressed with the fidelity of the slaves. Tears had come to Ida's eyes as she described to her parents the "eagerness with which they came to the manor house to hear from Mrs. Harding 'how Master was' and the tone deep feeling with which they spoke" of him.[25]

From late June until the end of August, when Mrs. Harding learned that Governor Johnson seemed willing to parole her husband, her primary objective was to visit him. Toward that end, she made numerous entreaties to Governor Johnson and plans for the trip. Each time she worked out the details, something prevented her departure. Early in July, Mrs. Harding got word that there was no point in going without the secretary of war's permission for General Harding to join her at the hotel on Mackinac Island.[26] Nevertheless, she planned to leave for Mackinac as soon as Federal troops could rebuild the bridge the Confederates had destroyed at Bowling Green.[27] However, John Hunt Morgan's sensational raid into Kentucky and Nathan Bedford Forrest's equally daring capture of Murfreesboro threw "Andy and Nashville into spasms," and her plans were postponed again.[28]

In a letter written to General Harding on July 22, his daughter-in-law, Mag Harding, described the pandemonium among the Federals in Nashville over Murfreesboro's capture and the appearance of Confederate forces as close as Mrs. William Nichol's plum orchard on the Lebanon Turnpike. Because Nashville was almost surrounded by Confederates, there was no chance, Mag said, of Mrs. Harding leaving. As a matter of fact, she mentioned that Governor Harris and the Confederates were "trying to come," and that Harris "will make a requisition for you as soon as he is in power, which can't be far off." Mag also told General Harding about her two-year-old son, William Giles Harding III. Mag said, "You'd be amused to see him, he's the biggest fellow of his age and size in the state; one day he calls himself 'Captain Morgan,' and the next he struts out [as] 'Stonewall Jackson,' and imagines he ought to go to the war and fight the Yankees for putting his dear Grandpa in prison."[29]

Elizabeth Harding had an appointment to see Governor Johnson on July 22 about the possibility of General Harding's being paroled to stay with her at a Mackinac Island hotel. In town, she found that Church Street had been barricaded at the depot "by tying wagons together." Directing her driver, Miles, to try the Charlotte Pike, Mrs. Harding was able to reach Capitol Hill. There, she and her daughters, who accompanied her, were alarmed by the cannons that "perfectly commanded it." Hesitant to follow through with her original plan to see Johnson personally, she wrote him a message that Miles delivered. When Mrs. Harding did not receive a response by 5:00 P.M. as had been promised, she started home.[30]

As their carriage passed William R. Elliston's place, Elliston's daughter, Josephine ("Joe"), who was sitting by the front gate, called out to Mrs. Harding to stop and spend the night since guards at Cockrill's Spring were turning back anyone who would not sign the oath of allegiance. Not dreaming that the pickets would stop a woman with only her two daughters and a driver, Mrs. Harding declined the invitation and continued out the turnpike. As her carriage neared the spring, "an inferior officer of Johnson's precious body guard" stood in the middle of the road and called to Miles to stop. After taking the pass from Miles, he turned to Mrs. Harding and asked her if she had read the oath on the

FORT MACKINAC, view from south rampart showing guardhouse and two officers' barracks. Courtesy of Mackinac Island State Parks

TENNESSEE STATE CAPITOL, held by Union forces and known during the war as Fort Andrew Johnson. Courtesy of Western Reserve Historical Society

back of her pass. She responded, "I have sir." "Do you have any objections?" he asked. Her answer was emphatic: "They are numerous and insuperable, sir, but why do you ask? My pass is correct, and renewed a few days since." He replied, "My orders are to let no one through, unless they take the oath, or have taken it." Mrs. Harding asked him why he did not inform people of that when they entered the city. He responded that he had no orders to that effect, and since Nashville was surrounded by Confederates, they must be very strict with both men and women.[31]

Just then, Miles intervened: "I showed Gov. Johnson my pass this evening and asked him if it would take us home, and he said 'yes.'" The soldier looked at Mrs. Harding for a few seconds and said, "Madam, will you give me your word you will not give any information to any Confederate cavalry that may visit your house, tonight or tomorrow, detrimental to us?" Mrs. Harding said that she would do so because she had no information to give. He then turned to Selene and asked her to promise the same thing. Selene answered very coldly, "I know nothing to communicate." Mary's turn was next; she offered a similar response. They were then allowed to proceed. When Mrs. Harding recounted the story to her husband by letter two days later, she said that "if Miles had not mentioned the 'all powerful name' we would have been turned back, as *every other* was."[32]

General Harding's nephew, David H. McGavock, was arrested in midsummer, charged with having ferried Confederate troops across the Cumberland and having operated his mill all night to provide meal for the rebels. Fortunately, he was able to prove his innocence and was released. David's arrest was only one of Mrs. Harding's many worries. As her sister, Mary Southall, wrote a few days later, "Everything is in such a state of worry and excitement, fearing each day that John [Harding, Jr.] will be arrested, and expecting also to be called upon for Negroes to work upon Federal fortifications, etc., we are kept in a constant state of excitement, and [I] cannot possibly say when she [Elizabeth] can get off." Mary also spoke of her sister's physical condition: "She is *overburdened* with care and—she shows it in her face—looks pale and careworn."[33]

There were plenty of reasons for Elizabeth Harding to look careworn that August. Mary Southall was slowly dying. Also, Mr. Hague, on parole from an earlier arrest, could be picked up again at any time. On the twelfth, the Federal post commander at Nashville called on Mrs.

Harding to furnish twelve "stout, able-bodied men" to build fortifications at Nashville. Mrs. Harding was also required to supply them with axes, shovels, spades, and daily rations. [34] She was so "shocked and appalled by this act of gross injustice and violence" that she temporarily gave up all hope of getting to Fort Mackinac. When the twelve conscripted slaves returned home the following weekend, they told Mrs. Harding that they did not "much like drilling and marching" but preferred handling the pick and spade. [35]

Hay wagons came daily to the plantation for forage for Col. William B. Stokes's Union cavalry regiment. Plantation owners were called upon to supply Stokes's troopers with horses. Mrs. Harding complained, in an appeal to Governor Johnson in mid-September, that "every suitable horse I had except my carriage horses" was taken. [36] Actually, Mrs. Harding was able to save her husband's Thoroughbred mares, as well as the colts and four stallions. In mid-August, Randal M. Ewing wrote General Harding that his mares, including Gamma, were "as well as when you left home." Similarly, Harding's four young stallions were reported to be all right, except that Loyalty's eyes were still a problem. [37] A few days later, Federal soldiers took six horses from the park, giving Randal Ewing, husband to Harding's niece, a receipt for them. None belonged to the Hardings, and Ewing promptly notified the owners. [38]

Randal Ewing and his wife, Ellen, helped her Aunt "Betty" in a multitude of ways. They and their children stayed at Belle Meade during August and volunteered to remain there while Mrs. Harding visited Mackinac. Every morning and evening, the Ewings took the Harding girls to Bosley's Sulphur Spring by a carriage hitched to General Harding's "long-eared greys," mules Randal said he would not trade for the best carriage horses in the state. When Randal first arrived at Belle Meade, he discovered that because of a cracked boiler at the gristmill Mrs. Harding had been unable to make meal for a couple of weeks. Accordingly, he and Mr. Beasley attached the mill "to the horse power at the barn." That saved the eight-hundred-dollar expense of a new boiler and enabled the Hardings once again to be self-sufficient in making their meal. [39] Elizabeth was deeply grateful for Randal and Ellen Ewing's assistance. Although she did not complain, she had experienced a recurring pain in her side, and through fatigue, worry, and overwork, she had lost a good deal of weight. Yet, she had not been "in bed one hour from sickness" since General Harding left. [40]

About the time of Randal Ewing's letter to General Harding, John Martin, a jockey formerly employed by Harding, came to Belle Meade and asked Mrs. Harding for help in getting home to South Carolina. Knowing that her husband was fond of John and had once "sent him to school," Mrs. Harding gave him an unruly gelding that the blacks on the place considered to be "incorrigible and dangerous." Before he could get out of Davidson County, however, John was arrested as a spy, suspected of "conveying letters or information to the Southern army." Hague found out about it and also that Mrs. Harding was suspected of sending letters by Martin to the south. Mrs. Harding immediately wrote Governor Johnson, explaining why she gave Martin the horse, denying her complicity in any type of espionage, and vouching for the young man's honesty and innocence. Mrs. Harding, probably through intervention by the governor, was exonerated. Martin's fate is unknown.[41]

During the latter part of August, marauders bothered the Harding family by shooting turkeys and sheep and by stealing watermelons and other crops. Susanna Carter, the house slave, reported the misdeeds to General Harding in a letter she wrote him, using "Mars Randal" as her "amanuensis." The consideration Mr. Ewing received from Susanna was "certain glasses of peach cordial, black-berry wine, and other knick-nacks." In her letter to her "dear and honored Master," Susanna said that "many servants have run away from their homes" but that "so far not one of yours has disgraced himself and you by such conduct." Susanna also expressed gratitude for a letter General Harding had recently written her and the other servants.[42]

The summer of 1862 was far more pleasant for Harding, though in prison, than it was for his wife. By sometime in June, he, Barrow, and Guild had moved from the Mission House into the officers' quarters at Fort Mackinac, just renovated to accommodate them. There, as the only prisoners in the fort, the three Tennesseans had separate rooms. They were under the custody of a Capt. Grover S. Wormer and the Stanton Guard, a Michigan militia company. Wormer and his guards liked the Tennesseans and treated them with respect and kindness. Wormer even allowed the prisoners to take a two-hour daily walk on the beach, accompanied by two armed soldiers.[43]

One day while on such a jaunt, Guild sauntered up to the courthouse where Indians, half-breeds, and whites were all "manifesting great interest" in the trial of a young Indian for the murder of another Indian. Guild, an experienced criminal lawyer, became interested in the case and soon realized that the defense lawyer was incompetent. With the permission of the court and the lawyer, Guild assisted the defendant by examining witnesses and making the final argument before the jury. Guild's participation had, by that time, attracted the whole town. After he returned to his seat, he was greeted with ringing applause. The jury, after deliberating only ten minutes, found the defendant innocent, and he was set free. As Guild hurried from the courthouse with his guard to return to the fort, friends of the Indian he had defended seized him, raised him to their shoulders, and carried him down the beach in a mood of exhilaration. Quickly, the word got back to Captain Wormer that there had been a row in town involving some Indians and one of his prisoners. In response, Wormer sent a dozen soldiers, with fixed bayonets, to quell the disturbance. After dispersing the crowd and returning Guild to his quarters, Wormer reprimanded Guild severely for "practicing law" and "raising a mob in the streets." However, after Guild explained what happened, Wormer dismissed him and never mentioned the matter again.[44]

A U.S. Army surgeon, a Protestant United States chaplain, Rev. J. Knox, and the latter's wife were also at Fort Mackinac. They were good company for the imprisoned Tennesseans. On Sundays, the chapel within the fort was open to the soldiers, the prisoners, and the townspeople. Since Knox was the only minister in the village, he provided a needed service for the one thousand residents. Barrow, Guild, and Harding were regular and attentive listeners. One Sunday, a Roman Catholic priest was invited to speak. In his sermon, he denounced Southern secessionists, calling them "rebels against the law, rebels in favor of slavery." In the middle of his denunciation, the three Tennesseans rose and left the sanctuary. According to a reporter who covered the story, the guards kept the prisoners from leaving the fort that day. They did not attend church the following Sunday, even though the Reverend Mr. Knox was to officiate. The reporter's final comment was, "They still seem to relish darkness, and hug the secession delusion."[45]

The fort's surgeon described Guild as "a self-made man, a very strange and erratic genius. . . . He observes everything, talks to everybody, and makes himself agreeable generally. The soldiers say that 'for an old secesh he is a pretty good old Brick.'"[46] Guild also wanted to go home.

On June 20, he solicited the aid of friends in Tennessee to secure his release.[47] Six weeks later, on August 1, Guild, having arranged for a ten-thousand-dollar bond to be posted, subscribed to an oath of allegiance to the United States. He was not released, however, until the end of September.[48]

Harding was also considering whether he could accept parole without sacrificing his honor. His wife, sister-in-law, and Randal Ewing did their best to convince him that he could. In a letter written in late August, Ewing explained carefully the "construction" that Governor Johnson placed on the parole and assured Harding that "a number of your intimate friends have been consulted" and thought he could accept it with honor.[49] A few days later, Elizabeth Harding wrote her husband that she had finally given up the idea of visiting him, but she offered the hope that "Gov. Johnson seems willing to parole you." The plan was for Mr. Hague to take the parole to Michigan. Mrs. Harding suggested to her husband that, before coming home, he purchase winter clothing in Canada or one of the Northern cities because everything in Nashville was offered at "enormous prices."[50]

The first two weeks of September 1862 were probably the worst of Elizabeth Harding's life. Mr. Hague was away, apparently headed to Fort Mackinac with General Harding's parole. Mary Southall was sicker than ever. Marauding soldiers killed sixty of the one hundred deer and all but one of the twelve or fourteen buffalo in their park. All the fowl were stolen, including those owned by the slaves.[51] At midnight on Friday, the twelfth, a company of one hundred men came to plunder Belle Meade, and they shot and severely wounded Bob Green when he protested their actions. The next morning, a captain's company of soldiers, possibly the same ones, appeared. They told Mrs. Harding that they had come to get a stallion. When she protested that the stallion, worth "at least $1,500," was "too fine a horse to use as a cavalry horse," they replied that they intended to make the horse a present to an officer. Desperate, Mrs. Harding showed them a document signed by General Thomas, the Union commander, offering a degree of protection to the place. That and the presence of a guard of four soldiers, detailed by Thomas, saved the Thoroughbred.[52] Mrs. Harding remained indebted to George H. Thomas for the rest of her life.

On the same day, pillagers entered the back acreage of Belle Meade and stole nine mules. When one of Mrs. Harding's nieces, probably Mary

Ellen Ewing, refused to give one of them a key to the smokehouse, he picked up an ax and threatened to "dash her brains out." Another soldier chased a black girl into Mrs. Harding's bedroom, and when Selene attempted to slam the door, he "stabbed at her with his bayonet and ran it in" to prevent her from closing it. Pillagers broke into the dairy on Saturday and took every onion, potato, and winter vegetable that Mrs. Harding had to feed her "family of 150 persons."[53]

By Sunday, Mrs. Harding was at her wit's end. Thirty-seven wagons were standing on the turnpike "getting ready to load up with the small amount of hay and oats left on the place." From the house, she could see the soldiers knocking down her stone walls. At least fifty soldiers were digging up a sweet potato patch, while other soldiers, without a commissioned officer in sight, were swarming around the house and the slave cabins, plundering at will. Already, soldiers had killed two cashmere goats that cost General Harding a thousand dollars each; taken all the corn, milk, and butter; and robbed the slaves, one of whom lost a gold chain and all the silver money she had.[54]

Mrs. Harding appealed to Governor Johnson in a lengthy letter detailing all the outrages mentioned above as well as the pillaging of Major Graham's place. Unless Johnson found a remedy for "this evil," she said, all the citizens "who desire to live in peace and quiet will have to leave their homes and leave the country an uninhabited waste." She told him that if he thought she was exaggerating her situation, he should ask Colonel Stokes, with whom she had already made an arrangement to provide all the forage on the plantation not already taken. Mrs. Harding closed her letter with the hope that "your Excellency will be able to do something to mitigate this monstrous evil."[55] It is not known what steps Governor Johnson took to aid Mrs. Harding. He probably did something because he was considered vulnerable to women, particularly if they were in distress. Mrs. Harding took pains to make it clear that she realized the acts committed at Belle Meade did not meet with his approval. A perceptive woman, she undoubtedly knew that Johnson was "highly susceptible to flattery, not only from ladies but also from representatives of the upper class."[56]

Ten days after Mrs. Harding penned her plea to Governor Johnson, General Harding wrote her from Detroit. Unaware of the harrowing experiences she and his daughters had suffered over the weekend of September 12-14, he unburdened himself by speaking of his "desponding spirits." For three weeks, he had expected to hear the order of his release. He said the problem was that, without the sanction of authorities in Washington, officials in Detroit would not honor Johnson's order for his release.[57] Approval from Washington may have arrived on the same day Harding wrote. The next day, September 25, he and Guild were discharged from custody.[58] Within a few days, they must have arrived home. Their fellow prisoner, Washington Barrow, still unwilling to sign an oath, was moved to Fort Johnson because it was deemed impractical to keep Fort Mackinac open to house one prisoner.[59] Captain Wormer disbanded the Stanton Guard, closed the fort, and went on to serve in various Michigan units, attaining the rank of brevet brigadier by June 1865.[60]

When word of Harding's arrival in Nashville reached his plantation, several of his slaves were so excited that they met him on the turnpike about a mile toward town. They insisted that he get out of his carriage so that they could put him on their shoulders for a triumphant processional to Uncle Bob's cabin. There Bob Green, recuperating from the wound he received a few weeks earlier, welcomed him. No end to the war was in sight, but at least General Harding was home.[61]

11 / The Long Ordeal

W HEN GENERAL HARDING RETURNED TO NASHVILLE IN the fall of 1862, he was ordered to report directly to Governor Andrew Johnson. There he learned firsthand the terms of his parole. Governor Johnson wanted to make certain Harding clearly understood his obligations. They were for Harding to "support the Constitution of the United States" and to bind himself "not to give any aid or assistance to the rebellion," including any "information to the 'enemy' which would forward their movements." Harding agreed to the terms, which did not call for him to pledge an oath of allegiance but merely to promise he would not use his liberty "to destroy the government of the United States." Harding intended to honor his parole, although his heart belonged to the South. He still wore the beard he had sworn to keep until the South won.[1]

Although his plantation had suffered severe damage and deterioration in his absence, Harding's spirits were lifted by being reunited with his family. His girls were fine, and Elizabeth would soon recover her strength as he lifted many of her burdens. However, his sister-in-law, Mary Southall, died at Belle Meade on October 22, soon after his return.[2] She lived just long enough to see her son Randal released from prison. He had been exchanged for a Union officer imprisoned by the Confederates before General Harding's release, but he was not a well man. On September 26, he was discharged from his regiment in Mississippi for disability.[3]

During the fall of 1862, Federal foraging parties continued to plague the plantations along Richland Creek, including Belle Meade. In September, DeGrice's Michigan Light Artillery took two wagonloads of corn and a wagonload of oats from Belle Meade. Two days later, the Eleventh Michigan Volunteers took twenty-five bushels of corn from General Harding's place.[4] The same month and again in November, Union

109

foragers raided Major Graham and appropriated eight wagonloads of corn and twelve loads of hay in their two trips to his plantation. Fannie Davis Harding, the widow of William Giles's uncle David Morris, was also hit. A train of eleven U.S. Army wagons stopped by her farm and took about seventy pounds of bacon, shoulders, hams, and sides; over four dozen chickens; twenty-nine turkeys; and some ducks and geese. They also took fourteen beehives, nine loads of corn, four mules, and a wagon.[5]

A much worse fate befell Dr. William Bass, the son-in-law of Squire William Watkins, Harding's neighbor to the northwest. A Confederate officer, Bass was murdered by Federal soldiers early in the morning of October 2 after they had learned, possibly from slaves at Belle Meade, that Bass would spend the night with his family at Watkins's home on the Charlotte Pike.[6]

Widespread marauding and Bass's murder—"without a word spoken, a demand for surrender or even to halt"—prevented the Hardings from seeing much humor in the Yankee occupation. One moment of comic relief, however, involved a Federal officer who seemed absorbed with his own dignity. He was attacked by a swarm of bees from the Hardings' beehive. He escaped only by running down the carriageway and rolling in the creek. That story about the Yankee officer was told in the family for several generations.[7]

Sometime after Gen. William S. Rosecrans arrived in Nashville in November 1862, Harding suggested that Federal authorities divide among the needy of Nashville "a number of condemned horses or mules, such as are totally useless to the government." His idea was that, without hurting the government, those poor people who had been deprived of their own horses for the army's use "would be permitted to retain them long enough to make their little crops." General Rosecrans accepted the suggestion and complimented Harding for it.[8]

Andrew Johnson was also concerned about the "helpless widows, wives and children" in Davidson County who, he said, "had been reduced to poverty and wretchedness in consequence of their husbands, sons, and fathers having been forced into the armies of this unholy and nefarious rebellion." His solution was to assess prominent secessionists who had, directly or indirectly, brought about the sad state of affairs. Johnson announced his first assessment against twenty-seven men in August.[9] A second and far larger assessment was levied against eighty-four prominent Nashville and Davidson County citizens and companies the following December; included were John M. Bass, Neill S. Brown, Archer Cheatham, Mark R. Cockrill, General Harding and his son John, Frank and David McGavock, John Overton, and Philip Shute. Harding was advised to contribute one thousand dollars over the five-month period given each assessee.[10]

Harding was in no hurry to pay his assessment. He was more concerned about controlling his losses. On the very day the assessment was issued, someone burned one of his large barns filled with hay. Fires had been set in other buildings at Belle Meade for several preceding days but had been put out.[11] As a matter of fact, very few of the assessed individuals and companies responded promptly. The following February, fifty-five were cited as being delinquent in making payments. By the end of the war, only 56 percent of the total assessment had been paid.[12]

The Hardings had reasons to be both sad and grateful during the 1862 Christmas season. The best news, of course, was that General Harding was home. Nevertheless, serious problems arose on every side. In addition to the deaths of Dr. Bass and Mary Southall, the pillaging, and the burning of a Belle Meade barn, four or five sutlers seized some rooms in John Harding's house on Church Street. It took a letter from General Harding to General Rosecrans to get them evicted.[13] The Hardings were cheered when news came that General Van Dorn's cavalry had slipped behind General Grant's forces at Holly Springs, Mississippi, and soundly defeated the Yankees. The Southern victory forced Grant to retrace his steps to Memphis and conduct a river campaign against Vicksburg.[14] As so often happened during the Civil War, however, the Confederate victory was followed by a loss. On the last day of the year, the Confederates seemed to be on the verge of a great triumph at Stones River near Murfreesboro, but by January 2 the pendulum had swung toward the Union forces. The carnage was terrible, with a total of twenty-four thousand casualties. General and Mrs. Harding's interest was not only in the well-being of the Confederate soldiers in Bragg's army, many of whom they knew, but also in the safety of Giles Scales Harding and his family, whose home was on the field of battle.

The battle surged around the house and across its grounds. When Union soldiers first arrived at the two-story log house, they took the bricks Harding had stockpiled for building a home to rival Belle Meade and used them to build breastworks. On another occasion, a group of Yankee soldiers came to Harding's home, put a noose around his neck, and prepared to hang him. Only the arrival of Federal officers saved his life.[15] At some point, Giles Scales Harding and his family were forced to leave their Rutherford County home, which was turned into a hospital for wounded Federal soldiers. A short time later, an accidental shelling of the house by Union artillery resulted in a cannonball entering the Hardings' parlor, killing several soldiers and damaging the family's grand piano. Years later, postcard pictures of the "wounded" Harding piano with the cannonball beside it were sold in Murfreesboro.[16] When the Giles Scales Harding family returned to their home following the battle, one wounded soldier was still there. After he recovered enough strength to leave, he gave the Hardings' daughter, Ellen Amy, who had nursed him, a $2.50 gold piece. Later, Ellen had it mounted in the center of a silver medallion given to her by her great-uncle John Harding of Belle Meade. The medallion had come from the saddle of Ellen Amy's great-grandfather, Giles Harding, Sr., whose initials were engraved on it.[17]

During the winter of 1862-63, William Giles Harding kept a low profile. He apparently did not even see his friend and former fellow prisoner Josephus Guild, although they lived only about thirty miles apart. On February 15, Harding wrote his other former prisonmate Washington Barrow, who was then on parole in St. Louis, where he had little to do but report to the provost marshal twice a week. In his response, Barrow wrote that he feared he would never get rid of a lameness he had developed and said he did not think there was "the slightest prospect of my being in Nashville again before the end of the war."[18]

General Harding did, however, frequently visit with his old friend and neighbor Maj. Daniel Graham. Harding was disturbed by Graham's plans to sell his property. The Grahams had been steady friends, and the major had been a great help to Elizabeth Harding during her husband's imprisonment. Harding apparently was unable to dissuade the major from leaving. The seventy-three-year-old native North Carolinian was ready to sell his plantation because continual Yankee raids had taken their toll on his and Mrs. Graham's spirits. Graham sold his nine-hundred-acre place to Howell Huddleston in early March.[19]

About the same time Graham sold his farm, General and Mrs. Harding gained two houseguests. John ("Jack") Ellerson Brown, a Federal soldier in the Fifteenth Pennsylvania Volunteer Cavalry, along with a member of a Kentucky regiment were ordered to Belle Meade as "safeguards to the person and property of General Harding." Many years later, Brown recalled the great courtesy extended them at Belle Meade. The young men were also impressed that General Harding detailed some of the servants "to look after us especially."[20]

Soon after Brown's arrival, a valuable stallion belonging to General Harding disappeared from a secluded paddock that was, according to family tradition, in the "high pasture." Learning the horse had been taken by a Federal cavalry officer, Harding obtained passes from General Rosecrans for himself and a servant to go to the front of the Federal lines at Murfreesboro to find the stallion. His search was successful, and the Union officer, much to his disgust, was forced to surrender the horse. Harding also had an opportunity to measure the strength and position of the Union army.[21] On the evening of Harding's return from Murfreesboro, Mrs. Harding asked him how many men General Rosecrans had. "Her ever courteous husband replied: 'My dear, I fully realize your question is an innocent one, and I do not doubt your discretion, but you must remember that I took the oath of allegiance as a paroled prisoner: also that I was treated as a trusted guest of General Rosecrans. It would, therefore, be extremely improper for me to disclose to any one—even my beloved wife—facts regarding the strength of the Union Army.'" Jack Brown, the Union guard, happened to be sitting in the library at the time and overheard their conversation. He concluded that General Rosecrans "had made no mistake in trusting to the good faith and absolute honor of his southern guest."[22]

Not long after Jack Brown formed his high opinion of General Harding's character, another event at Belle Meade nearly cost Brown his life and made him forever grateful to Mrs. Harding. One Sunday just before dawn, at a time when General Harding was away from home, Brown and his fellow guard heard a persistent knocking on their door.

> Hastily rising and opening it slightly, we heard the frightened voice of a faithful darky girl saying: "Hush! Don't make no noise, kas dere's a party of guerrilors outen the front gyard'n dase getting ready a rope to hang bothen you gemmens." Thanking her, we locked and bolted the door, and opening the shutters of the windows slightly, we looked out in the faint, gray light, and there sure enough was a party of horsemen, about a dozen, and some had already dismounted; and the truth had been told, as two of them were adjusting a rope over the limb of a large tree. . . . Then came a loud knocking at the front door, and a demand that the door be opened instantly

WILLIAM GILES HARDING, ca. 1865.
Photo by C. C. Giers,
Belle Meade collection

ELIZABETH MCGAVOCK HARDING,
1850s. Miniature portrait by John
Wood Dodge, Belle Meade collection

and the Yankees be delivered up. We were just about to open fire from the window, having secured our carbines and revolvers, when to our consternation we could see that the door had been opened, and there right out in front of the entrance stood brave Mrs. Harding, with a drawn pistol in her hands, covering the leader, and telling them all to begone! The leader could face men, but the sight of that lone woman, braving the entire band, appealed to his chivalry; and although the whole band had come prepared for any deviltry—all being more or less drunk—the leader drew back, took off his hat, and bowed to Mrs. Harding. Then turning to his men, he called: "Mount and get away boys! We don't want to disturb no lady as game as that!" A quick mounting of the ruffians, another word from the leader, and the whole band was off at breakneck speed, cursing and yelling as they ran. The Union soldiers hastily dressed and rushed downstairs to thank Mrs. Harding, who was, by then, surrounded by a group of admiring servants. After modestly waving aside the boys' thanks, she said, "But what else could I have done? General Harding being away, our fighting force was not strong enough for that number even if we shot from the window. I was therefore certain that if I went to the door, pistol in hand, they would at least pause: and then seeing one lone woman, they would be ashamed to do violence, for even the roughest men of our country have some good in them; and you see I was right."

Jack Brown immediately realized "from what source the Confederate soldier drew a double inspiration for his valor, backed as he was by the brave and self-sacrificing women of the South."[23]

During the spring, Ida Hamilton visited her close friend Lena Harding at Belle Meade. Jack Brown quickly became infatuated with Miss Ida even though she made it perfectly clear she had no use for Yankees. After Mrs. Harding mentioned, in her introduction of Brown, that he had participated in the Battle of Stones River, Ida coolly said, "Why, Auntie dear, he does not look so very dangerous! But then of course no Yankees are!" At dinner that night, matters between Ida and Jack went rather smoothly until the subject of the war came up. Ida made a disparaging remark about the bravery of Union soldiers, and Brown playfully retorted, "There will come a time, Miss Ida, when you will marry a Yankee soldier." That so infuriated her she stamped her foot angrily and fairly hissed, "I would rather marry a dog than a Yankee!"[24]

To avoid an argument, Brown rose from the table, bowed to the other guests, and withdrew to the veranda. General Harding followed him from the room, apologized for Ida's breach of hospitality, and told Brown to wait. He then returned to the dining room. After a few minutes, Ida appeared on the veranda and said, "My dear Mr. Jack! Please accept my apology for those horrid words at the table. I do not know what made me do it; and I am very sorry for saying what I did!" Knowing perfectly well the answer to his question, Jack asked, "Miss Ida, tell me truly, was that pretty apology of yours all spontaneous and sincere?" The little Southern spitfire replied, "No! I was compelled to make you an apology, for General Harding said that if I did not do so at once, I would promptly be packed right back to Mamma."[25]

Some weeks later, the two Union guards rejoined their regiments. After the war Jack Brown remained in Nashville. One day, while on a train, he happened to see a "tall and handsome gentleman" he recognized as Col. Gates P. Thruston, a Federal officer with whom he had seen considerable service. When Jack invited the colonel to visit with him in the smoker, the colonel declined, saying he was on his wedding trip. He then introduced Brown to "the handsomest and best little woman in the entire South." When Brown's eyes met those of Thruston's adorable bride, they "were mutually dumfounded." As he expressed it, she "was none other than our gallant little visitor, who had made such ravages in my heart at Belle Meade." When Brown started to say something about his wartime prediction, Ida put her finger to her lips and said, "Now, Jack, don't be horrid! Never mention a word of that to the Colonel; for I would die with mortification if he knew I ever made such a dreadful speech about Yankee soldiers."[26]

Harding was grateful for the protection of the two Federal officers, but his losses at Belle Meade before they arrived had been great. He was encouraged to hear on March 13, 1863, that General Rosecrans had established a Board of Claims consisting of two Federal officers and three citizens. Its purpose was to receive, review, and give advisory opinions on claims for damages sustained by the citizens of Nashville and the surrounding area "from the occupation of the place by the military force of the United States." Almost immediately, the board was inundated with claims. Among the claimants were most of Harding's neighbors. Although he was skeptical of receiving compensation, Harding filed, on March 28, claim 439 for $33,826. Before doing so, he apparently took an oath of allegiance. The claim listed seven horses and thirteen mules at $125 each, twenty-one asses at $21 each, one hundred deer worth $300, fifty goats worth $2,500, three buffalo, three elk, 1,650 feet of plank fence, ten acres of garden vegetables, 831 tons of hay, 295 ears of corn, six sets of harnesses, some picks and shovels, and 7½ cords of wood.[27] The horses taken did not include any of Harding's valuable brood mares. Later that spring, a Federal officer in the headquarters of the Army of the Cumberland at Murfreesboro sent a list of twenty-eight brood mares at Belle Meade to Washington. They were by such distinguished stallions as Albion, American Eclipse, Childe Harold, Epsilon, Glencoe, and Priam. In his report, the officer said the mares were exempted from impressment until the "will of government" was known.[28]

The Board of Claims in Nashville reluctantly recommended the following January that General Harding be awarded $27,617.42. In the file compiled on him, someone wrote, "Mr. Harding had not accumulated one dollar of his immense wealth by the fruits of his own labors but inherited it from his father, a slave trader. Slaves made it all."[29]

Harding had received no payment on his claim by March 1867. In the commission's report of that time, William Driver, the board's recorder, stated that "among the claimants are some of the most influential and wealthy men of this State, who not only voted for separation but stood prominently forward urging on the fearful ruin. Their purse, their voice, their all was pledged, if needed, to aid the accursed cause of rebellion." Specifically mentioned in that category were several well-known rebels, the first of whom was William Giles Harding. In addition, notations were made next to their names on the report to the U.S. Senate; beside Harding's claim were the words "chairman of the rebel military board." It was 1885 before the quartermaster general, U.S.A., acted on Harding's claim.[30]

A problem for General and Mrs. Harding in the spring of 1863 was the war's interruption of their daughters' education. Classes had been suspended at the Nashville Female Academy since shortly after the fall of Fort Donelson, and the war was still raging in Middle Tennessee. The Hardings, therefore, decided to send Mary to Nashville's St. Cecilia Academy and Selene to school in the East. Mrs. Felicia Porter agreed to take Selene to Groton, Connecticut, where she would spend the summer before entering Madame Masse's French School in Philadelphia in the fall. Selene's separation from home would be a little easier because she would be with Nashville friends Lucie M. Harris and Nannie and Willie Eakin.

SELENE HARDING, ca. 1866. TSLA

MARY ELIZABETH HARDING, ca. 1866.
TSLA

Harding's management of Selene's education illustrates the fascinating mixture of civility and belligerence that existed between North and South during the war. When Selene arrived at Groton with Mrs. Porter and her daughter on May 30, Lucie Harris greeted her with the news that she had already lined up a sailboat for the summer and that construction was under way on several bathhouses along the river. Quite a colony of Nashvillians gathered at Groton that summer. Mr. and Mrs. A. G. Adams, Mr. and Mrs. Henry Bruce Buckner, and Judge and Mrs. William F. Cooper, all of Nashville, were there, as was Lucie's father, Jeremiah George Harris, a U.S. Navy officer.[31] Although Harris's deceased wife, Lucinda, was a McGavock, Mrs. Harding had no use for him because of his stand for the Union. A year earlier, when she caught a glimpse of him sitting in the vestibule of Nashville's St. Cloud Hotel, Mrs. Harding "did not see him, but passed on" with her veil down.[32]

About the time the Hardings arranged for safe conduct for Selene's move to Connecticut, General Rosecrans's Army of the Cumberland published a "Police Record of Operations of Spies, Smugglers, Traitors, etc.," occurring within their lines. The record, written after the Battle of Stones River, included biographical sketches of some of the most prominent rebels of Nashville and Davidson County. Its characterization of General Harding was particularly demeaning. The write-up began by saying that "the old government was quite too oppressive upon him to be longer content." The scribe then sarcastically enumerated "the particular oppression under which this man groaned." Harding had, the writer said, "a little farm of some five thousand acres," with a mansion that would "vie with those of the old manorial estates of the English barons." The article discussed his wealth, estimated at $2,500,000; his fame as a stock fancier and breeder; and his buffalo, deer, and cashmere goats. It mentioned that he had acquired the title of general "without wading through any extensive ocean of blood," but admitted that his wife and daughters were highly esteemed by all and said that "police records contain not one word of reproach" against them.[33] Then administering the coup de grace, the police report said Harding was, despite his wealth and social prominence, "not eminently a man of brains, and had no reputation as a speaker or writer." To the contrary, "his ideas hardly rose above the eaves of his stables, and his tastes were upon a level with the roll of his grazing lands. He had just sufficient ability to conceive that horses and negroes are the *summum bonum* of this life, and that a separate and distinct

Southern Confederacy was the best form of government for rich men of his ilk."[34]

Though the Hardings could send a daughter North for schooling, conditions in Davidson County in 1863, as suggested by the police report, did not help Harding in his effort to reestablish Belle Meade as a producing plantation. President Lincoln's Emancipation Proclamation was an unsettling influence, even though it did not free Tennessee slaves. The proclamation and an unprecedented collection of free blacks, contrabands, and runaway slaves in Nashville obviously attracted the attention of the slaves at Belle Meade, although most, if not all, of them remained where they were. The depressing news of the death of Randal W. McGavock at Raymond, Mississippi, on May 12,[35] Confederate raids in the Richland Creek area, Union foraging parties, and Harding's indictment for treason in August by the grand jury of the United States District Court were additional burdens for a severely stressed household.[36] Still, Harding made some progress. In July, he shipped four cashmere goat kids to a customer in Granville, Ohio.[37] During the year, his farm produced 850 bushels of wheat, 1,500 of corn, 800 of oats, 60 tons of hay, and 2,500 pounds of bacon.[38]

A *Nashville Daily Union* article, "Severe Rebuke to an Ex-member of the Rebel Military Board," was another irritant. The article consisted primarily of an alleged conversation between Harding and Governor Johnson, said to have taken place in mid-August. Harding initiated the conversation, according to the article's author, by asking the governor what policy the Federal government intended to pursue with respect to enlisting blacks in the Federal army. Harding allegedly added that if the government was going to do that in Tennessee, he intended to keep Selene in school in Philadelphia indefinitely rather than bring her back to a state that would soon become "a theater of indiscriminate violence, robbery, rape, bloodshed and every species of outrage perpetrated by negro soldiers, who will have no regard for the lives, and property of citizens, or the chastity of women."[39]

At that point, Johnson supposedly lectured his former supporter on the outrages perpetuated daily by Harding's friends, about which Harding was silent. When Harding replied that he did not approve of those outrages either, Johnson allegedly castigated Harding for his role on the Military and Financial Board of Tennessee that, he said, made Harding "responsible for the murder of the flower of the youth of Tennessee, and the desolation of her households." Harding's reported response was that he had obeyed the dictates of his conscience in all he had done since the war began, just as he did when he held office under Johnson in earlier years. The governor was said to have retorted that he once thought Harding an honorable man, but now he considered him a traitor, an unrepentant enemy of his country, and a man instrumental in stirring up "mutiny, rebellion, and anarchy in this state." Johnson supposedly ended the conversation saying that the government was determined to put down the rebellion and equally determined to bring all traitors "to a strict and terrible accountability." Wealth and position would not, Johnson was quoted as saying, shield a traitor from the "avenging justice of the people."[40]

Although none of the letters Selene Harding wrote her parents during the year she was in Groton and Philadelphia have been preserved, several written by Lucie M. Harris to Nashville and Franklin relatives have been saved. In a letter written in September 1863, Lucie reported that she and Selene reached Philadelphia early that month. They arrived before the fall session started at Madame Masse's school, so they stayed with their chaperone at a hotel and dashed around town for a week. The girls went to the theater and enjoyed seeing *Macbeth*, starring a remarkable and popular actor named John Wilkes Booth. On the last weekend before school started, they moved to the La Pierre Hotel, where Nashvillians Mr. and Mrs. Robert Gardner, Mrs. John Bell and daughters, Mr. and Mrs. William Eakin, and Dr. and Mrs. Thomas Jennings were staying.[41]

When Madame Masse's school, located on Spruce Street, convened on September 20, Lucie and Selene were roommates. The two girls were among seven boarders, including the Eakin sisters. Presumably, there were also a number of day students from Philadelphia. They found they were expected to speak French exclusively, a challenge for Selene, who had begun taking French only the year before. In addition to their French lessons, Lucie and Selene took instrumental music and voice lessons from an instructor named Parrilli, whom Lucie praised as "the finest vocalist in America."[42]

Grimy, beleaguered Nashville presented a marked contrast to the cosmopolitan Philadelphia that Selene knew in the fall of 1863. A critical shortage of fuel plagued Tennessee's capital city. Contractors for the army and the Cumberland River steamboat trade hired black laborers to cut down trees in the woods surrounding the city.[43] In early October, Ernest M. Bement wrote Governor Johnson to complain that General Harding was selling wood at sixteen dollars per cord "with every prospect of an advance to twenty dollars." Complaining that poor people would suffer in the coming winter if forced to pay such exorbitant prices, Bement offered to sell wood at a reasonable price, after either buying it from loyal citizens or taking it from disloyal parties "on appraisal." Bement undoubtedly exaggerated the prices Harding was getting. Several weeks later, Harding and the assistant quartermaster in Nashville, Captain Perkins, reached an agreement calling for Harding to furnish the U.S. Army with one thousand cords of wood at four dollars per cord.[44]

That fall and winter, John Harding, Jr., and his family felt the wrath of an occupying army. In November, about fifty men of the Tenth Tennessee (Union) Cavalry stopped at Harding's home, Bellevue, on a foraging expedition. Brushing aside the "safeguard" John showed them,[45] they killed his chickens, carried off his garden vegetables, fired shots in his yard, and took all the food from his kitchen table. Two days later, the same party returned and stole all of Harding's milk and butter. One soldier, who appeared to be drunk, threatened to shoot Harding when he refused to cook dinner for him.

In the wake of the depredations, John Harding lodged a complaint about his mistreatment with a brigadier general in Nashville and identified the officer and sergeant who commanded the forage parties. A month later, Harding's "large and elegant mansion" on the Cumberland River bluff mysteriously burned. The fire, discovered early one Sunday morning, spread so rapidly that "everything was destroyed" and the family members were barely able to escape with their lives.[46]

After the dual defeats at Gettysburg and Vicksburg in July 1863, General Harding was convinced that the South would lose the war. Consequently, after carefully reading President Lincoln's proclamation of Amnesty and Reconstruction issued that December, he decided that he would voluntarily take the amnesty oath. Even the cowardly burning of his son's home did not dissuade him from doing so.

12/ Surrender, Loss, and Endurance

I N FEBRUARY 1864, GENERAL HARDING APPEARED BEFORE U.S. Commissioner E. R. Campbell and took the amnesty oath prescribed by President Lincoln in his proclamation of December 8, 1863. Harding swore to "faithfully support, protect, and defend the Constitution of the United States" and to "abide by and faithfully support all acts of Congress," as well as "all proclamations of the President made during the existing rebellion having reference to slaves." When the *Nashville Union* took note of Harding's action, the writer expressed the hope that other rebels would "break the fetters that bind them, and become free men in fact, as well as in name." As a result of Harding's move, the conspiracy charges against him were dropped, and he was discharged upon payment of court costs. About the same time, Harding's neighbor, Henry W. Compton, and his nephew, David H. McGavock, also took the oath.[1]

When General Harding took the amnesty oath, his younger daughter, Mary, was one of twenty-four pupils in their fourth year at St. Cecilia Academy. Often, on weekends, the nuns arranged outings for the girls, and they were pleased to accept an invitation from Mrs. Harding to a picnic at Belle Meade that spring. Some Federal officers heard about the affair and asked to furnish the picnickers with "their best band of musicians and the means of transferring them to the grounds and back. Accordingly, a train of carriages, thirty-nine in number, was in line in due time, with a band composed of splendid musicians." Just as the young people arrived at the deer park, where arrangements were made for games and amusements, rain moved in. Mrs. Harding, who had prepared food for her daughter's friends, immediately invited them to come into the house, saying, "My halls and balconies are spacious, they are at your

123

disposal. If the Sisters do not object to dancing, you may yet have a pleasant day."[2]

Suddenly, in addition to the invited St. Cecilia students, a crowd of people consisting of Federal officers and some civilians, both men and women from Nashville, came into the house, wishing to join the school party. Because the strangers' manner of dancing was "deemed neither proper nor modest," the schoolgirls retired upstairs, leaving the outsiders in full possession of the front hall. A little later, Mrs. Harding was heard to remark, "I am sure you young ladies are so disgusted with the sight you have seen that you will never indulge in the vulgar amusement of round dancing." In Mrs. Harding's view, she had little control because the strangers represented Federal authority.[3]

In early June, Selene returned to Nashville from Philadelphia as a sophisticated eighteen-year-old who had been exposed to an East Coast world of music, soirees, and theater. She found Nashville a swollen, brawling supply depot and rail head, teeming with contrabands, Midwesterners, refugees, Confederate prisoners, soldiers, and camp followers. Little was left of the gentility that had characterized much of life in the prewar city.[4]

As had been true before Selene left home, several Union soldiers were living at Belle Meade, assigned to protect the property. The setup drew the wrath of the editor of the *Nashville Daily Times and True Union*, who objected, in the July 22 edition of his paper, to the practice of allowing Southern aristocrats like Harding the protection of the oath and of guards as well. It was, he said, "permitting treason to be quite as respectable as loyalty and a great deal more comfortable." During the summer and fall of 1864, Andrew Johnson focused on abolition, which he now supported, and on his candidacy for vice-president of the United States on the Republican ticket. On October 24, 1864, there was a torchlight parade by Nashville's black citizens through downtown Nashville in support of the Lincoln-Johnson ticket. Johnson addressed the group, which had pressured him to issue an emancipation proclamation, from the capitol steps. To their delight, he proclaimed "freedom, full, broad, and unconditional, to every man in Tennessee." He also singled out the local aristocracy for monopolizing a disproportionate share of the "lands and wealth of Tennessee" and suggested that the state's loyal citizens would be well served if the landed estates of such men as William Giles Harding and Mark R. Cockrill were divided up and "parceled out amongst a number of free, industrious, and honest farmers." Johnson also lashed out at the aristocracy for begetting mulatto children, and promised to put an end to black "concubinage." Although Harding resented Johnson's speech, he undoubtedly knew that Johnson's public statements were often much more severe than his private utterances.[5]

In addition to the national election and the long-term issue of a more equitable land distribution in Tennessee, Johnson had an immediate problem. There were persistent rumors that John Bell Hood's Confederate Army of Tennessee was on its way to Nashville. Rumors and speculation increased when, on October 30, units of Hood's army crossed the Tennessee River both below and above Florence, Alabama.[6] By November 18, Hood's entire army had crossed the Tennessee.[7] Heavy marching, numerous skirmishes, and bitter fighting continued as Federal forces under Gen. John M. Schofield fell back through Lawrenceburg, Pulaski, and Lynnville to Columbia. After Hood's mysterious failure to attack Schofield's army at Spring Hill, where an easy victory was in prospect, the Union forces retreated to Franklin. There they occupied a strong defensive position on November 30. Feeling the frustration of having allowed the enemy to slip through his hands at Spring Hill, Hood hurled his troops against the entrenched Union army at Franklin in one of the Civil War's bloodiest battles. The Union forces were victorious, suffering 2,326 casualties compared to a staggering 6,202 for the Confederates. Despite having won, Schofield's army quietly deserted their works and retreated late that night to the safety of heavily fortified Nashville.[8]

When Elizabeth Harding learned of the carnage at Franklin, her first thoughts were for the safety of her family there. Her brother John McGavock, his wife Caroline, and their children Harriet and Winder lived at Carnton on the Lewisburg Pike. John had inherited the house after his mother's death in 1854. Elizabeth's other sister-in-law, Louisa Chenault McGavock, the widow of James Randal McGavock, was living with some of her children at Riverside across the pike and on the other side of the Harpeth River.[9] Mrs. McGavock waited out the battle with some of her family in the safe confines of Riverside's basement, while less timid family members watched the conflict from under a large oak tree on the brow of a hill overlooking the river.[10]

When Hood ordered his ill-fated attack on the Federal lines, Gen. Alexander P. Stewart's corps formed behind Carnton in McGavock's Grove, on the right wing of the Confederate army.[11] Carnton, designated a field hospital, was soon inundated with wounded and dying Confederate soldiers. Every piece of white linen, damask, and cotton in the house was used for bandages as Mr. and Mrs. McGavock assisted in the grisly work of ministering to the wounded and caring for the dead. Before the night was over, even the family clothes were used "to staunch blood and bind up wounds." Dawn found Southern soldiers filling all but one room in the spacious house, the rugs and floors soaked with their blood, and the bodies of four Confederate generals—Cleburne, Granbury, Adams, and Strahl—laid out on the home's long back porch. In a battle lasting but a few hours, Carnton gained its greatest fame in a way so ghastly no one could have imagined it.[12]

In Nashville, life went on but with an air of anxious expectancy as Confederate troops drew closer. The day before the Battle of Franklin, Mrs. Harding sent a message to Mary at St. Cecilia, saying that she would send some clothes by Daniel, her carriage driver, and bring her home for the weekend.[13] By that time, December 3 and 4, 1864, Hood had reached the outskirts of Nashville on his advance from Franklin. On Saturday, December 3, some Confederate cavalrymen rode through the Belle Meade grounds, passing between the cistern and the east end of the house. The place was quiet, "everything was covered with ice," and they saw no one at home.[14] The following week, ravenous Confederate troops slaughtered some of General Harding's Southdown sheep and Durham cattle and stole some of his Thoroughbred horses as well as some forage and provisions.[15]

On Saturday, December 10, the weather turned miserably cold, with a heavy snow followed by sleet. During the bad weather, Confederate Gen. James R. Chalmers and his staff made their headquarters at Belle Meade, having been invited to do so by the Hardings, according to Capt. James Dinkins, a staff officer who stayed there. In extending the invitation, Harding clearly violated the Union amnesty oath he took the previous February.

After the war ended, Dinkins remembered Mrs. Harding as "a lady of marked character and ability." He said, "She presided over that grand old home with unsurpassed eloquence, and I venture to speak for all the party, when I say they were never better or more hospitably entertained." On that particular weekend both Harding daughters, Mary and Selene, were at home. Selene, the older and prettier of the two, was an immediate hit with the Confederate officers. Dinkins commented that "she was capable of entertaining the most intelligent men of the party." Chalmers's chief surgeon, Dr. G. W. Henderson, was considerably more enthusiastic. One evening after retiring to his bedroom at Belle Meade, Henderson told his roommate, an officer named Bleecker: "I have at last found it. Here is a man with vast estates, surrounded by all the comforts and luxuries which the most cultivated mind can suggest, an accomplished wife and lovely daughters; what else can he desire?" The doctor thought Selene was "the most beautiful and interesting girl he had ever met," and Bleecker and Dinkins concurred.[16]

One night, Mrs. Harding made a large bowl of snow ice cream for her guests. Because Dr. Henderson was especially fond of it, she gave him a smaller bowl to take to his bedroom. After eating all he wanted, he placed the bowl on the window sill outside the shutters. Early the next morning, Henderson jumped out of bed and threw open the shutters, knocking the bowl to the stone walk below. The doctor, as much to himself as to Bleecker, complained: "If it had been an ordinary bowl, I could replace it; in fact, it would be unnecessary to do so. But it was a piece of that beautiful set of imported ware, which can not be matched in the world." He cursed his luck, rushing downstairs to pick up the pieces and make his apology to Mrs. Harding. To Henderson's delight, the bowl was not broken, having fallen into a snowdrift. Although Bleecker had promised not to mention the episode to anyone, he could not resist telling General Harding. Naturally, everyone in the house soon enjoyed the doctor's secret.[17]

After the winter storm, General Thomas ordered the long-awaited attack on the advancing Confederate army. The Federal juggernaut attacked Chalmers's thin line of troops on both the Charlotte and Harding Turnpikes. At about four o'clock on the afternoon of the attack, December 15, General Chalmers, who was near Davidson's Landing on the Cumberland River, decided to fall back in the direction of the Hillsboro Turnpike. He ordered Bleecker to move ahead as an advance guard, removing the headquarters wagons from General Harding's racetrack. Bleecker's escort company crossed the steep Walnut Ridge near

Belle Meade and passed about a mile beyond to the racetrack. There they found that fourteen wagons, containing baggage, papers, and records, had already been burned.[18]

As Bleecker's company moved out the Harding Turnpike, they saw about two hundred Federal soldiers, some mounted and some on foot, milling about in the Hardings' yard. Concluding that he had a good opportunity to surprise the Yankees, Bleecker moved his troops around and behind one of the barns and formed his men for a charge. Yelling and firing as they came, Bleecker's men killed nine and captured fifteen of the enemy before pushing the others into the deer park beyond the house. There, the Confederates ran into stiff resistance from a line of Federal infantry that had formed behind the stone wall paralleling Richland Creek. Forced to retreat, the Southerners returned through the yard close enough to the house that bullets were "clipping the shrubbery and striking the house." As Bleecker rode back, he saw Selene Harding standing on the stone arm of the front porch, waving her handkerchief: "The bullets were falling thick and fast about her, but she had no fear in her heart. She looked like a goddess. She was the gamest little human being in all the crowd." Bleecker passed and caught the handkerchief and urged her to go into the house, but she would not until the boys had disappeared behind the house.[19]

After the skirmish at Belle Meade ended and the scene of battle moved three miles or so to the southeast, the Hardings knew it was safe to let the small black children out of their hiding spot in the spring house. One of them was Joe Carter, the three-year-old son of Ike and Susanna Carter. More than three-quarters of a century later, Joe, then eighty-one years old, was interviewed by a reporter for the *Nashville Tennessean* about the old days at General Harding's. When questioned about the Civil War, the aged ex-slave said that he did not remember much except the Battle of Nashville. "They was shooting and fighting all over our land," Joe said. "They shut all us chillun up in the basement of the spring house so we wouldn't get hit by no stray bullets which was whizzing all around."[20]

Following the Confederate retreat from Nashville, a number of severely wounded Confederates, including Gen. William A. Quarles, were left at Carnton. Because Selene wanted to help them, Mrs. Harding requested permission of the Federal authorities for her daughter to travel by the Tennessee & Alabama Railroad to Franklin to take the soldiers a small box of hospital stores. Bvt. Brig. Gen. and Assistant Quartermaster

William G. LeDuc, who knew and admired General and Mrs. Harding, gave Selene the needed pass.[21] In 1903, LeDuc, then eighty years old, found the note from Mrs. Harding and mailed it to Selene from Minnesota as a memento of those "strenuous and trying" times.[22]

About the same time that Selene took medical supplies to the wounded Confederates, the *Nashville Daily Times and True Union* picked up where it left off the previous summer by protesting against the protection given notorious rebels, such as "that unmitigated rebel Gen. W. G. Harding." The article said that Harding "has had Federal soldiers to follow him about for more than a year as body-guards and lackeys." A petition circulated on the streets of Nashville in January stated that "in addition to this monstrous abuse [body-guards], these rebels have had protection papers by which they have been enabled to keep their stock, grain, and meat for private speculation while poor Union men have had to give up everything." The petition, signed by some of the most influential Union men in the state, asked commanding General Thomas not to tolerate "so gross an abuse."[23]

Once again, Federal authorities made no move to confiscate Harding's property. However, publicity given the inflammatory petition may have been a factor in the attempt of some Union soldiers to ambush him later in the month. On December 23, 1864, the *Nashville Daily Times and True Union* reported that General Harding "came very near losing his life the other day, at the hands of some highwaymen, who tried to shoot him." The article concluded by saying that Harding had done "all that was in his power three years ago to let loose desperados in this community. There is such a thing as retribution." Federal authorities were not so callous as the newspaper. The assistant adjutant general put a permanent guard at Belle Meade. The duty was assigned to soldiers who were "convalescents in hospitals at this post."[24]

A different form of retribution came a day or so after the newspaper account of the incident involving Harding and the soldiers. Federal authorities ordered both General and Mrs. Harding to explain why they should not be sent south through the Confederate lines to fend for themselves. Mrs. Harding responded, on January 27, 1865, to Col. John G. Parkhurst, provost marshal at Nashville, in the following manner:

> I am called on to state the reasons why I should not be sent within the lines of the enemy. I answer because I have done nothing detrimental to the

United States government from the commencement of the war to the present time, nothing whatsoever that the authorities could disapprove. Moreover, all my family ties, my kindred, and my dearest friends are here. I therefore hope I shall not be banished from my birthplace and home.[25]

In a more lengthy response to Colonel Parkhurst, General Harding admitted that his sympathies and friends were with the Confederacy but argued that he had, ever since General Buell took possession of Nashville and the surrounding countryside, been a loyal citizen of the United States and the State of Tennessee. He said that, when the oath was required by the government, he had been among the first to take and subscribe to it, and that he had faithfully discharged his duty to obey the authorized acts of the government even though he did not always approve of them. Harding said that if he had offended either civil or military laws, he was entitled to a lawful hearing before a civil or military court before being banished "from the comforts of a home in which I was born, and in which I and my fathers before me have lived . . . to become, with my wife and children, beggars and wanderers among strangers."[26]

The threatened banishment of the Hardings indicates that Federal authorities knew that General Chalmers made his headquarters at Belle Meade just before the Battle of Nashville and that he and his staff were welcomed there. Nevertheless, the Hardings were not driven from Belle Meade. Apparently, Colonel Parkhurst or his superior looked on forcing them from their home, when the war was all but over, as unnecessarily harsh.

With the Army of Tennessee's crushing defeats at Franklin and Nashville, and with Sherman's troops fanning northward through the Carolinas wreaking even more destruction than in Georgia, it was only a matter of time before the South would be forced to surrender. The end for the Army of Northern Virginia came at Appomattox Courthouse on April 9, 1865. Joseph Johnston's army, including three corps from the Army of Tennessee, surrendered on April 26 near Durham Station, North Carolina.[27] Finally, on May 9, Gen. Richard Taylor, C.S.A., surrendered the last Confederate troops east of the Mississippi River.[28]

The Civil War cost General and Mrs. Harding dearly. Their Confederate money was worthless, and they had lost thousands of dollars worth of livestock, produce, crops, and timber. Torn-down fences, a burned barn, and other property damage swelled the total. Still, the Hardings must have considered themselves fortunate. No one in their immediate family had been killed or injured. Their magnificent home was intact, and their property had not been confiscated. Amazingly, their slaves remained on the plantation. With an aged father and exhausted wife to care for, two teenage daughters to guide, slaves to manage and provide for, and a farm looking more like the battlefield it had recently been than the plantation it once was, General Harding had to look ahead, not back, and that is what he did.

13/ The Old Order Changes

O N April 10, 1865, the news of General Lee's surrender of the Army of Northern Virginia was posted on the bulletin board of the *Nashville Dispatch* on Deaderick Street. The announcement spread across the city and into the countryside. At Belle Meade, as on other plantations, blacks working in the fields probably paused momentarily to listen to the noise of the big guns at the Federal forts around Nashville as they blasted their victory salutes. The Belle Meade slaves must have received the news of the effective end of the war with relief and expectancy. Although they had remained loyally on the Harding plantation, most were eager to taste the fruits of emancipation, such as schooling for themselves and their children, and to have a place they could call their own. For the Hardings, the outlook was different. Among the Confederate dead and wounded were many good friends and neighbors. The recent past must have underscored for General and Mrs. Harding the uncertainty of their immediate future. Even so, they also must have been relieved that the long ordeal was over.

Some of General Harding's friends were determined to start over in Mexico or South America. If he considered that option, he never mentioned it. In the summer of 1865, Matthew F. Maury crossed the Rio Grande with a group of ex-Confederates and offered his services to Emperor Maximilian. Harding knew of Maury's appointment as the first immigration commissioner for the ill-fated Southern colony in Mexico known as the Carlota Colony.[1] However, with two teenage daughters, a devoted wife who loved her home and her family, an aged and incapacitated father, and 130 or so servants who were just as dependent on him now as they were before the war, Harding felt his place was at Belle Meade, working to recover from its substantial losses.

Had General Harding accompanied Maury to Mexico, he never would have seen his father again. John Harding, the founder of Belle Meade, died on September 16, 1865, a few weeks short of his eighty-eighth birthday.[2] His death was not even mentioned in the Nashville newspapers. They were Unionist in sentiment, and he was considered a rebel. Their silence ignored the contributions of a man who had earned, during his sixty-seven years in Davidson County, an enviable reputation as an excellent planter whose word was as good as a contract, a man fair in his dealings but firm for his rights. He would be remembered for his energy, industry, and his strong Christian faith.[3]

Harding was buried in the family vault at Belle Meade. The honorary pallbearers were old family friends, and the active pallbearers were black men, including Bob Green, most of whom were born and raised at Belle Meade. Although most of those at John Harding's funeral must have known that he built Belle Meade from a log cabin and 250 acres along a buffalo trail, few were aware that, at his death, he still owned more than 6,500 acres in Davidson County. The land included Belle Meade and a large adjoining tract west of the Richland Turnpike, extending all the way to the Mark R. Cockrill and Charlie Bosley lands. In his will, written before the war, John Harding left his two plantations, Belle Meade and Cliff Lawn, to his children, William Giles Harding and Amanda Harding McGavock, respectively. He left to his surviving Mc-Gavock grandchildren—David McGavock, Susan Smith, and Amanda Cheatham—three contiguous 100-acre tracts on the southeast side of the Richland Turnpike. David's tract was next to the deer park, Amanda's the middle tract, and Susan's the northwestern tract adjoining Col. Willoughby Williams's land. David also inherited his grandfather's town house on Church Street. John Harding had already given his 1,200-acre Stones River plantation to William Giles, who conveyed the property to John Harding, Jr., in May 1865.[4] Amanda inherited her father's 50 percent interest in a 188-acre tract that he and Johnson Vaughan owned along the Nashville & Northwestern Railroad in the gap south of Vaughan's "home tract." She also inherited a hilly "knob track of land called Trickem," where the third tollgate stood on the Charlotte Turnpike.[5]

About the time John Harding died, a stranger named Ned Pagette showed up at Belle Meade and introduced himself as a traveling agent for the newly created Bureau of Refugees, Freedmen and Abandoned Lands.

He was looking for the best site for a freedmen's school. Belle Meade was his first stop on an inspection tour of the southwest portion of the county. According to the agent's report made on September 29 to John Ogden, principal of Fisk School, Harding's reception was "as cool as an iceberg." Harding supposedly told him that the blacks could have a school, but he could do nothing to help it. Pagette had apparently already talked with the blacks on the place and said that they knew of an unoccupied house that could be used as a school room. Frustrated because General Harding emphatically denied its existence, Pagette went on to the adjoining plantation of Howell Huddleston, where he found seventeen freedmen eager to attend a neighborhood school. A few more in the employ of Mr. Demoss, Dr. Carter, Mr. Colton, and others would make "in all a school of 130 or 140 scholars," Pagette wrote in his report. That number included 100 or so freedmen living at Belle Meade. If Harding could be prevailed upon to donate the building referred to, if the bureau could find a teacher willing to board among the blacks and sleep in the school, and if books could be found, they could start.[6]

Pagette's response to his cool reception illustrates the tensions that arose under a changing order: "I found almost all the Planters afraid of and ready to denounce the Bureau and very few of them seem to understand the Equal Rights policy of the contract system, and are afraid to enter into any agreement with the Freedman, lest in case of difficulty with him he be hauled up before the Freedmen's Court, and wronged by the partiality of an 'Abolition clique.'" Pagette said, in behalf of the planters, that "none are so boisterous and vehement in their denunciation as the despicable ignoramus who never owned a negro or a foot of land."[7]

Under the contract system at Belle Meade, General Harding agreed to furnish his laborers with "quarters, fuel, sufficient and healthy rations of meal and meat, and to pay in money each one the sum agreed to by the parties." In 1879 (and probably in 1865 as well), "one half of the monthly wages, less the deductions for lost time, short work, neglect of duty, disobedience of orders and cash advanced," was paid at the end of each month. The remainder was paid at the end of the annual contract, "less the deductions for breakage or loss of tools, gear or other farm implements." Every other Saturday and every Sunday were unpaid holidays. The workday at Belle Meade began with the ringing of the plantation bell at daylight. Laborers were expected to be in the fields by dawn and work until sunset. When midday meals were served in the fields, workers could smoke. Otherwise, smoking was limited to the quarters lot or the employees' houses. Each family was allowed one male dog but no live-stock. Children were not to trespass "upon the garden, orchard, truck patch, or any field or other property of [the] employer." The laborers' wages were subject to deductions for various reasons, such as breaking or losing tools; abusing the stock; neglecting duty; shooting or trapping partridges, mockingbirds, or squirrels in the deer park; pulling rocks from the stone walls; or being sick.[8]

Although the contract system employed at Belle Meade seems in-credibly harsh, it was less so than systems in Deep South states where Black Codes imposed even harsher conditions on plantation workers. As a matter of fact, General Harding said that "with the kind of contracts he made he had but little trouble." He paid his efficient laborers twelve dollars a month, and two or three dollars a month extra during harvest, which he said was "as much as he could afford." That was well above the average annual wage of sixty dollars for black plantation laborers in the immediate postwar years. That Harding's black workers trusted him became apparent in 1870. When he paid them the balance of their wages that Christmas, a total of two thousand dollars, "they made him a kind of safety bank, and deposited about that amount with him, subject to their order."[9] Their actions refuted the argument advanced by planters that it was necessary to withhold part or all of laborers' salaries until the end of the year because, until their ex-slaves spent their money, they tended to slack on work.[10]

FARM WORKERS gathered by the smokehouse. Belle Meade collection

For 1865, General Harding's total net income was $7,819.40, $5,779.40 from his farming operation and $2,040 from rental income. Among his taxable articles were forty-five ounces of silver plate, three carriages, two gold watches, and two pianofortes, organs, or melodeons. His total federal income tax for the year amounted to $262.[11] The following year, Harding paid $20 to get a license to carry on the business of stallion keeper at Belle Meade so that Mark Cockrill's stallion Brown Dick might stand the 1866 season there. In October 1866, Harding paid the federal tax on the four tracts of land he inherited from his father in Davidson County's Eleventh and Twelfth Districts, totaling 3,379 acres.[12]

In spite of all the problems associated with putting their lives and plantation back together after the war, the Hardings did not wait long before finding a reason to celebrate on a grand scale. When ex-Confederate Gen. Benjamin Franklin (Frank) Cheatham married Anna B. Robertson in March 1866, the resilient General Harding and his daughter Selene entertained the couple with an immense party at Belle Meade for which seven hundred invitations were sent, fifteen of them to former Confederate generals. Gen. James Chalmers and his staff, including Capt. James Dinkins, all of whom had been headquartered at Belle Meade before the Battle of Nashville, were among the officers who accepted. According to one of her friends, Selene was the center of attention. A current rumor had it that Dr. Van S. Lindsley had proposed to her but had been rejected. For the party, which none of Selene's friends dared to miss, she was dressed in white with pearl beads in her hair. Her guests enjoyed the music of two bands, danced in the four main rooms downstairs, and ate a late dinner at tables that ran the whole length of the back galleries, both upstairs and down.[13]

Though Harding clearly took pleasure in the social display, he also addressed in a practical way the domestic needs and concerns of his household and wider family. Worried about Elizabeth's health and needing someone to help Selene and Susanna Carter with household responsibilities, General Harding invited Elizabeth ("Lizzie") Hoover, the thirty-two-year-old daughter of his first cousin, Martha Shute Owen, to live at Belle Meade. Harding also may have wanted to help the unmarried Lizzie, whose parents were dead. It was common in the nineteenth-century South for young women to be housekeepers or tutors for wealthy kinspeople.[14] Lizzie most likely became a resident of Belle Meade during 1866.

SUSANNA CARTER.
Belle Meade collection

COUSIN LIZZIE HOOVER.
TSLA, Hill McAlister Papers

WILLIAM GILES HARDING FAMILY, ca. 1867. Left to right: Selene, John, Jr., Mrs. Elizabeth Harding, W. G. Harding, Mary, Lizzie Hoover. Belle Meade collection

That October, Cousin Lizzie, General and Mrs. Harding, Selene, and Lucie M. Harris, Selene's roommate from Philadelphia school days, took the train to Franklin to visit Col. and Mrs. John McGavock. Also visiting McGavock then was Harding's friend Dr. Alexander Jackson. The group visited the two-acre cemetery the McGavocks had laid out near their home for the Confederate dead originally buried around town in hastily dug graves, and on the next day the battlefields around Franklin.[15]

Later in the fall of 1866, Dr. Jackson and his son, ex-Confederate Gen. William Hicks ("Billy") Jackson, visited Belle Meade. While there Billy bought a bay mare from General Harding for two hundred dollars. He also thoroughly enjoyed seeing Harding's nineteen-year-old daughter Selene. Soon afterward, General Harding invited Billy to return for a Christmas holiday reception to be given at Belmont by Adelicia Acklen in honor of Madame Octavia Le Vert of Mobile. General and Mrs. Harding attended the affair, which began at 11:00 P.M. and lasted until 6:00 A.M.[16] Whether Billy came back to Nashville for the reception is unknown. Unquestionably, he wanted to return because he was falling in love with Selene.

Because he could not come to Davidson County every weekend, Billy Jackson asked Henry Shapard, a Nashville friend, to keep him posted on Selene and her suitors. In March 1867, Henry wrote Billy that a group of about twenty young people including a Major McNairy had been at Belle Meade. Shapard stated that "Selene looked lovelier than usual, and you know how lovely she generally looks." He also said that during a game of twenty questions he and Selene were "selected to go out together." He took advantage of the privacy to tell Selene that he knew someone who loved her "with the whole strength of his nature." When she pleaded with him to name the young man, he yielded, "as I always do with her." Selene replied that she knew someone who loved her more than Billy ever did. Although she coyly refused to identify him, Shapard was positive she meant McNairy.[17] A month later Shapard was back at Belle Meade with a date, Josephine ("Joe") Elliston, Selene's best friend. He wrote Jackson that when he and Joe arrived at Belle Meade about 9:00 P.M., they "found company there of course." Henry wistfully remarked, "Who has ever gone there without finding company?" After a late supper of oysters and salad, the young people played draughts and enjoyed themselves thoroughly. Henry was ambivalent about Billy's chances: "Sometimes I think your chances are very good and sometimes I don't."[18]

While Selene was busy receiving beaux, General Harding was working long hours from daylight to dark. In addition to managing his Thoroughbred stud and farm, he continued to sell cashmere goats through the United Cashmere Company, a concern he and Robert Williamson owned.[19] He also gradually rebuilt the herd in his deer park, identified as the only wild animal park "worthy of the name" in the South or Southwest before the war. At his inaugural Thoroughbred stock sale on August 6, 1867, Harding was pleased that Billy Jackson not only attended but bought Hermitage, a bay filly by Highlander.[20]

Two days after the sale, Elizabeth McGavock Harding died.[21] She was only forty-eight years old, and the entire community was shocked. Her courage, particularly in 1862 when she ran the plantation by herself while her husband was imprisoned, was an inspiration to countless Tennesseans. Her attention to the needs of others, without concern for her own frail health, almost certainly contributed to her decline and eventual death. She faithfully looked after all who depended on her, including her father-in-law, John Harding, during his declining years; her own widowed mother, Sarah Rodgers McGavock; her invalid sister, Mary McGavock Southall; her children; and the sick or needy among the servants. Decades later, Elizabeth Harding's role during the Civil War would be eulogized in Katherine M. Jones's book, *Heroines of Dixie*.[22] After Elizabeth's death, General Harding tenderly put his arms around his daughters and said, "You have lost your mother; I will now be both a father and mother to you."[23]

That summer Billy Jackson was raising cotton at Walnut Grove, his father's 640-acre plantation six miles west of Jackson, Tennessee, as well as at another plantation his father owned in Madison County.[24] In addition to occasional visits to Belle Meade to see Selene, he kept in touch with several of his fellow Confederate officers. Ex-Brig. Gen. Peter B. Starke tried to interest Jackon in writing a history of his division, but Jackson turned down the invitation; he never wrote about his war experiences or those of his command.[25] He had received a similar request from John Pryor, who asked Jackson to send his military books and papers to him in care of Nathan Bedford Forrest at 272 Front Street, Memphis. Pryor wanted to borrow the material for the book he and Gen. Thomas

Jordan were writing, *The Campaigns of Lieut. General N. B. Forrest and of Forrest's Cavalry.* [26] Because no recognition was given contributors to the book, it is not known if Jackson did so. What is known is that Billy Jackson did not dwell on the past. His hands were too full with the present and future. He visited Selene when he could during the winter of 1867-68. By March, however, he had to give more attention to his cotton and to a shortage of labor. He spent four days in Memphis that month trying to employ "hands" through the Freedmen's Bureau. Undoubtedly, Billy sought General Harding's advice concerning the problems of employing freedmen. [27]

General Harding had worries of his own. In May, Quincy C. De-Grove formerly of Edgefield, brought suit in federal court in Nashville against General Harding and thirteen other defendants who, he claimed, harassed him into leaving Nashville in July 1861. DeGrove's lawyer argued that Harding and other rebel leaders, including Mayor R. B. Cheatham and John Overton, were members of an 1861 vigilance committee that ran out of town anyone who refused to support the Confederacy. When DeGrove's suit ended in a mistrial, his motion for a second trial was denied by Judge Trigg of the federal court. [28]

Freed from DeGrove's lawsuit, General Harding fretted about the possibility that Selene might soon marry and move away. Although he liked Billy Jackson and would be proud to have him as a son-in-law, he wanted his daughter at home. Billy's rival, thought to have been Major F. H. McNairy, was less of a threat than he had been earlier. Although McNairy still came around, he spent most of his time with General Harding out in the fields. "You know the Gen'l likes these fellows who don't mind the sun," Shapard wrote Jackson. [29]

By October 1, 1868, his thirty-third birthday, William Hicks Jackson knew where he stood. When he gave Selene an engagement ring, she was thrilled. On reflection, she wondered where Billy got the money to buy such a big, beautiful ring. The remote possibility that it might be a fake popped into her mind. To make sure it was not, she impulsively wrote her name in a windowpane in her father's office. If the gem cut the glass, as it was supposed to, she would know it was a real diamond. Selene was reassured! Her name still shows clearly in the windowpane.

If Billy was captivated by Selene, she was equally in love with her calm, sociable fiancé. There was still a little boy look about the blue-eyed, auburn-haired Jackson, who stood five feet nine and one-half inches tall and weighed 220 pounds. Very erect in bearing, he once heard a small black boy advise one of his friends to "rear back and throw out your chest like the general."[30] Jackson was already well known in Nashville because of his distinguished war record. General Harding knew it by heart.

The West Tennessean had graduated from West Point in the class of 1856, standing number thirty-eight in a class of forty-nine.[31] After a furlough home, Jackson spent the latter part of 1856 and a good portion of 1857 at the U.S. Army's Cavalry School at Carlisle, Pennsylvania. Upon completing that course, he and some fellow soldiers followed the Santa Fe Trail to New Mexico to join their regiment of Mounted Rifles.[32] On the two-month trip, Jackson killed his first buffalo near the "Plum Buttes" beyond Fort Riley. A companion, J. Cooper McKee, reminded him of the incident: "You had an old fashioned Mississippi rifle and were an excellent shot. . . . We crept up to a rock near or within 80 yards of the great animals, and they looked as big as elephants. . . . You made a fatal shot and the old fellow came down with a smash and crash."[33]

For the next three and a half years, Jackson served in New Mexico, Texas, and Colorado, protecting settlers and fighting Indians. For faithfulness in performance of duty and gallantry in the field, he was highly complimented by the War Department.[34] In 1857, near Fort Craig, New Mexico, Jackson saved the life of 2d Lt. William W. Averill of New York, later a Union general. In a hand-to-hand fight with a Kiowa Indian, Averill was knocked to the ground. From a distance, Jackson shot the Indian, saving Averill's life.[35]

The young soldier's experiences attracted the attention of Theodore Roosevelt, who wrote about one of them years later in *Hunting Adventures in the West*. He said that he had never heard of anyone duplicating "Red" Jackson's feat. While on a scouting party looking for hostile Indians, Jackson's troops roused a large grizzly bear. Because of the proximity of Indians and orders not to fire at game, Jackson carefully directed his horse so that its blind side was toward the beast, rode by at a gallop and, "with one mighty sabre stroke," killed the bear in the presence of the entire scouting party.[36]

When Billy Jackson learned that Tennessee's General Assembly had passed an ordinance of secession, he resigned his commission in the U.S. Army and turned over to the proper authority more than twenty-eight thousand dollars he held as assistant quartermaster.[37] With Col. George B. Crittenden of Kentucky, Maj. James Longstreet of South Carolina, and others, Jackson made his way to Galveston, ran the blockade, and sailed to New Orleans, where the group split up. Before leaving New Orleans, Longstreet, who was on his way to Richmond, promised to try to get Jackson a commission in Virginia.[38]

Jackson returned to his home in Jackson, Tennessee, to await word from Richmond. Not hearing anything and not wanting to fall behind his peers, Jackson accepted a commission from Gov. Isham Harris as a captain in the Artillery Corps of Tennessee.[39] When Billy reported for duty to Gen. Gideon J. Pillow, commander of Confederate forces in Memphis, he took with him his father's admonition to "be obedient to all authority over you, keep strictly sober, never borrow money unless you have the chance to return it immediately, never play cards, and pray to God for his blessings and protection at least every morning and evening that you may come out of the service at least as good a Christian as you went in."[40]

By September 1861, with 130 men under his command, Jackson was part of Gen. Leonidas Polk's line of defense near Columbus, Kentucky. During the Battle of Belmont, Missouri, in November, Jackson's horse was shot from under him, and he was seriously wounded in the side.[41] In a telegram sent to his wife the day after the battle, General Pillow said, "My gallant friend, Capt. Jackson, shot through the body, but I hope [he] will live."[42] When Dr. Jackson heard that his son had been shot, he made the trip to Kentucky in a boxcar to check on him. Within four days, Billy was able to drink some soup and milk, smoke a cigar, and eat some quince jelly. A week later, he was sent home to recuperate.[43] Returning to the field in February 1862, Jackson still carried the ball in his side. A week before the Battle of Shiloh, he was promoted to colonel for his gallantry at Belmont and given command of all cavalry in West Tennessee. During that spring and summer, Jackson preyed on Union forces almost at will by cutting off their supply lines, capturing trains, and diverting Federal cavalry units from their main objectives.[44]

On June 23, 1862, at a crossroads about nineteen miles east of Memphis, Jackson missed by less than an hour a chance to capture Gen. U. S. Grant, who was on his way to join his cavalry escort after stopping for water and a rest at the home of Mr. and Mrs. Josiah Deloach.

Residents living nearby told Jackson that a lone Federal officer had passed about forty-five minutes earlier. General Grant escaped only because Deloach, a Union loyalist, did not invite Grant to stay for dinner, suspecting that Confederate cavalrymen were in the area. After the war, Grant said that he came closer to being captured that afternoon than at any other time.[45]

Colonel Jackson was promoted to brigadier general by President Jefferson Davis on December 29, 1862, for his gallantry at the Confederate capture of Holly Springs, Mississippi. In that fight, Jackson's troops, who led the charge, captured and paroled 1,800 infantry and destroyed stores and supplies worth an estimated $6 to $8 million. They even captured General Grant's carriage, baggage, and some of his private papers and maps at Walter Place, a private home where the Grants were living.[46]

Throughout the late winter and spring of 1863, Jackson commanded a division of cavalry under Gen. Earl Van Dorn in Middle Tennessee. In early March, Jackson planned the battle at Thompson's Station, in which his division did all the fighting. In twenty minutes, 265 of his men were killed or wounded, but he captured Col. John Coburn's Federal brigade of 1,600 infantry.[47] A few weeks later, when Van Dorn was killed, Jackson assumed temporary command of his corps as the ranking brigadier general present.[48] When Grant's siege of Vicksburg tightened in the spring, Gen. Joseph E. Johnston desperately appealed to President Davis and Secretary of War James Seddon for reinforcements. In response, 2,000 cavalry from the Army of Tennessee, commanded by Brig. Gen. William Hicks Jackson, arrived from the north.[49]

Maj. Gen. Stephen D. Lee recommended Jackson for promotion to major general in December 1863. In a communication to Secretary Seddon, Lee described Jackson as "competent, reliable and gallant." He said that Jackson's division was the best disciplined and equipped in his command. Attached to Lee's recommendation were letters of endorsement signed by Generals Dabney H. Maury and Joseph E. Johnston.[50]

After increasing his already high reputation throughout the Vicksburg campaign, General Jackson served under Lt. Gen. Leonidas Polk in the Meridian campaign of February 1864. At that time, Jackson's cavalry captured a "goodly number" of prisoners and army trains and destroyed much of Sherman's supplies. That month, Polk added his support of Jackson's nomination in a communication to Seddon. Promotion still did not come. Jackson wondered if the delay had anything to do with his arrest of a young friend of Joseph Davis, the president's brother, for selling government cotton in Vicksburg for his own benefit. When Joseph Davis asked Jackson to release his friend, Jackson declined to do so. That was considered "a highhanded offense against the said Joseph Davis, who was all-powerful with his brother, Jeff."[51]

On May 17, 1864, Jackson's cavalry division joined the Army of Tennessee at Adairsville, Georgia, under the new command of General Johnston. Johnston assigned Jackson as commander of cavalry on his army's left wing. During the spring, the Army of Tennessee, despite tenacious fighting, steadily yielded ground to the numerically superior Federal forces. President Davis, who never had confidence in Johnston, replaced him in July with the impetuous General John Bell Hood.[52] Although General Jackson preferred continuing to serve under Joe Johnston, his command "participated actively and most gallantly" in the summer's fighting around Atlanta.[53]

Jackson's next assignment was as part of Forrest's corps in Hood's Tennessee campaign. Before the costly Battle of Franklin, Jackson appealed to his men to do their duty, behave like gentlemen, respect citizens and their property, and endure hardships "without a murmur." When his troops, in an offensive maneuver, crossed the Harpeth River near Carnton during the battle, they were confronted by the superior force of Gen. James H. Wilson's cavalry. Unable to hold his position, Jackson fell back to the south side of the river, and reported to Forrest at his headquarters on the Lewisburg Pike near Gen. Matthew Fontaine DeGraffenried's house. After four more hours of fighting, Jackson's ammunition was depleted. At 10:30 P.M., he was ordered to send to Forrest's headquarters for more and be ready to move at sunrise. Early the next morning, Jackson's troops crossed the Harpeth and advanced up the Wilson Pike. After a fight at Wilson's Crossroads, Jackson's division led the Army of Tennessee's advance to within two miles of Nashville.[54]

Before the Battle of Nashville, Hood divided Forrest's command and ordered him to take Buford's and Jackson's divisions to destroy the Nashville & Chattanooga Railroad and attack the Federal garrison at Murfreesboro. As a result, Hood fought the Battle of Nashville with only two undermanned cavalry divisions and with Forrest, the ablest cavalry commander on either side, thirty miles away.[55] Following the Confederate debacle at Nashville, Jackson's cavalry formed a rear guard for Hood's "ill-clad, bare-footed, hungry soldiers" as they retreated through the mud and slush to the Tennessee River. For his service in the Nashville campaign, where he bore the brunt of the retreat, Jackson was assigned command of all of Forrest's cavalry troops and the Texas brigade, giving him three brigades in all. Once again, he was recommended for promotion to major general, this time by Generals Dick Taylor and Nathan B. Forrest. Once again, there was no response.[56]

After the fall of Richmond, General Johnston requested Jackson's promotion one more time. Though the request was denied, President Davis asked Johnston to investigate fully the apparent complaint against Jackson involving the president's brother. Unfortunately, military operations were too "active and pressing" to allow Johnston to pursue the matter. Within days, his Army of Tennessee surrendered to the overwhelming forces of Sherman and Grant.[57]

On May 1, Gen. William Hicks Jackson addressed his troops. In response, the officers and men pledged to "stand by one another to the last moment," which was imminent. Within a week, Gen. Richard Taylor appointed Jackson a commissioner for the Confederate States of America in paroling soldiers in what was then called the Army of the Department of Alabama, Mississippi, and East Louisiana.[58] On May 9, 1865, Jackson and his Federal counterpart, Gen. Elias S. Dennis, issued to each Confederate soldier in that army a written parole. Nine days later, in Columbus, Mississippi, Jackson received his parole and headed home.[59]

Not long afterward, Jackson wrote President Andrew Johnson to apply for a pardon and amnesty. Pledging obedience "as a gentleman and soldier" to the laws of the land, Jackson added that his conduct during the war had been "strictly in accordance with the wages of civilized warfare, marked with kindness to all prisoners of war." For confirmation, he referred Johnson to General Sherman; Jackson did not know Sherman personally but had continually fought against him.[60] If the President had talked to Sherman or been able to read the general's memoirs, he might have learned that Sherman identified William Hicks Jackson, Nathan Bedford Forrest, Jeb Stuart, and John Hunt Morgan as prime examples of a distinctive class of Southerner. Sherman called them

> the young bloods of the South: sons of planters, lawyers about town, good billiard players, and sportsmen, men who never did work and never will. War suits them, and the rascals are brave, fine riders, bold to rashness and dangerous subjects in every sense. They care not a sou for niggers, land or anything. They hate Yankees per se, and don't bother their brains about the

past, present, or future. As long as they have good horses, plenty of forage, and an open country, they are happy. . . . They are the most dangerous set of men this war has turned loose upon the world. . . . These men must all be killed or employed by us before we can hope for peace. . . . I have two brigades of these fellows in my front. Stephen D. Lee is in command of the whole. They are the best cavalry in the world.[61]

Sherman's portrayal of Jackson as typical of the "young bloods of the South" was a half-truth. Billy's father was a planter, and Billy grew up riding horses. He was also brave, possibly to the point of rashness. He did not, however, hate Yankees, and he cared more for blacks than Sherman gave him credit for. Billy sided with the South because that was his home and its people were his people, not because of any deep-seated animosity toward the North. Sherman was more nearly correct in identifying Billy as a sportsman. No better evidence of Billy's fondness for sport can be found than the comments of his stepmother in a letter she wrote Dr. Alexander Jackson in 1852; she said that she wished Billy would put aside his "fondness for sport and idle amusements and prepare himself for some laudable pursuit." Billy's boyhood was drawing to a close. Only two months after his stepmother's complaint, he received an appointment to West Point to begin his career as a military man.[62]

Though General Harding dreaded losing Selene to marriage, he had great affection and respect for Billy Jackson. Selene and Billy's wedding took place at Belle Meade on December 15, 1868. Phillip S. Fall, minister of Nashville's Christian Church, officiated.[63] His involvement was important to Selene because he had been a religious mentor of her grandfather, John Harding. Before the wedding, General Harding asked Billy to make his and Selene's home at Belle Meade. In Harding's view, "There was plenty of room and plenty of work for them both, and because he was growing old he did not wish to be separated from Selene, who had charge of his household affairs."[64] Jackson accepted Harding's offer even though he knew that Lizzie Hoover was perfectly capable of looking after the General's household. He also knew how much Selene loved her family and Belle Meade.

Billy Jackson's penchant for competition and a boyhood spent in the rural South riding, hunting, and shooting had made him one of the Confederacy's best cavalry generals.[65] However, once the war was over, he put away wartime bitterness. With the same energy he had brought to his successful military career, General Jackson achieved, in private life, equal success as a horse breeder and plantation manager. He and General Harding established Belle Meade as one of the world's premier studs. As the old order passed and a new order began, Belle Meade continued to represent in the public's mind the hospitality and gracious living of the Old South.

14/ The Hardings and the Jacksons

WHEN SHE MARRIED WILLIAM HICKS JACKSON, SELENE was twenty-two years old. Friends used such words as *articulate, beautiful, vivacious,* and *refined* to describe her. With such a helpmate at his side, the able, outgoing Jackson was confident their future was bright. A few weeks after their marriage, Selene became pregnant and Billy was thrilled. During her pregnancy that spring, Selene enjoyed watching a group of Sunday school children from the Christian Church romp across the meadows.[1] As they laughed, sang, and played mumble-the-peg, she mused that soon her own child would be doing those things. Her pregnancy was uneventful until July, when she suffered an asthma attack.[2] Although the severity of the attack alarmed the family, Selene carried her baby for its full term and, on October 4, presented Billy with a daughter named Mary Elizabeth. The infant lived only a week.[3] Though stunned by the loss of their first child, the young couple rose to the challenge of helping General Harding rebuild Belle Meade.

The plantation had become a place very different from what it had been just before and immediately after the war. By the end of 1868, just a few black families were living there, a dramatic reduction from the number at the end of the war. The largest was the Harris family: Richard, Sr., Richard, Jr., Reuben, Chloe, and Phyllis. The first three were laborers, Chloe was General Harding's cook, and Phyllis was a child. Bob Green, a hostler, was the only member of his family mentioned in the 1870 census. The Vaulx family consisted of Jacob, a laborer; Hamit, the dining room servant; Alex, a carriage driver; and Milly, a child. Four Lees lived at Belle Meade—Julius, a carriage driver; Betsy, a house servant; and their children, Betsy and Monroe. The only other resident servant in 1870 was John Nichol, a laborer.[4]

Keeping farm laborers was a problem for Harding and Jackson just as it was for other plantation owners in the postwar years. To farm the 2,000 acres in cultivation in 1870, they relied primarily on laborers who lived off the place. Most of them probably were Harding's ex-slaves. During the year, he paid out $10,000 in wages; since the average wage was probably around $10 per month, that gives some idea of the size of their work force.[5]

The cash value of Belle Meade in 1870—including all buildings, 3,870 acres of which 1,870 were woodland, and livestock (but excluding $2,500 in machinery)—was $190,000. That figure was 30 percent less than it was in 1860. The total value of 70 horses, 37 mules, 20 milk cows, 100 other cattle, 150 sheep, and 150 hogs was calculated at $40,000. The farm produced that year $2500 worth of slaughtered animals, and Indian corn, oats, barley, hay, Irish and sweet potatoes, wool, butter, garden products, and fruit worth $28,245.[6]

Because he considered land to be dead capital after the war, Harding purchased property only three times during the last two decades of his life. One purchase was for two lots in town. The other two were for tracts adjoining Belle Meade that he bought from his neighbors Johnson Vaughan and John M. Joslin.[7] Although he claimed to be "anxious to sell" land, Harding sold only two small tracts during the same period, one each to neighbors James Page and Howell Huddleston.[8]

Damage from the war and new economic pressures were not the only challenges at Belle Meade during Reconstruction. In the spring of 1872, a tornado struck the Harding Turnpike at the second tollgate from town, a half mile beyond Belle Meade's front gate. The fierce wind demolished the tollhouse, and fences and trees along the pike from there to the deer park were knocked down. The storm uprooted many of the trees in the front yard and three-fourths of those in the park. Harding's workshop was blown down and two of his mares badly hurt. The house, which was somewhat off the path of the storm, was only slightly damaged by a few falling bricks dislodged from one chimney. Fortunately, no one on the farm was killed, although the storm left Belle Meade with an estimated five thousand dollars in property damage. The next day, Generals Harding and Jackson, their neighbors, and thirty or forty other men cleared fallen trees and debris from the pike, rendered impassable for over a mile.[9]

If the tornado of 1872 was the worst storm Harding ever experienced, the greatest controversy he ever faced erupted a year earlier. In January

1871, he gave a speech to the Davidson County Farmers' Club on immigration and its effects. The thrust of Harding's message was to advocate the use of black labor in preference to foreign labor in Tennessee. In a newspaper interview a few days later, Harding defended the reasoning behind the speech. First, he said, "The negroes were already here and citizens of the country. We raised them. They had been our slaves. We had enjoyed the fruits of their labor in the past. . . . Common justice demanded that we, their former owners, should give them a fair and patient trial." Harding then added those more traditional views of Southern planters. He said that "the negro from his organization, physical and mental, was better adapted to the drudgery of farm work than any other race of people, that we could board them cheaper [than we could foreigners], and that they were the most contented and happy race in their humble position, resulting from an organization that did not belong to any other people." Besides, he said, "They possess the capacity of enduring labor under a sun that would be distressing, if not unsupportable, to any other race." For those reasons and many others, Harding told the audience, "I do not think we would gain by exchanging the negro for the SCUM of the old world . . . daily landing on our shores." Harding added that black laborers should have "the rudiments of education, enough to protect themselves against the impositions of bad men." Further than that, he said, "I do not deem [education] necessary."[10]

Following Harding's speech, a portion of Nashville's foreign-born population was furious with him for having referred to the foreign element as the "scum and dregs of European society." A letter to the editor appearing in the *Republican Banner* on January 19 called on foreign-born citizens to protest. In response, a committee of local foreign-born citizens met at the state capitol and raked Harding over the coals, criticized the Farmers' Club for not having objected to his outrageous remarks, and censured the press for the same reason. Harding's friends advised him to drop the matter. After recalling Davy Crockett's motto, "Be sure you are right, then go ahead," he wrote a carefully worded defense of his position, directing it to the editor of the *Union and American*. Harding concluded by requesting "the leaders of my foreign friends at their next indignation meeting read, for the benefit of their audiences, this, my first and, I hope, my last essay on immigration."[11]

The matter died almost as quickly as it arose. Older Nashvillians knew Harding and remembered that, sixteen years earlier, he had run against a Know-Nothing candidate whose platform was anti-Catholicism and anti-foreignism. Interestingly, Harding was not criticized by Nashville's foreign-born group for his comments about black "organization" and education. In the Reconstruction South, many prominent men, such as Gov. Jackson Worth of North Carolina, did not believe in education for blacks.[12] Conservative whites did not believe that black people could be educated successfully and did not want to bear the cost of educating those who paid little or no taxes. Consequently, Harding's views were not unusual. Less than six months after delivering his "immigration and its effects" speech, Harding accepted another invitation to speak to the Davidson County Farmers' Club. This time, however, his topic was the blood horse.[13]

The arrival of a healthy grandchild diverted Harding from his wrangle with Nashville's foreign-born community. On February 8, 1871, Selene gave birth to a daughter, whom she and Billy named for Eunice Jackson, his stepmother.[14] Mrs. Jackson came to Belle Meade about the time the baby was born and stayed five weeks to assist the new mother. When she left, General Harding, Selene, Billy, Mary Harding, and Lizzie Hoover officially commended her for her skills as a "master Doctor woman for babies."[15]

After the freedom of having his own military command, Billy Jackson had to adjust to the constraints of working for a prominent and demanding father-in-law. One of Billy's first opportunities to manage Belle Meade alone occurred in the summer of 1871 when General Harding went to Hurricane Springs in Franklin County for a much-needed rest.[16] To establish his own identity in Davidson County, Billy joined the Tennessee Agricultural and Mechanical Association. Soon he was a stockholder and director.[17] One of his ideas was to establish a National Agricultural Congress so that delegates representing every phase of agriculture and every part of the country might meet annually to consider agriculture from a national point of view and deal with the national interests of the farmer.[18] The proposal gathered momentum when Hearn Watts, United States Commissioner of Agriculture, endorsed the idea. With Watts's support, Jackson founded the Congress, which held its first meeting in Nashville in October 1871.[19]

At the close of the Congress, attended by "many cultivated and distinguished gentlemen, mostly from the Southern states," General Jackson provided a barbecue dinner for the delegates. Among those present were Commodore Matthew F. Maury; Jacob Thompson, a member of President Buchanan's cabinet; Edmund D. Barbour, the inventor of the adding machine; Alfred H. Colquit, who would be elected governor of Georgia in 1876; and former Confederate Gen. John S. Marmaduke, editor of the *St. Louis Journal of Agriculture* and a future governor of Missouri.

A less well known delegate, Edward William West of Bellville, Illinois, recalled the hospitality of Jackson and Harding. West said that, before dinner, Harding pointed out the several paintings of horses in Belle Meade's front hall. The General was proudest of Gamma, the mare he said was the foundation of his success. Then General Jackson invited his guests to a sideboard filled with glasses and decanters containing liquors and wines of every description. When West explained that he did not drink, Harding put his hand on West's shoulder, looked him in the eye, and said, "with his gentle but peculiar Southern accent, 'Sir, I honor your candor, and your adherence to your convictions of propriety, and know, sir, that every gentleman in my house is privileged to act in perfect freedom.'"[20] Harding's comment may have signaled more than common civility. Though Harding was no teetotaler and made liquor available to visitors, some say he never invited a guest to join him for a drink. As the story goes, Harding's enemies saw his manner as stinginess, whereas friends saw it as a matter of sensitive conscience.[21]

When the Tennessee legislature passed an act establishing a Bureau of Agriculture in 1872, Gov. John C. Brown appointed General Jackson one of two commissioners of agriculture from Middle Tennessee. At the first bureau meeting, Jackson was elected president.[22]

Jackson helped plan the meeting of the National Agricultural Congress held in St. Louis in May 1872. He corresponded with Commodore Maury, who, after a nine-month stay in Mexico and two years in England, had been appointed professor of physics at Virginia Military Institute. At the invitation of the president of the Congress, Maury agreed to speak at the St. Louis meeting. However, because he had been ill over the winter, he asked Jackson, then a vice-president, to deliver the speech for him. Jackson did not do so because Maury, whose health had improved, "screwed up his courage" and delivered the message himself.[23]

General Jackson was also the primary organizer of the *Rural Sun*, the only weekly paper published in Tennessee devoted entirely to the state's agricultural and industrial interests.[24] General Harding had advocated its establishment at a meeting of the Davidson County Farmers' Club in 1871. He envisioned the newspaper as the means by which "the farmer could learn the value of his products."[25] Jackson was president and chairman of the Rural Sun Publishing Company's executive committee. J. B. Killebrew and Hunter Nicholson (of Knox County), fellow commissioners of agriculture, were editor and assistant editor, respectively. General Harding helped the *Rural Sun* get off to a good start in 1872 by contributing two articles to its first issue. In one, he advocated that farmers use a device to measure their rainfall; in the other, he discussed the problems of growing barley in Middle Tennessee.[26]

General Jackson was reelected to the board of the Tennessee Agricultural and Mechanical Association in April. Governor Brown also appointed him one of five commissioners to attend the 1873 World's Fair in Vienna, but Jackson turned down the assignment.[27] He was too busy and probably could not afford to go anyway. As soon as the Nashville spring races were over, he went to Indianapolis for the annual meeting of the National Agricultural Congress, where, to his considerable surprise, he was elected president.[28]

Soon afterward, General Jackson became seriously ill. He was concerned enough to telegraph his father, advising him of the illness. Dr. Jackson knew that cholera was present in Nashville, that Billy had been pushing himself, and that he was under stress because of his rapid rise to prominence in the agricultural world. Dr. Jackson reached Belle Meade from Jackson, Tennessee, after a trip full of delays that took thirty-four hours. The regular night train had been cancelled because of the cholera epidemic, and the schedule was disrupted. When he arrived, he learned that his son had endured a violent congestive attack. Billy gradually improved and, by July 3, felt well enough to go to Hurricane Springs to regain his strength.[29]

Jackson felt much better by August when he wrote an address to the farmers of Tennessee, which was circulated from the Maxwell House office of the *Rural Sun*. In September, at the Tennessee Farmers' Association Convention in Nashville, where General Harding was a delegate, Jackson was elected president, another honor he had not anticipated. In his presidential address, Jackson expressed "the clear opinion" that the plantation system of farming would soon pass away and predicted that it probably would be replaced by the tenant system. He also spoke out for "cheap" railroad transportation for Tennessee's products, direct trade with Europe through Savannah, and "a system of education suited to the wants of the farming population."[30]

During the fall and the following winter, General Jackson, restored to his usual good health, became increasingly involved with the Grange movement. In addition to his other offices, Jackson was Master of Tennessee Grange #64 in Nashville. Periodically, farmers wrote asking him to help organize Granges in their districts, to support their local causes, and to speak before their local groups.[31]

Earlier, on March 18, 1873, General Jackson's sister-in-law, Sophie Jackson, died of consumption, leaving his brother Howell to rear five children.[32] After six months or so, Howell visited Mary Harding at Belle Meade. Two weeks before Christmas, he wrote Eunice Jackson, his stepmother, to ask for advice. On the one hand, Howell did not want to "act with unbecoming haste," yet he hated his single life and yearned for the companionship of "a noble woman" like Mary. He asked Mrs. Jackson what she and Dr. Jackson thought about his going to Belle Meade over the holidays.[33] Wherever he spent the holidays, he proposed to Mary the following February. She accepted, and they broke the news to the family.

By that time, Howell had decided to leave his law practice in Memphis and begin anew in Jackson. Sophie's death, the local economic plight, and yellow fever and cholera epidemics were all factors in his decision. He thought it best, however, to leave his children in Memphis with his Molloy in-laws while he reestablished himself in Jackson. Mary agreed conditionally; she thought she should take charge of the children in Jackson as soon as she and Howell married.[34]

By mid-March the news of Mary's engagement to the forty-two-year-old Howell was widely circulated. One friend of the family went out to Belle Meade to satisfy herself that the marriage rumors were true. She told Mary that she did not believe them. When Mary asked why, the lady responded, "Because I thought you had too much sense to take the responsibility for five children." Mary retorted, "Well you see I have not, don't you?" One great-aunt, seventy years old, rode eleven miles to wish God's blessings on the twenty-four-year-old bride-to-be. So many friends showered Mary with affection that she began to feel uncomfortable and unworthy. She shared that and her other feelings with "Mr. Howell" in frequent letters.[35]

Howell and Mary were married at Belle Meade on Thursday, April 30.[36] For many of the wedding guests, it was their first time to see the

WILLIAM HICKS JACKSON and SELENE HARDING JACKSON.
Belle Meade collection

HOWELL E. JACKSON and MARY HARDING JACKSON. Photo by
C. C. Giers, TSLA; TSLA, Hill McAlister Papers

groom. "He was 5'8" tall and weighed about 150 pounds, had a strongly marked face, a compact, well-knit frame, and a stout, if not robust, constitution."[37] He was intelligent, though not as affable as his brother, and Nashville lawyers said he was held in high regard by his colleagues at the Memphis and Jackson bars. Before the wedding, General Harding said tearfully to Mary, "Well, my daughter, I have given you away and a hard thing it was for me to do, but I think I have done my duty."[38]

The bridegroom had received his college education at West Tennessee College and later at the University of Virginia. In 1853, he returned to Jackson and read law with A. W. O. Totten and Milton Brown. Following those clerkships, he enrolled at Cumberland Law School, where he excelled.[39] In March 1856, Professor Nathan Green, a former chancellor and state supreme court justice, thought so highly of Jackson's moot court opinion that he mailed Dr. Jackson a copy to show to Judge Brown and Judge Totten.[40] Following his graduation from Cumberland in 1856, Howell returned to Jackson, where his father had just completed his second term as mayor.[41] After practicing law there a year, he moved to Memphis where his association with David M. Currin, a well-known lawyer and Democrat, gave him his first exposure to a business and corporate practice. In May 1859, he married Sophie Molloy, daughter of a Memphis banker.[42]

In the late winter and early spring of 1861, Howell, like his father and brother, opposed secession, but as so often happened with Southern Whigs, all three men chose the South when Tennessee seceded. That summer, the United States Congress passed a law authorizing the confiscation of Southern assets in the North. In retaliation, the Confederate Congress passed similar legislation providing for the sequestration of Northern property in the South. The administration of the South's sequestration laws was placed in the hands of receivers appointed by the district courts, and Howell was appointed receiver for the Western District of Tennessee.[43]

After the war, Howell returned to Memphis to resume his law practice. Just as his brother had done, he wrote President Johnson requesting a pardon. In his petition, written June 18, 1866, Howell minimized his responsibilities as receiver of sequestered property, saying that he acted as receiver only through June 1862, which was not true. He added that he never served in the "Rebel Service as a soldier."[44] That Howell's application for pardon was denied was not unusual because few were granted that summer. He made a second petition the following December. Again, he minimized his participation in the "late unfortunate Rebellion." By then, pardons were being granted more freely and his was approved, which meant he could resume practicing law.[45] One of the first clients of Howell's firm, Estes & Jackson, was Nathan Bedford Forrest, who sought their services when he thought he was going to be indicted on civil and criminal charges. In the fall of 1873, Estes and Jackson took in a new partner, Henry T. Ellett, the first postmaster general of the Confederacy, and a postwar member of the Mississippi Supreme Court. Shortly after that, Jackson returned to his hometown to practice.[46]

The newly wed Mary assumed responsibility for Howell's four children—Henry, Mamie, William, and Howell, Jr.—ranging in age from six to thirteen. The fifth child, Sophie, had died of croup a month before the wedding. Fortunately, Eunice Jackson, Howell's stepmother, lived in Jackson and could help. Also the children received periodic invitations to visit kin, usually the Molloys in Memphis and, at least once, Uncle Billy at Belle Meade. Meanwhile, Howell was establishing himself as a leading member of the Jackson bar.[47]

While Howell was building his law practice, Billy continued his leadership role in the National Agricultural Congress. In 1874, he presided over the third annual meeting of the farm congress in Atlanta.[48] Soon after returning to Nashville, General Jackson, wearing his hat as president of the Tennessee Bureau of Agriculture, reported to the General Assembly and to Governor Brown that the first and second reports of the Bureau of Agriculture had been completed and published under the name *Resources of Tennessee.* Jackson praised J. B. Killebrew, secretary of the bureau, for his "good judgment, correctness, zeal, enthusiasm and untiring energy" in producing the two-volume work.[49]

Although his fourth child was born in the summer of 1874, General Jackson waited until General Harding's sixty-sixth birthday on September 15 to name him. That morning he told his father-in-law that his grandson would bear his name, William Harding. Billy said he named his son out of his high regard for General Harding and that he hoped William would follow his grandfather's example. Billy also stated his intention of "remaining with you and contributing, in every way, all in my power to lighten the burdens and depression incident to declining years."[50] That winter, Billy supervised much of the maintenance work done at Belle Meade, including extensive repairs required after Richland Creek flooded in March. Portions of the front fence, water gaps, abutments, bridges, and stone fences were washed away. It was, according to Selene, worse than the high water two years earlier.[51]

Billy was both a great help to his father-in-law and a considerate uncle. In March 1875, he invited Howell's son Billy to come to Belle Meade on his eleventh birthday to see Joseph Jefferson play Rip Van Winkle at the Grand Opera House.[52] The following month, he pinch-hit for General Harding while the latter went to Jackson to visit Mary. Because Howell was on the Court of Arbitration bench in Memphis, the lonely Mary thoroughly enjoyed her father's visit.[53]

Howell disliked being away from home and was clearly envious of his brother's pastoral life near Nashville. On April 3, he wrote Mary to say he was growing tired of city life and that he hoped "before long we can try country life near Belle Meade." While he was in Memphis, several prominent lawyers approached him about the possibility of his being placed on the Tennessee Supreme Court. He told them he would accept the position only if they could get the court permanently established in Nashville.[54]

The highlight of the fall social season for the Hardings and Jacksons was the marriage of David and Willie McGavock's twenty-three-year-old son Frank to Lula Spence of Murfreesboro. The Harding side of the family was represented by General Harding, General and Mrs. Jackson, and John Harding, Jr., and his daughters Sophie and Lena. The girls were fashionably dressed in their balsam-colored poplins trimmed in darker silk. Their aunt Selene wore her black silk with lace and her summer bonnet. Amanda Cheatham of Cliff Lawn was also in the delegation of sixteen who traveled to Murfreesboro from Nashville for the event. Selene said Amanda had on her "three buttoned kids from 'my man in Cincinnati'; [size] 5 and ½ she wore and it took her one hour to put them on and [she] perspired so we had to fan her vigorously." Selene's cutting remarks about Amanda's gloves were provoked by Amanda's opinion that Selene and her nieces were "entirely out of society."[55]

The wedding took place at the home of Lula's parents, David and Sally Spence. According to Selene, Mrs. Spence was so emotional that she could hardly entertain the forty or fifty wedding guests. Nevertheless, Frank looked handsome and Lula beautiful. After the ceremony and the reception, the Harding group took hacks to the hotel where they "snatched off" their party clothes and headed to the depot to catch the train to Nashville. After bidding the others in the party good-bye, General and Mrs. Jackson and General Harding caught a train to the Belle Meade station, arriving at 11:00 P.M. From there, they had a pleasant moonlight walk to the house.[56]

A few days after the McGavock-Spence wedding, General Harding was stricken with malarial fever. Dr. William T. Briggs, the Hardings' family physician and a distinguished Nashville surgeon who later became president of the American Medical Association, came out twice to treat him. Both times, he left instructions for the old gentleman to be given forty grains of quinine every six hours.[57] The doctor also treated five servants with malaria. One, Aunt Sucky, died. Although Harding had nearly recovered by the following weekend, General Jackson was so concerned about him that he canceled his trip to Cincinnati for the fourth meeting of the National Agricultural Congress, of which he was still president.[58]

By August 1876, two births at Belle Meade brightened a scene darkened temporarily by Selene's recurring asthma attacks and General Harding's sinking spell.[59] Both Mary and Selene Jackson delivered healthy baby girls. Elizabeth Jackson, Mary and Howell's first child, came just a week before Selene's baby, also named Selene.[60]

During the following winter, General Jackson helped his father-in-law root out the locust, sassafras, willow, black gum, persimmon, sedge-grass, and buckle-bush sprouts that annually grew up in Belle Meade's pastures and fields.[61] Realizing that the General's energy was giving out, Billy talked to him about the possibility of getting away from Middle Tennessee's heat to Hot Springs the next summer. Although nothing came of the idea, General Jackson was steadily assuming a heavier share of responsibilities at Belle Meade. He also continued to furnish leadership to several agricultural organizations. In the spring, he was elected vice-president of the Tennessee Stockbreeders Association.[62] Less than a year later, he was nominated for the presidency of the organization. Noting that his friend Maj. Campbell Brown of Maury County had also been nominated, Jackson immediately withdrew.[63]

Billy and Howell's father, Dr. Alexander Jackson, died in January 1879. He had shown symptoms of apoplexy for years but had been in downtown Jackson on the day he died. General Harding felt keenly the passing of his old friend. They had a great deal in common. Although

Dr. Jackson was a physician, he had not practiced medicine since 1847. Like Harding, he was a farmer. Both had family roots in Virginia, and both had been imprisoned during the war. Jackson was interned at the military prison in Alton, Illinois, at the same time Harding was held at Fort Mackinac. Charged with being a Confederate spy, Jackson was released after a few months.[64] An editorial in the Jackson *Tribune and Sun* following Dr. Jackson's death described him as a remarkable man "who carved success from the hard rock of self reliance." The writer said that Dr. Jackson was "certainly the finest conversationalist we ever met, and an hour with him in his prime, was worth a year of ordinary study."[65]

In the early fall of 1879, General Jackson took Selene to Colorado Springs, where asthmatic patients were thought to benefit from the climate.[66] Accompanying them were their daughter Eunice, then eight years old; Selene ("Lena") McNairy Harding, John Harding, Jr.'s, unmarried daughter; Dr. Collins, Selene's physician; and Joanna, the cook. Jackson, who had not been in Colorado since 1858, visited horse breeders across the state.[67] Before returning to Belle Meade, he saw to it his family members had everything they needed, particularly since Dr. Collins had advised Selene to stay in Colorado until spring.[68]

When he returned from Colorado, Billy threw himself into farm work at Belle Meade, including sowing wheat. He also dealt with Richland Turnpike matters and corresponded with Howell about the possibility of improving their Summer Street property so that, in the event of their deaths, Selene, Mary, and the children would have comfortable incomes. But Billy seldom went to town, and he and Howell did not pursue the property matter.[69]

As fall turned to winter, General Jackson knew that Selene was homesick. Accordingly, he arranged for Lizzie Hoover to have pictures of William and Selene taken and tinted. He planned to mail them to her already framed. However, three-year-old Selene refused to sit for her picture; Cousin Lizzie would have to take her back to town for another try, Billy explained to his wife. He also reported suffering from a liver problem and recovering from a recent hunting accident when his leg was sprayed with birdshot. On a more positive note, Billy told Selene that he had made "quite a reputation among the negroes on the place" by successfully defending Reuben and Dick before Squire C. B. Chickering, his neighbor and a justice of the peace.[70]

In December, Billy and General Harding supervised their annual hog killing. They killed their last sixty-four hogs on the twelfth when a cold spell struck. The next day they cut out, salted, and packed away the meat. The net weight was 14,530 pounds, an average of 227 pounds. The total meat put up at Belle Meade for 1879 was 17,770 pounds "with a good remnant of old meat in the smokehouse."[71]

With Selene still in Colorado on their anniversary, December 15, Billy wrote the following letter to her on that special day:

My own beloved and lovely wife,

Though separated, we are truly united on this the anniversary of our happy wedding day. Time has but the effect of adding intensity to the love we bear each other. I ask for nothing on earth to fill our cup of happiness except a restored health to your dear sweet self, for we are blessed beyond most on earth. . . . And as for your dear self, I can truly say that my love for you is deeper and more earnest than the day we were married, for then it was based on first impressions of your beauty, vivacity and sprightly conversational powers, but after living with you for eleven years, I find underlying the whole of these—principle true and unswerving—Christian witness of the highest possible order. . . . If Heaven is peopled with any better than yourself, I know not from what country or clime they were drawn. . . . You admire Eunice for all her graces and gentle qualities and thinking powers. And so do I. She draws them from you, for she is just like you. May the blessings of God the Father and His Son, our Saviour, guard, protect and keep you in health and unite us again to live together to a ripe old age is the prayer of my heart. Happy Xmas greetings to one and all in your present household. A kiss for my lovely daughter and a father's tenderest love ever accompany her, and for your noble, devoted self, the truest, the strongest and the everlasting love, springing ever warmer from your husband's true heart shall be your portion. Love to Lena. Kind regards to Dr. Collins and the others.[72]

Though the family was not all together, 1879 ended on a happy note for General Jackson because of the attention he gave the children. On Christmas morning, William and Selene went into Grandpa Harding's bedroom to find what Santa Claus had left them. Selene's favorite toy was a doll she named Louise. William was "most pleased with his engine with cow catcher and bell." Later on Christmas Day, when several young boys had arrived from Nashville, the children shot off firecrackers and sky-rockets. The next day, General Jackson went bird hunting with two of the boys. On December 27, Jackson sent Joe Carter, Susanna's son, over to Mr. Davidson's to borrow his hounds so the boys could chase deer in the mill woods. One of the boys, Jimmie Taylor, shot and killed a deer. When the young man returned to Nashville by train the next day, he proudly carried with him the skin, a quarter of the deer, and part of the saddle. The following night, General Jackson wrote his daughter Eunice to tell her all about Christmas and to congratulate her on helping her mother and studying so well. As a reward for her good behavior, he sent her the smallest diamond ring Calhoun's Jewelry Store had. It was the only one he could find that would fit his eight-year-old daughter's hand.[73]

15 / Home of the Racehorse

J ACK MALONE, A CHESTNUT FOAL OF 1858 BY LEXINGTON, was the first stallion General Harding bought after the war. The sire's first season at Belle Meade was in 1867 when he was offered to the breeding public for a fee of one hundred dollars.[1] Nashvillians got to see Jack Malone that August when Harding held his first Thoroughbred yearling sale. The "celebrated racer" was shown to the buyers and spectators who came to the sale from Nashville on a special train. Prices for the get of Brown Dick, Bill Cheatham, Childe Harold, Highlander, and Loyalty were "below average" that day because of the scarcity of money in circulation and "the costly character of the thoroughbreds." The *Union and American* reported that, despite the low prices, General Harding planned to hold similar sales annually.[2] A *Republican Banner* correspondent was impressed enough to call Belle Meade second in importance as a stud only to the "Alexanders' place" in Kentucky, and second in beauty to none.[3]

Horsemen in attendance sensed that, in inaugurating the auction system of selling bloodstock in Tennessee, General Harding was laying the foundation for the most successful breeding and distribution of Thoroughbred stock the state would ever see. Although essentially a stock raiser, Harding had won more purses with his own horses than any man then living in the United States. Turfmen respected his knowledge of horseflesh. As the buyers enjoyed their barbecue lunch following the auction, several commented on the possibility that Harding's establishment might become one of the leading studs in the country.[4]

Harding's role in the 1868 racing season was prominent, not only as an owner of horses but as an official of the body controlling horse racing in Nashville. Harding's Skirmisher, by Loyalty, was an entrant on the first day of the spring races.[5] That same day a report circulated that the owners of Maggie Hunter tried to rig one of the races. Harding, a vice-president of the Nashville Blood Horse Association, issued a statement that the testimony given the club owners "utterly failed to substantiate the charge" and that "the public might rely on not being swindled in betting their money."[6] When the fall races came around, Harding entered three horses—a bay colt by Highlander, a bay filly by Highlander, and Skirmisher. The bay colt was scratched; the bay filly placed third in her two heats. Skirmisher came in third and distant.[7]

Though there was no Belle Meade yearling sale in 1868, Harding aggressively advertised the next sale, to be held on the last Thursday in April 1869. Billy was there to help him. In addition to offering a fine selection of yearlings and two-year-old colts and fillies sired by Lexington, Brown Dick, and Jack Malone, Harding had some mares, Aldernay bulls and heifers, Berkshire hogs, and Lancaster lambs he wanted to offer the public.[8]

Among those present at the sale were Dr. Alexander Jackson, Governor Dewitt C. Senter, Gen. Abe Buford of Midway, Kentucky, Col. Balie Peyton, Gen. Frank Cheatham, Gen. Lucius J. Polk, and John Overton. At 10:30 A.M., the crowd filling the house and grounds moved over to the deer park, where the sale took place. About that time, a special train on the Nashville & Northwestern Railroad brought an enthusiastic group from the city, swelling the crowd to several hundred. Well-known horse auctioneer T. W. Barnes conducted the auction, which brought General Harding $6,775 on sixteen yearlings and two-year-olds. Gen. Joseph A. Mabry of Knoxville paid the top price of $1,010 for Helmet, a bay colt by Lexington. Following the sale, the mares, bulls, heifers, pigs, and sheep were sold. Then the guests enjoyed a magnificent barbecue, a tradition Harding continued as long as he held yearling sales.[9]

Edward Troye visited Nashville in November, and Harding asked him to paint likenesses of the sires then standing at Belle Meade. Troye, who was on his way home to Alabama, painted two portraits of Brown Dick, one for Harding and the other for Col. B. F. Cockrill. He also painted Vandal, Harding's most recent addition to his stud.[10] In December, Troye displayed his newly executed paintings in Nashville in hopes of getting more commissions. When Thomas Barry of Gallatin saw them, he was so impressed that he wrote the editor of *Turf, Field and Farm* to say how magnificent they were and to declare Troye "the best painter and artist in the world."[11]

General Harding, who subscribed to *Turf, Field and Farm*, read Barry's flattering comments. He also read with interest another letter to the magazine's editor, written several weeks later, in which a Virginia reader advocated a return to longer races. The general fully agreed. Harding, who identified himself as one of the oldest Tennessee breeders, wrote in support of having more three- and four-mile heats. He first advanced the premise that the strongest argument for turf racing was to improve the horse. He next argued that all who use horses, whether for riding, for the plow, or for the harness, would agree that strength and durability are their most valuable characteristics. In support of his theory, Harding once demonstrated at Belle Meade that the Thoroughbred horse was less affected by stress than the mule, long considered impervious to heat and fatigue. "He worked the mule to one plow and the thoroughbred to another, and drove them in alternate furrows in fields of corn so high as to shut out the breeze, and in every instance the mule hoisted the sign of distress long before the horse."[12]

How then, he asked, can we induce breeders to develop those characteristics? Harding answered his own question by suggesting a radical change in programs. Instead of short races, "popular with gamblers and like characters who follow after race horses," he advocated a return to the earlier system emphasizing longer heats. When this change is made, he said, breeders will immediately change their system of breeding "more for game and less for speed." This would, he concluded, "improve the game and stamina of our blood horses and likewise elevate the tone of our turfmen." Harding clearly wanted to turn back the clock to the "olden times" when "to train and run race horses was a passport to the confidence of the community and a badge of honorable distinction."[13] Harding had strong feelings on the subject, and on July 1, 1871, the issue dominated his speech before the Davidson County Farmers' Club.[14]

Another of Harding's theories was that his best success in breeding came when he matched his stallions to mares that had not been exhausted on the track. Instead, his preference was to breed mares whose bloodlines showed success on the track but which had never been raced. Over the winter of 1869-70, General Harding arranged for such mares to be put to his senior stallions Vandal and Jack Malone the following spring. One of his repeat customers who appreciated Harding's breeding principles was Col. Alfred R. Wynne of Castalian Springs, Tennessee. In a letter to Wynne in March, Harding told him Vandal and Jack Malone were both in "fine health and good condition," but that Vandal had only one vacancy. Harding said he "would as soon you would fill it as anybody."[15]

In the spring of 1871, General Harding took Selene to the Memphis races, where several of his horses won purses. The Memphis *Public Ledger* reported that another objective of General Harding's visit was "to arouse among our people a greater desire for finer stock and elevate the race track to the dignity to which the moralist can take no exception."[16] A week later, at his own yearling sale, General Harding sold twenty-one yearlings for an average price of $321.[17] The two best-known breeders in attendance that year were Jackson's old friend Abe Buford and Capt. T. G. Moore, whose famous mare Mollie Jackson, by Vandal, was described by contemporaries as "the best mare of any day."[18] A few weeks after his sale, General Harding attended the St. Louis races.

Both Vandal, the head of Harding's stud, and Jack Malone died in 1872. The loss of Vandal, regarded as second only to Lexington among living American sires, was particularly damaging.[19] He was put to sleep in April after rheumatism in his hind quarters completely disabled him.[20] Consequently, at his yearling sale three weeks later, Harding talked with Col. Sanders D. Bruce, publisher and founder of *Turf, Field and Farm,* Hosea Ball of New York, and other turfmen about promising sires that might be available. The sale, which took place in the creek bottom across from the stables, resulted in seventeen yearlings changing hands for an average price of $356. Vandalite, a filly by Vandal out of Vesperlight, was the star of the auction, bringing $1,015 from Mr. Ball.[21] The horse proved to be a good investment, becoming the champion three-year-old of 1874. Her exploits on the track and as the dam of future stakes winners brought acclaim to Belle Meade and caused racing people to remember her illustrious father.[22]

About the time that Vandal died, an itinerant racing correspondent wrote an article on an insignificant stud thirty-five miles north of Chicago, named Glen Flora Farm. He lamented the fact that so fine a horse as Bonnie Scotland, in second place on the list of winning sires in 1868 and 1871, was doomed to the obscurity of such a place. Harding was alerted. He knew that Frogtown, a Bonnie Scotland get, had earlier in the year lowered the American record for a mile and a quarter. In June, he and John Harding, Jr., traveled to Glen Flora Farm and made a deal with C. C. and R. H. Parks. For "a good round sum," Harding bought

Bonnie Scotland, a stallion that would found a dynasty and make Belle Meade famous. Harding also bought a painting of the horse done by Edward Troye in November 1865. When Bonnie Scotland reached Nashville, he was exhibited to the Nashville public at Sam Black's stable.[23]

During the 1872-73 racing seasons, Harding's best horse was Euchre, a chestnut filly by Brown Dick. At the fall 1872 meeting of the Nashville Blood Horse Association, Euche was the favorite in the club purse for four-year-olds held on the second day. Euchre made Harding look good by winning the mile heats in times of 1:46.75, 1:46.5, and 1:47.5.[24] The filly's loss of an eye the previous spring, from a boy's carelessly thrown rock, had not impaired her racing ability.[25] The spring 1873 meets at Lexington and Nashville conflicted. "As evidence of the stronger attractions" at Nashville, the editors of the two leading horseman journals in the country, *Turf, Field and Farm* and the *Spirit of the Times*, were present at the Nashville meeting.[26] Harding's Euchre, trained by Theodore Alcock, won three races—one on Wednesday and two more on Friday and Saturday.[27]

Usually, the Belle Meade sale preceded the Nashville spring meeting, but a writer for the *Spirit of the Times* noted that General Harding had postponed it until September. The correspondent said that would "prevent many Eastern buyers from coming out, for by that time the most important stakes will have closed."[28] A likely reason for the postponement was that the "hard times" facing Tennessee farmers that spring were turning into a financial panic.[29] Another problem arose with the approach of fall. Because of a severe drought, Harding was at his wit's end to know where to get water for his stock, particularly his hogs.[30] Possibly for those reasons, Harding canceled at the last minute the sale of his "fine lot of yearling colts," which had been advertised to take place at the Nashville Race Course on September 27.[31] On that Saturday, instead, Harding was in Columbia at the Maury County Fair, where his Torpedo won a premium in the "Aged Stallion, Thoroughbred Horse" category.[32]

Hard times or not, General Harding remained a gracious host to the many visitors to Belle Meade. One day during the 1870s, a guest wanted to see one of the stud's fine horses. When General Harding had Bonnie Scotland brought to the front of the house, the man asked, "General, is that a runner or a trotter?" The General bowed and said, "Walk into the house. I will endeavor to entertain you in the parlor, sir."[33]

The 1874 Belle Meade yearling sale was another disappointment. A downpour, lasting until the train left the Nashville & Chattanooga depot, caused many to think the sale would be postponed. Accordingly, attendance was small. Only seven yearlings were sold before the auction broke for dinner. Afterward, General Harding decided not to resume the sale because of the slow bidding. The highlight was the exhibition of Bonnie Scotland. When the great horse was first brought to the United States, it was said of him, "He stands full sixteen hands high, he has the longest shoulder, deepest heart-place, best forehand, shortest saddle-place and the most powerful quarters of any horse now before the public."[34]

By the spring of 1875, Harding and Jackson were encouraged by an improving economy. Both men were optimistic about the chances of the six horses from their stable—Ventilator, Camargo, Voltigeur, Planchette, Bounding Doe, and Vocalist—that were taken from Belle Meade to the Nashville track on April 28 for training for the spring meeting of the Blood Horse Association.[35] Then too, Bramble was foaled at Belle Meade by Bonnie Scotland, dam Ivy Leaf, in the spring of 1875.[36] At the time, Harding did not realize that Bramble would be his next star.

The 1875 Belle Meade spring yearling sale went off very well. The crowd was larger than usual and included several distinguished out-of-state visitors. A reporter for the Union and American noted the presence of Ben Bruce of the Kentucky Livestock Record, Col. Sanders D. Bruce, who compiled the first acceptable American Stud Book, and Meriwether Lewis Clark, president of the Louisville Jockey Club and Racing Association. Clark had established the organization the previous June. While at the Belle Meade yearling sale, he undoubtedly spoke to Middle Tennessee horsemen about investing in the new enterprise and attending its inaugural meeting two weeks later.[37]

It was rumored that Col. W. H. Johnson, as agent for Pierre Lorillard of New York, bought stock at the Belle Meade sale. Rumor or not, Harding's efforts in developing Thoroughbred stock were drawing some national attention. His lead stallion Bonnie Scotland deserved much of the credit. He was the sire of all but one of the yearlings sold that spring.[38] At the spring 1875 meeting of the Blood Horse Association, Harding's Voltiguer won on Saturday. However, Camargo, after winning the first heat of his race, got a terrible start in the second heat, having his head down when the starter, Col. W. H. Johnson, tapped the drum. Though apparently out of the running, Camargo closed much of the gap and impressed everyone, coming in third.[39] Though Harding was narrowing his interests to focus on breeding, his reputation as a trainer and racer of horses was well established.

A week after the Blood Horse Association meet ended, General Harding planned to attend the meeting of the Louisville Jockey Club and "to sell his [racing] stable out—consisting of Ventilat[or], Voltigeur, Camargo and Bounding Doe."[40] That marked the beginning of Harding's retreat from racing and training in favor of breeding. Some of his Middle Tennessee racing friends, including James and A. C. Franklin of Sumner County and Archer and R. B. Cheatham of Davidson County, also had horses entered there. Harding shipped his horses to Louisville in care of their trainer a few days before he was to leave. His daughter, Mary, made a surprise visit to Belle Meade the weekend before the Louisville meeting. She and her stepson, Howell Jackson, Jr., arrived on Saturday. The next morning, Billy and Selene's baby, William Harding, was christened at McKendree Methodist Church. Everyone but General Harding, who was not feeling well, and Mary attended the ceremony. Mary stayed at Belle Meade to keep her father company. In the meantime, he decided not to go to Louisville but to send Billy instead.[41]

General Jackson probably caught the express to Louisville that left the North College Street Depot at 1:40 P.M. On Monday, Mary heard from Howell, who spoke of giving up his law practice in favor of farming. When Mary told her father about Howell's dream, General Harding's advice was for him to stick to what he was doing: "He knows nothing about it and there is no money in it. Don't you ever let him go to farming."[42]

General Harding and Mary also talked about the races in Louisville. That Monday the first Kentucky Derby was held, and Billy was there. If Harding's Camargo won, the General estimated the purse would be about three thousand dollars. That, he told Mary, would mean Camargo would sell for about five thousand dollars. Mary told her father she did not think the Kentuckians would ever let a Tennessee horse win the race, "if cheating would keep him from it."[43] As it turned out, Camargo did not start in the Derby. Of the fifteen horses that did, however, six had or would later have close ties to Belle Meade. G. H. Rice's Volcano, by Harding's Vandal, placed second. The fifth-place finisher, McCreery, owned by General Jackson's wartime compatriot Gen. Abe Buford, was from a dam by Harding's Bonnie Scotland. J. B. Rodes's Searcher, coming in eighth, was also from a dam by Bonnie Scotland. A. B. Lewis and Company's Vagabond, finishing third from the last, was by Vandal, out of Gem by Harding's Childe Harold. McCreery and Searcher were by Enquirer, a stallion Harding would acquire in 1879. Enlister and Bill Bruce, the sixth- and eleventh-place finishers respectively, were also by Enquirer.[44]

Camargo was one of seven three-year-olds to start in the Falls City Stake on Friday. Before the crowd of fifteen to twenty thousand, Camargo won with times of 1:42.75 and 1:43.25.[45] On Sunday, Voltigeur won the Clark Stake, a two-mile dash, beating ten other starters with a time of 3:50.75.[46] After the races, General Jackson visited with other owners in Clark's quarters, which served as the clubhouse, and accepted congratulations for General Harding's two winners. Voltigeur's victory was the last ever run by a horse belonging to Harding. In June, he sold Camargo, Ventilator, and Voltigeur for $8,500 and retired from racing to devote his full energies to breeding horses for others. General Jackson, who probably negotiated the sale, saw two good results: General Harding received fair prices for the horses, and he was "retired from training horses forever."[47]

Harding may have had several reasons for quitting racing, the most important being his age. It was time for the sixty-six-year-old horseman to slow down. Another factor may have been that, unlike many of his racing friends, Harding never bet on a horse race in his life. He used the racetrack as a proving ground for the strains he wished to promote in his horses. He cared little about amusing the public. His interest in racing was never in the race itself, so frequently the case among trainers, but in what the race could teach him about breeding. A related factor, though a minor one, was his disapproval of the role professional gambling was beginning to play in the sport. He preferred that racing continue to be run by amateurs and gentlemen.[48]

Ironically, Harding made his last race at the Louisville Jockey Club during its inaugural and during the same week that the first Kentucky Derby was held. Just as a new day in horse racing dawned for Kentucky, one closed for Belle Meade. The stud farm's maroon racing silks, active since John Harding's early racing days at the Nashville Jockey Club, were put away. General Harding was still in debt as a result of the Civil War, but Belle Meade's future as a stud was brighter than ever. As Mary Jackson said in a letter written from Belle Meade to her husband,

"Tennessee has forced Kentucky to take a back seat." She added, "I suppose you saw the accounts in the Memphis papers. The Nashville papers are full of it and the public generally seem to rejoice in father's victories." When General Harding first brought the good news of his horses' successes in Louisville to Mary, he was typically restrained. He simply said, "My daughter, I reckon Mr. Howell will be glad to hear it."[49]

The Jacksons celebrated the new year of 1876 with a dinner at Belle Meade. The last guests to arrive were George W. Darden, secretary of the Nashville Blood Horse Association, and a writer for the *Spirit of the Times,* who used the pen name Albion. After greetings were exchanged, Col. W. H. Johnson and George W. White proposed visiting the Thoroughbreds. The group, also including Col. B. F. Cockrill, W. T. Link, J. T. Burt, General Jackson, and General Harding, took the short walk to the paddocks. There Uncle Bob Green, the longtime hostler, had two or three of his assistants bring out the nineteen colts then present. One that drew little attention when favorites were chosen was Bramble, "a small compactly built, hardy-looking bay colt." He was brought out a second time by Uncle Bob, the only one who liked him.[50]

Two new stakes were established at the spring meeting of the Nashville Blood Horse Association—a one-and-a-half-mile dash to be held at each spring meeting and a two-mile dash to be run at each fall meeting. Both were named the Belle Meade Stakes in honor of the stud and in appreciation for the 40 percent funding of the purse that Harding had agreed to underwrite personally. The purses for the Belle Meade Stakes were set at five hundred and seven hundred dollars. The *Daily American* of April 30 complimented Harding and praised the association for contributing the other 60 percent, stating that "a more important work for the advancement of the Association, and of local breeding interests has not been achieved since its inauguration."

Despite a cold, drizzly rain, a large crowd gathered for General Harding's 1876 yearling sale, including about 150 people who came out on the train. Many of the buyers had come to see and bid on the get of Bonnie Scotland and Harding's new sire John Morgan. The young stallion, bought to stand with Bonnie Scotland, was by Sovereign and had been bred in 1858 at Woodburn Stud, Woodford County, Kentucky. John Morgan remained in service at Belle Meade through the 1880 season.[51] Among the most prominent horsemen were Col. Sanders D. Bruce, Maj.

Uncle Bob Green. Belle Meade collection

Joseph Elliott of the *New York Herald,* Maj. Ben Bruce, and Capt. T. G. Moore, who with a partner had won the San Francisco Stakes. Harding's sales totaled $8,580 for nineteen yearlings auctioned by Captain Kidd. General Harding had given all of Bonnie Scotland's get, constituting most of the sale, names beginning with the letter B. Thomas W. Chadwell of Nashville surprised the crowd by advancing his bid for Bramble to $450.[52] When the clerk charged the little colt to Chadwell, no one suspected what fame he would win for his owners, for Harding, and for Belle Meade.

The night before the spring races of the Nashville Blood Horse Association began, bidding at the gambling pool auction at the Maxwell House was spirited. The *Daily American* of May 2 reported that "a dense throng of bidders and speculators" packed the place. Auction pools, the only method of gambling in 1876, were handled by an auctioneer who invited bids on each horse in the race, giving the highest bidder the claim to that horse in the pool being auctioned. As soon as one pool was completely sold, the auctioneer started others until there was no more demand. The individual holding the winning horse in each pool received the entire pool less the auctioneer's commission.

In September, Howell Jackson read in the Louisville papers that Belle of the Meade, a Belle Meade product, was a winner of the two-year-old stakes at Lexington, beating twelve to fifteen competitors.[53] Because of Belle of the Meade's success and that of other Bonnie Scotland get during the fall 1876 racing season, observant horse fanciers, and breeders particularly, anticipated General Harding's yearling sale the following spring. Horse magazines and newspapers began covering Belle Meade as part of their regular beats. A correspondent for *Turf, Field and Farm,* in an article reprinted in the *Daily American* on January 31, 1877, gave the total Belle Meade acreage at 3,780, of which 150 acres were bluegrass paddocks for the two stallions Bonnie Scotland and John Morgan, the forty brood mares, and the many yearlings. The author said that Belle Meade was "run by thirty farm hands and three hands in charge of stock, all negroes, and constantly superintended by General Harding and his son-in-law, Gen. W. H. Jackson, who are in the saddle from sunrise to sunset daily."

In terms of attendance and prices, Harding's 1877 yearling sale was his most successful yet. There were also more visitors of note than ever before: Gov. James D. Porter; Marshall Polk, Tennessee's treasurer; Col.

Sanders D. Bruce; Phil Dwyer of New York; and H. B. Bruce, A. Keene Richards, Col. Jilson P. Johnson, Peter Fox, and Attorney General Moss, all of Kentucky. The sale took place on the west lawn of the mansion, where Captain Kidd's auctioneer stand was surrounded by an amphitheater of seats constructed for the event. Desks for the press were arranged in front of Captain Kidd's stand. Twenty-two colts and fillies by Bonnie Scotland and John Morgan sold for a record $11,755, an average price of $534. With more visitors than usual in town for the Belle Meade sale and the Nashville Blood Horse Association races the next day, bidding sessions were described as heavily attended.[54]

The Young America Stakes No. 1, held in Nashville on May 1, marked the first public appearance of Bonnie Scotland's bay colt Bramble. He ran the half-mile dash in :50.5, placing a good second to Milan in a field of nine. Three days later he won the six furlongs Young America Stakes No. 2 in the mud in 1:20, beating Milan and five others.[55] On May 29, his owner sold him to the Northern firm of Crawford and Puryear for $1,000, and he was shipped to Saratoga, where he stirred more laughter than serious interest because of his immense girth, stumpy tail, short body, and equally short legs. Soon he was dubbed the "Tennessee Conestoga." Bramble was surprisingly fast, however, and on July 31, he won the Saratoga Stakes, worth $3,700, in 1:17.5; placed third in the Kentucky Stakes; and, in the final race of the season, was beaten by Pique in a special sweepstakes in 1:16.75. On the day Pique beat him, Bramble was sold to the Dwyer Brothers of Brooklyn for $2,200. That surprised many horse people who thought the colt's two wins as a two-year-old were flukes. Phil Dwyer, who had seen Bramble win in the mud at Nashville, obviously disagreed with that evaluation.[56]

Nobody followed Bramble's career with more interest and pride than General Harding. Although he was no longer racing, his enthusiasm for horse breeding remained intense and probably accounts for his alertness and activity even though his health was beginning to fail. Back in the fall, his spirits had been lifted by Belle of the Meade's setting a course record for the mile at the Louisville Jockey Club, with a time of 1:44.25.[57] In January 1878, he found the energy to accept his election as a director and one of three vice-presidents of the Nashville Blood Horse Association.[58] In anticipation of the 1878 yearling sale, General Harding constructed a new sale barn 112 feet long and 75 feet wide. Located in a wooded lot across Richland Creek to the west of the house, the barn enclosed an open court 66 feet square used as the display ring. In the center of the court was a trough fed through iron pipes from the Red House Spring. The stables on the inside contained thirty-two stalls, each ten by twelve feet. There were feed rooms in the building's four corners. The exterior of the barn was broken and relieved by ten gables and by two towers, placed on the north and south ends. [59]

The press was represented at the 1878 sale by brothers Sanders D. and Ben G. Bruce, and Frank Worley, turf correspondent of the *Cincinnati Enquirer.* Phil Dwyer, president of the Brooklyn Jockey Club, was back, and there were several well-known Kentucky racing enthusiasts and breeders, including Dan Swigert, whose colt Spendthrift was undefeated that year, and Colonel Clark. Despite the presence of the prominent horsemen, prices for the twenty-five yearlings were well below the average of recent Belle Meade sales. Observers blamed the poor showing on a sour economy. [60]

Several weeks after the disappointing sale and in spite of the poor economy, Harding's innate generosity manifested itself. That May, he shipped two hundred fawns by train to the Blooming Grove, Pennsylvania, Hunting and Fishing Club. Harding made the gift because of his friendship with Col. Sanders D. Bruce, who had attended Harding's yearling sales since 1872 and admired Harding's deer park. As a founding member of Blooming Grove, Bruce asked Harding if the club might have some fawns to start a herd. Harding complied with the request of a friend who only a decade and a half earlier had been of great assistance to Union Gen. George Thomas in winning the Battle of Nashville. [61] The Tennessee deer venture was obviously successful because descendants of the Belle Meade fawns are still at Blooming Grove.

About the time Harding's fawns reached Blooming Grove, Bramble made his first appearance as a three-year-old. On May 30 at Jerome Park in Fordham, New York, he placed second in the Withers Stakes. Five days later, he won a one-mile handicap sweepstakes of five hundred dollars in 1:48.5. After a disappointing loss attributed to his jockey's poor handling, Bramble moved to Saratoga, where he won eight out of twelve races. His magnificent performances there raised him in the eyes of the racing public to a preeminent position among the nation's three-year-olds. His owners, the Dwyer brothers, thought him superior to any three-year-old in the country. On August 31, they sent him south to engagements at Louisville and Nashville. In Louisville, he won the Great

American Stallion Stakes, one and three-quarters miles, in 3:14.25, and was second in a mile and a furlong at the same place, giving up five pounds. The race, won by Warfield in 1:56, was the fastest time at the distance that year. Bramble and Warfield met again at the Maxwell House Stakes in Nashville where Bramble won both mile heats in 1:43 and 1:44. Bramble then went to Baltimore, where he placed second to Bonnie Wood. In his defense, he was stale from his long trip to the East.[62]

Following the 1878 racing season, Maj. J. R. Hubbard, racing editor for the Spirit of the Times, heaped praise on Bramble: "General Harding has been long on the American turf, and he has bred some horses of distinguished merit, but he never bred a better colt than Bramble. Even the celebrated Vandalite, with all her reputation, was not the equal of this remarkable colt, and a tougher, better, or more reliable one will probably not be bred anywhere in a decade."[63] Hubbard's enthusiasm for Bramble was shared by John L. Hervey, a later generation's chronicler of horseracing history. Writing for the Thoroughbred Record in October 1934 under the pen name of Salvator, Hervey said that Bramble was the greatest of the Bonnie Scotlands and the greatest product of Belle Meade, as racehorse and progenitor.

For the 1878 season, Belle Meade's old hero Bonnie Scotland stood second only to Lexington among American sires in the amount of winnings. Bonnie Scotland actually outranked Lexington in winners as a percentage of starters and in the number of horses finishing second. That year, twenty-four of his get won eighty-four races worth $49,552. Bramble led with $11,885. Of his twenty-one races, he won twelve and was second nine times. His win at the Great American Stallion Stakes was the largest stake of the year, netting him $7,325.[64]

Harding's interest in Bramble's racing career never wavered, but he concentrated his efforts on breeding future winners. In December, he sent General Jackson to New York to meet the ship bringing Great Tom from England. The stallion, purchased from Lord Falmouth, stood sixteen and a half hands and was a beautiful golden chestnut with his two hind legs pure white halfway to his hock and a blaze from the center of his forehead to the end of his nose. Harding's plan was for Great Tom to succeed the aging Bonnie Scotland at the head of his stud.[65]

During the winter foaling season, Harding's mare Blondin, by Commodore, foaled a bay filly by Bonnie Scotland. The good news was negated only a day or so later by the accidental death of Burlesque, a two-year-old filly by Bonnie Scotland out of Nubia. Burlesque got out of her paddock at night and wandered onto the railroad track adjoining the lot. There she was struck and killed by a train.[66]

At the 1879 Belle Meade yearling sale, General Harding expected a big crowd. His latest import, Great Tom, was the special attraction. When Uncle Bob brought the big stallion out with Bonnie Scotland at ten o'clock on the morning of the sale, the crowd gathered from all portions of the grounds to see him. As one admirer remarked, "He is all horse and no mistake."[67]

Selene and Lizzie Hoover did not have time to marvel at Great Tom. To be sure they had enough utensils, Lizzie had rented ten dozen plates and dishes and twelve dozen tumblers. Susanna Carter had cooked sixteen pones of light bread. Although Selene and Lizzie did not think they were thick enough, the number came out exactly right. Eighteen lambs and seven shoats were barbecued, twelve hams were cooked (six too many), and 150 gallons of buttermilk were on hand. Although bidding continued through lunch, preventing a long line, Lizzie and Selene were worn out when the day was over. They concluded that the next year they were going to put Susanna in charge with four assistants, and with three hired policemen to control the crowd.[68]

Everyone else seemed to enjoy the sale. Col. Sanders Bruce was back to cover the event and to thank General Harding for the fawns he gave to Blooming Grove. Phil and Mike Dwyer also returned to share with Harding the congratulations they had received for Bramble's remarkable racing performances. The usual large contingent of Kentuckians came, including Peter Fox and Robert Cathcart of Louisville. Gen. George B. Buell and Asa Burnham were there for the first time. Burnham, a successful cheese manufacturer and coal dealer from New York, turned out to be one of the largest buyers at the sale. Often he was in spirited bidding duels with Colonel Bruce, who was representing James R. Keene, another wealthy New York horseman. In all, twenty-nine yearlings sold for a record total of $14,145.[69]

Even though Great Tom drew the largest crowd at the yearling sale, Bonnie Scotland was the one eulogized by Captain Kidd, the auctioneer. He said the sire had sent forth more winners during the previous two years than any horse alive.[70] A few weeks later, Herbert S. Kittredge painted a picture of Bonnie Scotland and Uncle Bob Green.[71] A copy,

BONNIE SCOTLAND AND BOB GREEN. 1956 copy painted by Stewart Treviranus of 1879 original by H. S. Kittredge. Belle Meade collection

JACK MALONE. Painting by Edward Troye, 1869. Collection of Mr. and Mrs. Donald U. Bathrick, Jr., Nashville

BRAMBLE. Painting by Henry Stull, 1878. Belle Meade collection

executed by Stewart Treviranus in 1956, now hangs in Belle Meade's front hall.

By 1879, the success or failure of the Belle Meade Stud rested on General Jackson's shoulders. He felt the weight of the responsibility and realized how difficult it was "to keep up with this breeding establishment to anything like a paying basis." To do so, he felt Belle Meade needed the most popular sires he could find. John Morgan would continue in service only one more year. Bonnie Scotland's career was also nearly over, and Great Tom was unproven. Consequently, Jackson believed the stud needed another stallion. By June, he had found the horse he wanted—Abe Buford's Enquirer, the bay son of imp. Leamington and Lida, by Lexington. Jackson had been convinced by Col. W. H. Johnson and other horsemen that if Belle Meade had Enquirer at its head, "We would have the lead in America, in a word we would have the track."[72]

On June 3, Jackson invited Colonel Johnson and John Harding, Jr., to dinner at Belle Meade to help him persuade General Harding to go along with the idea of buying Enquirer. Having learned that the horse could be obtained for ten thousand dollars, Jackson's plan was for Howell, John, and Jackson himself to buy the stallion, with General Harding furnishing John's third. Since Howell was in West Tennessee, Jackson wrote him outlining the plan and asking for his support on the matter of "highest importance."[73] By mid-June, a deal had been struck for General Harding to buy Enquirer for ten thousand dollars from Billy's ex-Confederate friend Buford. General Harding paid four thousand and Billy and Howell paid two thousand each. Either John Harding, Jr., paid the remaining two thousand or his father paid it for him. Neither the Hardings nor the Jacksons had the cash to make the purchase, so Billy arranged a loan of six thousand dollars through Nashville's Fourth National Bank at 7 percent. Elated at what he considered a coup, Billy wrote Howell to say that "Enquirer stands higher in public favor today than Bonnie Scotland" and that he would rather spend two thousand dollars on him than risk the chance of having a drop in sales, should Bonnie Scotland "drop off" and should Great Tom "not meet with public favor."[74] That October, General Harding commissioned Henry Stull to paint a likeness of Enquirer. At the same time Stull painted Falsetto, an Enquirer colt Harding admired.

As the decade closed, General Harding and General Jackson felt comfortable with their efforts to propel the Belle Meade Stud to the top of the breeding world. They had two sires, Great Tom and Enquirer, that looked capable of taking over whenever Bonnie Scotland died. They also had witnessed throughout the 1879 racing season a continuation of Bramble's startling success as a three-year-old. In 1879, the four-year-old started twenty times. Of those, he won fifteen times, came in second twice, third once, and was unplaced twice.[75] Recognition of Belle Meade as one of the nation's premier studs extended as far west as Denver. In the fall of 1879, a correspondent for the *Denver Tribune* wrote that only Colonel Sanford's and Col. A. J. Alexander's studs in Bourbon and Woodford counties, Kentucky, could approach the Belle Meade Stud in magnitude.[76]

Ever since the first of the Belle Meade-bred get of Bonnie Scotland came out as two-year-olds in 1876, the stallion's climb up the ladder of great American sires had been rapid. Bonnie Scotland's two great rivals, Lexington and Leamington, died in 1875 and 1878. Following their deaths, Bonnie Scotland ranked first among all living American sires in both 1878 and 1879.[77] In 1880, he finally captured the crown as the leading American sire. That season his get won 137 races and $135,700, erasing the records of 102 wins and $120,360 Lexington had established ten years earlier. Unfortunately, Bonnie Scotland did not live to wear his crown. He died at Belle Meade on February 1, 1880. His blood line established through his son Bramble, however, was conspicuous in the pedigrees of American Thoroughbreds for decades to come. The "Tennessee Conestoga," first purchased for $450, made Belle Meade a national landmark.

16/ Family and Friends

DURING THE GLOOMY WINTER OF 1879-80, GENERAL Jackson did not have enough money to visit Selene twice in Colorado as she requested. In fact, he could not leave Belle Meade at all unless Howell relieved him. It looked as if that might not happen until the first of July. Even his going then did not suit General Harding, who complained that he and Howell "make a poor do as I can't manage negroes; neither can Howell." Billy sarcastically wrote Selene that Howell might want to practice law the month of June just to pay his travel expenses from Jackson to Belle Meade. Billy added, "You know that pecuniary affairs weigh quite heavily with our dear brother and sister."[1]

Billy and General Harding spent much of the winter directing twenty or thirty black farm workers in "fencing and cleaning up grass land and seeding." Billy may have overextended himself; he spent a few days in bed "considerably afflicted" with a boil.[2] Despite that frustration, he did his best to cheer up Selene. She had one operation behind her and was facing a second in March.[3] In February, General Jackson wrote her that William knew his ABC's, some poetry, and part of *Robinson Crusoe*. Billy told her how he would lie on the little bed in the back parlor in the evenings and tell William stories from his army days about buffalo, bear, and antelope. Billy also kept Selene posted on plans for rental houses they were building on some of their city property and mentioned that rainy weather would delay sowing oats and planting corn.[4] Billy also sent Selene a picture of the new Nashville Centennial Exposition Building downtown. During Selene's long convalescence in Colorado, her minister, Dr. D. C. Kelley, visited her. When he asked her why she did not live in Colorado permanently, Selene replied, "I would not give five years at Belle Meade for twenty anywhere besides in this world."[5] She was home before the end of May.

Before Selene's return, Billy invited his old army friend Gen. Joseph E. Johnston to stay with him when he was in town for the Centennial Exposition. Johnston replied that he had already accepted an invitation from Capt. A. J. Porter, but that he looked forward to seeing Jackson more than "any other man, soldier, or civilian" and hoped to meet Mrs. Jackson. Unfortunately, she was still in Colorado when Johnston reached Nashville on May 18.[6] When Johnston's special train pulled into the depot, a welcoming committee was already on the train, having boarded at an earlier stop. The city gave Johnston a grand reception, including a reunion with his comrades from the Army of Tennessee. On Wednesday afternoon, Johnston visited General Jackson at Belle Meade.[7]

The big event of the 1880 Christmas season for the Belle Meade Hardings and Jacksons was the marriage of General Harding's granddaughter, Selene ("Lena") Harding, the twenty-three-year-old daughter of John and Mag Harding. Lena's bridegroom was Charles P. Curd, a twenty-nine-year-old professor of Latin at Washington University in St. Louis. They met when Curd taught high school Latin and German in Nashville.[8]

Howell Jackson's election to the United States Senate in January 1881 was another cause for celebration. Billy was proud of his brother. Only a few years earlier Billy had come close to embarking on his own political career. During the seventies, the Farmers' Association of Tennessee wanted to nominate him for governor, but he declined, saying that the position of the private American farmer was preferable to the governorship.[9]

With summer came the usual stream of visitors. Henry W. Grady, editor of the *Atlanta Constitution,* arrived in July with E. P. Howell, also of the *Constitution,* and some Georgia political figures, including the speaker of the house, a state senator, and several legislators. The Georgians left Nashville "charmed by Middle Tennessee, Nashville, and the great stock farm."[10] In November, Lysander Flagg of Rhode Island was equally enchanted with Belle Meade. While at the 3,785-acre plantation, Flagg commented on the stallions, brood mares, colts, and fillies and reported that "about 100 negroes, old and young, cultivate this rich domain." In an article Flagg wrote for the *Daily American,* he said, "We didn't know there was such a place in America. Here they do all for themselves, saw at their own mills their own logs, and grind their own corn and wheat. The Jersey cows give them rich milk and butter for the place." General Harding, he said, "trains no mares. His noble old race course is in wheat." Finally, he wrote that "although General Jackson rode with Forrest and could 'hit hard,' and can't vote yet, I never found a warmer welcome, nor had a more cordial invitation to come again."[11]

Amid all the comings and goings of the adults, life for the Jackson children included school at home. For several years, "Miss Lizzie" Elliott, the daughter of educator Collins D. Elliott, came to Belle Meade and held school for Eunice, William, and Selene. In November 1880, Mrs. Jackson wrote her stepmother that Eunice was as far advanced in her studies as a fifteen-year-old, that William was "high on the road to fame," and that Selene "reads quite well." Miss Lizzie was replaced as governess for the Jackson children by Lucy Chambliss of New Orleans. Later, Eunice and Selene attended Dr. Price's School for Young Ladies in Nashville.[12]

During the 1882 Christmas holidays, the children enjoyed watching some workers build a new mill on Richland Creek. They also had great fun with "their guns and popping crackers, torpedoes, etc." Christmas day went off quietly except for the "fuss of the children and the drunken negroes."[13] Late Christmas morning, Selene and Billy attended the funeral of cousin Sallie B. Ewing at Mt. Olivet. General Jackson was apprehensive about leaving the plantation because all the blacks were drunk. He did so, however, because he was afraid that if Selene drove in alone, her horses might be frightened by firecrackers.[14]

General Jackson looked forward to a winter break. He had planned to go hunting for a week in West Tennessee with his half brother Robert Jackson, but business commitments forced him to cancel the trip.[15] Selene worried about him because he "had more to do than any two men I know of and never has any rest." She mused that a U.S. senator "has a much better life and better pay for his services." As so often happens in families, Selene and Billy envied the lives Howell and Mary led in Washington, while Howell and Mary longed for the peace and quiet of Belle Meade. So drawn to Belle Meade were the Howell Jacksons that they bought property nearby and moved from their West Tennessee home. Howell and Mary arrived in mid-March to stay for a month while they fixed up the old Tealey place.[16]

By the time Mary and Howell moved to Davidson County, General Harding had suffered a stroke and was not only feeble but spoke with great difficulty. No longer able to ride his horse, he rode around the farm twice a day in his buggy. He wanted Selene nearby all the time, and caring for him left her little time for herself or her children. Selene was miffed that none of those responsibilities seemed to fall on her sister. She quoted Mary as saying, "Well, sister, you will have to stay at home, as no one else can manage father. He is the hardest-headed man I ever saw."[17] With all her duties, it is little wonder Selene was so sick with "a terrible spell of asthma, congestion of her lungs, and nervous prostration" after the 1883 yearling sale that she swore she would never again invite guests at that time of year. With the help of morphine and atropine prescribed by her doctor, however, Selene recovered.[18]

Almost immediately, she and General Jackson started the first reno-vation of the house since General Harding expanded it in 1853. Billy and Selene were so impressed with how beautifully Howell and Mary were restoring the Tealey place with every modern convenience that they decided to remodel Belle Meade.[19] The plan included replastering and repainting the interior of the house despite the aggravating effect paint fumes had on Selene's asthma. Other alterations included converting General Harding's office and an adjacent pantry into a downstairs bed-room and bath for him, converting the upstairs linen room into a family bathroom, and putting water and sinks in the dining room and kitchen. Because she did not want to lose all her closet and linen space, Selene built a new linen room above the dining room in the kitchen house. She had the stairs taken out of that room and made the old press in the dining room into a pantry.[20] Selene anticipated that the work would take two or three months to complete. Accordingly, she tried to talk her father into spending some of the time at Mary's house, but he preferred to stay at home.[21]

After exactly three months of work, the house was, as Selene put it, "new from garret to cellar." Mr. Dorris, a correspondent for the *Nashville Banner,* spent a day at Belle Meade in order to describe the renovation of the house for his readers. In his article of July 20, 1883, he said that Belle Meade conveyed "the idea of comfort and convenience." The exterior was painted a stone color with a darker shade on the shutters and cornices. On the top of the cornice, Oman & Stewart, the stonemasons, placed beautiful stone shell scrolls "with smaller scrolls supplementing the larger one in the centre."

Inside, the entrance hall walls had been painted a rich smoke color, which the artist John Wood Dodge had selected as being particularly effective as a background for pictures. The double parlors, Dorris wrote, are elegant, commodious rooms, connected by folding doors. The walls of the parlors are painted robin's egg blue, with ceilings a beautiful tint of sweetgum. The projecting points of the cornice are a darker shade of blue than the walls, with a finish of gilt moulding. Nothing could be more beautiful than this shade of coloring, certainly the most delicate and elegant of colors. Even the blue-room of the White House does not surpass it in delicacy of coloring and artistic finish.[22]

On the other side of the hallway, the library and the sitting room walls were painted café au lait. The woodwork in each room was painted to resemble walnut; gilt molding with special hooks made it easy to hang pictures. The library and the sitting room were separated by folding doors grained to resemble walnut. In both rooms, chandeliers hung from cream-colored ceilings. Dorris made no mention of new rugs or draperies in any of the rooms, so it seems likely they were not replaced in 1883.

The renovation produced changes in private rooms as well. The woodwork in General Harding's new bedroom, where the old plantation office had been, was grained to resemble oak. The walls were painted a light olive, with the ceiling a lighter shade of olive. The bathroom, formerly the pantry, contained "every possible convenience" for a gentleman of Harding's age. Its woodwork was fashioned to resemble walnut. Upstairs, the *Banner* correspondent found the family rooms decorated with handsome gilt paper. The schoolroom was papered with Mother Goose stories and entertaining legends to assist Miss Lizzie in instructing Selene.

Water for the bathrooms, kitchen, and dining room was supplied from a well by an Erickson hot-air engine in the cellar. From there the water was conveyed to an eight-hundred gallon tank on the long gallery upstairs. In the kitchen, where a new wrought iron range from Webb, Stevenson & Co. of Nashville was installed, the walls were painted a rich terra cotta, and the ceiling a shade of sweet gum; the floor was stone. The adjoining dining room was furnished with a sink that had both cold and hot water. Finally, a sink was put in the milk cellar for Sarah, a servant.

Soon after the renovation was complete, General Jackson's West Point classmate and wartime associate, Stephen D. Lee, visited Belle Meade for a few days with his sixteen-year-old son. General Jackson, his son William, and Howell took General Lee and his son to see Battle of Nashville sites near Traveller's Rest.[23] Not long after Lee's visit, Billy, Howell, and Mary went to Louisville to attend the Southern Exposition and to the fair in St. Louis. Selene stayed at home because of her asthma. While General Jackson was away, she gave a party for Eunice and Selene. About twenty girls went hickory nut hunting and then ate a "very nice dinner" at the Red House Spring. General Harding and Lizzie Hoover went along as did William, who was perfectly confident nothing would happen to his sisters as long as he was there.[24]

General Harding made the short trip to the Red House Spring even though his health remained precarious. Impressed by his frailty, he made arrangements for his children to receive the remainder of their inheritance during his lifetime. Harding gave his daughters and their husbands his land in Davidson County and his personal estate, excluding his bloodstock. In his will, Harding said his desire was that the farm should "remain as a whole in the common use and possession" of Selene and Mary without division "as long as it may suit their convenience." He added that, should they prefer a division, Selene should have the tract on the east side of the turnpike, including the house, and Mary should receive the tract lying west of the turnpike, as well as "all that portion of the Finney tract lying south of the Red-house place and west of what is known as the Lower Franklin Road and also two or three small tracts adjacent to the Finney tract."[25]

General Harding presented his Thoroughbred horses, eighty-odd brood mares, four stallions, and forty-nine weanling colts and fillies to his son, John Harding, Jr., and to his two sons-in-law. He stipulated that, by relinquishing his property then, he reserved for himself an annual salary of twenty-five hundred dollars, Howell and Billy paying one thousand each and John five hundred. His sons-in-law were also asked to pay his future debts, taxes, and costs of repairs at Belle Meade. About the same time, he quitclaimed a lot in Southfield to his daughters, Selene and Mary, for "the love and affection" he bore them.[26]

Harding wanted his administrators and heirs to understand why he gave the more valuable portion of his property, including his home and its furnishings, to Selene: "I have counted the board of Genl. W. H. Jackson and family, since he has resided with me, as compensation in part for his services as manager of my affairs and further state, that if there appear any inequity in the provisions of my will in favor of said W. H. Jackson and wife, that I intend it as the balance of compensation for his services, which have been very valuable to me."[27] The favoritism shown Selene and Billy in Harding's will was justifiable. Since his stroke, he seemed "so sad" whenever Selene left his side. Her steadfast attention to him in his declining years made his life bearable.[28] Without Billy's help in managing Belle Meade, the General could not have built a stud of such importance. The increasingly conservative patriarch and his aggressive son-in-law made an excellent team.

Billy Jackson was particularly valuable to Harding in maintaining good relations with the workers. A story told several years later illustrates his rapport with his employees. Once, Jackson recalled that he had "forgotten, or neglected but one promise made to a hand." That was, he said, when he promised George Thornton a pair of pantaloons. As Billy stepped out of his buggy after coming from town, George was waiting, perfectly confident he would receive them. When Jackson realized he had forgotten them, he said, "I am sorry, George; and the only way I can rectify it is to give you the money, which I now do, and loan you my saddle horse to ride to the city and get them." George accepted the offer, perfectly satisfied.[29]

Belle Meade's hospitality in the 1880s was extended to Northerners, Southerners, foreigners, blacks, and whites. In May 1884, sixty New England newspaper editors visited Belle Meade. General Jackson, whose penchant for public speaking was well known, welcomed them and said that, despite having fought against the North, he had no animosity toward Northerners or Easterners. He said that he fought for the South because of the accident of his birth and the location of his home. The visitors were so touched by his remarks that "tears trickled down every cheek." They realized that he was a loyal American, even though they had been told he was one of only thirty ex-Confederate officers who had never been pardoned by the federal government.[30] Another guest was Lord Tarbot, third son of the Duke of Sutherland. While at Belle Meade, he joined in a deer hunt "in the English fashion."[31]

For seven years beginning in the late 1870s, a social organization named the Ugly Club, composed of some of the most prominent African Americans in Davidson County, held picnics at Belle Meade. In 1885, fourteen members were present, along with twenty-nine guests, including a number from out of town.[32]

General Jackson, Senator Jackson, and General Harding invited the Harding Light Artillery to a day of activities at Belle Meade in September, 1884. The former Confederate company, which Harding had armed and equipped, had been reorganized as an "independent company

BELLE MEADE'S ENTRANCE HALL, ca. 1900. Belle Meade collection

HARDING LIGHT ARTILLERY REUNION, 1884. Belle Meade collection

of artillery under the old name" on January 12, 1884. The artillerymen, their wives, and girlfriends were accompanied to Belle Meade by the Porter Rifles, the Hermitage Guards, the Cantrell Guards, and others. Most came by a special train, but others traveled in carriages, drags, and buggies. The morning was spent dancing on the grass in a grove beside Richland Creek. At two o'clock, a barbecue dinner was served to the several hundred attendees. After eating, the guests visited the deer park, danced, or listened to the cannonading of artillery and the music of the Enterprise Cornet Band of Nashville. Later, some of the men played baseball. After the game, the band members asked General Harding for permission to change their name to the Harding Light Artillery Band, a wish he naturally granted. Then, after expressing appropriate thanks and having their picture made in front of the house with their hosts, the group returned to town in railroad cars sent out from the Nashville & Chattanooga Depot.[33]

A few days later, a committee of the Harding Light Artillery adopted a resolution of thanks to the Harding and Jackson families for their kindness. The resolution was in addition to an earlier testimonial signed by all its members:

TO GENERAL WILLIAM G. HARDING Friend and Patron, The Earliest, Truest and Best of THE HARDING LIGHT ARTILLERY by him organized and equipped for the Confederate Service January 12, 1861. It participated in thirty-seven regular engagements and over three hundred skirmishes. Re-organized January 12, 1884 as an independent company of artillery under the old name, by the surviving members, aided by recent recruits, no less worthy, who join, with equal fidelity, in this memorial pledge of their love and gratitude. Still be the living like the dead our loved ones gone before, who nothing of dishonor shed on the brave name they bore.[34]

When the Harding Light Artillery met at Belle Meade, a Gothic dairy house was under construction there. Earlier that year, General Jackson had employed Con Callaghan, a Nashville stonemason, to build the structure on the north side of the front lawn. After the dairy house opened in the spring of 1885, workers brought cream to it directly from the separator in the dairy barn. At one end of the dairy house's cream room was an oblong stone basin through which flowed a stream of cold water, siphoned from a nearby well. After being thoroughly cooled and aerated on a "Star" aerator, the cream was set aside by the buttermaker in cooling cans to ripen for churning. In an adjacent octagonal room, an engine drove the shaft to operate the butter churns. By 1899, the Belle Meade Dairy with its one hundred or more cows and its modern equipment was called "easily the finest and most complete in the South."[35] Howell Jackson also operated an up-to-date dairy, but it was never included in his Belle Meade partnership with Billy and John Harding, Jr. Howell's stone dairy building still stands in the front yard at West Meade.[36]

For his own physical and mental well-being, Billy tried to cut back on his extensive speaking engagements, civic activities, and business interests. He was not particularly successful. In October 1884, he resigned as president of the Safe Deposit, Trust and Banking Company, after having served one year.[37] Several months later, Jackson attended President Grover Cleveland's inauguration in Washington[38] but declined an invitation from Stephen D. Lee to make the annual address at the June commencement of the Mississippi Agricultural and Mechanical College.[39] He did agree, however, to become a trustee of the Nashville YMCA.[40]

A significant event of a different nature occurred that spring. In May 1885, Gen. William Giles Harding, then seventy-six years old and sick in body, accepted Jesus Christ as his Lord and Savior. Harding's conversion took place in a gospel tent pitched at the corner of Broad and Spruce Streets in Nashville by Georgia evangelist Sam Jones. Soon afterward, Harding was received into membership in the Vine Street Christian Church by the Reverend R. Lin Cave.[41] A few days later, Dr. D. C. Kelley of McKendree Methodist Church called on General Harding to offer his congratulations. Harding slowly repeated three times to Dr. Kelley, "I have been more comfortable since then than ever before in my life." The hope expressed nearly a half century earlier by a dying Mary Selena Harding that her husband would someday "obtain the promise of salvation" finally came true. Harding's conversion was also a dream come true for Selene.[42]

General Jackson was equally moved by Sam Jones. During a service at the Broad Street Tabernacle, Jones invited those who "had a word of praise on their lips" to stand up and "say it." When Jackson stood up, Jones asked him to come forward to the platform. The general told the audience he had never been so moved by a religious service in his life and wanted to give his testimony. Jackson said that although he was tempted

PICNIC AT BELLE MEADE for Confederate veterans, 1884. Seated, right to left: Selene Harding Jackson, General Harding, Giles Scales Harding. Standing (from right edge) Mary Harding Jackson (4th from right), Howell E. Jackson (7th from right, with beard). Front row, left to right: General Jackson, Elder Lin Cave. Belle Meade collection to accept Christ many times during the war, he had not done so because he knew his motive was fear. Following the war, however, he said he investigated Christianity and determined for himself the authenticity of the Scriptures. He said he was converted by Bishop James D. Andrew in Jackson, Tennessee, and since then had tried, despite being far less than perfect, to live a Christian life.[43]

At another revival meeting, Jones caught Jackson's attention by saying, "There's many a man here that's going right straight into hell on a blooded horse. I reckon you think though it's better to go that way than to walk." Jackson was sufficiently impressed by what Jones said that night and throughout the revival that he raised ten thousand dollars to buy the evangelist a home in Nashville. Jackson knew that Jones was interested in moving to the official home of Southern Methodism. Jones reluctantly refused the check because his wife did not want to raise their seven children in a city with saloons. When Jackson insisted that he keep the money, the evangelist gratefully did so and spent a portion of it adding to his small house in Cartersville, Georgia.[44]

General Jackson spent New Year's Eve 1885 exactly the way he wanted. He, William, and several guests including B. F. Cockrill hunted foxes all day. Soon after starting out at 8:00 A.M., their twenty-five hounds jumped a red fox, which led them on a long chase around the hills of Belle Meade to the bluff of the Cumberland River on Mark Cockrill's place. Three other foxes were jumped that afternoon.[45] Jackson was so enthusiastic that he purchased two foxhounds from the Ashworth brothers of Wilson County to improve his pack. They were Brownlow, "the famous leader of the Barton Creek pack," and David Crockett, widely considered the most promising foxhound ever raised in Wilson County.[46]

ASSEMBLED FOR AN 1870s HUNT. Left to right: 2. David H. McGavock; 4. General Harding; 5. General Jackson; 6. John Harding, Jr.; 7. Frank O. McGavock (from *Outdoor America*, Dec. 1926)

About the same time Jackson went fox hunting, Belle Meade was brought to the center of a bizarre criminal investigation. Frank Arnold, an aged black man at Belle Meade, had mysteriously disappeared. In January, a headless body was found in Nashville at the trestle on Line Street. Two *Nashville Union* reporters who had been hanging around the police station heard about the story and, through their own detective work, concluded it might be Arnold's corpse. They "shadowed the Belle Meade Farm" after confiding in General Jackson, who agreed to aid them "in every way possible." On the Sunday following the discovery of the body, the reporters told Chief of Police Kerrigan they felt the headless victim was Frank Arnold and that they suspected his murderer was an unsavory character named Ben Brown, who was then living at Belle Meade in the cabin where Arnold formerly lived.[47]

The reporters accompanied Kerrigan to Belle Meade, where he confronted Brown. Under questioning, he confessed. He had murdered Arnold in order to obtain a quitclaim deed to three acres of land Arnold had pledged to him in the event he failed to repay a $190 loan. Apparently, Arnold repaid the loan and reclaimed the mortgage. Kerrigan did not arrest Brown at that point because a corpse without a head was little better, as evidence, than no corpse at all. However, link by link, a chain of circumstantial evidence was built indicating that Brown murdered Arnold and that several other black men staying at Belle Meade were involved. At midnight on January 26, 1886, officers and one of the reporters as guide "swooped down" on the farm and captured five of the six men. Only Ben Brown escaped.[48]

A few days later, a reporter and a group of officers went to the little farm Arnold had mortgaged to Brown. There, in an old beehive, they discovered Arnold's severed head. That same night Ben Beasley, a private citizen, captured Brown at the mouth of Richland Creek. The indictment and subsequent trial of Ben Brown and his co-murderers resulted in a death sentence for Brown, penitentiary sentences for four of the five others, and the release of the fifth man, who turned state's evidence. Justice was served thanks to the "persistent and determined work of the newspaper reporters in unearthing the crime." The newspaper work was called "unquestionably the finest ever done in Nashville, and very likely in the entire South."[49]

Eighteen eighty-six brought with it several events that widened the fame of the Jacksons and Belle Meade. Theodore Roosevelt came to Nashville in March to gather material for his book *The Winning of the West,* published in 1889.[50] Roosevelt is said to have called on General Jackson at Belle Meade. The two men shared a love of the outdoors and hunting, and Jackson accepted Roosevelt's offer of membership in the Boone and Crockett Club, reserved for men who had brought down one of the big game of North America.[51]

In early April of 1886, General Jackson read in the newspapers that President Cleveland wanted to appoint Howell to a vacancy on the Sixth Circuit Federal Court and that Howell declined it because he had presented other names from his constituents. Billy immediately wrote Howell to ask if that was true. If so, he advised Howell to forget about any "supposed case of want of delicacy" and accept the position. Howell took Billy's advice and, on April 15, resigned his seat in the United States Senate and accepted the judgeship.[52]

Howell Jackson began his judicial career in his hometown of Jackson, Tennessee, on April 26. After concluding his work there, he hurried to Nashville to see his new house, West Meade, which was nearing completion. It replaced the old Tealey place he and his family had occupied since 1883. The Jacksons' new two-story Victorian house had rooms fourteen feet high and inside brick walls twelve to fourteen inches thick. The contract with the builder called for the house to be built at a cost of $12,900 and a smokehouse to be constructed for $750. The inside woodwork was of yellow poplar, and the great paneled doors were made exclusively for West Meade at a local shop.[53]

Late in 1886, the eminent author, editor, and humorist Charles Dudley Warner visited Nashville. On Saturday, the day he arrived, Warner accepted General Jackson's invitation to spend the night at Belle Meade. After Sunday dinner with the Jacksons, he attended a Sunday school class that fifteen-year-old Eunice Jackson had been holding for black children at Belle Meade since she was nine years old.[54] On Monday, Warner toured Fisk, Vanderbilt, and Ward Seminary before returning to Belle Meade for lunch. At the plantation, he took in everything—the stallions, mares, colts, and cashmere goats; the deer park; the log cabin where General Harding was born; and, from a distance, a deer hunt. Mrs. Jackson impressed Warner as being "a very positive woman, a great Methodist," and a prohibitionist. Warner wrote in his diary that General Harding was ill during his visit, and that the two daughters were "lovely."[55]

While in Davidson County, Warner made efforts to evaluate the new condition of Southern blacks. In Nashville, he met with eight prominent black citizens, including Henry Harding, a prosperous furniture store owner whose wife had been a slave at Belle Meade, James Carroll Napier, a black lawyer, and Napier's father, William C. Napier. "They talked about their race" and the gall they felt at being excluded from the hotels and cars.[56] At Belle Meade, Warner asked if he might see a "real Southern mammy." General Jackson rang the bell, and Aunt Susanna, "a small gray-haired, light-skinned colored woman," responded. Jackson asked her to tell their guest where she hid the family silver during the war. Susanna said to Warner, "Ain't you from the North?" When he said he was, she replied that she could not tell him where the silver had been hidden because there might be another war and he would know where to look for it. Susanna also told Warner that along with advantages, like education, freedom had brought its own set of problems and anxieties. Of formal education, Susanna's view was that "they used to learn more that was useful in the family than [they now learn] in the school." When Warner asked directly if she preferred freedom to the days of slavery, the loyal ex-slave reflected her many years as a house servant on a plantation during a time when life was different. Her answer was meant as hers alone, one she qualified as no general view. Susanna said "she [would] like slavery back, that is for her. It is better for some, freedom, not so good for others." Following his visit, Warner said that "the colored woman Susanna I met at General Harding's was the most remarkable thing I saw in the South."[57]

17/ Palmy Days

BONNIE SCOTLAND, GAME TO THE LAST, DIED SUDDENLY in his paddock early on Sunday morning, February 1, 1880. His brilliant career as a sire ended in his twenty-seventh year. The hero's death was considered a near national calamity because his winning sons and daughters were already legendary. Descendants of Bonnie Scotland include such illustrious Thoroughbreds as Nijinsky II, Roberto, and Never Say Die, all winners of the English Derby; and Johnstown, Needles, Iron Liege, Carry Back, Northern Dancer, Majestic Prince, Canonero II, Forward Pass, Dancer's Image, Riva Ridge, Secretariat, and Sunday Silence, all winners of the Kentucky Derby. In 1990, Margaret Lindsley Warden, a Nashville Thoroughbred authority, determined that of the fifty-three Thoroughbred Horses of the Year between 1937 and 1989, forty-six were descended from Bonnie Scotland. Officials of Vanderbilt University took notice of his death by requesting his skeleton for display in their museum, and Harding agreed.[1]

Soon after Bonnie Scotland died, Henry Grady, a writer for the *Philadelphia Times,* recorded his impressions of Belle Meade. He said the front hall was a picture gallery of horses, mostly by Stull, but the most prominent picture was Kittredge's portrait of Bonnie Scotland and Bob Green. He also noticed Gamma's portrait and was impressed by a large mahogany case in which were displayed purses and plate won by General Harding in his racing days. Grady was told that "up until a few years ago, the Belle Meade colts were trained on a private track for the turf and entered by General Harding in all the principal races" but that "Harding has withdrawn from the turf and breeds only for sale."[2]

The 1870s and 1880s were a special time for Belle Meade-bred Thoroughbreds. Years later, James Douglas Anderson wrote, "In the opinion of many people, Belle Meade, in its palmy days, in the 1870's

196

and 1880's, was the greatest attraction of its sort anywhere in the United States. This was true because it was one of the few places where the Old South was brought over into the new and continued on an elaborate scale; and, because, as a Thoroughbred nursery, it was a great success."[3]

Both Great Tom and Enquirer were exhibited before the 1880 yearling sale, which netted modest proceeds. Twenty-eight yearlings sold for an average price of $329. On hand for the event were Vernon K. Stevenson of New York; Kentuckians Ben Bruce, S. D. Bruce, Milton Young, and Peter Fox; and Frank Burns of Waynesboro, Tennessee. General Harding had known Burns's family for fifty years. A prominent newcomer was Charles Reed of Saratoga, New York.[4]

That spring, another Bonnie Scotland colt bolted to the front. Luke Blackburn, a three-year-old out of Nevada by Lexington, was burning up the tracks. Bred by James and A. C. Franklin of Sumner County and owned by the Dwyer brothers, Luke went on to become the crack three-year-old of 1880. That season he won twenty-two of twenty-four races. The little son of Bonnie Scotland won all the great stakes that year, including the Tidal, Long Island St. Leger, and Great Challenge Stakes at Sheepshead Bay; the Grand Union Hotel and United States Hotel Stakes at Saratoga; the Champion Stakes at Monmouth Park in Long Branch, New Jersey; and the Kentucky St. Leger and Great American Stallion Stakes in Louisville. His race in the Champion Stakes was called the best ever run in the United States over a mile and a half. Luke Blackburn's final race of 1880 in the Great American Stallion Stakes "put an end to his wonderful campaign and virtually closed his turf career. In pulling up he injured one of his feet and later had a violent attack of epizootic. Though he started twice the next year, he was never himself again."[5] After Luke's racing days were over, General Harding purchased him for fifteen thousand dollars and brought him to Belle Meade, where he stood his first season in 1883 for one hundred dollars a service.[6]

Baron Favorot de Kerbreck and Captain De la Chere of France toured Belle Meade in the spring of 1881 as representatives of the French government inspecting horses and breeding establishments in the United States. In their report, they said that "the best specimen of the Thoroughbred horse" was at General Harding's. "We saw a crop of Thoroughbred yearlings there that surpassed anything we had ever seen in England or France."[7] After reading in the *Spirit of the Times* that Harding had named a colt in his honor, Favoret wrote Harding to thank him for doing so and for his family's hospitality.[8]

The 1881 spring yearling sale at Belle Meade coincided with the month-long Nashville Industrial Exposition. Everyone in the Tennessee turf world knew that the spring sale, with or without the exposition, would be exciting and, perhaps, record-setting. Bramble's and Luke Blackburn's magnificent performances on the track had stimulated great buying interest in the last get of Bonnie Scotland, including Joe Blackburn, a full brother to Luke Blackburn. The sale would also feature the first of Great Tom's get, all with names beginning with a T, to be offered to the public.[9] Between a thousand and fifteen hundred people showed up, including more notable horse enthusiasts than ever before. Others sent their agents. Colonel Johnson of Nashville represented Pierre Lorillard of New York, while Mr. Alcock represented Pierre's brother George.[10]

Some guests spent the night before the sale at Belle Meade. One of them was Jacob McGavock Dickinson, Selene's second cousin once removed. That evening the conversation centered on the sale and the probable price Joe Blackburn would bring. Because of the unsurpassed achievements of Luke Blackburn in 1880, it was obvious that bidding would be high for his brother. The consensus was that he would probably sell for more than $1,000. Up to that time, any price above $500 was considered extraordinary. The next day, the bidding for Joe Blackburn was spirited. It began at $500 and quickly went up to $3,500. When someone bid $3,750, General Harding stood up and said, "No untried colt was ever worth any price like that. I will stop this foolishness, and not permit the horse to be sold. Mr. Auctioneer, please withdraw him." According to Dickinson, the crowd yelled, "General Harding, there has been a second bid on him and he belongs to the crowd." Harding sat back down and the sale went on; the colt brought $7,500.[11]

As he had done for some years, Bob Green exhibited the stallions before the sale. Both Great Tom and Enquirer were "in fine form and spirit." Then at 11:15 A.M., Captain Kidd extolled the virtues of the Belle Meade Stud in an effort to generate even more buying excitement. Just before asking Uncle Bob to lead out the yearlings, he reminded the audience that Bonnie Scotland's get won $130,000 in 1880, which he said "was $60,000 more than realized by the representatives of any other stallion on American soil."[12]

The sale crushed all previous records. Thirty-four colts and fillies brought $38,530, an average of $1,133 per yearling. The eleven Bonnie Scotlands sold for $21,050, a breathtaking average of $1,914. The two highest-priced colts sold were Joe Blackburn, the chestnut brother of Luke Blackburn, and a bay colt that was a brother of Glidelin. Harding and James and A. C. Franklin of Sumner County's Kennesaw Stud were joint owners of both colts.[13]

Howell Jackson had hoped to attend the sale, but his plan to bring Senator Thomas F. Bayard of Delaware with him was canceled when it became obvious that Congress would be in session until well into May. Four days after the sale, Howell wrote Mary he had read in the newspapers that "your father had a glorious sale. The best one made in the U.S. I am rejoiced at his good fortune. He will now be able to pay himself and John [John Harding, Jr.] out of debt."[14]

General Harding was looking for a stallion that spring with the potential to sire another Iroquois. That same spring Iroquois, by imp. Leamington, became the first American-born, American-bred horse to win the English Derby. Owned by Pierre Lorillard, the bay stallion also won the Prince of Wales and the St. Leger Stakes, becoming the first horse ever to win all three premier English events.[15] Harding's choice was Bramble, the great son of Bonnie Scotland. Just after Bramble ran his last race at Baltimore on May 26, Harding purchased him for a reported five thousand dollars. In that race, Bramble had finished lame in the second heat, although he still managed to come in second. His racing days were over, but he was going home to Belle Meade to father future winners.[16]

Both Senator Bayard and Commissioner of Agriculture John B. Loring came to Belle Meade for the 1882 yearling sale. They and Senator Gorham of Maryland arrived a day or two early to see the city. General Jackson, Senator Jackson, J. W. Childress, and Gen. Frank Cheatham took the visitors sightseeing on April 28. The group visited the state capitol, where they met Gov. Alvin Hawkins, and saw Mrs. Polk's home, Vanderbilt University, and Belle Meade.[17] While they were at Polk Place, Mrs. Polk expressed her appreciation to Senator Jackson for successfully introducing her name for a federal pension.[18]

At the yearling sale the next morning, the crowd of nearly two thousand people was even larger than in 1881. Among the Kentuckians present were Daniel Swigert, a breeder whose stud produced a rival of Luke Blackburn named Hindoo; Milton Young, who acquired his famous

McGrathiana Stud that year; and Col. Meriwether Lewis Clark of the Louisville Jockey Club, whose track would, in 1883, be named Churchill Downs.[19] All three Belle Meade sires—Enquirer, Great Tom, and Bramble—were exhibited immediately before the sale in the main stable. Thirty-seven yearlings out of Enquirer and Great Tom were sold for $23,355, an average price of $631. A surprise buyer was Mrs. Charles Reed of Saratoga, New York. The *Daily American* reported that with her purchase of a Great Tom-Woodbine filly she became the first woman to purchase a horse at a yearling sale in the United States.[20] A year later, Mrs. Reed's husband, Charles, bought the Fairvue Stud in Sumner County from Adelicia Acklen Cheatham for $50,000.[21]

Following the sale, Howell returned to Washington, and General Jackson redirected his efforts to managing Belle Meade. That spring within the borders of Belle Meade's sixteen-mile-long stone fence he planted 50 acres in barley, 200 in clover, 350 in corn, 200 in oats, 100 in orchard grass, 400 in timothy, and 200 in wheat. In addition, there were 150 acres in paddocks sown with barley and blue grass, 1,300 in woodland pasture sown with orchard and blue grass for beef cattle and sheep. (The 425 acres in the deer park remained uncultivated.) The average produce per acre at Belle Meade in 1882 was 40 to 50 bushels of barley, 50 to 60 bushels of corn; 1.5 to 2 tons of hay, 40 to 50 bushels of oats, and 27 bushels of wheat.[22] Those yields compared favorably with the average yields for the same crops on the best farms elsewhere in the county.

To prevent wearing out his land, General Jackson followed the practice, initiated many years earlier by General Harding, of rotating crops. After a two-year stand of red clover, he put in wheat, followed by corn for two years, and then oats and clover. Both Jackson and Harding used red clover as a fertilizer and soil-builder, a practice recognized as progressive even today. For "worn out spots" Jackson planted peas. Some of Belle Meade's fields in continuous cultivation for seventy years were in better shape in 1882 than they were originally.[23]

Following his visit to Belle Meade in 1882, Joseph H. Reall, editor and publisher of the *Agricultural Review and Journal of the American Agricultural Association,* wrote an article hailing it as the greatest farm in America.[24] If Belle Meade were to live up to the high expectations set by Reall's pronouncement, General Jackson knew he had to do more than rely on red clover and proper crop rotation to get the highest yield per acre. He also needed the best farm equipment. Consequently, he arranged for a demonstration of harvesting machines sold by the McCormick, Osborne, Buckeye, and Wood Harvesting Machine companies to be held at Belle Meade. After watching each machine, pulled by mules, cut a field of barley and then a field of green wheat, Jackson chose an Osborne and a McCormick harvester.[25]

Henry Stull, the well-known painter of horses, visited Belle Meade in June. His drawings of scenes and people there were published in *Frank Leslie's Illustrated Newspaper.* The caption below the pictures identified Belle Meade as "the mecca of American horsemen." Earlier, Stull had painted Trifle and Luke Blackburn, portraits in the Belle Meade collection today.[26]

Early in the summer, General Jackson sold 111 head of cattle to Perry & Lester, livestock traders, for $8,637.80, took 155 head of cattle from Perry & Lester to graze until October, and bought 3 yearling calves, bringing the Belle Meade herd to 74. Jackson paid for the cattle on an account he and Howell jointly maintained, indicating that the cattle belonged to them and not to General Harding.[27]

Two Sundays before the 1883 Belle Meade sale, a flood prevented General Jackson from opening the front gate and temporarily cut the house off from the turnpike. Just upstream, the new sale barn was in "an island of water." As the flood subsided, everyone plunged into preparations for the annual yearling sale, "with its usual anxieties and troubles." Selene could always tell when it was near because Billy invariably began to "get nervous and bilious."[28]

The Jacksons' houseguests for the sale were Senator Thomas Bayard and his two daughters. They arrived early so the girls could see the farm. A highlight of the visit for the girls, both of whom were good riders, was a gallop through the 425-acre deer park. After his four-day visit to Belle Meade, Bayard was so impressed with the hospitality extended him that in parting he called Belle Meade "a fine type of America's best civilization." It was a home, he said, where the governess and seamstress were so courteously served and so freely intermingled with honored guests that "no one dreamed that they were less than peers of the best."[29]

Despite rain, a train with seven cars and many private conveyances came out from town for the sale. Selene recalled that they fed one thousand people. The sale was held outside the large stable in a new amphitheater, designed to hold more people than the stable. Of forty-two yearlings sold, there were eleven colts and eleven fillies by Enquirer,

ENQUIRER. Painting by Henry Stull, 1879

LUKE BLACKBURN. Painting by Henry Stull, 1880

IROQUOIS AND SAM NICHOLS. Painting by an
unknown artist.

Belle Meade collection

eleven colts and seven fillies by Great Tom, one colt by Bramble, and one by Fellowcraft. The yearlings brought an aggregate of $27,430, or $653 per yearling. By far the most popular were the Enquirer get, which brought an average of $867.[30]

The 1883 racing season once again demonstrated the quality of Belle Meade breeding. Yet another Bonnie Scotland colt distinguished himself. George Kinney, out of Kathleen by Lexington, won twelve of eighteen starts, with four second-place and two third-place finishes. The bay stallion, owned by the Dwyer brothers, was named the champion three-year-old of the year.[31]

Before the next yearling sale, the *Spirit of the Times* reported, on April 26, 1884, that men "frequently associated with racing" said there was no chance for men of moderate means to get good colts at yearling sales such as at Belle Meade, Runnymede, Fairvue, Woodburn, and Elmendorf because rich men, notably the Dwyers, James R. Keene, A. J. Cassatt, and the Lorillards, outbid them. According to the article, the sentiment was so common that owners of small stables did not attend the yearling sales. This was not a surprising development in a day when a well-made man's hat could be purchased in Nashville for $1.50 and a boy's suit for only $5 or $6. Despite the adverse publicity, the 1884 spring yearling sale, conducted jointly by General Jackson, Senator Jackson, and John Harding, Jr., was well attended, if only moderately successful. The average price fell below that of the previous three sales. The highest price was two thousand dollars paid by the Dwyer brothers for a Bramble colt. Because of the increase in the number of yearlings to be auctioned, Billy held the sale outside the stable in a ring over which he erected a large tent. In addition to the usual contingent of wealthy out-of-state buyers, a good number of local breeders, trainers, and general horse fanciers turned out, including Gov. James D. Porter. General Harding, still not recovered from the effects of his stroke, did not attend.[32]

The Tennessee breeders' sale of Jersey cattle was held at Belle Meade in May. Area dairymen viewed the sale as an initial step in organizing a statewide breeders' association. The auction included Jerseys from Thomas H. Malone's Richland Grange Farm, Matt Gardner's Lynnwood Farm, and William J. Webster's Columbia Jersey Cattle Company.[33] Belle Meade's herd of forty to fifty grade Jerseys was kept only for the purpose of supplying milk for the family and help. Since the herd did not represent an emphasis on breeding, General Jackson did not participate in the sale.[34]

Shortly after the cattle sale, Commodore Jeremiah George Harris, U.S.N., brought for a visit to Belle Meade Nelson Dingley, the editor of the Lewiston (Maine) *Journal.* The pleasure Dingley took in the visit indicates the healing process taking place between North and South during the mid-eighties. General Jackson's warm welcome formed in the Maine newspaperman the impression of the general as a man of great dignity "with equal cordiality and courtesy." When Commodore Harris told him Jackson had never been pardoned, the New Englander was surprised, particularly since Jackson expressed the view that "the South is better off than it could have been had the Confederacy succeeded." Jackson went on to praise the development of self-reliance and energy among Southern young men and women as remarkable. In an article written for the *Daily American,* Mr. Dingley called Luke Blackburn, the graceful son of Bonnie Scotland, "the most famous racer in the world." He said that the Kingdom of God "must be a wonderfully nice place to go to if it is any more celestial in atmosphere and radiant in beauty than Belle Meade."[35]

Despite the success of the Belle Meade Stud brought about by the remarkable performances of Bonnie Scotland's get, Billy and Howell Jackson were not yet out of their financial quagmire. When they and John Harding, Jr., took over the estate from General Harding, they had no cash and had to borrow money to purchase beef cattle and sheep. Billy's efforts at making the Belle Meade Farm profitable included allowing companies to use the Belle Meade name. In the early 1880s, Nashville boasted a Belle Meade Tobacco Factory—manufacturers of Belle Meade twist and Belle Meade Smoking Tobacco—and a Belle Meade Distillery— producers of bourbon and rye whiskies.[36] By January 1885, the strain of running the big agricultural machine, with its debt and absentee partners, was frustrating Billy. He bristled when Howell apparently wrote expressing his concern with a critical tone. In a letter to Howell that January, he agreed with his brother's hope that the sale of their beef cattle and yearlings would get them out of debt. He also said he did not understand Howell's comments about the operation of the farm and hoped "no fault or censure on me is implied." General Jackson added, "I am doing the best I know how & shall endeavor to limit expenditures all I can."[37] The local public had no inkling that citizens as prominent as John Harding, Jr., and the Jackson brothers might have financial worries. To them, Belle Meade was a wonderland of deer, Thoroughbreds, and fashionable society. Large numbers enjoyed the deer park and saw the stallions on weekends. There often were so many on Sundays in good weather that the grooms would earn sizable sums in nickel and dime tips for holding the visitors' horses and showing the stallions.[38]

Though less and less vigorous, General Harding gave up activities grudgingly. Even though his stroke two years earlier limited his activity, he often braved bad weather and ignored his infirmities to accompany a visitor to the stables to admire and show his stock.[39] He also attended the 1885 yearling sale. Naturally, many of the visiting turfmen and reporters spoke to him. Although he was quite feeble, he expressed his deep gratification at seeing them once more, reminisced about the days when Bonnie Scotland was king, and took a great interest in the proceedings. As usual, Bob Green exhibited the stallions—Bramble, Enquirer, Great Tom, and Luke Blackburn. A *Nashville Banner* correspondent said Bob "strolled the yard a veritable autocrat." Although Great Tom had lost his sight in one eye the previous fall, he was otherwise in good form, as were the other sires. The sale was successful; forty colts and fillies brought an average price of $558.[40]

That was also a good season for Belle Meade youngsters on the nation's tracks. Enquirer stood eleventh on the list of winning sires, his get earning $45,055, with 70 first places, 62 second, 50 third, and 195 unplaced. Editor and Inspector B were his largest winners, earning $9,275 and $5,552, respectively.[41]

Among the colts and fillies making their appearances at Belle Meade early the next spring were two of promise by the great American stallion Iroquois. The last week in March, Bric-a-Brac, by Bonnie Scotland, dropped a brown colt forty-three inches tall. About the same time, Martica, the dam of Economy, dropped a forty-six-inch bay colt. There were a dozen colts and fillies by Iroquois at Belle Meade, and General Jackson was ecstatic. He told a reporter that "the foals dropped to Iroquois are positively the finest I have seen at Belle Meade in the history of the establishment."[42] His statement foreshadowed a time when the name of Iroquois would signal an even closer connection to Belle Meade.

The press announced that the nineteenth Belle Meade yearling sale would be held on April 27, 1886. The sale was the best since 1881. Forty-seven yearlings sold for $38,125, an average of more than $811 per horse. Buyers were eager to "capture the progeny of Luke Blackburn and Bramble as representatives of the blood of the immortal Bonnie Scotland." For an hour before the sale, Uncle Bob's crew exhibited Enquirer, Luke Blackburn, Bramble, Great Tom, and Plenipo, the most recently acquired Belle Meade sire.[43] The stallions had a combined estimated value of $85,000, ranging from $25,000 each for Enquirer and Luke Blackburn, down to $5,000 for Plenipo.[44]

General Harding was present but too infirm to mingle with the guests. Nevertheless, all the notable visitors sought him out to pay their respects. Among those in attendance were "Big Ed" Corrigan of Kansas City and Sam Bryant of Louisville. James Ben Allen Haggin of Rancho del Paso, near Sacramento, was one of the heaviest buyers. Although he did not attend in person, he had a representative on hand. His Ben Ali won the Kentucky Derby that spring. Another change was that William Easton of New York replaced Capt. P. C. Kidd as auctioneer.[45]

With an excellent sale and with Great Tom's get Swift and Telie Doe finishing the season as two of the fastest mares in the country, 1886 shaped up as a banner year. Confirmation of the stud's status as one of the country's premier Thoroughbred horse nurseries came from the second contingent of Frenchmen to visit Belle Meade in five years. In September, Vicomtes de la Motte Rouge and DeCoumout, inspectors general of the Ministère de l'Agriculture of France, stopped at Belle Meade after seeing ten Kentucky studs. Before leaving Nashville, the Frenchmen said that "nothing we have seen anywhere is comparable to Belle Meade in the number of good horses to be seen there. Even the mares are of a superior kind. Harding's is indeed the best place we have seen in America." The Frenchmen also mentioned to a Daily American reporter that the Kentucky breeders encouraged them to come to Belle Meade and were "very warm" in their praise.[46] It is interesting that the Frenchmen spoke of Belle Meade as being General Harding's stud rather than General Jackson's or, more correctly, a stud belonging to the Jackson brothers and John Harding, Jr. Regardless of where title lay, as long as General Harding was alive, the public considered it his home.

The visit of the Frenchmen provided a brief change of pace for General Jackson. As usual, he had plenty on his mind, primarily Pierre Lorillard's auction of all the horses at his fabulous Rancosas Stud in Jobstown, New Jersey. Lorillard had decided to dispose of his Thoroughbred holdings because of the press of other business. The most famous horse he owned, the great sire Iroquis, was in the group. That definitely caught Jackson's attention. He, Billy Cheatham of the Cliff Lawn Stud, and C. H. Gillock, secretary of the Nashville Blood Horse Association, went up for the sale. The *Spirit of the Times* correspondent covering the event described Jackson for his readers:

> Gen. W. H. Jackson, of Belle Meade, in his slouch hat of the trooper days, his eyes dancing merrily beneath his bushy brows, enlarges to his auditors upon the merits of Mortimer as a diversion from his intended coup d'état on Iroquois, as he leans forward and leans on his stick and chews the end of his cigar, which goes out at regular intervals of five minutes.[47]

The auction brought $149,050 for an American record average of $5,520. The filly Dewdrop, champion two-year-old of 1885, topped the bidding at $29,000.[48] Close behind was Iroquois, 1881 winner of both the English Derby and the Doncaster St. Leger Stakes. That feat would not be duplicated by an American horse until Never Say Die won both events in 1954. Iroquois went to General Jackson for $20,000. In a short speech, Jackson explained that he bought "the carrier of American colors on foreign soil for fear he might be taken away." Jackson spent another $5,330 on five brood mares.[49]

When Belle Meade's new Thoroughbreds reached Nashville in October of 1886, they were exhibited at Black's stable on North Cherry Street.[50] More than half a century later, Lee Roy Jordan, who was a barefoot boy of eleven in 1886, recalled the excitement of the arrival: "When Iroquois was brought in people stood around and sung songs. They hollered and they yelped. They made up one song to the tune of Casey Jones, tell[ing] how Iroquois had whipped the British, and they sung it all over the country. It was a happy day." According to Jordan, who worked at Belle Meade for twenty years, both whites and blacks of the section gathered to celebrate the great runner's arrival.[51] General Jackson was clearly delighted with his purchase and the promise it held for the future. He was also delighted with the present: the 1886 winnings of the get of his stallion Enquirer nearly doubled those of 1885. In 1886, Enquirer's get won 97 races, came in second 68 times and third 71 times, and were unplaced 22 times. Their total winnings were $87,017.[52]

In the fall, the *New York Sportsman* learned from General Jackson and C. H. Gillock that racing in Nashville would unquestionably become established on the firmest of foundations. Earlier that year, the old Nashville Race Course had closed because of its inaccessibility and tendency to flood.[53] The newspaper understood that the Nashville Blood Horse Association and investors interested in the street railroad "have combined to beautify a piece of ground in easy reach of the city."[54] The executive committee would control racing, and spring and fall meetings would be held at the new track, named the West Side Park Club, where Centennial Park is located today. It opened in 1888.[55]

On December 15, 1886, Gen. William Giles Harding died at the age of seventy-eight. He had grown increasingly weak during the summer. By the fall, his eyesight was failing, and within a few weeks, he was totally blind. He probably never saw Iroquois. As a horse breeder, master, employer, parent, grandparent, and neighbor, he had been loved and respected, his honesty, humanity, and modesty winning him wide esteem. "His ruling trait in life was a faith in the innate resources and native greatness of Tennessee," particularly its middle section.[56] Few had done more than he to add to the renown of Nashville and Tennessee. The plantation he managed with skill and persistence for forty-four years was famous the world over as a stud. His stallions Epsilon, Priam, John Morgan, Vandal, Bonnie Scotland, and Enquirer were equally well known. From 1870 to the close of 1885, their get had won $1,163,869 in stakes and purses. With the probable exception of Woodburn Farm, Spring Station, Kentucky, Belle Meade was considered America's greatest breeding establishment.[57]

Newspapers across the country took notice of Harding's death. The *Daily American* said of him: "His moral nature was pitched upon a plain of great height. He was genial and lovable of nature, and dies without an enemy in the world." The *St. Louis Daily Globe-Democrat* commented that the country "is incalculably indebted to his sagacity and enterprise for the value and superiority of its Thoroughbred horses." The *Chattanooga Times* called him a "monarch on his own domain."[58]

The common citizens of Davidson County also praised him. The gatekeeper on the Harding Turnpike recalled that Harding "was the honorablest wealthy man in the world. He was my friend and the friend of every workingman. His soul stands clean, without a spot, before the judgment today." Henry Harding, a black Nashville furniture store proprietor, had made it a point to praise General Harding while he was still alive. During the previous summer, he was heard to say to Harding: "You have been the truest friend to me and my race I have ever known."[59]

Jacob McGavock Dickinson's feelings about General Harding were still strong in 1926 when he wrote: "He was of that style of man that exists no longer in the South, and so far as I know no longer in the world. . . . Wrought in the mould of republican institutions, schooled in the principles of civil liberty and self-government, proud of the history of their fathers, believing that to be an American was greater than to be a King . . . they were a race of men who, in the splendor of their characteristics, were equal to the best that any time has produced."[60]

On the morning of his funeral, General Harding's body lay in state in the front hall at Belle Meade. On his cedar casket were three simple designs of fresh flowers. One carried the dedication "Old Master," from the General's servants, the second the word "Father," and the third "Grandpa." The only other floral arrangement had the letters "H. L. A." inscribed on it. It had been provided by members of the Harding Light Artillery. The service was conducted by the Jacksons' former pastor, Dr. D. C. Kelley, assisted by Elder R. Lin Cave of the Christian Church. At the conclusion of Elder Cave's remarks, Dr. Kelley offered a prayer, and twelve black men, some quite old, took up the coffin and reverently bore it to the family mausoleum. Among them were Tom Harding, the General's faithful manservant, and Bob Green. Ahead of them marched the Harding Light Artillery and the honorary pallbearers, who were either old friends of Harding's or their sons. Behind the active pallbearers came the family, friends, and servants. After a brief service, Harding's body was "gathered to his fathers" inside the tomb and placed near the body of his father, John Harding, the founder of the plantation and stud that William Giles so ably expanded and improved.[61]

The curtain of gloom enshrouding Belle Meade extended beyond Nashville. Many thought Harding had done as much for the breeding interests of Tennessee, and perhaps for all America, as any man in the nineteenth century. A consolation for his loss was the fact that Belle Meade was alive and well. The *Spirit of the Times* correspondent, who visited Belle Meade two months after Harding's death, wrote that nowhere else in America could be found "a quintet of sires whose blood and speed lines" compare with Iroquois, Enquirer, Great Tom, Luke Blackburn, and Plenipo.[62]

Historian George Bancroft visited Nashville in April 1887 to examine the papers of former President James K. Polk. Bancroft, who had been both Polk's secretary of the navy and minister to the Court of St. James's, stayed at the Maxwell House with his German valet Hermann. On the last morning of his visit, the eighty-five-year-old gentleman, accompanied by a committee of the Tennessee Historical Society, drove out to Belle Meade.[63] General Jackson and Judge Howell Jackson met their distinguished guest on the lawn. The group then went into the house where the Jackson women and children were waiting in the parlors to be introduced.[64]

After thirty minutes of conversation, Jackson invited Mr. Bancroft to drive through the deer park. Half a dozen horses were quickly saddled and brought to the front door, along with several carriages for those, including Bancroft, who preferred them. A reporter for the *Daily American*, who had come along on the outing, noticed that Hermann seemed "as unexcitable and immovable as stone until taken through the park." However, when "a drove of perhaps 200 deer" dashed past, "Hermann exclaimed in excited ecstasy, 'Well, did you ever see anything like that?' Bancroft's voice trembled as he replied 'Never in my life.'"[65] The Bancroft party next saw the Thoroughbreds at the "imperial" stables before returning to the mansion. They were again entertained in the parlors, and one of the young ladies asked Mr. Bancroft to tell them something of Goethe, Byron, Von Humboldt, Bismarck, and Von Moltke. He obliged his attentive audience for fifteen or twenty minutes before excusing himself in order to keep a noon appointment with Mrs. Polk. Before leaving, Mr. Bancroft undoubtedly mentioned the colt General Harding named for him in 1878.[66]

The 1887 yearling sale was remembered for its enormous crowd of four to five thousand. Sanders D. Bruce was the auctioneer for the event, held in a tent with "circular amphitheater seats." When Bob Green exhibited the stallions, Iroquois drew the most attention. Immediately before the sale, Uncle Bob was introduced to the crowd. He responded by politely taking off his hat and saying he had been at Belle Meade some sixty years and "in the royal family's employ for thirty years." He then promised to show the crowd the best lot of yearlings he had ever handled.[67]

Despite predictions of an outstanding sale, the results were disappointing. Some thought it was because the Kennesaw and Fairvue sales, preceding Belle Meade's, depleted the purses of many buyers. Forty yearlings sold for an average price of only $564. The highest price was paid by Ed Corrigan, a wealthy investor with wide-ranging interests in the horse business.[68] The swashbuckling tycoon's turf empire included seventy to eighty Thoroughbreds, and interests in racetracks in California, Chicago, Hot Springs, Kansas City, New Orleans, and St. Louis.[69]

A train of seven cars went to Belle Meade for the 1888 yearling sale. The fifty-two yearlings represented the largest number ever sold at Belle Meade; unfortunately, the average price of $478 was even more disappointing than the previous year. Following the sale, General and Mrs. Jackson invited visiting horsemen, their families, and a number of local guests to the mansion, where they enjoyed "a substantial and highly enjoyable luncheon." That was a change from previous years when barbecue luncheons were served to the entire crowd.[70]

Because the 1888 yearling sale did not produce the income Billy and Howell were counting on, they were forced to borrow twenty-five thousand dollars from New York's Chase National Bank through the help of Charles McClung McGhee, a Knoxville friend and financier. The loan was made in the name of Jackson Brothers, the partnership Howell and Billy formed to manage the stud.[71]

Successes of Proctor Knott and other Luke Blackburn get on the 1888 racing circuit encouraged the financially plagued Jacksons. During that season, Luke's get started 447 times, came in first 81 times, placed second 68 times, and finished third 55 times. Their total winnings were $100,339, and he was the fourth leading sire in the country.[72] His son Proctor Knott, named for a Kentucky governor, won the first Futurity at the Coney Island Jockey Club before forty thousand people, bringing great acclaim to Belle Meade. After the race, a newspaper correspondent called Proctor Knott the greatest horse ever bred in Tennessee and "probably the best horse that ever looked through a saddle."[73] General Jackson proclaimed Proctor Knott "a greater horse than Luke Blackburn and the best he ever saw. Unless some accident should befall him, the three-year-old stakes of America are at his mercy."[74] Proctor Knott got his chance to prove Jackson correct at the great spring meeting at Nashville's West Side Park Club on May 2. He and Come to Taw were the favorites in a new stake, the Two Thousand Sweepstakes— so named because of the size of the purse. Although Proctor Knott won his preliminary heat, he lost by a neck to Come to Taw in the five-horse field.[75]

Proctor Knott's next opportunity was at that year's Kentucky Derby, where he was the favorite at odds of two to one. Before the race started, the fractious horse false started several times and twice almost threw his rider, Pike Barnes. However, he got away clean and rushed to the front at the first turn. Halfway down the backstretch, Proctor Knott had a three-length lead. At the last turn, the race evolved into a struggle between Proctor Knott and Spokane with the former having the best of it by about two lengths. A little beyond the eighth pole Proctor Knott's lead had been cut to about a length. Just then the gelding suddenly broke to the outer rail, and was caught at the finish line by Spokane, a ten-to-one shot.[76] A majority of the spectators thought the finish was a dead heat. The judges hesitated before awarding one of the most disputed victories in Kentucky Derby history to Spokane. "Thousands of Tennessee hearts and purses" were said to have been broken. G. Chapman Young of Louisville, who was at the race, described what caused Proctor Knott to lose his lead. He said that, as he was watching the race from the infield, "a Negro wadded up a newspaper and threw it out on the track in front of Proctor Knott, causing the horse to bolt." It is recognized that a horse running within the pack is not easily distracted, but when a horse has a good lead, with only the track in front of him, he can easily be diverted. Pike Barnes, the jockey, did not see a newspaper thrown. After the race, he called Proctor Knott the greatest horse he would ever ride. He said that "if I could have held him he would have won, hands down. In the stretch he swerved badly to the outside, and I was too light to hold him, and so he got off his stride and lost the race."[77]

Despite Belle Meade's reputation as one of the country's greatest studs, General Jackson was frustrated. His relationship with Howell was deteriorating over financial and management matters, stud expenses were high, he was in serious debt, and he was not sure of how to improve his cash flow. With his love for entertaining and public attention, it is not surprising that he hit upon the idea of inviting the president of the United States to Belle Meade. If Grover Cleveland accepted, the Belle Meade Stud would receive national publicity that could boost his yearling sales to new heights.

18 / New South, Old South

O N MAY 14, 1887, WILLIAM HICKS JACKSON WROTE HIS
friend Secretary of State Thomas F. Bayard inviting him,
President Grover Cleveland, and another member of Cleveland's cabinet
to Nashville on May 27. The proposal was that Cleveland speak during
the "inaugural ceremonies incident to the opening of the Grand Manufacturing enterprises" in West Nashville, commonly referred to as New
Town. Given such short notice, it is understandable that the president
declined.[1] Toward the end of July, however, the Nashville press announced that President Cleveland might come to Nashville in the fall on
his way from Memphis to Atlanta. Judge Jackson wrote the president that
"myself and brother General W. H. Jackson will be delighted to entertain
you at Belle Meade, our country home, of which the Secretary of State
will give you an account." A few days later, the president responded,
opening the possibility of a visit.[2]

While the Jacksons and Nashville awaited confirmation of the president's plans, both brothers spoke out in favor of a five-hundred-thousand-
dollar subscription by the citizens of Davidson County for common stock
in the Midland Railroad, which proposed to build a road through Davidson County connecting the rich coalfields of the Cumberland Mountains with the iron and timber belt west of Nashville. The subscription,
bitterly opposed by the powerful Louisville & Nashville Railroad (L&N),
was defeated despite widespread support, including that of Mayor Kercheval, former Gov. Albert S. Marks, the Jacksons, and several prominent
black leaders. On the day following the election, the *Daily American*
charged that the L&N brought in illegal voters from such places as
Murfreesboro, McMinnville, Columbia, Bardstown, Kentucky, and
Bridgeport, Alabama, to vote against the subscription. Although indignation meetings were held at the Maxwell House and on the public

214

square, the decision stood.[3] Though disappointed by the defeat of the proposed railroad, the Jacksons turned full attention to the presidential visit.

By September, Cleveland's stay in Nashville from October 15 to 17 had been agreed upon. On October 1, General Jackson went to St. Louis to extend a personal invitation to the president to stay at Belle Meade for "a quiet, home-like reception" and to make final arrangements with Cleveland's press secretary, Col. Daniel S. Lamont. The idea of a quiet weekend as guests of the Jacksons appealed to the Clevelands. The president made it clear that he did not want any visitors on Sunday but that he and Mrs. Cleveland would like to call on Mrs. Polk.[4] Accordingly, Jackson informed a spokesman for a group of Mexican War veterans that their best bet to meet the president would be at the capitol on Monday morning.[5]

John Thomas, president of the Nashville, Chattanooga and St. Louis Railroad (NC & StL) seized an opportunity to be the first Nashvillian to greet the chief executive. He arranged to meet the presidential party at McKenzie and pull the president's train to Nashville behind his personal steam engine, *The Tennessean.* The only problem was that when the train left McKenzie the president was not aboard. He was still shaking hands with the estimated five thousand people who came to the depot to see him. The train was almost a mile away before the engineer realized what had happened and began backing his train to pick up its distinguished passenger.[6]

Late that afternoon, preparations at Belle Meade were nearly complete. Boys and men were hanging hundreds of Japanese lanterns along the carriageway from the front gate to the house. The special train was expected to arrive around 9:15. For two hours before that, General Jackson and Judge Jackson entertained the press in the library at Belle Meade.[7]

One of the reporters managed to slip out of the library long enough to interview Mrs. Jackson. He found her to be "a most charming woman, thoroughly Southern in every instinct." During the interview, she remarked,

> We don't intend to put on one bit of extra display. We are giving him as good entertainment as we know how. I haven't put bouquets into every nook and crevice in Mrs. Cleveland's room because I know that she has literally

tramped upon the choicest of flowers since she left Washington. We are not going to put on any extra style in eating either. We have a long table and all our old family servants. Our visitors will sit down to regular old-fashioned meals. All of the food will be on the table when we sit down and not served in courses in modern day style. Then if the President doesn't like battercakes he can have waffles, and if he doesn't like birds, he can have venison.[8]

A little before nine, General Jackson ended his entertainment of the press and he, Judge Jackson, and the group of reporters walked down to the station. In a few minutes, they heard the shrill whistle of a locomotive, and "afar in the distance a light shone down the track." Scarcely had the presidential train arrived than Judge Jackson bounded up the steps of the car, the Alfaretia, with General Jackson right behind him. After appropriate introductions were made, the party left the train. Four handsome carriages, which had been waiting in the shadows with liveried servants standing at each door, drove up on General Jackson's signal. President and Mrs. Cleveland and her maid got into the first carriage and left for the mansion. General Jackson, accompanied by Lamont, Cleveland's secretary, followed in a second carriage. The other two carriages went with Judge Jackson and four other members of the presidential party to West Meade, a mile away.[9]

At Belle Meade, General Jackson introduced his distinguished guests to Mrs. Jackson, Eunice, and William. Soon thereafter, the Clevelands retired to the double bedrooms on the second floor. The president's room, opening on a large veranda, was furnished in pink, including the carpet, pillows, spreads, and hangings. He slept in a large canopied bed that had been in the family for years. Mrs. Cleveland's room was furnished in blue, with blue pillows, silk spreads, toilet cases, and carpet. The curtains in both rooms and throughout the house were of lace.[10]

On Sunday morning, the Clevelands, Jacksons, and Lamont had a leisurely breakfast topped off with quail and venison shot by twelve-year-old William. After breakfast, General Jackson took his guests to see his stallions. The president, dressed in the Prince Albert coat he habitually wore, and Mrs. Cleveland, attired in an exquisite gray walking costume, were anxious to see "the most noted home of the Thoroughbred in the South." Accordingly, Jackson called for Uncle Bob Green and introduced him, with considerable praise, to the guests. When Bob shook hands with President Cleveland, he said, "I is proud to be able to show de President de royal family." Next, the group sauntered to the paddocks where they admired the royal family—Iroquois, Bramble, Enquirer, Luke Blackburn, and Great Tom. They then visited the weanling stables.[11]

General Jackson had one more treat for the Clevelands. He suggested that they walk in the woods east of the house. Then, without their knowledge, he had Uncle Bob and some helpers corral the deer and drive them past the chief executive. Suddenly, two hundred deer burst into view, much to the delight of the Clevelands. The president turned to Jackson and said, "That was a splendid sight, General; it made my nerves tingle; I never saw such an exhibition before."[12]

PRESIDENT CLEVELAND, viewing the Belle Meade deer. *Harper's Weekly*, Oct. 29, 1887

After President and Mrs. Cleveland left Belle Meade, a writer asked Bob Green what he thought of the guests. "Lor me," he exclaimed, "I'se been nigh unto sixty-five years on dis place, and to shake hands wi' de President is great satisfaction." When asked his opinion of the corpulent president, Bob said, "Well, sah, he certainly is a hearty looking man." Asked about Mrs. Cleveland, Green said, "She certainly am a queen, and goody goodness, but she does like a fine hoss. Dat pet of mine (Luke Blackburn) seemed to cotch her eye. I like dat lady I do."[13]

Before the Clevelands' visit to Mrs. Polk, Judge and Mrs. Howell Jackson were hosts at a luncheon for the presidential party at West Meade. During a moment of privacy, Cleveland told Judge Jackson he would like to name him to the Supreme Court, but because of political pressure he would have to name someone from the large district encompassing Texas, Louisiana, Alabama, Georgia, Florida, and Mississippi.[14] When the luncheon was over, the Clevelands' party drove to town in two elegant carriages pulled by jet black horses. The groomsmen and footmen, dressed in livery, were reported to be "so exalted by their coveted positions as to feel that the President himself had less cause for emotions of pride." All along the route buggies were waiting, ready to join the chase to town. Before two miles had passed, "at least 200 buggies, carriages, drags, and all manner of vehicles" were pounding along in a dust so blinding that sometimes the vehicle ahead was invisible.[15]

President Cleveland had requested that the call on Mrs. Polk be as informal as possible. Because of that and because it was a Sunday, "no ladies and only a few gentlemen" were invited to attend. Large crowds lined both Spruce and Vine Streets since people did not know which entrance the presidential party would use. The crowd on Spruce Street extended all the way down to Broad Street and out two miles to Vanderbilt University. Both President and Mrs. Cleveland were attentive to the eighty-five-year-old widow of the nation's eleventh president. The vast difference in their ages did not prevent them from enjoying each other's company. After the visit, the presidential party returned to Belle Meade for a quiet supper with their hosts.[16]

On Monday morning, the president and his party went by train to West Side Park, where they were greeted by Gov. Robert Love Taylor, Mayor Kercheval, and other dignitaries. After a short reception at the club house, the party entered carriages for a grand procession to Vanderbilt. There Chancellor Garland and the students briefly welcomed the Clevelands. Next, the party progressed to Hillsboro Pike and from there along Broad Street to town. General Jackson was grand marshal for the event, which drew enthusiastic crowds along the route. At the state capitol the president met various state officials and the Mexican War veterans before being officially welcomed by the governor and giving his own speech. Following his address, a public reception was held for him on the capitol grounds. Concurrently, a reception for Mrs. Cleveland took place at the Maxwell House. Following those events, the presidential party rode in carriages to the Union Depot, where they boarded the Alfaretia for Atlanta.[17]

Middle Tennesseans recalled the presidential visit in various ways. Joe Carter, Susanna's son, always remembered having shaved the president. For the rest of his life, Joe kept the razor he used and the paper dime tip the president gave him.[18] Elizabeth Jackson regretted that she was on crutches during the visit as the result of a foot infection. Mrs. James E. Caldwell recalled the beautiful reception for Mrs. Cleveland at the Maxwell House.[19] Miss Mannie Baxter cherished an autographed picture that Mrs. Cleveland gave her.[20] Judge Jackson remembered that his former law partner, Judge H. T. Ellett of Memphis, died five minutes after President Cleveland left the reception given him in Memphis on the fifteenth. Only a few minutes earlier, Judge Ellett had officially welcomed the president to the Bluff City.[21] General Jackson was relieved that the only criticism he received was Col. A. S. Colyar's complaint that the president should have responded to Chancellor Garland's remarks at Vanderbilt. Dr. Charles F. Smith, a professor of modern languages who coordinated the university visit, said Colyar's criticism was unwarranted because Jackson "carried out to the letter" their agreement concerning the president's stop there.[22] A nationwide readership followed the visit in national magazines, including *Harper's Weekly* with its illustrations of the visit to Polk Place and of Uncle Bob driving the deer at Belle Meade.[23]

The following spring, 1888, the new West Side Park, located between the Harding and Charlotte turnpikes two miles from town, was the scene of a sham Civil War battle. General Jackson and ex-Confederate Brig. Gen. Joseph B. Palmer were selected to command the opposing sides. When Jackson "in full uniform and riding a thoroughbred dark bay" appeared among his men, some of whom had served under him in the real war, they greeted him with a rebel yell. In an article in the *Daily American* on May 24, entitled "The Red Fox of the Confederacy," Jackson was said to have had "the longest continuous service without leave of any general officer in the army." Although Jackson's side lost the sham battle, he did not mind. Egmont, one of Enquirer's sons, won the Kentucky handicap that day within a half second of the record.

Sometime after the battle at West Side Park, General and Mrs. Jackson and Judge and Mrs. Thomas H. Malone decided to send their daughters, Eunice and Ellen ("Nellie"), on an extended trip to Europe, chaperoned by a Miss Tilden.[24] Eunice wrote her family at Belle Meade frequently while in Europe. In fact, she sent so many letters that her parents became uneasy. In time, the Jacksons and the Malones sensed that Miss Tilden was part of the problem. Despite her devotion to the girls, she was such a worrier and an uneasy traveler that she got on their nerves, particularly Eunice's. The situation deteriorated to the point that Judge Malone made plans to go to Europe, discharge Miss Tilden, and bring the girls home himself.[25]

On his arrival at Antwerp, Judge Malone found a letter from Nellie written from Sorrento, Italy. She was pleased he was coming and implied that Eunice wanted to go home immediately. Malone traveled by train through Germany and the Alps to Naples, where he caught a steamer for Sorrento. When the ship got within half a mile of shore, it cast anchor and the passengers went ashore in rowboats. Both girls were so glad to see Malone that they all cried. As he walked arm in arm with Nellie and Eunice to the hotel, the hotel staff, both men and women, shouted, "Papa, papa!"[26]

Malone found the situation to be about as he had thought. Miss Tilden, despite her good intentions, was totally unfit to be in charge of the girls. He paid her salary and bought her a ticket to Berlin. He also sent a cablegram to General Jackson, saying that he had arrived, the girls were enjoying themselves, and all was well. Eunice's spirits seemed to improve by the minute. Malone's diagnosis was that "over half of her trouble has been poor food, & nearly all of the other half home-sickness."[27] To be certain that Eunice was well enough to travel, Malone and the girls stayed at Sorrento a few days before visiting Pompeii. That trip went so well that they left the next day for Rome, where they spent two days. From there, they visited Florence, Venice, and Paris before sailing for America.[28] Eunice arrived home too late to attend the April marriage of her Uncle Bob Jackson to Miranda ("Mannie") Louise Baxter. Mannie, a good friend of Eunice's, was the daughter of Nashville financier and businessman Nat Baxter, Jr.[29]

The following November, General and Mrs. Jackson gave a dinner at Belle Meade in honor of Nellie Malone. That evening several hundred guests welcomed Nellie and Eunice into society. Belle Meade was "brilliantly lighted" for the occasion, and "the appointments were in keeping with the liberality that has always characterized this house."[30] Although there was no dancing, musicians played soft music, and an elaborate supper was served after eleven o'clock.[31] The party was one way General and Mrs. Jackson could show their appreciation to Judge Malone for his errand of mercy.

During that elegant social affair, General Jackson, Judge Jackson, and Judge Malone managed to get away from the guests long enough to chat briefly about one of their favorite pastimes—fox hunting. Because Howell was usually in Cincinnati every week, he particularly enjoyed weekends at home hunting with Judge Malone, whom he called Captain because of Malone's Confederate service. On such a weekend late one December, Judge Jackson called Malone to arrange a fox hunt. Malone told two servants, Isaac and William, to have his hounds ready to go by daylight the following morning.[32]

Before dawn, Captain Malone, Isaac (a former slave in charge of Malone's dogs), and William, "closely followed by the coupled hounds, halted at the West Meade gate where the Judge awaited them." After greetings were exchanged, a decision was made to hunt a fox that kenneled in Belle Meade's high pasture. The high land was a favorite hunting site and provided a commanding view of the region, particularly since General Jackson had contracted with the state of Tennessee for convicts to clear out the undergrowth, leaving only the big timber. When they reached the high pasture, Howell noticed that Isaac had brought along Little Rachel, "a poor, little, black, weakly thing" that had "inherited neither the size nor the vigor of her father nor the matchless grace and beauty of her mother." Isaac said the Captain told him to bring Little Rachel because every dog has "got to have a fair show." Isaac added, "If they don't come up to his notion I've got to kill 'em. I've killed 'em till I'm mos' shamed to look an honest dog in the face and now its pore Little Rachel's turn."[33]

As soon as the dogs were off, followed by Isaac on horseback, the Judge and the Captain seated themselves on a log near a hole where the fox had so often found safety. As they sat facing the east, "an increasing light along the line of the Granny White hills told them that the sun would soon be up." After a few moments spent contemplating the beauty of the scene, William recognized the bark of Vic about a mile to the west near Vaughn's Gap. Another cry indicated that "Old Mack has struck it ahead." As the hounds pressed to Mack's incessant call, the Judge and the Captain recognized the distinctive sounds of other favorite hounds. The cry grew fainter as the chase led to Ed Hicks's farm before turning toward the Hillsboro Pike. In a little while, the fox doubled back and was headed for the high pasture. The Captain heard them first. "Here they come," he said. "They've crossed the ridge—they are in the high pasture—he's headed straight for his earth, the coward." [34]

"Here he comes; here he comes! Stand by the hole, William," shouted the Judge. In a flash, the fox went by with a two-hundred-yard lead over the leader of the pack, Old Mack. Refused admittance to its den, the fox sped away to the east, across the Page Place, over the Harrison knob, across Hillsboro Pike, and toward the Granny White Hills. Thinking the dogs had lost him, the Captain and the Judge lighted their cigars and, seated on the log with their feet to a fire, were soon engrossed in a legal discussion. [35]

The hounds had been running an hour, "when William, who had been standing some distance from the fire, approached and said: 'I heard Isaac, sir.' 'Where?' 'On the Granny White Hills, I thought, sir.'" Although the hounds were four miles away, the Captain and the Judge soon picked out the voices of Little Vic and Old Mack. In succession, the fox, pressed by the hounds, crossed the Granny White and Hillsboro Pikes, raced across the Compton lands and the rear of Honeywood, and sped through the deer park and across the Belle Meade meadows. " 'William,' suddenly cried the Captain, 'there are eight hounds five hundred yards ahead of the pack. Don't you hear them?' 'I do,'" the Judge said, slowly ticking off their names. He recognized all but one. A long, shrill, clear cry from one of the lead dogs sounded suspiciously like Little Rachel. As the fox jumped the Marlin wall, the Captain got a glimpse of his red hide. Soon they saw that Little Rachel was one of six hounds racing side by side "with heads up and tails down" across the pony pasture. When the fox took the pasture wall, the Captain and the Judge watched for the hounds. Suddenly, the Captain "snatched off his cap and wildly waving it above his head, yelled out: 'Damn the fox! Damn old Mack! By the Lord, it's Little Rachel!'" [36] Without any of the obvious signs of a champion, she had come from nowhere to lead the pack across the hills, fields, and meadows of one of the great plantations and farming communities of the central South. It was Little Rachel's day.

As 1889 came to a close, General Jackson was fifty-four years old. In a land where he could not vote, he had become widely known as a successful planter and knowledgeable spokesman on farm issues. He enjoyed the respect of his community and the self-respect of a man with nothing more to prove. The Belle Meade Stud never stood in higher esteem, and he enjoyed the satisfaction of having as friends such distinguished Americans as Thomas Bayard, Charles Dudley Warner, George Bancroft, Theodore Roosevelt, and Grover Cleveland. Jackson loved the limelight and involvement in civic activities. Selene, who worried about his health, knew that getting him to slow down was beyond her.[37]

Billy and Selene were also proud of their household and attentive to its joys, sorrows, and growing pains. One Sunday in November 1889, twenty-two young gentlemen called on Eunice in the parlor. Mrs. Jackson was pleased that her elder daughter was in much better health and was receiving suitors. As a matter of fact, Eunice was going to the opera on both Thursday and Friday nights that season. On another occasion when Eunice was entertaining James H. Kirkland, a young Latin professor at Vanderbilt, General Billy paced protectively outside the parlor doors wondering if any romance was budding. Hearing his footsteps, Eunice opened the door and said, "Come in, father; we are discussing the Pentateuch." After Kirkland left, Jackson warned his daughter about young men who courted with the Pentateuch.[38]

With her delicate older daughter's health somewhat better, Mrs. Jackson had others to think about. Both Lizzie Hoover and Susanna Carter had become sick following the party honoring Nellie Malone. Selene, who had great affection for Susanna, feared that her old servant and friend would never be well again, having suffered a hemorrhage of the lungs.[39] Then there were those Selene cared for in other ways. Old Confederate soldiers and countless boys came to Belle Meade for Selene's advice. With a charm none of them could resist, she lifted their spirits, pointed out their faults, offered them practical counsel, and made them feel welcome.[40]

Fortunately, the Jacksons' younger children, William and Selene, were in boarding schools and doing well. William was at the Webb School in Bell Buckle. Selene, who had grown to her full height of about five feet, three inches and who had blue-gray eyes and beautiful blonde hair, was boarding at Dr. Frankie Pierce's house and attending Dr. Price's School on Vauxhall Place. When she came home on weekends and during vacations, she often entertained friends by skillfully playing popular music on the piano. General and Mrs. Jackson were proud of their children. Jackson expressed his pride with an analogy any experienced turfman could appreciate. The man who had spent more than two decades in developing one of the finest studs in the country said, "This . . . stock is hard to beat and the pedigree is so pure, you know."[41]

SELENE AND WILLIAM HARDING JACKSON in one of the carriages, ca. 1888. Belle Meade collection

19/ Tennessee Day

Proctor Knott's exciting 1888 Futurity victory may have prompted William Easton to make a proposal to General Jackson that would significantly affect the future of the Belle Meade Stud. The offer came at a time when Jackson was growing increasingly concerned about the whole plantation's financial future. Easton wanted Tennessee's leading horse breeder to ship his yearlings to New York for a sale in the spring of 1889.[1] Although Tennessee breeders were not accustomed to taking their yearlings to the East to sell, Easton had a point. Jackson knew he was correct in saying that, since the Civil War, the East had become the center of racing and that more of the larger buyers were there than in the South or West. Instinctively, Jackson must have thought of Phil and Mike Dwyer of Brooklyn, Sam Emery of New York, and S. S. Brown of Pittsburgh. During the past few years they had been among the heaviest buyers at the Belle Meade yearling sales. Jackson also reflected on his lagging sales in 1887 and 1888.

Easton undoubtedly told Jackson that he had approached or would soon get in touch with J. B. A. Haggin of Rancho del Paso near Sacramento, Milton Young of Kentucky's McGrathiana Stud, and Daniel Swigert of Elmendorf Stud in Lexington, Kentucky, about selling their yearlings in New York. Those men were Jackson's biggest competitors. He knew their sales catalogs almost as well as they did. Of the three, only Swigert had beaten the average prices Jackson got at that year's Belle Meade sale. Jackson's competitive instincts simply would not allow him to say no to Easton.[2]

During December, correspondence between Easton and the country's leading breeders, including Jackson, focused on the shipment of their yearlings to the New York market. Jackson had briefed his partners in the Belle Meade Blood Horse Department, Howell Jackson and John Harding, Jr., on Easton's proposal. The three men were interested, provided Easton could assure them that their yearlings would be transported safely and expeditiously to New York. Easton was working on that. He conferred with Col. John Hoey, president of the Adams Express Company, about giving concessions to Jackson and other breeders.[3]

On January 14, 1889, Hoey wrote Easton that he would carry the Belle Meade yearlings at three hundred dollars per loaded car, which could be "fitted up by the shipper," with the weight of the car not to exceed ten thousand pounds. Hoey also promised to give Jackson a special rate "if a sufficient number of cars, say not less than seven, is offered, to make a special train." Easton verbally accepted the proposition and wrote Jackson about it. Jackson decided to accept Hoey's offer.[4] He shared his decision to do so with the famous philanthropist Andrew Carnegie when he visited Belle Meade in February. Carnegie, who found Belle Meade to be "exactly the sort of place I like" and who joked that he was going to ask General Jackson for a job so he could live there, thought Jackson made a wise decision. In Carnegie's view, "Gen. Jackson will sell to better advantage there than here, but nothing can take away Tennessee's reputation as a fine country for stock-raising. In that line, you can't be beat."[5]

When Jackson wrote Easton on April 22, he was in an upbeat mood. He asked Easton to thank Colonel Hoey for "the rates he has given us and his obliging disposition." He also asked Easton to announce the sale of "20 very superior Shetlands [ponies]" in the sale catalog Easton had earlier agreed to produce. Jackson went on to predict that his yearlings would bring better average prices "than the Haggin lot." He closed his letter by saying, "I think I have the best looking and best grown lot of yearlings in America today."[6]

With approval from Jackson, Swigert, Young, and Leslie Combs, another Kentucky breeder, Easton completed plans for the great New York sales of Thoroughbred yearlings. The first sale would take place on Kentucky Day, May 14, 1889, at Easton's new sales paddocks at Hunt's Point, Long Island. On Tennessee Day, June 17, fifty-seven yearlings from "the historic Belle Meade Stud" and yearlings from Cliff Lawn and Charles Reed's Fairvue Stud were to be sold. Finally, on July 1, 103 yearlings from Haggin's Rancho del Paso Stud would be auctioned. Sales catalogs were printed, and publicity was generated in the *Spirit of the Times* and various horse journals.

On April 25, Jackson went to West Side Park to inspect a Burton baggage car similar to ones Hoey proposed that he use. Satisfied that the car was well ventilated and otherwise suited for the transportation of his yearlings, he struck his deal with Colonel Hoey. Jackson's understanding of the contract was that the Adams Express Company would furnish him with four red baggage cars, "such as were used by the Pennsylvania Railroad Company," his horses would be carried at "express rates of speed," the time in transit would not exceed forty-eight hours, and the train would be run as a special under the charge of an agent of the Adams Express Company for the entire trip. The route would be over the L&N Railroad to Cincinnati and from there to New York on the Pennsylvania Central Railroad, passing through Columbus, Pittsburgh, Philadelphia, and Jersey City to Hunt's Point.[7]

Jackson told Easton in mid-May that he planned to ship his Thoroughbreds on June 5. He also told Easton that he would not bring any Shetlands because they had distemper. In that letter or in an earlier one, Jackson mentioned that some of his friends felt that he was making a mistake and predicted a disastrous sale. In his reply, dictated on the twenty-second, Easton said that 150 copies of the Belle Meade catalog were on their way to Nashville by express mail. He added that, on the basis of what several good judges of horseflesh had told him, "I can confidently predict a higher average for the Belle Meade yearlings than any have previously earned." Easton also reported that the Kentucky Day sales were "extremely encouraging" and that Swigert and Young were "highly pleased at the averages obtained." He assured Jackson that the Kentucky yearlings "arrived without a scratch" and advised him to move his shipment date up a few days so that his yearlings would arrive at Hunt's Point a fortnight before the sale. Easton had seen the Kentucky yearlings show "marked improvement from day to day" after their arrival.[8]

An act of God in Johnstown, Pennsylvania, prevented the shipment of Jackson's Thoroughbreds on June 5. Under the pressure of heavy rains, a dam holding the South Fork Reservoir burst. Over two thousand people were killed, property damage exceeded $10 million, and twelve miles of the main Pennsylvania Central Railroad track and roadbed were completely destroyed. Nearly forty locomotives and a large number of boxcars and passenger cars were lifted off the tracks and badly damaged or destroyed. Railroad traffic was interrupted until June 16.[9]

Jackson read about the flood on Saturday morning, June 1. He did not know that three of the four baggage cars designated for the shipment of his yearlings were east of Johnstown at the time of the flood and, therefore, inaccessible for his use. Because he was concerned that the flood would alter his plans, Jackson quickly got in touch with D. C. Pierce, agent of the Adams Express Company at Nashville. On June 3, Pierce telegraphed J. W. Graham, superintendent of the express company at Louisville, to inquire whether the flood would change the date of departure for Jackson's horses.[10]

Graham replied that he had a telegram from Superintendent Rigney stating that the Pennsylvania Central lines east of Pittsburgh were "in such condition that they would be absolutely unable to handle any business for at least three or four days." On June 4, Graham directed Pierce to find out if Jackson was willing to wait four or five days "or whether he wishes his shipment to go through other lines." Graham also sent a route agent named Brachy to Nashville to go with Pierce to see General Jackson. Their meeting on Tuesday morning was unproductive. Jackson was adamant about not delaying the shipment of his horses beyond Thursday night, June 6. He could not postpone the sale because it was already heavily publicized. He asked Pierce and Brachy how they would transport his horses to Hunt's Point. Neither man could tell him. Brachy and Pierce telegraphed Graham that Jackson insisted on leaving Thursday night. The same day, Graham sent Pierce a telegram: "Will send Jackson via Pittsburgh & Lehigh Valley, if cars can possibly be gotten. Will advise." Pierce immediately communicated the information to Jackson. By Wednesday, five baggage cars were standing at the Belle Meade siding, where Jackson's carpenters worked feverishly outfitting them with stalls.[11]

At 8:30 A. M. on Thursday, Jackson wired Easton that "our cars are all ready, awaiting the locomotive to take us to the loading place—we will begin loading in half an hour or hour." Jackson expressed concern that the Adams Express Company "did not furnish us the kind of cars they promised—some of them good—some very indifferent." Jackson stated further that Mr. Pierce said the Adams Express Company would "carry our train via Pittsburgh, Pennsylvania, thence by the Lehigh Valley Road." Jackson apparently never learned whether that line led into the New York Central and down the Hudson or by Philadelphia to Jersey

City. He ended the telegram by asking Easton to "have everything ready and not keep our train waiting as Swigert had to wait."[12]

After sending the telegram, Jackson spent much of the day watching the loading of his fifty-seven yearlings, which was done under the supervision of Bob Green and Jackson's wife's nephew, William Giles Harding III. Green, Harding, Joe Carter, and three other grooms would accompany the yearlings. That way, at least one groom would be in each of the four Belle Meade cars. Will B. Cheatham's Cliff Lawn yearlings were loaded into the fifth car.[13] The previous evening, a prayer service was held at the servants' quarters. There, Bob Green supposedly said, "Goodbye, Lord. I'm going to New York."[14]

By 3:00 P.M. the yearlings had been loaded without a scratch, and a relieved Jackson sent Easton a telegram to that effect. From the little Belle Meade Station, the special train moved slowly toward Nashville on the NC & StL. From Nashville the train continued to Reed's Fairvue Stud near Gallatin. There Reed's fifteen or more yearlings were loaded into two empty baggage cars that had been dropped off earlier. With a representative of the Adams Express Company aboard, the train pulled out of Gallatin at 6:00 P.M. on the L&N. The Gallatin-to-Cincinnati leg took thirteen hours. After a thirty-minute stop there, the train spent all day moving up the state of Ohio on the Pennsylvania Central Railroad. According to Bob Green, they reached Pittsburgh about sunset on Friday. Up to that point everything had gone well.[15]

Unknown to Jackson, the Adams Express Company did not ship his horses the most direct available route to Jersey City from Cincinnati. Instead, the express company chose a much longer route through Pittsburgh. The court record of Bob Green's testimony recounts what happened after the train left there:

> I think we went out from it a piece. . . . I thought we were in the woods. . . . Nearly all that night we lay there if I am not mistaken, and I know I hollered to the train man to please take the cars away. . . . The colts all got upset, and were going on so I had to take one out of his stall to get him quiet. He was just as wringing wet as if he had swum the Cumberland River. I took him out and rubbed him off and put him back, and he began the same thing again, and I brought him out and rubbed him off again, and I stood there and held him in my hands until we got to New York, and right

after that another one got in the same fix that night, and I had him to take out, and I had to stand there. I stood right there and held them colts in my arms plum till I got to New York.[16]

The Adams Express Company turned responsibility for the seven carloads of yearlings over to the Wells Fargo and Company at Pittsburgh to be carried over the Pittsburgh & Western Railroad to Leavittsburg on the New York, Pennsylvania, & Ohio Railroad. From that point the train was to proceed to Elmira, New York, "where the Adams company would again take them in charge and carry them over the Lehigh Valley Railroad to New York." But no steam engine was available, and no agent of the Wells Fargo and Company was on hand to accompany the horses. So the seven baggage cars were hooked up to a coaling train headed for Leavittsburg, seventy-two miles away. The ragtag train left Pittsburgh about eight o'clock that night. The trip to Leavittsburg took twelve hours, during which time "there was much switching, jerking, and bumping of cars, noise and smoke from passing engines." In consequence, "the horses took fright, reared, plunged and became unmanageable, and many of them were thrown down, crippled, bruised, and roughly treated."[17]

The long haul from Leavittsburg to Elmira, New York, took a little over fifteen hours. A few miles east of Elmira, the Adams Express Company resumed responsibility, and the train, once again run as a special, moved uneventfully down the Lehigh Valley Railroad. It reached Jersey City around noon on Sunday. When asked how they got from the railroad/ocean terminal at Jersey City across twelve miles of open water to Long Island, Uncle Bob Green said that they ran the cars on "something that took us over there and I never knowed it."[18]

After being carried on barges fitted with rails and towed by towboats to the Harlem River Station on the Harlem River Branch of the New York, Hartford & New Haven Railroad, the weary Tennesseans and their yearlings were nearly through their ordeal. They reached Hunt's Point close to four o'clock Sunday afternoon, seventy-three hours after leaving Belle Meade. Bob Green said of his yearlings when they were off-loaded at Hunt's Point, "They looked rugged—just butchered."[19]

Uncle Bob was downcast, but he did not give up. After he and the other Belle Meade groomsmen put the yearlings in their stables, they got saltwater brine and washed down all fifty-seven of them before going to bed early Monday morning. A few hours later, they were back up trying to get the colts and fillies ready for the sale. For the week between their arrival and the sale on June 17, Bob said, "I never left the yard only to get my meals, and came back and worked as faithfully as ever I did in my life to get them colts in shape."[20]

On Tennessee Day, June 17,1889, there was "quite a large gathering of racing men, breeders, owners, trainers, etc.," on hand for the event. After the men inspected the horses, a luncheon was served; then everyone adjourned to the sale room. William Easton made a few appropriate remarks, "calling attention to the proud records of Belle Meade as a sale establishment, and the fact that this would be the first great offering of the get of Iroquois since the Derby winner had become a public stallion." He then introduced Uncle Bob Green, who as the handler of Priam, Vandal, Jack Malone, and many other stallions had become "one of the celebrated characters of racing." The sixty-three-year-old retainer of the Harding-Jackson household, who had never been East before, was invited to speak. He said:

> Gemmen, two years ago I sed dat buyin' yerlins at dis here sale was like buyin' tickets in the Louisiana lottery, 'cept dat dey was all prizes an' no blanks. Well, gemmen, Prockor Knott, what done gone an' win de Futurity, was in dat sale. Now I repeat dat statement 'bout dis yere sale. Dis is de best lot o' yerlins I ever seed at Belle Meade. I traveled all de way East 'long wid 'em. Tell you wot, when I got on de water I was skeered like, but I says 'Bob, if de yerlings go down you go down wid 'em, too.' Since I been out heah I seen a pow'ful lot o' people—believe I've seen de entire people ob de East.[21]

Bob Green then led, one by one, his prized colts and fillies into the ring. As he did so, he noticed the buyers pointing out the flesh wounds the yearlings received on the trip. Twenty-nine colts sold first, bringing $25,175, an average of $868. Twenty-four fillies did not sell "anything like as well as the colts. Some of them went very cheap." They brought $11,000, an average of $458. The crack of the sale was a bay colt by Enquirer, dam Bribery, by Bonnie Scotland. It brought $3,500 from the Dwyer Brothers. Overall, fifty-three Belle Meade yearlings brought a total of $36,175, an average of $683.[22]

General Jackson knew, well before the sale was over, that the prices were nothing like those Easton had told him to expect. To say that he was disappointed was an understatement. His average price turned out to be only 10.5 percent greater than the average of his three most recent yearling sales at home and did not come close to the record 1881 sale when thirty-four Belle Meade yearlings sold for $38,530.[23]

Following the Belle Meade sale, Billy Cheatham's yearlings were brought into the ring. His eleven colts and fillies brought $4,000, an average of $364. The Fairvue yearlings sold "very cheap," bringing an average price of only $261. A *Spirit of the Times* reporter said that "most of Mr. Reed's were from mares practically young and untried, and hence sold low."[24]

On Tuesday General Jackson allowed Uncle Bob and the other grooms to see the sights of New York City. Meanwhile, he made arrangements for taking care of his four yearlings that did not sell and a bay filly he bought at the Cliff Lawn sale. Bob Green recalled that he remained in New York eleven days.[25]

General Jackson came home without having paid the Adams Express Company for transportation charges. Before shipping his yearlings to New York, he had asked Pierce "to allow the horses to go 'charges collect,' thinking he could get Mr. John Hoey to make a reduction because of the expense of putting stalls in the cars." When the express company rendered the bill to Mr. Easton for $300 per car, or $1,200, Easton informed Jackson by telegram that he intended to pay it, presumably as Jackson's agent. Jackson did not like that at all. He advised Easton to tell Hoey "that you are in no wise responsible for our action or debts." Jackson added, "In this section of the country we believe in the rule of having corporations, as well as individuals live up to their contracts. I have submitted this whole question to the clear, cool legal mind of Judge Jackson and he says not to pay the full bill of Ex. Co. since they have not done the service which they agreed to do. This is our business, Mr. Easton, not yours."[26]

The disagreement between the Blood Horse Department of the Belle Meade Farm and the Adams Express Company remained unsettled that winter. In December, Jackson wrote Easton to ask that he return "by fast freight" some brushes, curry combs, and buckets that Bob Green left with the foreman at Hunt's Point. As a postscript, Jackson added, "Whenever the Adams Express Company are ready to recognize the equity of our claim for rebate on transportation of our yearlings to New York, we are ready to settle, or if they would prefer us to bring suit for damages to us here, will do that."[27]

The rebate was still at issue when Jackson held his next two yearling sales at Belle Meade. Both produced good prices. The day following the 1890 yearling sale, at which sixty-one yearlings sold for an average of $1,055, a writer for the *Daily American* wrote, "The breeders hereabouts made a mistake by shipping their youngsters hundreds of miles at big expense, and realizing no better prices than they had been receiving at home." The following spring, Jackson sold forty-four yearlings at home for an average of $1,074. [28]

Having given up all hope of resolving the dispute with the express company, the two Jackson brothers and John Harding, Jr., brought suit on January 23, 1891, in the Davidson County Circuit Court against the common carrier. Their claim was for ten thousand dollars, "the amount of damage claimed to have been suffered by them on the shipment of their yearlings to Hunt's Point." The declaration filed by the plaintiffs' attorneys contained two counts: a breach of contract and a breach of conduct. [29] The express company pleaded the general issue not guilty, invoking an act of God as their defense, and said that they did the best they could under the circumstances. There was a verdict and judgment in favor of the plaintiff for eight thousand dollars. The defendant appealed to the Supreme Court of Tennessee. On March 4, 1893, nearly four years after the alleged damages to the Belle Meade yearlings took place, the Tennessee Supreme Court upheld the circuit court's verdict. The supreme court ruled that "the act of God which will excuse a common carrier from liability, must be the proximate, not merely the remote, cause of loss or injury. Hence, the Johnstown flood, having occurred and being known before the shipment was undertaken, could not excuse the carrier from liability for loss occurring in the course of transportation, voluntarily undertaken with full knowledge of the situation." [30]

Although William Easton was a witness for the defendant in the original lawsuit, there was no animosity between him and Jackson. He was the auctioneer for Jackson's successful 1891 spring yearling sale. [31] When Easton's deposition was taken the following September, he was managing director and auctioneer of Tattersalls, New York, Ltd. [32]

The next spring Jackson had enough confidence once again to ship his yearlings to New York. On Friday, June 24, 1892, at Tattersalls' Sale Repository in New York City, the twenty-fifth annual sale of Belle Meade yearlings took place. The *Spirit of the Times* reported the next day that "everyone prominent in the turf world was present, and the galleries were filled with ladies, who followed the sale with great interest and seemed greatly to enjoy 'Uncle Bob's' extemporaneous speeches. The grand total of the evening was $110,076, an average of $2,076 for the Belle Meade yearlings." It was the greatest Belle Meade yearling sale ever held. Uncle Bob was happy and smiling. His prediction that the sale "was bound to be a hummer" was, as usual, correct. All of the bitterness of Tennessee Day, June 17, 1889, was gone.

20/ Cracks in the Foundation

E VEN BEFORE THE TENNESSEE DAY FIASCO, HOWELL Jackson had decided to get out of the breeding business. He negotiated with Billy and John Harding, Jr., about selling them his interest, but they never settled on terms. Finally, Harding, who was usually pinched for funds, agreed to sell his one-third interest to his brothers-in-law. General Jackson then offered to buy Howell's 50 percent interest. However, they could not agree on the value of the horses. To break the stalemate, Howell insisted that the Thoroughbreds be offered at an open sale so that the public "might set a value on the stallions and mares." Billy agreed to go along. Held the day after the successful 1890 yearling sale, it was heralded as "the greatest sale ever held on the soil of Tennessee" and "probably the greatest in America."[1]

Despite the hoopla, the sale of the brood mares generated only moderate interest and somewhat depressed prices. Ninety-eight mares brought $77,300, an average of $789. General Jackson bought many of the best ones. The sale of the sires was another matter. When General Jackson outbid Reuben Payne of Shepherd's Bush Stud for Luke Blackburn, Uncle Bob was thrilled. "Three cheers for Tennessee!" he cried. Iroquois was the next stallion to be auctioned. Jackson found himself bidding against George E. Wheelock, a bookmaker. Jackson claimed the horse with a bid of $34,000. By that time everyone realized Jackson was determined to keep all his stallions. After scaring off several prospective bidders, he claimed Bramble, Enquirer, and Great Tom. The five stallions cost him $56,500. When the sale was over, General William Hicks Jackson was the sole proprietor of the Belle Meade Stud.[2]

General Jackson still had enough cash or credit left to buy another stallion. In November, he went to Elizabeth, New Jersey, for the Dwyer Brothers' sale where he purchased Inspector B for $10,000. General

Harding had bred the bay horse by Enquirer in 1883.[3] During his racing days, Inspector B had been one of the top "cracks" in the country. He won three races as a two-year-old, earned nearly $40,000 at three, and continued to win regularly through his sixth year. At Belle Meade he proved to be a successful sire. His daughter Espionage had forty-four wins through the 1902 season and a son, Endurance, was one of the best two-year-olds of 1901.[4]

With General Jackson's purchase of the Belle Meade Stud came the breakup of Belle Meade into two separate entities—Belle Meade and West Meade. Following the split, the Belle Meade Farm contained 2,167 acres, including 400 in cultivation, 300 in permanent meadows, and "265 acres well fenced off into mare paddocks of from 4 to 20 acres." Each paddock was provided with ample water and shelter for the stock. The soil was rich, the land was well watered by Richland Creek, and there was "a thorough system of water works."[5] The somewhat larger and equally productive West Meade Farm that Mary Jackson inherited would henceforth be managed by Judge and Mrs. Howell Jackson.

The division of the farm was traumatic. A dispute involving Billy's employment of Howell's dairyman led Howell to write his brother the following letter in January 1891:

> It is proper for me to state definitely my cause of complaint against you and the attitude I shall assume toward you in consequence thereof. You crossed the line of neighborly treatment, as I think, in offering inducements to my dairyman and his wife . . . to leave my service and go into yours. You persisted in this after my written and formal remonstrations and succeeded in getting them away from me to my great discomfort, inconvenience and disadvantage if not serious injury. I would not have treated any neighbor, much less a brother, that way. I feel greatly aggrieved by this treatment, and my sense of the wrong thus done is aggravated by the reflection that you have not, in the past, shown a proper regard for either my rights or my feelings, but have repeatedly disregarded both. . . . While I have no disposition to seek revenge . . . or to subject you to loss or injury of any sort . . . I am equally indisposed to submit tamely to this new wrong and injustice, manifesting, as it does, a total disregard for my feelings, comfort, and interests, when they conflict with your own. . . . You courted the butter maker in my employment, and secured her without regard to my wants knowing that for me to lose her would subject me to much inconvenience and probable loss. Under these circumstances I am constrained to adopt the only course left open to me consistent with self respect, of manifesting my opinion of your unneighborly

treatment, which is to have no further formal or business relations with you except such as may be necessary to clear up unadjusted matters. . . . The course I have thus determined on . . . is taken more in sorrow than in anger, but I feel impelled to it by a sense of wrong and injury, and because I am unwilling to submit longer to improper treatment from you. . . . Mary, while feeling keenly the unneighborly treatment, which deprives her of her dairy help and forces her into the dairy in order to protect, to some extent, her interests, still prefers to submit to wrong rather than be estranged from her sister.[6]

Despite Billy's serious dispute with Howell, Belle Meade's dairy flourished. It was considered one of the South's finest, with one hundred or more Jersey cows, a well-arranged barn, and the most modern equipment available. Each afternoon, the cows filed into the dairy from their pastures and, with an accuracy that astounded visitors, found their proper places in the long line of stalls. When all cows were in and quietly eating, the black milkers began their work. Perfect silence reigned, "except for the quaint old Southern melodies" the milkers sang to their cows and the patter of the streams of milk filling the buckets. The milk was poured from the buckets into a conductor projecting through the wall from the cow sheds into a skimming room. From the receiving vat in the skimming room, the milk flowed to the separator where the cream was first extracted and poured into large cans to be taken to the dairy house to be cooled, aerated, and churned. The separator, large even by modern standards, could handle twenty-five hundred pounds of milk per hour. Meanwhile, the skim milk flowed through a conductor back to the cow shed, where it was drawn out through a "perfection" gate and fed to the calves.[7]

A writer for the *Memphis Weekly Commercial,* who visited Belle Meade in the spring of 1891, wrote a long article published on April 23 covering the recent history of the farm. The correspondent wrote that legal complications following General Harding's death "threatened for a time to overthrow the great establishment. However, dissatisfied parties interested in the estate were finally appeased and by forced sale the place passed into the possession of its present proprietor, Gen. W. H. Jackson." The dissatisfied parties were Howell E. Jackson and John Harding, Jr. The writer praised Belle Meade as being, in many respects, "the most remarkable breeding establishment in the world." To support his claim, he said that "in acreage no other stud farm devoted exclusively to the breeding and raising of the thoroughbred horse in America surpasses or even equals it." Also, Proctor Knott, a Belle Meade product, was "the largest winning gelding in the history of the American turf." His final argument was that Iroquois was the highest priced Thoroughbred horse ever sold at auction in America exclusively for breeding purposes.

Belle Meade's reputation was enhanced through a stroke of good luck. Because Tennessee escaped the spread of a disease causing mares to lose their foals that swept Kentucky and other states, Belle Meade had the usual crop of yearlings in 1891. That crop was larger than the combined production of Kentucky's Fannymede, Woodburn, and Elmendorf studs.[8] Horsemen in Tennessee and Kentucky anticipated that Jackson's sale would bring higher prices than usual, and their assessment proved correct.

During the 1891 racing season, 125 horses by Belle Meade sires won more than 450 races, totaling over $300,000 in purses. Iroquois's get alone won $99,097.[9] In the wake of that success, General Jackson acquired Tremont, bringing the number of stallions at Belle Meade to seven. Tremont proved to be "mean as sin," but Jackson kept him through the 1899 season.[10]

In the spring of 1892, two of Iroquois's get, Red Banner and Haydee, placed first and second in the Lassie Stakes at Memphis. Jackson was there to watch them.[11] Iroquois headed the list of American sires that year when thirty-four of his get won 145 races and $179,447.[12] Jackson ran a large ad in the *Spirit of the Times* that spring, publicizing the stud services of his stallions. Iroquois, Luke Blackburn, and Tremont were advertised as being available at $300 each, while Inspector B and imp. Loyalist, a bay horse foaled in 1885, were offered to the public for $150 each. Enquirer and Great Tom were listed as private. Bramble had been sold the previous August to Eugene Leigh of La Belle Stud near Lexington, Kentucky, for $4,000 in cash and brood mares worth equally as much.[13] Leigh, who had a well-known fancy for Bramble, said Jackson preferred big, handsome yearlings that were "eye-catchers at the sales." Bramble's offspring were apparently not big enough to suit him. With the addition of Loyalist, acquired in November, and the sale of Bramble, the Belle Meade stallion count remained at seven.[14]

The *Spirit of the Times* ad also carried lavish endorsements of Belle Meade from three prominent newspapers—the *New York Sun*, the *Philadelphia Record,* and the *Chicago Tribune*. The *Sun* said that Belle Meade had well earned the title "home of the race-horse." The *Record* noted, "In many respects Belle Meade is the most remarkable breeding establishment in the world." The *Tribune's* language was equally grand: "The oldest in years, Belle Meade has always kept in the front rank as America's greatest thoroughbred nursery."[15]

The ads no doubt boosted Jackson's 1892 yearling sale held at Tattersalls' Sale Repository in New York. Jackson sent his yearlings up that year in the care of his son, William Harding Jackson, Bob Green, and Mrs. Jackson's nephew, William Giles Harding III. General Jackson went by a later train. All were pleased with the impressive results—never more so than when one of Iroquois's colts, a dark bay, sold for $10,250.[16] The success of the sale apparently prompted Jackson to purchase two more sires. He bought Clarendon, by imp. St. Blaise, in November at the F. A. Ehret sale in New York City,[17] while Gleneig arrived early enough in 1892 to have one filly in the 1893 yearling sale.[18]

At some point before 1895, probably following his successful 1892 yearling sale, General Jackson built an enormous carriage house/stable at Belle Meade. The elegant wood frame building, which still stands, incorporated two large sections under a slate roof crowned with three cupolas. The stable portion included fourteen handsome box stalls, which housed the Jacksons' carriage horses. The tongue and groove walls of each stall slanted outward so that the horses could not rub their valuable coats against the sides. Each had its own gas jet light and running water that flowed by gravity from a reservoir Jackson built on a hill to the east. Green wire screens, adorned with gold-painted finials, were installed across the top of the stalls. The second floor of the stable "was used for hay storage with openings through which hay could be dropped into the feeding stations that straddled each pair of stalls."[19] The front section was a carriage house. The first floor included two tack rooms and a large room where as many as eighteen carriages were kept. Upstairs were rooms for the stud farm's seven resident grooms and visiting horse trainers and grooms. The carriage house/stable was a Victorian wonder unlike anything else in the South.[20]

Naturally, Jackson was proud of the imposing structure. He also felt so good about his stallions that he turned down an offer from an English syndicate of $150,000 for Iroquois. He made that decision with his heart, not his head, because he was still in debt. In the spring of 1893, an opportunity arose to address that problem, aggravated no doubt by his having spent $30,000 on the carriage house/stable. Jackson knew that

VIEW OF BELLE MEADE FROM THE PADDOCKS, 1890s. Left to right: outbuildings, carriage house/stable, smokehouse, and mansion. TSLA

CARRIAGE HOUSE/STABLE and a few of the carriages. Belle Meade collection

Richard Croker, the millionaire New York City political boss, had been interested in visiting Tennessee and purchasing a stud. Croker, who had undoubtedly been given glowing descriptions of Belle Meade by Charles Reed, the New York gambler and owner of the Fairvue Stud, came to Belle Meade in March. He was so impressed with what he saw that he offered Jackson $250,000 for a half-interest in his Thoroughbred stock. Because he had not contemplated selling an interest in the stud, Jackson asked for time to consider the proposition. Croker said: "Let me know in the morning." The next day Jackson accepted the deal that called for Croker to pay Jackson $3,000 annually to act as general manager of the stud and additionally to compensate him for the keep of the horses.[21]

When Nashvillians read about Croker's purchase, many were stunned. Old friends and admirers of General Harding did not think he would have approved of Billy's selling an interest in Belle Meade to any-one as controversial as Croker; by "honest graft" he had succeeded Tweed as boss of Tammany Hall. People wondered if Tammany, one of Jackson's 1889 yearlings by Iroquois out of Tullahoma, had been named to honor Jackson's apparent friendship with Croker. Tammany was the champion three-year-old of 1892 and the only $100,000 winner bred by General Jackson; he earned $113,290.[22]

A few weeks later, Jackson welcomed a horseman with social creden-tials quite different from those of Richard Croker. He was Sir Tatton Sykes, an unconventional horse breeder from Yorkshire, England. Sir Tatton, whose Sledmere Stud was older than Belle Meade and equally famous, was on the southern leg of a trip to the United States.[23] Members of the Yorkshireman's party told the Nashville press they preferred the South over the North because Southerners were more like the English and because the countryside between Lexington and Nash-ville, with its "beautiful forests and country homes," reminded them of Yorkshire. During the visit, Jackson told Sykes he was planning to come to England "to learn from them something about their conduct of breeding farms."[24]

An economic panic, precipitated in part by the decline of the U.S. gold reserve below the $100 million mark, hammered the entire country in 1893. On May 5, stocks on the New York Stock Exchange dropped sharply. Jackson worried about the impact of the developing economic crisis on his spring sale to be held at Tattersalls' in New York on June 19. Fortunately, it went off well. Fifty-eight yearlings sold for a total of

$79,400, an average second only to his record sale of 1892. An innovation was that the sale was held at night under electric lights.[25]

Jackson also considered the recession's effect on his stud fees. He had raised Iroquois's stud fee for the season to $500, moderate considering Iroquois's great reputation. Still, the decision represented a business risk. When Edwin S. Gardner and his son, Edwin, Jr., signed an agreement in June to breed ten of their best mares to Iroquois at the elevated fee, Jackson was relieved. As part of the agreement, he promised to breed no more than forty mares to Iroquois that season, including the ten from the Gardners' Avondale Stud.[26]

The year 1893 was a watershed. After that, the average prices Jackson received at his annual yearling sales were lower, and the winnings of Iroquois's get became progressively smaller. In 1893, the stallion's offspring won $138,865, placing Iroquois third among American sires.[27] The following year, Jackson and Croker decided to keep the stud fees for their sires—Luke Blackburn, Tremont, Inspector B, Loyalist, Clarendon, and their newest acquisition, Longstreet—at the moderate level of $150, but to raise Iroquois's fee to a whopping $2,500 and make him a private sire. They would limit his outside service to ten mares.[28]

Both General Jackson and Uncle Bob Green made their usual appearances at the 1894 Belle Meade yearling sale, held at the American Horse Exchange in New York City. Before the sale, Jackson gave a short speech in which he mentioned Croker's interest in his horse nursery. Although the $7,100 August Belmont II paid for a chestnut colt by Iroquois was within a few hundred dollars of the highest price paid in 1893 for a yearling, sales slipped a little. Sixty-eight yearlings brought an average price of $1,262. Bob Green was "cheered lustily" when he bought a filly by Iroquois for $550. The Easterners were surprised but pleased that Belle Meade's head groom had the money to make the purchase.[29]

In the spring of 1895, Mrs. Osborne Ellis of New York, a great-granddaughter of Gen. James Winchester of Cragfont, visited Belle Meade and later offered her recollections for an article in the *New York Sunday Mercury*. Mrs. Ellis described each stallion's stall as "a veritable small house, with windows and six feet of cedar wainscoting and sliding doors, which stand open throughout the day." She recalled that the mares had less imposing stalls, which, along with their one-acre paddocks, were across the road. Mrs. Ellis was greeted at the paddocks by Sam Nichols, one of Uncle Bob's assistants. Nichols, who had been born on the place as a slave, was content to remain there as a "keeper of the royalty." He told Mrs. Ellis he had turned down opportunities to leave, such as when Mr. Charles Reed offered him "a goodly price" to take care of his stallion, St. Blaise, at Fairvue. According to Mrs. Ellis, Nichols told Reed that General Harding had raised him and that he had fared well "whar I was. I wus satisfied." Sam then proudly showed Mrs. Ellis the sires, including Great Tom, Luke Blackburn, and Iroquois. As he fastened a lead to Iroquois's halter and led him from the stall, Nichols remarked, "He kin bite de sweet out o' a pie."[30]

Mrs. Ellis learned that Belle Meade was the center for the smaller stock raisers of Tennessee. Being somewhat skeptical of Northern or Western stockmen, they relied on General Jackson by consigning their yearlings to his sales. According to her informants, during the early 1890s Tennessee breeders and their grooms would assemble at Belle Meade and go North together. Jackson would be responsible for making up the sales catalogs and attending to advertising before putting his and their yearlings in the hands of William Easton for sale. Mrs. Ellis also learned that the little railroad station at Belle Meade was "almost solely a horse depot." At the time of her visit, it was "fenced about and supplied with inclined planes to facilitate the shipping of the horses."[31]

Mrs. Ellis's impression of Belle Meade was that, except for its deer park, it lacked the luxurious landscaping, greenhouses, and statuary of the most important Northern studs. However, she concluded that the stud lost none of its charm because of such quaint touches as "a buttress of hen's nest, constructed of rude boards," placed high enough in a tree to be safe from General Jackson's hunting dogs sleeping away "an idle existence" in a fence corner. And she was clearly charmed by such scenes as "a company of high-stepping turkey hens, strutting gobblers, a flock of ragged, lately-plucked geese, and white ducks turning somersaults in an earthen basin, sunk in the middle of a blue grass pasture."[32]

Richard Croker's enthusiasm for the Belle Meade Stud was short-lived. He was preoccupied with an even larger investment—trying unsuccessfully to prove that American-bred Thoroughbreds could defeat their English counterparts on English turf.[33] In January 1895, he gave Jackson an option to repurchase his one-half interest in the Thoroughbreds for $50,000. Jackson did not exercise the option, which was for forty-five days and called for Jackson to pay $25,000 three months from the date of purchase and the remaining $25,000 three months later.[34] When Jackson went to New York in May, he and Croker probably talked about their joint venture. Upon his return, Jackson told the Nashville press only that he discussed the racing situation with some leading horsemen of that section and "everything in the racing line" was rosy. Horsemen in the East seemed satisfied, he said, that new laws to control racing more tightly had been tested and proved to be practical.[35]

Jackson decided to divide his 1895 yearling crop by shipping half of them to Chicago for sale and selling the remainder at Easton's sale paddocks at the Sheepshead Bay Race Track on Long Island. A notice in the *Spirit of the Times* indicated that Eugene Leigh would sell the Chicago consignment of forty yearlings in late June.[36] The other forty-one yearlings were sold during a two-day sale at Sheepshead Bay. The New York lot brought an average price of $1,052, which was better than "any other lot which has been sold this year," said the *Spirit of the Times*.[37] Either the Chicago sale never materialized or prices were so low that a number of the yearlings did not sell. To dispose of twenty-six colts and fillies still on his hands, Jackson arranged to have them sold by Woodard and Shanklin, a Lexington, Kentucky, auction house, at the Oakley Race Track outside Lexington on October 1. They were sold there for an average price of only $285.[38]

The next year, General Jackson shipped all his yearlings to Sheepshead Bay for sale by William Easton. Despite the presence at the three-day sale of many prominent owners and trainers, including Phil J. Dwyer, John Mackey, and Eugene Leigh, prices were poor, and "some rare bargains were secured." Sixty-nine yearlings sold for an average price of $428, the lowest since 1880.[39] Jackson felt better when Ben Brush, one of Bramble's best colts, won the Kentucky Derby that spring.

Although General Jackson's energy was beginning to wane, "he still looked the fighter, the auburn still bore down the gray in leonine hair and moustache and there was no trace of defeat or surrender in his stirring eloquence."[40] Though he participated less in the physical labor of running the farm, he had no more time for leisure. A delegation of Cincinnati businessmen came to Nashville in December 1896 to inspect the Centennial grounds; they were planning a Cincinnati exhibit at the Tennessee Centennial Celebration, which opened May 1 and closed October 30, 1897. As a member of the Centennial Celebration's Executive Committee, Jackson was host for the group at Belle Meade.[41]

Entertaining at Belle Meade was a way of life for him. Daily, according to an 1897 newspaper account, "anywhere from a dozen individuals to deputations of fifty to a hundred" visited the place. The same article listed among Belle Meade's notable visitors of the recent past Robert Todd Lincoln and Generals U. S. Grant, William T. Sherman, and Winfield Scott Hancock.[42]

On May 1, 1897, a correspondent for the *Spirit of the Times* wrote that General Jackson "is looking fairly well, but his many duties as director of this and chairman of a dozen other things, keep him busy." The writer said Jackson would not attend his yearling sale on June 21 and 22 because he would be getting ready to leave for a European vacation the following week. Prices paid for yearlings at the sale, again held at Sheepshead Bay, were seriously depressed. Forty Belle Meade colts and fillies sold for an average of just under $300. One Enquirer colt went for only $65 and a filly by Iroquois for $150.[43] Temporarily forgetting his financial woes, Jackson enjoyed the company of a group of New Englanders while crossing the Atlantic on the U.S.M.S. *Paris*.[44] In England, he visited breeding establishments, undoubtedly including Sir Tatton Sykes's Sledmere Stud, and enjoyed seeing the get of one of Croker's sires run. He also discussed with Croker, who operated his own stud in England, the possibility of buying back Croker's interest in the Belle Meade stock.[45]

General Jackson was still in Europe when representatives of the *Cincinnati Enquirer* came to Belle Meade to honor the memory of his stallion Enquirer, the newspaper's great namesake. The famous son of Leamington had died two years earlier and was buried in his paddock where he had so long roamed as "monarch of all he surveyed."[46] In the general's absence, his son, William H. Jackson, was host to the large group that came out from the Centennial grounds by train. At Enquirer's old paddock, Sam Carey, editor of the *Enquirer*, introduced the speaker, Howard Baxby, a well-known writer for the paper. In his address, Baxby called the handsome granite monument the "most enduring tribute to a dumb animal to be found in this country." The monument was then unveiled while Weber's band from Cincinnati played "The Enquirer March."[47] At the Tennessee Centennial Celebration that night there was a spectacular fireworks display in which the image of Enquirer was shown in "colored fire . . . the greatest pyrotechnics of the age," by the A. L. Due Company of Cincinnati.[48]

General Jackson returned from Europe in September. Sometime be-fore November, probably while he was in England, he bought two imported sires—Madison, a bay horse foaled in 1895 by Hampton out of Democracy, and Tithonus, a brown horse by St. Simon out of Immor-telle. The two sires stood at Belle Meade through the 1902 season.[49] About the first of November, Jackson also purchased Croker's interest in the Belle Meade Thoroughbreds. Though the terms of the sale were never disclosed, the assets of the stud were once again entirely in Tennessee hands.[50]

At the Tennessee Centennial Celebration one day, General Jackson admired a large buck elk in a midway show. The elk, named Ben Yaka, stood nearly sixteen hands high and weighed as much as a horse. Jackson decided that Ben Yaka was just what his deer park needed, so he bought the elk along with its mate, Nellie. The two were taken to Belle Meade when the Centennial closed. Jackson renamed the male Tommy, and he was soon Belle Meade's most notorious resident. Before long, Jackson and park visitors realized that Tommy's disposition was anything but shy. One spring he was particularly rambunctious and turned over a buggy. On another occasion, two well-known Nashvillians happened into the park and strolled too near Tommy: "They were forced to take to a friendly tree and only escaped after Tommy had decided he had kept them aloft long enough."[51]

One of Jackson's neighbors was Joel W. Carter, president of the First National Bank and proprietor of the J. W. Carter Shoe Manufacturing Company. Carter, who was known for his frugality, lived on the Hillsboro Turnpike beyond Henry W. Compton's lands. Occasionally, he would drive out the Harding Turnpike in order "to approach his farm from the rear, thus surprising the farm hands if they were loafing on the job." In doing so he passed through the deer park. One day in the rutting season, Tommy ran him up a tree: "There he sat for two or three hours with no defense except to spit tobacco juice in the elk's eyes." Mr. Carter enjoyed telling the story, but he always left out the part about slipping up on his farm hands.[52]

Tommy, Nellie, and their five descendants roamed the deer park at will until it closed. No one dared to dispute their claims to it. In the fall of 1904, Marshall Morgan, a writer for the *Nashville Banner*, tried to photograph Tommy for an article he was writing about the demise of the deer park. Before Morgan could snap his picture, the elk charged and chased him around a tree. Morgan escaped by jumping back in his buggy.[53]

In 1898 Nashville businessman Percy Warner decided to sell his Thoroughbred mares. General Jackson bought them all, including "some of the most grandly bred in the country today." To make room for them, Jackson moved more of his stock to West Meade's pastures leased from his sister-in-law, Mary Jackson. To Nashville observers, Jackson seemed to be possessed with "improving the seemingly unimprovable blood of his thoroughbreds."[54]

Jackson sent another "grand looking lot" of yearlings to the Easton Company's sale paddocks on Sheepshead Bay in 1898. The pick of the lot was a bay colt by Iroquois, dam Trade Wind, who was purchased by Eugene Leigh for $2,500. Twenty-four youngsters sold for an aggregate of $13,350, a considerably better average than Jackson got the two previous years but still a far cry from his outstanding sales in the first half of the decade.[55]

On September 15, General Jackson's lease of West Meade expired. Because he had more stallions, brood mares, weanlings, yearlings, Shetland ponies, and Jersey cattle than he could pasture at Belle Meade over the winter, he held a three-day auction sale at Belle Meade. He sold 171 head of stock of various kinds for $27,665; included were 110 head of Thoroughbreds, brood mares, weanlings, and yearlings. Madam Reel and Tule Blackburn, two great mares, brought the highest prices—$7,500 and $4,100. Jackson sold his stallion Dandie Dinmont to C. H. Gillock for $1,500. He also wanted to sell Tremont but when he received only one bid, he withdrew him. According to a newspaper correspondent, "Taken as a whole, the sale was a very satisfactory one," though later it was learned that Gillock had bought in Dandie Dinmont for General Jackson.[56]

About the same time, William Harding Jackson, the general's son, built a mile-long training track across the turnpike "in the woods flat belonging to his West Meade aunt and cousins." Young Jackson loved nothing more than being with horses and horsemen. He was "affable, entertaining, full of fun and gentlemanly," but to some members of Nashville's hardworking set "he lacked serious interests."[57] After graduating from Webb School and attending business college, Jackson turned his attention to breeding horses. In March 1899, a reporter for the

Nashville American reported that General Jackson was spending much of his time with his guns and dogs and that he "had about given up the direction of affairs, except in a general way," to William. Though William's responsibilities at Belle Meade increased, he was hardly single-minded. Young Jackson and his wife went to Saratoga Springs for the 1899 racing season.[58] William also enjoyed his role as president of the Oakdale Hunting Club, a group of local gentlemen who owned and boarded horses, and he enjoyed "riding to the hounds" and racing his own horses. His colt Invictus finished second in the Hawthorne Stakes in 1900.[59] The following spring, young Jackson employed H. J. Gerhardy, who had been a popular jockey, to train his stable of horses for seventy-five dollars a month. Their agreement called for Gerhardy to receive 10 percent of the income from their winnings or from their sale. Soon, Gerhardy began training the last yearlings of Iroquois for the 1902 season.[60]

Though the old general was growing less involved in farm affairs, he remained attentive to livestock markets and never lost his interest in marketing. In 1899 General Jackson did something different with respect to his fillies foaled the previous year. Sometime before the yearling sale, he privately sold twelve of his best fillies to Bruce Seaton for shipment to England, where Seaton intended first to race and later to breed them. Jackson also held out the few remaining yearling fillies at Belle Meade for private sale and shipped only colts to New York for the thirty-second annual Belle Meade yearling sale at the American Horse Exchange. That meant he should get much higher prices for his yearlings. The market was also stronger in New York, and Jackson was encouraged by the success there of the earlier sales of yearlings from the Kentucky studs. The *Spirit of the Times* buoyed his expectations by appraising his consignment as being "the equal of any that ever came from that famous thoroughbred nursery."[61] Prices for the fifty-four Belle Meade colts proved to be better than they had been the past few years. The highest price, $5,200, was paid by Fleischmann & Sons for a chestnut colt by Iroquois out of Terbera.[62]

Iroquois, the great stallion that stood at the head of the Belle Meade Stud, died "of an acute affliction of the kidneys" on September 17, 1899. His death came as a surprise and a severe blow to General Jackson. At twenty-one, the sire seemed to be in the prime of life. With his death the racing world lost one of its most famous champions. Among the outstanding horses sired by Iroquois were Huron, Tammany, G. W. Johnson, White Frost, Bangle, Julius Sax, Addie, and Red Banner. Newspaper articles recalled that, as a three-year-old, Iroquois was nearly invincible, winning the English Derby, Prince of Wales Stakes, the St. Leger, and the Great Champion Stakes.[63] General Jackson removed two hooves of the famous stallion and had them made into inkwells, finely mounted by Tiffany & Company of Union Square, New York. Iroquois was buried in his paddock at Belle Meade. Although turfmen in the East long talked about erecting a monument to the horse, it was never done.[64]

General Jackson's good friend C. H. Gillock took the Belle Meade yearlings to Sheepshead Bay in 1900 for the stud farm's thirty-third annual sale.[65] The fine-looking lot consisted of the get of Clarendon, Huron, Inspector B, Iroquois, Longstreet, imp. Loyalist, Luke Blackburn, Tithonus, and Tremont. Prices were good, and the forty-three colts and fillies sold for an average of $923.[66]

Belle Meade-bred yearlings performed well during 1900. Indian Fairy and Iroquois Belle were both stake winners. Irritable, a third Iroquois get, won the Great Eclipse Stake for two-year-olds, while Bonita, another two-year-old, was a winner in England. Still another Belle Meade product, Chappaqua, had twelve wins that season.[67]

In the summer of 1900, the Belle Meade Stud was again bursting at its seams. There were so many brood mares and weanlings that Jackson simply did not have room for them all that next winter. Consequently, he held a reduction sale at Belle Meade in September to bring his stud to a manageable level. His old friend William Easton of the Fasig-Tipton Company handled the event, which drew about seven hundred prospective buyers and onlookers. In all, twenty-three weanlings, six yearlings, thirty-four brood mares, and two stallions were sold. The stallions—Clarendon and Dandie Dinmont—went for the ridiculously low prices of $250 and $75; Dandie Dinmont went so low because he was too old to be of much service. The prices of the other stock sold were satisfactory, according to Jackson.[68]

Occasionally people would ask General Jackson if he thought Belle Meade would last forever. He said he certainly hoped so. If he had any doubts about his son's ability to manage the farm after he retired, he kept them to himself. One key to future success was the acquisition of top-flight sires to stand at stud. Just before Iroquois died, Jackson bought

Huron, an Iroquois son out of Mariposa, one of his best mares.[69] Unfortunately, Mariposa died the same week as Iroquois.[70] Jackson made what turned out to be his last major investment in a stallion in June 1901. He bought The Commoner, considered one of the most promising sons of Hanover, from a syndicate composed of John B. Ewing of Nashville and two out-of-towners for $15,000.[71] During his racing career, The Commoner had started thirty-two races, winning eighteen times, placing second five times, third five times, and finishing unplaced in only four starts. He had met and defeated the best of his time.[72]

The 1901 Belle Meade yearling sale was held in New York's Madison Square Garden for the first time. Thirty-two yearlings sold for $25,050, an average of $783. The star of the sale was a "handsome bay by the English Derby winner, Iroquois, out of Wanda." James R. Keene got him for $6,500. A disquieting factor was that nine of the horses did not sell. Later that year, Jackson was encouraged that The Parader, by Longstreet, was one of the top three-year-olds of the season. The Parader was the last superior product of Belle Meade.[73]

Because all his yearlings did not sell the previous spring and because he needed to scale down the size of his stud even more, General Jackson scheduled a fall sale at Belle Meade of "a splendid collection of Shetland ponies and thoroughbred weanlings and yearlings." The *Nashville American* reported on October 10 that "there will be a splendid barbecue, one of the kind always served at Belle Meade, and everyone is invited to come, eat, and bid for bargains. . . . Who knows," added the writer, "but what there may be an Endurance by Right?"

"Hidalgo," a well-known turf writer, came to Nashville with his wife a few days before Christmas. A telephone call to General Jackson prompted an immediate invitation to Belle Meade. The day was "bitter cold and sleety," so Jackson sent his carriage to Nashville to pick up the visitors. When Hildago arrived, General Jackson met him at the door "with that cordiality that is part and parcel of his nature." During a lull in the storm, the two men went outside to look at the stallions. The Commoner was there, along with Inspector B, Longstreet, Tithonus, Madison, Loyalist, Luke Blackburn, Huron, and Mont d'Or, Jackson's most recent acquisition. When Hidalgo left in the Belle Meade carriage, he felt he was leaving behind, possibly forever, "the sweetest old home and most genial host in all the sunny South." In a December 23 article in the *Nashville American*, Hidalgo reported that Inspector B was "the handsomest horse on the farm, if not in all America," and that Belle Meade was the oldest organized breeding farm in America, established in 1807. The compliments were warm, but the tone was nostalgic, as if recalling past greatness.

21/ The Last Hurrah

I F THE EARLY 1890S BROUGHT THE STRESS OF FINANCIAL worry and family friction, they also brought many causes for celebration as well. Highlights of those years included several family marriages, the Tennessee Centennial Celebration, and Howell Jackson's appointment to the Supreme Court.

In the fall of 1891, Selene and her daughter Eunice planned one of the grandest social events of the decade at Belle Meade. More than eight hundred engraved invitations were mailed inviting guests either to a reception in the afternoon or to another that evening. All in all, it was the most elaborate party at Belle Meade in thirty-four years. The first reception was in honor of Eunice's recently married friends Mary Belle Keith Maddin and Nellie Malone Magruder. The evening's honoree was Miss Hattie Nichols, the youngest daughter of Gov. Francis T. Nichols of Louisiana.[1] For the parties, fresh flowers filled the parlor and the drawing room, and Japanese umbrellas and lanterns hung from the ceiling of the gallery between the house and the kitchen house. The gallery, also decorated with rich rugs, palms, and vines, had been temporarily closed and converted into a refreshment room. Responsibility for the receptions fell largely on Eunice; neither Cousin Lizzie Hoover nor Mrs. Jackson was well enough. One of General Jackson's responsibilities was to have water hauled from the Red House Spring because a drought had dried up the cistern. When the formally attired guests arrived for the evening reception, their carriages approached the house through "long lines of Japanese lanterns" flanking the carriageway. Inside, Mrs. Jackson and Eunice, assisted by Mrs. Howell E. Jackson and a number of friends, received them. Punch and lemonade—but no liquor—were served from cut glass bowls in the hall. As the guests in their "handsome winter toilets" mingled, an Italian band played "sweet strains from a recess."[2] Eunice had a wonderful time. At the party's end, Mrs. Jackson and Cousin Lizzie, exhausted and relieved, were so happy for Eunice that they wept.

Following the reception, the ladies kept busy social schedules through Christmas. In November, Eunice attended a *bal poudre* given by Martha Dickinson. For the occasion she powdered her hair and wore a Martha Washington watteau gown of white silk and embroidered roses with her grandmother Harding's jewelry. The next evening, Mrs. Jackson and Cousin Lizzie attended the Jesse Overton-Gladys Williams wedding, which Selene described as "the most swell wedding since the McNairy-Clifton wedding in 1869." General Jackson and Will B. Cheatham escaped to the races.[3]

Although General Jackson enjoyed horse races and fox hunting as much as Selene and Lizzie enjoyed weddings and parties, he rarely seemed to have time for either. Nevertheless, he allowed his neighbors, such as the Morgans, to hunt at Belle Meade. "The more rabbits you kill," Jackson said, "the less chance there will be of trespassers treeing them in my walls and tearing them down to get the rabbits out."[4]

Born in 1882, Tom Morgan recalled that during his youth Mays's Store on the Hillsboro Turnpike was a voting site and community center. On election day, voters in the eleventh district came to the store in buggies and wagons, on horseback and mules. He vividly remembered once seeing "fifty or sixty Negroes, each mounted on a fine mule," come in a long procession led by General Jackson driving his phaeton.[5]

From 1883 until 1895, Joshua Compton, mulatto son of Jackson's neighbor Henry W. Compton, served as a magistrate and deputy tax assessor for the district. Jackson and a number of the other large landowners supported him politically. The Belle Meade hands, whose poll taxes General Jackson probably paid, voted "straight for Josh" and for anyone else Jackson wanted them to.[6]

As 1891 drew to a close, illness troubled the Jackson household. Over the Christmas holidays, General Jackson caught influenza but recovered by mid-January. About the same time, Eunice suffered a depression, reminiscent of, but much more severe than, the one she suffered during her trip to Europe. By mid-January, she was "weak as a babe" and could not raise her head from her pillow.[7] Dr. William T. Briggs was called in, and Mrs. Jackson employed Miss Emma Barksdale, a trained nurse, whose treatment of Eunice included a nightly massage. When Eunice did not improve, she was moved to Dr. Briggs's infirmary on South College Street opposite the medical school grounds. Mrs. Jackson, disregarding her own rheumatic problems, and Miss Barksdale accompanied her. William and Selene came by each afternoon after school, and Eunice and her mother talked to General Jackson each evening by telephone.[8]

Eunice and her mother were at Dr. Briggs's infirmary nearly three months. By the time they left late in the spring of 1892, everyone there had fallen in love with Eunice.[9] Yet, she was far from well. In mid-June, after two fainting spells, she told her mother for the first time that she had given up all hope of recovering. On one occasion it took thirty or forty minutes to bring her back to consciousness. A week or so later Dr. Briggs put her in quarantine. Her treatment consisted of absolute rest, doses of cod-liver oil, glasses of beer, and the application of six leeches every other day.[10]

Despite the disruptions caused by Eunice's illness and the severe drought of the previous fall, the Jacksons remained active and optimistic. General Jackson went about his business of running the stud and attending to numerous other affairs. When Thomas Nelson Page came to town early in the spring, General Jackson was in attendance at Watkins Hall when brother Howell introduced the noted Virginia writer as the evening's speaker. The next day Selene Jackson left Dr. Briggs's infirmary long enough to assist Mrs. E. W. Cole at a reception Colonel and Mrs. Cole gave for Page at their home on Terrace Place.[11] Mrs. Jackson may have told the famous author that Aunt Susanna had memorized "page after page of his delightful dialect stories" and charmed visitors to Belle Meade by reciting them.[12]

General Jackson attended the third annual meeting and reunion of the United Confederate Veterans in 1892. He played significant roles there as commander of the Tennessee Division and chairman of the site selection committee for the next meeting.[13] When he was out of town on business, Jackson always tried to catch a train home in time to attend church with Selene. On one of the last occasions Mrs. Jackson was well enough to attend McKendree Methodist Church, she planned to meet him there. Not seeing him in the vestibule, she entered alone and sat in their pew. A friend seated nearby noticed that she seemed to be trying to reserve the seat next to her. The lady inquired, "Are you looking for someone?" Selene answered, "Yes, General Jackson will be here presently. I have never attended church without him since we were married."[14]

General Jackson and Judge Jackson were still not speaking in the summer of 1892 because of "all kind of hard feelings on both sides."[15] A major disagreement concerned the division of the Belle Meade stock, deer, carriages, and vehicles. Howell declined to accept Billy's invitation to come to Belle Meade and inspect the books with R. C. Brien, General Jackson's farm manager. Howell insisted on the right to examine for himself "any books and papers into which I have an equal right with yourself." He wanted to do so at his convenience and with the assistance of his own accountant if he needed help.[16]

Though their relationship was strained, the two brothers continued separately to excel at their work. General Jackson worked diligently at Belle Meade and by early in the decade had brought the stud to prominent fame. His personal renown and popularity among a broad range of citizens reached a high point as well. In July of 1892 as chairman of the Democratic Platform Committee for Tennessee, he wrote a statement of the platform, calling the Democratic party a friend of the farmer and the laboring man and accusing the Republicans of trying to drain the wealth of the South.[17] Howell Jackson was the first presiding judge for the Sixth Circuit Court of Appeals in Cincinnati, having been appointed to that position in 1891. While on the circuit court and the court of appeals, he wrote more than ninety opinions; perhaps the most important was one of the first constructions of the Sherman Antitrust Act of 1890.[18]

In the summer of 1892, the William Hicks Jacksons decided to remodel and refurnish Belle Meade.[19] The plan included the conversion of Mrs. Jackson's sitting room into a dining room and, more than likely, the construction of the porte cochere. To lengthen the dining room, she and General Jackson gave up some of their back porch. In early November, General Jackson had business in New York, and he took Eunice and Cousin Lizzie with him because, in Selene's words, they "were both almost broken down" by living in the midst of all the building and painting for two months.[20] Though Selene remained at home, she, too, was ill, and more seriously than anyone at first suspected.

A couple of days after they left, Mary and Howell insisted that Selene, who was then staying in town, move to West Meade. They were alarmed because her condition seemed to have deteriorated since they had last seen her. Judge Jackson reminded her that West Meade was sunnier and drier than Belle Meade. She agreed to do as they asked.[21]

BELLE MEADE DINING ROOM, ca. 1900. Belle Meade collection

Selene's nurse, Miss Barksdale, was a great help, bathing and dressing her and combing her hair. After a week, Selene was able to sit up for three or four hours at a time. One day she felt strong enough to ride to Belle Meade "to take a look." As her driver turned into the carriageway, she noticed that the sign reading "No stock exhibited and no visitors received on Sundays" was missing.[22] At her insistence, it was replaced. Although Selene did not get out of the carriage, her daughter Selene came out to see her. Not understanding how ill her mother was, Selene said, "Mother, we are doing so nice; everybody does as they please." The November rally was temporary. Certain that she was not going to recover, Selene said to Miss Barksdale, "Your attention has come from the heart, and I prize it as I would a daughter's." When Mrs. Jackson recovered some strength only a few days before she died, she told Miss Barksdale, "Our Father must have something more for me to do here, or he would not have called me back. His will be done, but it was so sweet to think of spending a Christmas in Heaven, with plenty of breath and no pain."[23]

Two days before Selene died, General Jackson was up all night with her. During those long hours, she asked him to write Eunice Jackson to tell her that "she loved her, how sick she was," and that she would meet her in heaven.[24] Near the end, Selene took communion from Dr. Kelley. At that time, she told Susanna Carter, her old and increasingly feeble servant: "You have been one of the most faithful and trusted of my friends, you are true to the last. We will eat together in our Father's house." Among the last words Selene spoke were to her beloved husband: "General, you have ever since our marriage had a hard struggle with debt. Now that prosperity seems to dawn, don't allow any ostentation, frivolity, or social pomp to come into our home."[25]

Selene died of complications related to her chronic asthmatic condition on December 13, 1892, at age forty-six. Her own diagnosis, made a month before she died, was that anxiety about Eunice caused her breakdown. She had no fear of dying and "rather wanted to go."[26] General Jackson delivered a eulogy at her funeral held at Belle Meade. Josephine Elliston Farrell, her lifelong friend, directed the singing. The active pallbearers were black men long identified with Belle Meade. For Uncle Bob Green, it was the third time he had served in that capacity.[27]

Eunice promptly stepped forward to assume a more active role in household affairs. General Jackson's sister-in-law Mannie Baxter Jackson said Eunice "bears her trouble wonderfully well, is so brave and sustains her father so much."[28] Selene's death left a terrible void in General Jackson's life, although he later jokingly called himself a "young widower." To relieve his loneliness, Jackson immersed himself in all kinds of outside activities. In January, he arranged a luncheon for Adlai E. Stevenson, vice-president-elect of the United States.[29] The same month, he also went by private railroad car to Winchester, Tennessee, to convince Gov.-elect Peter Turney to name J. B. Killebrew head of the Office of the Bureau of Agriculture, Statistics, and Mines.[30]

By the summer of 1893 Billy and Howell were speaking again. As a matter of fact, they were sufficiently reconciled for Billy to announce the construction of an office building they would erect at the corner of Church and Sumner Streets. General Jackson had already spent many hours with architects from the firm of H. J. Dudley & Son formulating plans for the building that promised to be the handsomest ever erected in Nashville.[31] The fireproof structure would be Nashville's tallest, with seven floors—each supported by steel columns, girders, and floor beams—

and a roof garden lighted electrically. As it rose above the low Nashville skyline, then dominated by church spires, the Jackson block drew the attention of the entire city.[32] The structure was built on land originally owned by Randal McGavock and featured a first floor built of limestone from the Belle Meade quarry and upper floors of fire brick with terra cotta and cut stone trimmings. When completed in 1895 at a cost of $157,091, the building's first floor contained space for up to four stores on Church Street and one on Sumner Street. Floors two through four were available for offices; the top three floors were designed as apartments.[33] Although the two brothers shared equally in the cost of the building, Billy assumed most of the responsibility because of Howell's appointment to the Supreme Court of the United States in 1893, which was quickly followed by his terminal illness.

After his defeat by Grover Cleveland in the 1892 presidential election, but before his term expired early the next year, President Benjamin Harrison had an opportunity to fill a position on the Supreme Court. Word soon reached Judge Jackson that he was being considered for the position by his former associate in the United States Senate. Howell had not sought the job, and he was astonished that a Republican president would consider a Democrat, a friend of President Cleveland, a Southerner, and a former Confederate. Harrison nevertheless submitted Jackson's name to the Senate for consideration. Jackson was quickly confirmed and took his seat on March 4, 1893.[34]

Massachusetts Senator George F. Hoar took credit for persuading Harrison to appoint Jackson. He argued that it was politically expedient to name a Democrat of "admirable judicial quality" rather than nominate a Republican who was doubtful of being confirmed in the equally divided Senate.[35] Harrison stated that he "never believed in a partisan judiciary" and picked Jackson because, among other reasons, Jackson's views of the Constitution and the powers of the Federal government were similar to his. He was also impressed with Jackson's reputation as a God-fearing man and a conscientious and industrious judge. Finally, Harrison hoped picking Jackson would broadcast the message that he was "most sincerely desirous of obliterating all sectional divisions."[36]

Justice Jackson's children were thrilled. Howell, Jr., felt like "just shouting for joy."[37] Dr. Alexander Jackson would have been proudest of all had he been alive to see his son's appointment. He once said that Howell was born to be on the Supreme Court. The only unhappy family

Left: JUSTICE HOWELL E. JACKSON, 1893. Belle Meade collection

Below: JACKSON BUILDING during construction, 1894. Drawing from *Art Work of Nashville*

member was Howell's wife, Mary. She had no social aspirations and was troubled about Howell's health. Knowing his tendency toward self-denial, she knew he was likely to push himself beyond his physical abilities. As a Washington friend of hers said, "I guess you rue his appointment more and more every day."[38]

Howell's professional colleagues uniformly supported his appointment. His fellow Sixth Circuit Judge William Howard Taft wrote, "I can not tell you how gratified I am. . . . And yet I ought not to put it that way, because we shall miss you dreadfully on this bench. You have served to give the court of appeals a standing in the country and it has been a great honor to me to have my name linked with yours."[39]

In Nashville, seventy-two of the city's most influential political and business leaders gathered at a banquet at the Maxwell House to honor the first citizen of Tennessee to be elevated to the Supreme Court in fifty-six years. After an elaborate dinner, Jacob McGavock Dickinson, the master of ceremonies, rose to signal the beginning of toasts. At their conclusion, Justice Jackson, who was deeply touched by his friends' expressions of approval, responded by saying that his aspiration was to become a judge "who has a Godly fear of doing wrong and entertains a just regard for the rights of every fellow being, without distinction of persons, whether rich or poor, high or low, humble or exalted." In closing, Jackson expressed the hope that "the great ruler will give me the wisdom, the grace, and the strength to heed and to follow a high and enlightened sense of duty in the new sphere to which I have been so unexpectedly called."[40]

A number of Jackson's friends and acquaintances specifically wished him "long life and health" to serve in the high station he had obtained, but that was not to be.[41] The ever-conscientious Jackson overtaxed himself in his first months on the bench. By August he was in a sanatarium for treatment of a lung problem. He was also worried about the "stability and soundness" of Nashville's American National Bank, where all his available funds were deposited. He wrote Mary to have Billy "check the situation out."[42] Although Howell was released from the sanatarium in time to be in Washington for the next term of the court, he was still sick. In January 1894 he was well enough to escort Mary to the White House to dine with President and Mrs. Cleveland.[43] However, his illness soon forced him to leave Washington for a six-weeks' stay in St. Petersburg, Florida, accompanied by his wife and Eunice, his niece. The warm climate did not restore Jackson's health, and he returned to West Meade that spring.[44]

While the Howell Jacksons were in Florida, General Jackson, Nat Baxter, Jr., and Inman, Swan and Company of New York bought controlling interest in the Nashville Street Railway Company.[45] Jackson and Baxter, who were good friends, had other business relationships. Baxter had once borrowed money from Jackson to buy an interest in a street railroad company in Birmingham, Alabama. When Jackson declined to renew the note, meaning foreclosure on the collateral, Baxter became furious. He got in his buggy, drove to Belle Meade, and appeared at Jackson's door with the renewal note and a shotgun in his hands. When Jackson came to the door, the shotgun caught his attention. After Baxter asked if he would renew the note, Jackson said, "Yes," and with the new note in hand, he retrieved the old one from his office and gave it to Baxter. For some time afterward, bankers in Nashville, upon seeing any note executed by Baxter, joked about the "shotgun note."[46]

Despite a gradual decline in his health, General Jackson remained active in civic affairs. In the spring of 1894, he attended the fourth annual meeting and reunion of the United Confederate Veterans in Birmingham. There, with his usual eloquence, he introduced General Miller, department commander of the Grand Army of the Republic, one of the principal speakers. Jackson was also the spokesman for the nominating committee. His nomination of John B. Gordon for commander in chief was accepted. In recognition of Jackson's leadership of the organization, the June 1894 issue of the *Confederate Veteran* carried his picture on its front cover.[47]

Meanwhile, the Jackson-Harding clan was sizing up Eunice's fiancé, Albert D. Marks, a promising young Nashville attorney. One family member described Marks as "about 25 years old, a good looking young man, quite talented and very ambitious . . . industrious, sober and energetic." She added that Eunice seemed to be "very much in love with him and has agreed to go to the Cumberland Presbyterian Church."[48] Henry ("Speedy") Green, Uncle Bob's son, thought Marks was "pretty as a woman," with dimples in his cheeks and chin.[49] Eunice and Albert were married at Belle Meade in June. Following the service, a quiet affair witnessed by family members and a few intimate friends, they spent a three-month honeymoon in Europe, then set up housekeeping at Belle Meade.[50]

While Eunice and Albert were on their honeymoon, Justice Jackson took Mary, their children, his physician, and several friends to California in a desperate effort to recover good health. He made it back to Washington for the October session, but had to excuse himself again to go to a less severe climate. In November 1894, Howell wrote Judge Taft that leaving the bench "was the worst trial of my life."[51] Justice and Mrs. Jackson occupied an elegant five-bedroom house named Southside Villa, on twenty acres of land outside Thomasville, Georgia, a popular vacation spot for wealthy Easterners.[52] The pine-scented air there was supposed to alleviate respiratory distress.

Jackson was not sure he had "the patience to spend the winter doing nothing but sitting in the sun." To keep mentally alert, he read newspapers daily and corresponded with other members of the court, Judge Taft, U.S. Attorney General Richard Olney, and Jacob McGavock Dickinson.[53] Aware that he would likely have to retire, Jackson told Mary that his choice for a successor was his friend Taft, whom he described as "an able lawyer, a just judge, and an indefatigable worker."[54]

Howell and Mary also discussed their precarious financial situation. If Jackson could not resume his seat on the bench, he would lose his income at a time when he owed money on the Jackson Building and when his medical expenses were the highest they had ever been. In March, following their return to West Meade, Howell borrowed fifty thousand dollars from the Northwestern Mutual Life Insurance Company, using West Meade as collateral.[55]

Jackson's last public act was perhaps his most courageous. In March 1895, a tax case came before the Supreme Court (Pollack v. Farmers' Loan & Trust Company). Jackson was absent at the time without any expectation of being able to return. The remaining eight judges were evenly divided and a reargument was ordered. Summoning all his strength, Jackson went to Washington expecting to cast the deciding vote in favor of the tax. On reconsideration, however, one of the other justices changed his mind, and by a vote of five to four the act was held unconstitutional. Jackson delivered his dissenting opinion with labored breath, but his clear and masterful reasoning forced everyone present to recognize that his mind was as bright as his body was weak.[56]

Howell, his daughter Louise, General Jackson, and Eunice and Albert Marks all went to Cincinnati in June for the wedding of Howell's son, William H. Jackson, and Caroline Dickson.[57] The trip exhausted the rapidly failing Justice Jackson. Eight weeks later, on August 8, 1895, he died of tuberculosis at age sixty-three. At his own request, his funeral service was simple, but it was well attended at Belle Meade, which was better suited than West Meade for the large crowd. Local friends and visiting dignitaries arrived by private conveyance and by a special train of five coaches. Presbyterian minister James H. McNeilly and R. Lin Cave, an elder in the Christian Church, conducted the service. Chief Justice Melville W. Fuller and Associate Justice David J. Brewer represented the Supreme Court. Among the honorary pallbearers were Judge Thomas H. Malone and Judge Charles M. Blackford of Lynchburg, Virginia, Howell's college roommates.[58] Jackson's daughter, Elizabeth, was not present. She always regretted that she was on a "grand tour" of Europe when her father died and did not know of the seriousness of his condition.[59]

By telegram from Pointe-au-Pic, Quebec, Judge Taft expressed to General Jackson his sorrow over Justice Jackson's death. In a subsequent telegram to Mrs. Jackson, Taft called his former colleague

> a rare man so loved, so gentle, so firm, so courageous, so full of the keenest kindliest humor, that association with him was nothing but a constant pleasure. His power of application which amounted to genius, his marvelous and quick perception, and his capacity for sustained logical argument made him one of the great judges of our country, and the Supreme Court has lost a member who in but one term impressed all his colleagues as a leader among them.[60]

When the news of Justice Jackson's death reached the two circuit courts in Nashville, they immediately adjourned. The Nashville, Memphis, and Chattanooga bars published resolutions of respect. On August 14 the Supreme Court adopted a similar resolution. Newspapers across the country carried the story of his death. In Cincinnati the "most representative aggregation of legal talent" ever seen assembled in the U.S. Court of Appeals to pay their last respects. The *Cincinnati Commercial Gazette* said of Jackson, "His logical facility was so great, his perception so quick, his moral force so great, his mental energy so intense, and his judicial quality so fine that he could sit on no court in which he did not exercise a recognized influence."[61]

Aware that his own health was increasingly frail, General Jackson relinquished two significant business responsibilities about the time his brother died. He stepped down from the presidencies of the Nashville Gas Light Company, furnishing Nashvillians with gas, and the Nashville Street Railway Company, furnishing "rapid transit to different portions of the city."[62] In December 1896, Charles M. McGhee, a Knoxville and New York financier, bought out Jackson's one-third interest in the Nashville Street Railway Company, equity said to be worth four hundred thousand dollars.[63] Two months earlier, General Jackson took another step toward retirement by conveying Belle Meade to his children. Possibly without his knowledge, they promptly used the farm as collateral to borrow sixty thousand dollars from the Northwestern Mutual Life Insurance Company.[64]

General Jackson's last great contribution to his native state was his significant help in planning and executing the Tennessee Centennial Celebration. In 1892 Douglas Anderson, a Nashville lawyer, suggested the idea of celebrating the hundredth anniversary of Tennessee's statehood. A year later, Capt. William C. Smith, a Nashville architect, urged the Commercial Club of Nashville to take the lead in holding a celebration of the centennial anniversary of Tennessee's admission into the Union.[65] That resulted in a committee of twenty-five men being named and a Tennessee Centennial Exposition Company being chartered. Jackson was a charter member, chaired one of the permanent committees, and served on the Executive Committee.[66] On July 30, Maj. Eugene C. Lewis was named director general.[67] He conceived the idea of constructing among other exposition buildings a replica of the Parthenon in Athens as a focal point for the Centennial. An ad hoc committee, consisting of Lewis, Centennial Board President Maj. John Thomas, Jackson, H. W. Buttorff, and W. L. Dudley, was appointed to recommend to the executive committee the plans and architects for the Parthenon, Transportation Building, and auditorium.[68] Their selections were approved in November. The West Side Park site was chosen that August.[69]

The nationally known artist George Zolnay was chosen to sculpt the figures on the Parthenon frieze. The Hungarian-born Zolnay also made busts of Sam Davis, the boy hero of the Confederacy, and William Hicks Jackson. The bust of Davis created a sensation at the Centennial and led to Zolnay's commission in 1908 to do the full-length statue of Davis standing today on the Capitol grounds. The bust of Jackson is at Belle Meade on loan from the Tennessee Historical Society.[70]

Over the winter, an act incorporating the Centennial Exposition as a city was passed into law. General Jackson was one of the new city's aldermen. On opening day of the Centennial, May 1, 1897, Jackson's old cavalry division flags were displayed in the Confederate Exhibit in the History Building, and Belle Meade was designated as a place to be seen by all visiting delegations.[71] During the Centennial, General Jackson rode in the presidential procession from the Maxwell House to the Celebration grounds when President McKinley visited, gave a welcome speech to visitors on Cincinnati Day, and was chief marshal for the parade on Confederate Day, deliberately scheduled to coincide with the annual meeting and reunion of the United Confederate Veterans held in Nashville on June 22-24, 1897.[72]

General Jackson was back from his trip to England in time to be a judge for the Tennessee Centennial Flower Parade on Kate Kirkman Day in late September. In October, he participated in the programs on Chicago and Illinois Day, and he was grand marshal for the second time on John W. Thomas Day, an event featuring the exhibition of some of Belle Meade's blooded horses. Finally, Jackson spoke during the Centennial's closing exercises on October 30. In his remarks, he paid tribute to Mrs. Van Leer Kirkman and other ladies on the Women's Board.[73] J. B. Killebrew noted in his memoirs, "I should say that J. W. Thomas, Judge [Horace] Lurton, W. H. Jackson, and W. C. Collier did more than any other men to get it [the Centennial] on its feet." Jackson's dedication to it was, in Killebrew's opinion, "genuine."[74]

The pace of events did not immediately slow after the Celebration. General Jackson's son, William Harding Jackson, married Annie Davis Richardson of Nashville at McKendree Methodist Church less than a month after the Centennial closed. He was the last of the Jackson children to marry. The wedding, thought to have been attended by more guests than any ever held in that sanctuary, was such a highlight of the social season that twenty-five policemen were needed to keep the crowd back and "prevent a great crush."[75] Church Street was lined with carriages on both sides for several blocks. As the guests left McKendree to go to the Richardsons' home on Park Place for the reception, the organist began playing "There'll be a hot time in the old town tonight," the theme song of the Centennial Celebration.[76]

Eighteen months earlier, William's sister Selene had suddenly married William R. ("Billy") Elliston, a personable and socially prominent

Left: ANNIE D. RICHARDSON JACKSON, 1877-1954. Belle Meade collection

Below: WILLIAM HARDING JACKSON, 1874-1903. Belle Meade collection

son of an old Nashville family. The Elliston family home, Burlington Place, was a local landmark. The Jackson-Elliston wedding at Nashville's Church of the Advent came as a shock to General Jackson and to many of the young couple's friends because only a handful of people were aware of their intentions. No one from Selene's family was invited. General Jackson learned about the wedding when Selene called him from the Duncan Hotel where a postwedding luncheon was held for the bridal party. Selene and Billy accepted the general's invitation to spend the night at Belle Meade before leaving on their wedding trip to New York.[77]

For a brief period, General Jackson and his children and their spouses occupied four separate apartments at Belle Meade. Each family had its own servants and vehicles. At meals, one servant's sole duty was to stand behind the general's chair and wait on him. One or two others served meals to the rest of the family. On Sundays, General Billy enjoyed having two-hour breakfasts, including venison and quail. By that time, "his once auburn hair was touched with gray, and his once ruddy face was no longer quite so florid."[78] He was obese and had difficulty walking. To get around the farm, he relied on a carriage. He also had forgotten the warning Selene gave him about shunning "ostentation, frivolity, or social pomp" at Belle Meade. Similarly, he disregarded the suggestion of his son-in-law Albert Marks to modify his style of living.

After getting out of the street railway business, General Jackson gradually turned over his financial affairs to Albert, a move he would live to regret. Jackson had more confidence in Marks's business acumen than he did in Billy Elliston's or his son William's. Unlike Albert, neither Billy nor William had shown much interest in working. The clean-shaven Elliston was described as "fairly tall, graceful in figure and movement," and a young man who "dressed like a fashion plate." He and the dainty Selene made a handsome couple, who enjoyed a more spirited social life than did the more sedate Markses.[79]

General Jackson's first grandchild was born on November 30, 1896, when Eunice gave birth to a son, Albert Marks, Jr. Soon after the baby's birth, Eunice's close friend, Nellie Malone Magruder, and her husband, William, came to Belle Meade to bring a baby present. Nellie noticed that the baby seemed unusually lethargic. An investigation revealed that the baby's nurse had been giving him paregoric or some similar medicine to keep him from crying.

Eunice got a brief respite from worrying about her sick baby in February when she, Selene, and General Jackson entertained a friend, Myssie Brown of Murfreesboro, with a luncheon on the day before Myssie's marriage to the the Honorable Archibald J. Marjoribanks of England. For the gala affair, the dining room tables were decorated with large silver bowls filled with white lilies. After Majoribanks's death several years later, Myssie married Lord Douglas Hogg. Their son, Quintin, became Lord Hailsham and Lord Chancellor of England.[80]

After the Brown-Marjoribanks wedding, Eunice's maid of honor, Mary Felix Demoville, grew increasingly worried about the Marks baby's delicate health. Mary knew that Albert, Jr., had never been baptized because Eunice and Albert had been unable to agree on a church home. Fearing that he would die unbaptized, Mary told Eunice that "with my church (Roman Catholic) anyone may baptize someone about to die." When Albert, Jr., showed signs of being terminally ill, Eunice sent for her friend Mary. The child had already died when Mary arrived, but Eunice told her that she had baptized him herself. Hearing of the child's death, the Magruders wondered if the medicine contributed to it.[81] Six months after little Albert's death, Selene gave birth to a son, William Jackson Elliston. William would be the next to last member of the Jackson family born at Belle Meade.

Selene's brother, William Harding Jackson, was gregarious like his father. Decades later, one of Bob Green's sons recalled that "going to town was what William liked best."[82] Billy and his brother-in-law, Albert Marks, were avid sportsmen and excellent shots, who particularly enjoyed trapshooting. Practice shoots were held every week or so at Belle Meade's gun club, an otherwise unused one-room house on the farm. At least annually, big shoots were held there. In 1898 General Jackson, William, and Billy Elliston were hosts for two live shoots. In May, five hundred pigeons were killed in the all-day shoot interrupted only for a barbecue dinner given by General Jackson.[83] That fall, following a "big shooting tournament" in Dayton, Ohio, where Elliston divided the first-place money, many of the nation's crack shots came to Nashville for what was described as the "greatest shooting tournament ever held south of the Ohio River." Elliston again "did himself proud" by coming within a single shot of tying the great Kansas City champion, J. A. R. Elliott, in a dual match.[84] Elliston killed forty-nine out of fifty birds under difficult conditions.

General Jackson and William Harding also competed against a national field in the two-day open shoot. Along with extensive coverage of the trapshoot, the *Nashville American* on October 17 carried pictures of William Jackson and Billy Elliston. The caption under Elliston's picture described him as "a coming American champion."

While her husband and brother were engrossed with the sport of trapshooting, Eunice Jackson Marks was mulling over a decision that, if she made it, seemed destined to estrange her from her friends and invoke the "lifelong displeasure" of her father.[85] Undoubtedly influenced by guilt feelings over never having had her baby properly baptized, Eunice began studying the Roman Catholic faith. She was encouraged in her interest in Catholicism by her friend Mary Demoville and by her husband's first cousin, Marks Handly, who was then studying for the priesthood at the College of St. Thomas Aquinas at Catholic University in Washington, D.C.[86] Eunice and Albert, who earlier had taken a neutral position on the matter, were baptized in the Catholic faith on May 22, 1899 at St. Mary's Church in Nashville. Her sponsors were the Reverend Marks W. Handly and Mary Demoville.[87] Fortunately, Eunice's fears concerning her father's attitude proved to be unfounded.

In January 1900, one of the strangest events in the history of the Jackson family occurred. General Jackson, Billy and Selene Elliston, and Joseph H. Acklen went on a fox-hunting weekend at the farm of Squire Moses Wall, eighteen miles from Russellville, Kentucky. Billy Elliston's brother-in-law, Edwards Sinclair, met them there Friday afternoon. At one o'clock the next morning, after all the guests and family members had retired, Elliston left his and Selene's bedroom and went downstairs to the room occupied by Moses Wall and Edwards Sinclair. They were ready for bed when he walked in and offered each a cigarette. He then picked up Wall's pistol from the mantelpiece and pointed it at his host. Elliston then suddenly turned and shot Sinclair four times, severely wounding him in the neck and side. After the shooting, Elliston asked his father-in-law what to do. Jackson told him to leave, which Elliston did. The next morning he was in Nashville, where he saw Albert Marks. Elliston told Marks what had happened and asked him to notify the police chief and the sheriff that he "was willing to surrender whenever he was wanted." Elliston was not arrested, but he soon left town.[88]

Elliston's reason for shooting Sinclair is still a mystery. One theory holds that he was temporarily insane. A fuller explanation is that Elliston shot Sinclair because he thought his brother-in-law was paying too much attention to Selene.[89] Anyway, Elliston fled to London. In December, Selene filed for divorce in the Davidson County Chancery Court on the grounds of Elliston's desertion and failure to provide support for her and their child. The divorce was granted and Selene was given custody of the child.[90]

In 1900, a divorced woman, even one from a prominent family, was virtually a social outcast. Abandoned by her husband, Selene turned to a Catholic priest for counsel, probably either the Reverend John B. Morris or Father Marks Handly. On April 24, she was baptized a Catholic. Four days later, her little boy, William Jackson Elliston, was also baptized according to her new faith. That Eunice had already become a Roman Catholic undoubtedly made it easier for Selene to make the change.[91]

By the turn of the century, Eunice and Albert Marks had moved from Belle Meade to a home of their own at #3 West End Park. There Eunice lived a quiet life because health problems, probably related to those she had in 1892, returned to plague her. Subject to fainting spells, she habitually used smelling salts and drank strong coffee. Though she was confined to her bed much of the time, she maintained a regal air. One day her aunt Mary Jackson brought her three-year-old grandchild, Mary Harding Buckner, to see Aunt Eunice, who was in bed propped up with a pillow. When they left, little Mary Harding said to her grandmother, "She looks like a princess."[92]

When Eunice became too ill to go to church, Father Morris brought Holy Communion to her. A short time later, Eunice said that her wedding gifts "have never been put to so good a use as in adorning the table prepared for Him." Her increasing spirituality focused her thoughts on death:

> I have a feeling of hastening, of having more to do and more to become than I can perhaps accomplish, and the question of what I have done or failed to do with my opportunities looms up terrifically before me. But if in the remainder of the time I can only have the strength, courage, resolution and continuity of purpose to do what God intends for me, I believe I could die in peace.[93]

Eunice died in her thirtieth year on March 25, 1901. According to the *Nashville Banner*, she "had been in ill-health for several years and her death was not unexpected." Eunice's funeral was held at St. Mary's

Catholic Church, with requiem high mass conducted by the Right Reverend Thomas S. Byrne, bishop of Nashville, celebrant, and the Very Reverend John B. Morris, assistant priest. Her remains were placed in the mausoleum at Belle Meade. Eunice's will, made in 1896, included bequests of annuities of one hundred dollars each to her cousin, Carrie Ewing, and her dearest friend, Mary Demoville. Eunice left all her property to her husband if he survived her. Albert inherited a one-third interest in Belle Meade and a one-sixth interest in the Jackson Building and six adjoining houses downtown.[94] Decades later, Jackson family members recalled hearing rumors that Albert killed Eunice by feeding her ground glass. General Jackson's family circle was reduced to Selene; her son, William Jackson Elliston; William Harding Jackson; his wife Annie whom everyone called "D"; their baby, William Harding Jackson, the general's last grandchild; and Albert Marks. All but Albert lived at Belle Meade.

Annie D. often invited friends to spend the night at Belle Meade. Willie Evans Fall, her cousin and maid of honor, came frequently. When there, Willie noticed that Selene was seldom seen. She usually stayed in her own suite of rooms with her own servants. Willie's most exciting visit to Belle Meade came on a rainy afternoon. Because of the bad weather, General Jackson sent his carriage for her. As the carriage came back out Broad Street by the new Union Station, the curtains that had been closed to keep out the rain suddenly parted and a stranger jumped in beside her. He told her that if she would be quiet he would not harm her. In a few moments the man disclosed to the frightened young woman that he had killed a man and needed to leave town. Recognizing the Belle Meade carriage, he had quickly made up his mind to hop a ride. Before the carriage reached Belle Meade, the man jumped out and was never seen or heard from again.[95]

D's younger sister Henrietta and their mother also regularly visited her at Belle Meade. Several days before their departure for such visits, Mrs. Richardson would usually tell her carriage driver, Anthony, to allow the horses extra rest because he always drove them as fast as he could to beat the train. If the carriage and the train got to Belle Meade at the same time, the noise from the steam engine frightened the horses. Among Henrietta's most vivid memories of Belle Meade were of riding about the farm in a wicker seat pony cart. The pony would invariably pull the cart into the middle of Richland Creek, stop, and refuse to move. No matter where the journey began, it always ended with someone rescuing Henrietta from the creek.[96]

The opening of Nashville's Union Station in October 1900 was just the sort of event General Jackson thoroughly enjoyed. It combined two favorite activities—civic hoopla and parading in a carriage. In the parade that morning, August Belmont, chairman of the L&N board, and Jackson rode in Jackson's Brewster rig.[97] Another person who enjoyed buggy riding with Jackson was ten-year-old Jeannette Acklen, whose father was on the ill-fated trip to Moses Wall's farm when Elliston shot Edwards Sinclair. In 1984, Jeannette recalled visiting Belle Meade frequently as a child. Near the end of her long life, her memory of Gen. W. H. Jackson was crystal clear. She said he allowed her to sit in his lap and twist his moustache in the shape of two horns. Jeannette also enjoyed riding around the farm with General Jackson. Her responsibility was to jump out of the buggy and open and shut each gate. As a wiry and well-coordinated tomboy, Jeannette thought she was good enough to ride one of Jackson's largest horses. When a groom protested, she convinced him that General Jackson had given her permission to ride any horse she wanted to. The horse she chose was too strong for her and ran away with her. For a considerable period afterward, she was content to ride ponies.[98]

Another person who passed on stories of Belle Meade to later generations was Zack Boyd Singleton, who was born in 1884 on his father's farm adjoining Belle Meade. As a young man, Singleton ran a blacksmith shop on the south side of the Harding Turnpike. One of his best customers was General Jackson. Singleton's favorite Belle Meade story was about a bull that loved to terrorize travelers on the turnpike. The bull met his end when he tried to intimidate a train on the NC & StL line to Memphis.[99]

Both General Jackson and Albert Marks wrote their last wills and testaments in 1901. Having already conveyed his farm to his children, Jackson named William Harding Jackson his executor and left him his entire estate with the exception of a pair of horses, the brougham, the surrey, the rockaway, the "volaine" coach, the harnesses for the horses, and the furniture and pictures in Selene's room, which were left to her.[100] Albert left his mother a life interest in his home in West End Park and bequeathed almost everything else to the Right Reverend Thomas S.

Byrne, Catholic bishop of Nashville. Byrne was named executor of the will replacing one written in 1891.[101]

Selene increasingly turned to the Catholic Church for support. Once while vacationing in St. Augustine, Florida, she wrote Bishop Byrne thanking him for his prayers and kindness. In her letter, Selene spoke of her loneliness and her weakness and said she prayed "that God will hold me close in his arms." Later, the bishop learned that Selene had made a will in his favor. In the spring of 1903, Byrne wrote Nashville attorney John J. Vertrees to ask him to return the will to Mrs. Elliston, who thought the bishop had it. Byrne said that he had never seen the will and thought Mrs. Elliston was foolish to have left her estate to him. He also "absolutely and unconditionally" surrendered any right or claim he might have under it.[102]

General Jackson's two surviving children, William and Selene, refinanced their mortgage on the 2,167-acre Belle Meade Farm with Northwestern Mutual in 1901. By executing a new ninety-thousand-dollar loan at 5 percent annual interest, they repaid the original loan of sixty-thousand dollars made four years earlier.[103]

Without being aware of Belle Meade's precarious financial condition, General Jackson invited the thirty-member executive committee of the Tennessee Centennial to a ten-course dinner with wine.[104] As Jackson's guests enjoyed his hospitality, some must have reflected on the changing times. Certainly "Old Red" missed his wife Selene and his daughter Eunice. A number of them knew the farm was mortgaged. Some were also aware that the county would soon purchase the Harding Turnpike, of which Jackson was a principal stockholder.[105] Although that represented progress, it also signaled the end of an era. Most wondered whether or not William was capable of carrying on the great stock farm that had been in his family for three generations. Jackson was as gracious as ever, but his thoughts tended to wander. As much as he hated doing so, his declining health dictated that he let William try his hand at running Belle Meade. He would wait until the new year to do that, however. For the moment, he had guests to entertain.

22/ End of an Era

WILLIAM HICKS JACKSON RETIRED IN 1902 AND GAVE his son William responsibility for the Belle Meade Stud. It must have been with a certain sense of relief that the battle-scarred veteran, then in his sixty-seventh year, went to Florida for a rest.[1] An era ended when the internationally known and respected breeder relinquished the reins of one of America's greatest studs.

An immediate priority for William was completing all arrangements for sending the yearlings to New York for the stud's annual sale. A problem was his lack of funds to pay for the shipping fees. To remedy that, a "Jackson note" for $2,500 was executed with Nashville's Union Bank and Trust Company.[2] The sale at the Fasig-Tipton Company's paddocks at Gravesend, New York, was disappointing. Although most of the prominent buyers were present, prices were well below what William had expected. Forty-one head sold for $35,700, an average of $871 per head. The next day twenty-five yearlings from the Rancho del Paso brought an average price of $1,300.[3] Getting whipped that badly in head-to-head competition with J. B. A. Haggin's stud was something General Jackson would not have tolerated a decade earlier when he was in better health. Things had definitely slipped.

General Jackson did not attend the New York sale. He may not even have left his room that day. He was still in shock from the suicide of his son-in-law, Albert Marks, a week earlier. On the morning of June 14, Marks had walked into the telegraph editor's room of the *Nashville American*, sat in a chair, and fatally shot himself behind the right ear. Friends, not knowing of any financial difficulties, speculated that Marks was temporarily insane. Front-page stories about his death appeared in the Nashville newspapers for days as reporters scrambled to run down rumors and separate fact from fiction.[4]

Father Morris denied a rumor that Marks had given $30,000 to the Roman Catholic Church. To the contrary, he said Marks was indebted to the church for several thousand dollars. It was rumored that Marks had lost money on the New York Stock Exchange and owed the estate of his late brother Arthur $35,000. Although Marks had negotiated the sale of the Richland Turnpike Company to Davidson County for $32,525, neither General Jackson, the principal shareowner, nor any of the other owners received his fair share of the proceeds. Some obtained nothing; others got fifty cents on the dollar. No one knew what Marks, who was the company's attorney, did with the money. It was also discovered that Marks had mortgaged his interest in Belle Meade to Nashville's Union Bank and Trust Company.[5]

Many people recalled a radical change in Marks's behavior the last week of his life. He was also said to have spent an inordinate amount of time kneeling in front of the altar at St. Mary's Church. When it was learned that he had executed promissory notes amounting to nearly $1,200 to servants at Belle Meade, a reporter pursued the story. He found that Marks had borrowed $550 from Reuben Harris, the night watchman; lesser amounts from Lee Bradley, Amanda Akin, and Bettie Elliston; and over $300 from the Belle Meade Sunday School and Sick Society, an organization that grew out of the Sunday school class Eunice Jackson Marks had taught as a teenager. Harris told the reporter that Marks had the confidence of all the servants, but they were naturally eager to know if they would be repaid.[6]

By the last week in June, more and more questionable transactions were disclosed. Marks had forged General Jackson's name on checks made out to Nashville banks, and he had victimized the Nashville Trust Company and out-of-town institutions as well. Although those matters had not been revealed when Marks was buried at Calvary Cemetery, his burial apart from Eunice at Belle Meade indicates that General Jackson knew enough.[7]

Following Marks's death, his home was sold and his personal belongings auctioned, including Eunice's gloves and even the pistol he had used to shoot himself. At Belle Meade, General Jackson seldom strayed from his private quarters on the first floor, although he reluctantly spoke to the press. When a reporter asked if it was true that "the well-known millionaire" George Gould would buy Belle Meade, Jackson denied having talked to Gould and said Belle Meade was not for sale.[8] Privately, he and

William considered their options. They concluded that, since the farm was heavily mortgaged, they had no choice but to scale down the size of the stud considerably. Notice that their horses were "to go under the hammer" in October appeared in the *Nashville American* on August 5. The front-page story, including pictures of Generals Harding and Jackson, said Jackson was retiring because of old age and continued ill health. Every Thoroughbred on the place, including 9 stallions, 139 brood mares, 15 yearlings, 75 weanlings, 12 two-year-olds, 1 three-year-old, and 1 four-year-old, would be auctioned.[9]

The Jacksons arranged for the sale to be handled by the Fasig-Tipton Company of New York. Their friend, William Easton, was the auctioneer. Each day of the sale, trains brought prospective buyers out from Union Station in midmorning and returned them after the sale. Nearly a thousand horsemen were present when Easton eulogized the stud. He said he had visited all the great breeding establishments in the world and that Belle Meade was the equal, if not the best, of them. He also praised General Jackson for his long and honorable career and prophesied that future generations of Jacksons and Hardings would add still more fame to the already world-famous stud.[10]

The Commoner, Hanover's great son and the head of the stud, was "knocked down" to Edwin S. Gardner of Avondale Stud for $41,000. Gardner also got Loyalist and the best of the brood mares. In all, 7 stallions and 136 brood mares were sold. The stallions brought an average price of nearly $8,000, while the brood mares averaged just under $600. It was generally known around the sales ring, however, that Gardner and a number of other friends who made purchases were acting as agents for William Harding Jackson and that The Commoner, Huron, Inspector B, Loyalist, and many of the brood mares would remain at Belle Meade.[11] Many speculated that the sale was really a way for General Jackson to give his horses to his son and that William never actually paid for them. Later, General Jackson was quoted as saying that, prior to the sale, he had never helped William financially as he had his two daughters and their husbands.[12]

During the fall and early winter, General Jackson was quite ill and remained secluded. His ebullience, his pride, his iron constitution, and his spirit were gone. Despite his illness, Jackson visited briefly with his young friend Jeannette Acklen. He was fond of the twelve-year-old tomboy, and he promised to give her a pony.[13] Before he got around to

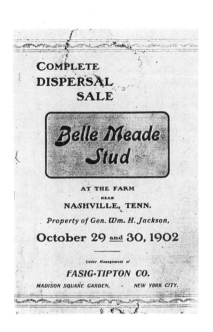

Left: DISPERSAL SALE CATALOG.
Collection of Ridley Wills II

Below: GENERAL JACKSON AND
GEN. FITZHUGH LEE, Jan. 1903.
Belle Meade collection

doing so, however, he was stricken with "a form of nervous prostration" and was confined to his room. He rallied in January when his old West Point classmate, Gen. Fitzhugh Lee, visited him. After reminiscing for several hours about their boyhood days at West Point, life in the old army, and their years of Confederate service, the two old soldiers posed for a final photograph sitting in rocking chairs on the front walk of the house. When Fitz got up to leave, he promised to return and spend more time at Belle Meade. His host replied in a tender tone, "Fitz, you had better come quick."[14] On March 30, 1903, General Jackson died of Bright's disease at age sixty-seven. His last words were "I want Joe's hand." Joe Carter, one of Susanna's sons, was quietly sitting by the bed. He promptly offered his hand. When Jeannette Acklen learned about her friend's death, she asked her father, Colonel Acklen, about the pony. He told her to forget it.[15]

The Nashville *Daily News* may have offered the best summary of Jackson's contributions:

> Perhaps of all of Tennessee's distinguished sons, none have come nearer the fulfillment of the sentiment, "first in war, first in peace, and first in the hearts of his fellow citizens." The renown which he gained through his long career as a soldier, whether in fights with Mexicans, Apaches, or in the long struggle of the Civil War, he did not suffer to grow dim when peace was declared. Though in a different field, his achievements have been hardly less conspicuous, and his renown even more widespread.[16]

The *Banner's* page-one story on March 31 commented that Jackson "filled probably the most unique place in the history of Tennessee" as a soldier, the proprietor of Belle Meade, a citizen, and a statesman. Under his guidance, according to the newspaper, Belle Meade was "one of the places where the chivalric and open-handed customs of the old South were never suffered to lapse. In him, one of the monumental remnants of the antebellum South crumbled and the state suffered a loss which can never be repaired." The *Nashville American* noted that, while Jackson's greatest fame came from his long tenure as proprietor of Belle Meade, his reputation would rest on his record as a soldier, which ranked him among the best the country had ever known. It also drew attention to Jackson's devotion to McKendree Methodist Church and said that he faced death philosophically and with the confidence of "an upright Christian man."[17]

The funeral, conducted by Dr. D. C. Kelley, was held at Belle Meade, with interment in the family vault. That may not have suited Jackson. He once mentioned that he wanted his final resting place to be at Mt. Olivet because Confederate soldiers were buried there. Among the many telegrams and letters received by the family were ones from Gen. Fitzhugh Lee; Mrs. M. C. Goodlett, president of the United Daughters of the Confederacy; and the officers of McKendree Methodist Church, among whom Jackson had served.[18]

With his father gone, William Harding Jackson was determined to fulfill William Easton's prophecy that someone in his generation would bring added luster to Belle Meade. Regrettably, determination was not enough. In late June, soon after returning home from a trip to New York and Chicago, Jackson came down with a high fever. Annie D. summoned Dr. Richard Douglas, whose diagnosis was that Jackson had contracted typhoid fever on his trip. Jackson's fever never abated, and he suffered an internal hemorrhage on July 15. From then until his death four days later, he slipped into and out of consciousness. During one of his lucid moments, he called Bob Green to his bed and said, "Uncle Bob, take care of Miss Annie. Let the horses alone tonight and make her your first care." At midnight, Annie D., not knowing of her husband's instructions to Uncle Bob, found the old servant waiting at the bedroom door. "The horses, Uncle Bob," she said, "are they all right?" "I don't know, Miss Annie," he answered. "The master told me to take keer of you, and I'm gwine ter mind him long as he's above ground."[19] Uncle Bob stayed at his post the rest of the night.

William Harding Jackson was only twenty-nine when he died. His sole ambition had been to make Belle Meade the greatest Thoroughbred breeding farm in the world, and he had shown some promise of doing just that. The *Nashville American* said he had won the love of the employees at Belle Meade and was equally admired and loved in Nashville.[20] Unassuming in manner and uniformly courteous, Jackson obviously had matured considerably since his brother-in-law's suicide. He had matched a new seriousness of mind to his amazing knowledge of horses. It was frequently said of him that, if the two or three hundred horses once on the Belle Meade Farm had been turned out into one lot, he could have called every horse by name and given its pedigree for several generations back. His two-and-a-half-year-old son, William, inherited his one-third interest in the 2,091-acre Belle Meade Farm. His sister, Selene Elliston, already owned a one-third interest as did the Catholic Church, although Albert Marks's debts to 147 creditors meant that the church would go away empty-handed.[21]

In West Tennessee an old Jackson family friend observed, "Belle Meade perhaps will never be again what it has been."[22] Annie D.'s father, James B. Richardson, was the administrator of his son-in-law's estate. He knew the place would have to be sold. The problems were daunting: his daughter could not manage Belle Meade; there was no one else left to take over; lawsuits were pending involving Albert Marks's bankrupt estate; and the farm was deeply in debt. Because Richardson did not want to move too fast, his statements to the press were cautious. He simply said that "he was not in a position to give a definite statement just yet, but for the time being the farm would continue to serve the breeding world as of old." He also said the dairy would be continued. Nevertheless, rumors persisted that the farm would be sold or that Mrs. Jackson would run it on a smaller scale.[23] William Harding Jackson's aunt, Mary Jackson, considered buying Belle Meade, but her son-in-law, Hill McAlister, dissuaded her.[24]

Richardson could not wait long. To obtain a desperately needed infusion of cash, he soon decided to sell the Thoroughbreds. He contracted with Fasig-Tipton to sell at Sheepshead Bay the four best stallions—The Commoner, Loyalist, Inspector B, and Huron—as well as sixty-one brood mares, a yearling, and twenty-eight weanlings. Although the sale was extensively advertised, it was a keen disappointment; prices were well under those realized at the sale eleven months earlier. The Commoner was bought in for Annie D. Jackson by Charles P. Gaither of Boston for $15,000. A year earlier The Commoner had been bought in for William Harding Jackson by Edwin S. Gardner for $41,000. Loyalist, bought in for Jackson by Gardner the previous year for $4,000, went to George P. Hendrix of Canada for $1,200. Inspector B was bought by Milton Young for $1,000, while Huron, only fourteen years old, was sold for the depressingly low sum of $200. The other prices were not as bad. One of the highest prices for a yearling was the $1,150 paid for a son of Loyalist and Augusta III. The total proceeds amounted to approximately $63,000.[25]

Richardson next arranged for Walter O. Parmer, a prominent Nashville horseman, to auction off in November at Belle Meade most of the remaining Thoroughbreds, some half-breeds, Shetland ponies, farm stock, vehicles, implements, and so on. About four hundred people showed up on the first morning of the two-day sale. Ninety-four horses, including fifty-four Shetland ponies, were sold. Several of the ponies were bought in for Mrs. Jackson's son, William. The sale's most touching moment came when Uncle Bob entered the ring with the saddle horse he had ridden around the farm for many years, Bob Taylor. Uncle Bob said he had brought Bob Taylor to be sold. Before the old black man could finish, someone suggested that the bidders buy the horse and present him to Uncle Bob. Richardson interjected that a public subscription was unnecessary and immediately made a bid of twenty-five dollars, at which time Parmer announced that the horse was sold. Richardson then said to Green: "He's yours." Uncle Bob's face was wreathed in smiles. Luke Blackburn, the remarkable son of Bonnie Scotland, was booked to be sold, but because of sentiment he was not brought into the ring. On the second day of the sale, twenty-four mules were sold in the morning. Only one went for less than a hundred dollars. That afternoon, plows, tractors, portable engines, mowers, threshers, and binders were sold by another auctioneer who specialized in selling farm equipment.[26]

The dispersal sale brought in about thirteen thousand dollars. It also convinced Nashville newspaper readers that Belle Meade's end was near. Friends and acquaintances speculated about how long Annie D. and her little boy would stay at Belle Meade. William B. Cheatham offered to help. Ellen Marshall, a friend, thought Annie D. would find Will very useful to her if she decided to spend the winter at Belle Meade, "not only for protection but in looking after the animals." Mrs. Marshall said of Will: "Working with horses is the only thing Will does know and he knows that better than any man. He has graduated in the race horse business and has his diploma of bankruptcy duly certified." Philosophically, she added, "Why should men go crazy over horses?"[27] Annie D. stayed at Belle Meade only a few weeks longer. Early in 1904, at her father's insistence, she and her son Billy moved to Lockland, her family's home in East Nashville, where she went into seclusion.[28]

The last family members were gone, so the servants had to leave, too. Uncle Bob's heart was nearly broken. To leave Belle Meade, the only home he had ever known, and to leave the only family he had ever served was asking too much. He pleaded with tears in his eyes to be allowed to spend his remaining days in the cabin by the creek where he had lived so long. With difficulty, the family persuaded him to go with all the rest.

He and his family moved to a little house he already owned on Kayne Avenue.[29]

In the summer of 1904, Annie D. decided to get away for a while. She made plans to take her son to a resort hotel at Narragansett on Rhode Island Sound. When Uncle Bob heard about it, he went to see her to ask a favor. "I may not be here when you come back, Miss Annie," said Bob, "and I want you to say you will take me back to Belle Meade when I die." Mrs. Jackson promised to do what she could.[30] At Narragansett little William was homesick. He missed Belle Meade and his ponies. When R. C. Brien, the longtime superintendent at Belle Meade, heard about Billy's anxieties, he wrote the little boy, assuring him he was not forgotten and that his ponies were in the pony lot nibbling grass. He added that if "Gee and Sam undertake to sell them while you are away, they will have a pretty tough time of it as I have constituted myself my little friend's agent."[31]

By the time his daughter left Nashville, Richardson had set a price on the Belle Meade Farm and was actively seeking prospective buyers. One was Walter O. Parmer, who had handled the dispersal sale the previous November. Parmer was a cofounder of the Highland Park Jockey Club, which controlled racing on the Northern circuit at Fort Erie and Detroit. He had also established his own stud, called Edenwold, a year or two earlier on the Nolensville Pike. Parmer was interested in Belle Meade and made a number of offers to buy the house and a large block of land. He and Richardson never could get together on terms, however. Other potential buyers also looked at the estate but were unwilling to pay Richardson's price.[32]

Finally, at a meeting in New York City, Parmer and Richardson struck a deal. On October 12 Richardson sold to Parmer and several associates, including Edwards Sinclair, The Commoner, a dozen brood mares, and seven weanlings, all belonging to Mrs. Jackson. With the sale of the horses, all going to Parmer's Edenwold Stud, the *Nashville American* announced that Belle Meade's long career as a breeding establishment had ended.[33]

The final sale in November was especially poignant. Some three thousand people were present, many having come by a special train and others by automobile or "with teams." Only five Thoroughbreds were left. The only stallion remaining was Luke Blackburn, the twenty-seven-year-old sire of Proctor Knott, who once brought $30,000 at auction. The horsemen seemed wary of making bids for the old stallion. However, just before he was led back to his stall, he was knocked down to W. H. Allison of Bellevue for $20. Before the old horse was led away, Annie D. had Bonnie Scotland's blanket put on him. The other four Thoroughbreds (three mares and a colt) also went cheap. When the last of the Belle Meade Thoroughbreds was sold, Richardson informed the crowd it was over. The audience accepted the news in silence. To change the subdued mood, Richardson held up a handsome bridle formerly worn by The Commoner and presented it to Mr. Parmer, the owner of the stallion. The dairy utensils, farm equipment, 109 Jersey cows, some bulls, and nine mules were also sold the first day. Some of the prices were "ridiculously low." On the other hand, the cattle netted something over $3,000, a "very satisfactory figure" in Richardson's opinion. The household goods that had belonged to General Harding were not sold. Selene Jackson Elliston had gotten an injunction restricting Richardson from selling any of them.[34]

Later in the week, a splendid array of household furniture, historical relics, and one of the best racehorse libraries in the country were sold. The furniture was of particular interest to those with an eye for the many antiques. They were not disappointed. Mrs. James B. Richardson picked up an inlaid table for $20, while Mrs. Samuel R. Sanford bought a rosewood marbletop table for $27. Mrs. Walker Edwards got two mirrors for $90 and $130. Mrs. Hamilton Parks bought a massive oak hatrack and two mirrors, including a gilded one from Eunice Marks's room. Mrs. E. A. Hale paid $300 for a Steinway grand piano, while Mrs. John E. McCall came away with a carved library table for which she paid $40. A number of gentlemen also made purchases. Edwin Warner bought two carved walnut chairs, and W. J. Cummins outdueled Dan Buntin for a tiger skin rug by paying $300.[35]

For most of Friday, people hauled away everything that had been sold. By evening the house was completely dismantled except for some goods belonging to the Jackson estate. The family was able to buy some of the oil paintings by Henry Stull, Edward Troye, Thomas Scott, and others, and some of the furniture. Mrs. Howell E. Jackson bought a portrait of her husband, a cherry dresser, a washstand, and a music box. Annie D. made quite a few purchases, and Selene Jackson Elliston bought portraits of her parents and a wine press.[36]

An account in the *Nashville American* stated that only General Harding's household effects and a herd of 250 deer remained. There were also seven elk in the park. Frank Avent, secretary of the Tennessee Railroad Commission, made an offer for the deer on behalf of J. M. Avent, the manager of an 18,000-acre hunting preserve in Hardeman and Fayette counties. Richardson's negotiations with Avent fell through, however.[37]

The Nashville public took an interest in the deer. One man suggested that a subscription be held to purchase the deer and turn them loose.[38] Col. Joseph H. Acklen, state game warden, thought it was a good idea and started a movement toward that end. Earlier, Richardson had sold twenty of the deer to Moses H. Cone, a North Carolina cotton merchant who wanted to place them on his estate at Blowing Rock.[39] When an attempt was made to capture about a dozen by driving them into a corral, the frenzied animals dashed themselves against the sides of the enclosure and were either killed or so severely maimed that they had to be destroyed. One big buck sprang into the air and cleared the twelve-foot-high fence "as though it were a small log."[40] Richardson gave up on the idea and called off the deal. He also was determined not to sell the animals for slaughter.[41]

It was not until May 1906, when work began on building roads through the deer park, that the deer were finally bought by the state for six hundred dollars and turned loose. The *Nashville Banner* had taken the lead by contributing twenty-five dollars toward the successful public subscription. Colonel Acklen said that Tennessee's laws to protect deer, which provided a fifty-dollar fine and three months in jail for killing them, would be rigidly enforced.[42]

Acklen acquired one elk and took it to his home, Acklen Hall, in West End Park where it remained for some time as a pet. Finally, dogs severely injured the animal, causing the Acklens to have one of its legs amputated. Because it was no longer possible to keep the elk at his home, Acklen gave it to the inmates at the Tennessee State Prison. They fashioned an artificial leg for the pet animal and kept it for a long time.[43]

Luke Blackburn died in late December 1904. After leaving Belle Meade in November, the old horse steadily grew more feeble, and death came as a relief. Horse fanciers liked to tell that the horse always stood in his paddock in Bellevue facing east toward Belle Meade. In 1925, Luke Blackburn was compared favorably to Man O' War, perhaps the greatest American racehorse of the first half of the twentieth century.[44]

In March 1905, the final dismemberment of Belle Meade took place. Selene Jackson Elliston sold her one-third interest to Nat Baxter, Jr., for

$47,000, agreeing as part of the deal to pay her one-third of the mortgage on Belle Meade amounting to about $75,000.[45] Baxter then sold his interest to James E. Caldwell, who in turn sold it to Robert T. Smith, representing a syndicate composed of Jacob McGavock Dickinson, Jesse M. Overton, J. C. Welling, J. T. Harahan, and Stuyvesant Fish.[46] The same group purchased, also through Smith, the interest of Annie D. Jackson and her son. They also bought from Bishop Thomas S. Byrne all his rights to Belle Meade land formerly owned by Albert Marks. The $45,000 purchase was made through Goodloe Lindsley, trustee for the Belle Meade Land Company, incorporated the previous February to "purchase and hold" properties owned by its trustees. The total cost of acquiring Belle Meade was approximately $185,000.[47]

One of the new owners, Judge Dickinson, had a special love for Belle Meade. Not only was he kin to the Jacksons through his mother, Ann McGavock Dickinson, but he had enjoyed Belle Meade's hospitality on many occasions going back to his childhood. Before the Battle of Nashville, he bivouacked at Belle Meade as a fourteen-year-old Confederate cavalryman in the Army of Tennessee. A few weeks later, he saw Confederate Cavalry Gen. W. H. Jackson in an entirely different environment. The occasion was the wedding of Confederate Gen. Stephen D. Lee at Verona, Mississippi, where Jackson served as Lee's best man. Dickinson—small, young, and impressionable—would never forget the occasion for another reason. Confederate Gen. Abe Buford attended the wedding on crutches, having just been released from the hospital. At the reception, the giant Buford, who was said to weigh 280 pounds, fainted. Young Dickinson, standing beside the general at the time, instinctively jumped out of the way. In doing so, he bumped against a grande dame holding a full glass of punch consisting of parched sweet potatoes and rye flavored with a little captured coffee, causing her to spill it all over her silk dress. Naturally, young Dickinson got the blame and a tongue lashing.[48]

With such a sentimental attachment to Belle Meade and its family, it was no surprise when Jacob McGavock Dickinson, general counsel for the Illinois Central Railroad, bought the house and forty acres from the Belle Meade Land Company. At the same time, May 19, 1906, he also purchased all rights to the waters of the Red House Spring, including pipes, pumps, pumping station, and the reservoir on the hilltop.[49] By early fall, Dickinson's son, Overton, was at Belle Meade supervising

renovations. As soon as they were complete, the younger Dickinson
moved in with his wife and daughter.[50] Meanwhile, the Belle Meade
Land Company, having built and graded four miles of road through the
deer park, offered tracts of from five to twenty-five acres for sale.[51] The
transition was complete. The Belle Meade Plantation, owned for nearly a
century by members of the Harding-Jackson family, passed into new
hands.

Sometime before James B. Richardson relinquished his responsibilities as administrator of William Harding Jackson's estate, he burned all
the farm and horse records without explanation. Even so, their loss did
not erase the accomplishments of the plantation's founder, John Harding,
or of his successors, William Giles Harding and William Hicks Jackson.
Those three men, their supportive and capable wives, and many black
workers—most of whom, unfortunately, remain nameless—cleared,
built, and maintained for nearly a century a plantation and stud that
became known around the world. Such a feat, accomplished through
decades of labor, anguish, and devotion, will likely never be repeated.
The agrarian order of planters and horsemen, like the Hardings and
Jacksons, long ago gave way to a new economic order dominated by
businessmen and urban commerce. To step onto the Belle Meade property today is to step across time and cultural history into a world remote
from our own. But it is a world approachable through both imagination
and historical scholarship, a world that warns with its mistakes and
charms with its recollection of Southern civility and style.

Epilogue

In the fall of 1951, the Association for the Preservation of Tennessee Antiquities (APTA) was organized. Creating the group was the idea of Mrs. Louisa Van Ness, who had recently returned to Nashville from a trip to Richmond, Virginia, where the Association for the Preservation of Virginia Antiquities has its headquarters. A year later, Mrs. Van Ness, first president of APTA, announced that the Meredith Caldwells, owners of the Belle Meade home and twenty-four acres since 1932, had offered APTA an option to buy the historic site. The Caldwells were also considering an offer from the Belle Meade Methodist Church, which proposed to build a new sanctuary there. Two weeks before that announcement, The Nashville Chapter of APTA was created with Mrs. John Keith Maddin, a great-granddaughter of William Giles Harding, as its first president.[1]

In November 1952, the *Nashville Banner* announced the opening of a campaign by APTA to raise funds to buy Belle Meade.[2] Concurrently, Mrs. Guilford Dudley, Sr., a longtime Nashville civic leader and wife of Guilford Dudley, a founder of Life and Casualty Insurance Company, led an effort to persuade the state legislature to appropriate $125,000 for the purchase of the house and twenty-four acres. On March 25, 1953, a bill authorizing the expenditure passed the House of Representatives. The following day the bill was signed into law by Gov. Frank Clement. Belle Meade was then deeded by the state, in trust, to APTA to be preserved "as a monument to the Old South."[3] Since 1953, the mansion, its outbuildings, and the land have been faithfully maintained by the Nashville Chapter of APTA.

In July 1986, APTA's Nashville Chapter participated in a Homecoming 1986 project sponsored by the State of Tennessee. All known descendants of families who once owned Belle Meade were invited to the homecoming, and approximately 130 people attended. At about the same time, APTA's Nashville Chapter began a $1,500,000 capital funds drive to restore the mansion, the carriage house/stable, smokehouse, and dairy. By July 1988, the campaign goal had been exceeded by more than $100,000, and restoration was well underway. By that fall the first floor of the mansion had been carefully restored to appear as it did after the renovation of 1883. The outside of the house was stripped of an inappropriate surface of thick latex paint, repaired, and repainted; inside, storm windows with protection against ultraviolet light were installed. The exterior of the carriage house/stable was also stripped and repainted after rotten wood was replaced, and the first floor of the stable was restored. The Tennessee legislature appropriated funds in August 1988 to replace the roofs on the dairy and the smokehouse. That September, a contract was let to rebuild the 1890s-era porte cochere and upstairs porch, with the state participating in the cost of the project on a two-for-one match with funds raised by the Nashville Chapter of APTA. The Belle Meade Mansion, now beautifully restored, has consistently been the most heavily visited of the eleven sites maintained by APTA. In 1990 nearly one hundred thousand visitors passed through its gates.

In 1985, Larry Wallerstein, a Los Angeles art collector, bought three Southern portraits at a gallery there. The dealer thought that two of the paintings were of a Mr. and Mrs. Archer Cheatham but said that he did not know the name of the man in the third portrait or where the portraits came from. However, the dealer knew that the paintings had been owned by a Mrs. Lipscomb, whose maiden name was Cheatham. Wallerstein launched an effort to identify them. One telephone call he made to museums in the South was to the Tennessee State Museum in Nashville. Greg Anderson, a curatorial assistant there, recognized the Cheatham name and volunteered to help if Wallerstein would send him photographs of the paintings. Anderson immediately identified one of the photographed portraits as that of John Harding. When Anderson was in high school, he had worked part-time as a docent at the Belle Meade Mansion and was familiar with the Harding family.[4] Sue Olsen, the Belle Meade director, and Irene Jackson Wills, president of APTA's Nashville Chapter, also compared the pictures of the California portraits with pictures and portraits of various Harding family members. They concluded that the portraits were of John, Susannah, and William Giles Harding. After their identifications were confirmed by Harding descendants, Ellen Wills Martin of Washington, D.C., a great-great-granddaughter of General Harding, bought the portraits and, after having them restored, gave them to the Nashville Chapter of APTA. The Washington Cooper portraits of John Harding, Susannah Shute Harding, and William Giles Harding now hang on the walls at Belle Meade for the first time since the 1840s.

The story of Belle Meade would not be complete without explanations of what happened to the family members and the farm after 1906. It also seems appropriate to add comments on the legacy of the blooded horses that brought international fame to the Belle Meade Stud, and on the development of the city of Belle Meade and Percy Warner Park on the site of the plantation.

William Harding Jackson's young widow, Annie Davis Jackson, remarried. Her second husband was Maxwell Stevenson of Hempstead, New York. Annie D. and Maxwell had no children. Annie D. and William's son, William, whom Uncle Bob called "the little Governor," was educated at St. Mark's School in Southboro, Massachusetts, Princeton, and Harvard. Admitted to the New York bar in 1932, he practiced law in New York City for several years before becoming a successful investment banker. After William Jackson died in Tucson, Arizona, in 1971, his remains were brought to Belle Meade. His funeral services were held in the home where he was the last member of the Harding-Jackson family to be born and where he and his mother were the last members of the family to reside.[5]

William Robert Elliston lived in London for some time after deserting Selene in 1900. A representative of a rifle manufacturer, he lived at a fast pace and numbered among his friends the Duke of Windsor.[6] Elliston later moved to California, where he committed suicide in 1909. His remains were returned to Nashville for burial at Mt. Olivet Cemetery.[7]

After leaving Belle Meade, Selene Jackson Elliston and her son, Billy, moved a number of times. During 1905 and 1906, they lived at Nashville's Tulane Hotel. Afterward, they briefly lived at 318 22nd Avenue North, before settling in a small house at 2007 Murphy Avenue. There, Selene employed several family servants to look after the house and care for her son. Her furnishings included some of the furniture and paintings from Belle Meade. One summer, she went to Monterey, California with Mary and Annie Demoville, who had been asked to look after her by Eunice shortly before she died. Tragically, Selene was estranged from her family. When any of them called, she instructed her servants to say that she was not at home. Her aunt, Mary Jackson, who realized that Selene was mentally ill, would put her foot in the door and go in anyway.[8] In 1910, Selene executed a new will, leaving her estate to her son. In it, she appointed her godfather, the Right Reverend John B. Morris, then the Roman Catholic bishop of Arkansas, as guardian for

William during his minority.[9] By the fall of 1913, she was so addicted to narcotics that one of her servants telephoned her first cousin, Louise Jackson McAlister. Mrs. McAlister and George Parks, a black servant, came and took Selene to Stevens Sanitarium, where she died several weeks later. Selene's remains were taken to West Meade, the home of her aunt, who had unsuccessfully tried to help her. Selene's funeral services were conducted by Dr. Carey E. Morgan, Mrs. Howell E. Jackson's pastor at the Vine Street Christian Church. Her remains were buried, at her request, in the Jackson family lot at Mt. Olivet Cemetery.[10] Selene's son, Billy, who attended Culver Military Academy, grew up to marry twice and have four children. He physically resembled his father, having the same graceful walk and slender build.

General Jackson's other daughter, Eunice, and her husband, Albert Marks, had only one child, Albert Marks, Jr., who died in infancy. Consequently, that line of the Jackson family ended with Eunice's death in 1901.

When Jacob McGavock Dickinson bought Belle Meade in 1906,[11] he used it primarily for entertaining. Although he never resided there, his son, J. Overton Dickinson, lived in the mansion with his family until 1909. Not long after the Dickinsons moved in, Uncle Bob Green died. Jacob McGavock Dickinson remembered Uncle Bob's last wish and granted permission for the faithful servant to be buried at Belle Meade. There, on November 10, 1906, friends, both black and white, gathered around Green's grave as the pastor of the Harding Pike Church held a brief service. While the choir sang "Nearer My God to Thee," his remains were lowered to his last resting place in the servants' cemetery at Belle Meade, the home of his heart. Howell E. Jackson, Jr., represented the family as a pallbearer.[12]

Historic Belle Meade, which had been the scene of so many brilliant gatherings in the past, added another notable event in May 1908 when Judge and Mrs. Dickinson and young Mr. and Mrs. Overton Dickinson entertained Secretary of War William Howard Taft and the members of the Tennessee Bar Association, their wives, and friends with a barbecue. The sounds of a dinner bell greeted the nearly two hundred guests as they arrived at the Belle Meade station on a special train provided by the NC & StL Railroad.[13] Taft, who stayed at Belle Meade, gave the principal address that evening at the twenty-seventh annual meeting of the Tennessee Bar Association at Nashville's Vendome Theatre.[14]

JACOB MCGAVOCK DICKINSON (left) and WILLIAM HOWARD TAFT at Belle
Meade. Collection of the National Park Service, William Howard Taft Historic
Site, Cincinnati

Early in 1909, Dickinson turned down an offer from William S. Bransford to buy Belle Meade, but he agreed to sell to Bransford's nephew, Johnson Bransford, some lots in the deer park and the Red House field, including the ever-flowing Red House Spring. In September 1909, Overton Dickinson's wife, Helen, died of complications resulting from the birth of her second daughter, also named Helen. Because of that family tragedy, the mansion became "a house of sorrow" to Jacob McGavock Dickinson. He was also worried about his son Overton's poor health, resulting from injuries caused by his horse falling on him.[15] Consequently, Dickinson sold the place to James O. Leake, a well-known Nashville capitalist, whose wife, Bessie Lea Leake, was Judge John Overton's great-granddaughter. Leake bought the property, including four hundred acres, on October 19, 1909, for $110,000.[16]

During the six years that he and his family lived at Belle Meade, Mr. Leake used the carriage house as a garage for his Duryea touring car.[17] Following the death of their nine-year-old-daughter, Esther, from diphtheria in 1916, Mr. and Mrs. Leake felt uncomfortable living there. Leake sold the house to Luke Lea, Bessie Leake's first cousin, who, in turn, offered the house and two tracts of seven and fifteen acres for sale at a public auction that May.[18]

Leake owned only one hundred acres of Belle Meade when he sold the property to Colonel Lea. Earlier, he had sold three hundred acres to W. S. H. Armistead, who also purchased the other Belle Meade tract of 1,255 acres and all the associated rights-of-way from the Belle Meade Land Company. To make those purchases, Armistead and some associates created the Belle Meade Company with capital stock of $200,000. Armistead deeded the Belle Meade farm property to the new company, which assumed responsibility for making payments to Leake and the Belle Meade Land Company.[19]

Contracts were let, by the Belle Meade Company, to cut a road from Harding Pike to the Lower Franklin Road, three miles away, and to pave what would soon become Jackson Boulevard from Harding Pike to the newly cut road, today's Belle Meade Boulevard. Contracts were also let to build a road from Belle Meade Boulevard through the old Chickering farm to the Lower Franklin Road, a distance of one and a half miles.[20] The roadways for the subdivision to be known as Belle Meade Park were laid out by Ossian Cole Simonds, who was considered America's premier cemetery landscape architect.[21]

The Belle Meade Company experienced financial difficulties almost immediately, which resulted in Luke Lea, Telfair Hodgson, and David Shepherd buying out the interests of Armistead and C. B. Horn. From that point onward, Luke Lea was the controlling stockholder in the Belle Meade Company. In December 1910, he proposed to the Nashville Street Railway and Light Company that it construct a four-mile-long single-car track from the end of its Broadway and West End line at Wilson Boulevard to the present entrance of Percy Warner Park on Belle Meade Boulevard. Percy Warner, president of the Railway and Light Company, agreed to the proposal, under which Lea agreed to underwrite the entire cost of both the streetcar line and a macadam boulevard twenty feet wide on either side of the car line.[22]

Between 1911 and 1914, during which time Lea directed operations from Washington, where he was a U.S. senator, the Belle Meade Company remained active. In 1911, the company bought the 505-acre high pasture from Mrs. Howell E. Jackson, who was still living at West Meade.[23] Sixteen years later, the high pasture became the heart of an 868-acre tract that Colonel and Mrs. Lea deeded to the city of Nashville for a public park.[24] When Percy Warner, Lea's father-in-law, died a few months later, Lea asked the Park Board to name the park for Warner, who had been its chairman. The board unanimously voted to name it Percy Warner Park. Lea's company also sold lots in Belle Meade Park to a steadily increasing number of people. A water pipe laid from Charlotte Pike to the deer park enabled Belle Meade Park residents to tap into city water.[25]

Colonel Lea made an equally strategic move when he convinced the Nashville Golf and Country Club in 1913 to accept a gift of land in the Belle Meade Company's new subdivision as a site for a new club and golf course. Construction of the new clubhouse began in 1914 and was completed in 1916. Building the eighteen-hole golf course took considerably longer; it was not completed until 1922.[26] A problem for the designers was that an old Harding family cemetery, established about 1835, was situated in the middle of the proposed course. That was solved by disinterring the caskets of Giles and Charlotte Harding and eight others and moving them to a new Harding lot in Spring Hill Cemetery.[27]

Colonel Lea held the Belle Meade house and the twenty-four adjoining acres only a short while. He sold the place to Walter O. Parmer in 1916 for fifty-five thousand dollars. Parmer, who had been the auctioneer

SOUTHWEST NASHVILLE (1984), showing the acreage covered by Belle Meade Plantation (ca. 1884). Courtesy of T.V.A.

at the 1903 dispersal sale, moved his Edenwold Stud to Belle Meade and began to revive the Belle Meade stock farm.[28] Before moving in that fall, he made some renovations, including installing paneled partition walls and windows in the heretofore open breezeway joining the main house to the kitchen house.[29]

For a while before the United States entered World War I, Parmer also leased the West Meade Farm. During that period, he sold a few of his yearlings each autumn at Saratoga, New York.[30] Sometime after the United States entered the war, he shipped all his Thoroughbred horses to Lexington, Kentucky, where they were sold at public auction. Then he let the West Meade lease go. Following Parmer's death in 1932, the Belle Meade Mansion was sold to Mr. and Mrs. Meredith Caldwell. They lived there for twenty-one years before selling the property to the state of Tennessee.[31]

The residential development of Belle Meade by the Belle Meade Company received enormous boosts from the construction of new streets and water mains, the Nashville Golf and Country Club, and a streetcar line that put people at the end of the line only forty minutes from downtown. Soon, prominent Nashvillians, using outstanding architects, were building homes throughout Belle Meade Park. At least two of those homes were built with stone from the Belle Meade quarry. In 1916, Miss Ida E. Hood and Miss Susan L. Heron, founders of Belmont Collegiate and Preparatory School, today's Belmont College, built a large home named Braeburn overlooking Richland Creek on Deer Park Drive.[32] Today, the home is the residence of Chancellor and Mrs. Joe B. Wyatt of Vanderbilt University. Another house built of Belle Meade stone was a smaller, two-story home built by George A. Livingstone, the golf professional at the Belle Meade Club. Some of the stones in his house came from the quarry on the present fourth hole of the golf course; others were picked up from the fairways and hauled to the building site in wheelbarrows.[33] A third home with direct ties to the Belle Meade Plantation is a frame house at 506 East Bellevue. According to its present owner, Melinda Sneed Brink, the original portion of the house was built in the 1890s by General Jackson and used as the house for the deer park's gatekeeper.[34]

In 1925, a group of young parents who had moved into Belle Meade Park appealed to the superintendent of the Davidson County Schools to build a grade school in the Belle Meade area. The school system responded favorably to the idea and negotiated with both Luke Lea and Walter Parmer for an appropriate location. A site owned by Parmer was acquired, and by November 1927, a small one-room clapboard building well back from Leake Avenue was ready to receive students. The school was named for Mr. Parmer. A modern brick building containing four classrooms replaced the original school by September 1928.[35]

The city of Belle Meade was established in 1938 when the residents of Belle Meade Park voted by a margin of more than two to one to incorporate. A year later William Jackson, who was not related to the Belle Meade Jacksons, made the first wrought iron street signs for the newly incorporated municipality. As a salute to the stud, his design included outlines of Belle Meade Thoroughbreds.[36] Fifty years later, the Tennessee Historical Commission and the Nashville Chapter of APTA erected an historical marker at the intersection of Deer Park Drive and Belle Meade Boulevard to commemorate the history of the deer park.

The city of Belle Meade is, and has been almost since its inception, Nashville's premier residential area. Its streets carry the names of such distinguished Belle Meade stallions as Clarendon, Enquirer, Iroquois, Luke Blackburn, and Bonnie Scotland. Paddock Place is located where paddocks once stood, and deer and elk once roamed where Deer Park Circle and Deer Park Drive now curve. Harding Place, Harding Road, Page Road, and Chickering Road all recall early days when those families were friends and neighbors, and Belle Meade Boulevard cuts through the heart of the old plantation. In Edwin Warner Park,[37] the Iroquois Steeplechase annually reminds thousands of Middle Tennesseans that Iroquois was the first American-bred, American-owned horse to win the English Derby. The bell that traditionally has been rung to signify the start of the final steeplechase race once rang at the Belle Meade Plantation.[38]

West Meade was the last of the Belle Meade Plantation landholdings to be retained by the family of General Harding. Mary Harding Jackson, though not blessed with her sister Selene's beauty, had an indomitable will. She and her three children, Elizabeth Jackson Buckner, Louise Jackson McAlister, and Harding Alexander Jackson, paid off their mortgage and gained a clear title to West Meade in 1909. A few years later, Mrs. Jackson's health began to fail. When she died at West Meade in 1913, Dr. Carey Morgan, her minister at Vine Street Christian Church, conducted her funeral service. She lived a relatively long life of sixty-three years, which was almost exactly as long as Justice Jackson lived. In her will she left her three children West Meade, her one-half interest in the Jackson Building, and her five-sixths interest in six houses on Fifth Avenue North directly behind the Jackson Building. Among her bequests was a thousand-dollar gift to Transylvania College in Lexington, Kentucky, to complete and furnish two rooms for divinity students. Mrs. Jackson asked that the rooms be named for the two places she loved best in all the world—Belle Meade and West Meade.[39]

It was not until 1944 that Mary and Howell Jackson's children sold West Meade to a group of investors, headed by E. A. Wortham and Brownlee O. Currey. Those Nashville businessmen had incorporated a company under the name West Meade Farms, Inc., to take title to the property they acquired for $175,000. At the time of the sale, the purchasers announced plans for the development of part of the 1,750-acre tract, with the remainder to be cut up into small farms. They soon sold 50 acres of the farm and the house to Mrs. Ronald L. Voss.[40] West Meade remains in her possession today. The small farms have long since disappeared in favor of the post-World War II homes comprising today's West Meade section of Nashville.

Belle Meade should be remembered as the home of the American Thoroughbred. Although the Belle Meade silks of solid maroon remained dormant after the breakup of the Belle Meade Stud in 1904, they reentered the racing world some years later under the guidance of Howell E. Jackson III of Bull Run Stud, Middleburg, Virginia.[41] The grandson of Judge Howell E. Jackson, Howell III was a trustee of the New York Racing Association and the National Museum of Racing at Saratoga Springs. He raced the Belle Meade colors on tracks in the United States and Europe for many years, gaining additional fame. After his death in 1973, his widow, Dorothy Patterson Jackson, officially retired the colors, the oldest registered racing silks in America, ending a dynasty of 150 years. At the National Museum of Racing, there are portraits of Howell E. Jackson III and General William Hicks Jackson. Also hanging there are the Belle Meade racing silks and portraits of five Belle Meade horses: Priam, Vandal, Iroquois, George Kinney, and Proctor Knott. Though his portrait is not included at the museum, Luke Blackburn, a sixth Belle Meade horse, is a posthumous member of the museum's Hall of Fame.[42]

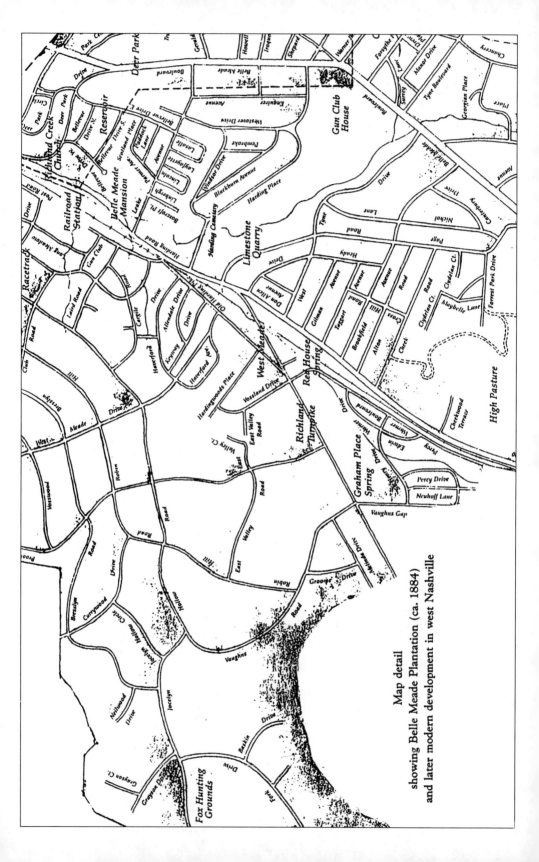

Map detail
showing Belle Meade Plantation (ca. 1884)
and later modern development in west Nashville

Abbreviations

Originals of many unpublished documents cited in the notes and once owned by members of the Harding and Jackson families are part of the Southern Historical Collection (SHC) at the University of North Carolina, Chapel Hill, or in the Jean and Alexander Heard Library at Vanderbilt University, Nashville, or the Tennessee State Library and Archives (TSLA), Nashville. Copies of those documents in SHC are available at TSLA. When copies rather than originals have been consulted because of convenience of location, the library's abbreviation is included with the citation, along with that library's cataloging notation. Where no depository is given in the note, the reader should refer to the abbreviation table below or to the Bibliography for the primary location.

AJP:	Andrew Johnson Papers (unpublished), Library of Congress
APTA:	Association for the Preservation of Tennessee Antiquities
BHAPTA:	Sherrill Jane Kilgore, "Brief History of the Association for the Preservation of Tennessee Antiquities and its Belle Meade Historic Site," Master's thesis, Middle Tennessee State University, 1981
CBRC:	Civilian and Business Records of the Confederacy, National Archives
CDEP:	Collins D. Elliott Papers, Tennessee State Library and Archives
CMR:	Confederate Military Records, National Archives
DCCM:	Davidson County, Tennessee, Court Minutes
DCCR:	Davidson County, Tennessee, Court Records
DCD:	Davidson County, Tennessee, Deeds
DCMR:	Davidson County, Tennessee, Marriage Records
DCRWI:	Davidson County, Tennessee, Records of Wills and Inventories
GCC:	Grover Cleveland Collection, Library of Congress
GCRDW:	Goochland County, Virginia, Record of Deeds, Wills, etc., Goochland
GPO:	Government Printing Office
HEJP:	Howell E. Jackson Papers, Tennessee State Library and Archives
HFP:	Hayes Family Papers, Tennessee State Library and Archives
HFR:	Harding Family Records (privately held)
HJFR:	Harding-Jackson Family Records (privately held)

HJP:	Harding-Jackson Papers, Southern Historical Collection, University of North Carolina
HMP:	Hill McAlister Papers, Tennessee State Library and Archives
IGHP:	Isham G. Harris Papers, Tennessee State Library and Archives
JAHL:	Jean and Alexander Heard Library, Vanderbilt University
JFR:	Dr. Alexander Jackson Family Records (privately held)
JHL:	John Harding's Ledger, Harding-Jackson Papers, Southern Historical Collection, University of North Carolina
JMDP:	Jacob McGavock Dickinson Papers, Tennessee State Library and Archives.
MFBT:	Letters and Telegrams of the Military and Financial Board of Tennessee, Tennessee State Library and Archives
ROQG:	Records of the Office of Quartermaster General, National Archives
RPM:	Records of the Provost Marshal, National Archives
TMT:	Transcript Middle Tennessee, 1892 Tennessee Supreme Court Case
TSLA:	Tennessee State Library and Archives, Nashville
WCCM:	Williamson County, Tennessee, Court Minutes, Franklin
WCD:	Williamson County, Tennessee, Deeds
WCRW:	Williamson County, Tennessee, Record of Wills
WGHL:	William Giles Harding Ledger, Harding-Jackson Papers, Southern Historical Collection, University of North Carolina
WHJP:	William Hicks Jackson Papers, Tennessee State Library and Archives
WHL:	William Hague Letters, Nashville Room, Ben West Library, Nashville
WHTC:	William Howard Taft Collection, University of Tennessee, Knoxville

Notes

Chapter 1. Dunham's Station

1. W. W. Clayton, *History of Davidson County, Tennessee*, 412; Josiah S. Moore, ed., *Annals of Henrico Parish*, Addenda, 78; Agreement between Sarah, Giles, and William Harding, and will of William Harding, GCRDW, bk. 10:376-77.

2. Clayton, *History of Davidson County*, 412.

3. "British Mercantile Claims, 1775-1803," 73.

4. GCRDW, bk. 1:27, 37; bk. 17:45, 84. Sarah LaForce Harding was a daughter of Sarah and René LaForce of Manakin Town, Virginia. Dr. LaForce, a physician, was a French Protestant who came to America during the reign of King William III. He prospered in Virginia and left his descendants a considerable estate in his will.

5. Mary Kegley, "The Big Fort," 16-17.

6. Suzanne Burrow, G. Fred Hawkins, and Joe P. Distretti, "The Old Island Road," 17.

7. See Samuel D. Smith, "Fort Southwest Point, A New View," 17; Joe C. Guild, *Old Times in Tennessee with Historical, Personal and Political Scraps and Sketches*, 93.

8. DCD, bk. E:54, 57.

9. Microfilm records, miscellaneous files, bk. 7:H-18, TSLA.

10. Giles Harding's oldest son, George, never moved to Tennessee. George married Elizabeth Baker in 1798. They lived in Goochland County, Virginia, until 1814 when they and their children moved to Powhatan County, Virginia, where George died in 1822 (*Richmond Enquirer*, Sept. 24, 1822). Robert Page was married to Giles Harding's oldest daughter, Sarah.

11. DCD, bk. G:189, bk. O:145; Paul Clements, *A Past Remembered* 1:36.

12. DCMR, bk. 1 (1789-1837): 76. Thomas Harding died in 1805, leaving a widow and nine children (DCCM, July Session, 1805, p. 212).

13. DCMR, bk. 1:57; Clayton, *History of Davidson County*, 412.

14. James Veech, *The Monongahela of Old or Historic Sketches of Southwest Pennsylvania to the Year 1800*, 90-93.

15. King George III's proclamation of 1763 prohibited settlement west of the crest of the Appalachian Mountains (Veech, *The Monongahela of Old*, 90-93).

16. Fayette County, Pa., Deeds, bk. A:38, 130. The land the Shutes occupied in Pennsylvania was part of the vast area ceded to the English by the Chiefs of the Six Nations at Fort Stanwix, N.Y., on Nov. 5, 1768 (Franklin Ellis, *History of Fayette County, Pennsylvania*, 64).

17. Memoirs of Philip Shute, in "Buckner and Wills Families," p. 15R, HJFR collection of the author. Philip and Elizabeth's son William, born Dec. 26, 1768, was thought by the family to be the first white child born west of the Allegheny Mountains (Fayette County Courthouse Records, Uniontown, Pa.; Shute Family Records, collection of Mrs. Grady W. Leach, Jr.).

18. Memoirs of Philip Shute, p. 15R, HJFR collection of the author. See also DCD, bk. C:47; Genevieve W. Bartlett, *Forefathers and Descendants of Willard & Genevieve Wilson Bartlett and of Allied Families*, 184). Shute named his place Belle Meade (beautiful meadow).

19. DCMR, bk. 1:57; DCD, bk. G:192.

20. North Carolina Land Grant #173, bk. 7-G:91, 92, TSLA.

21. A. W. Putnam, *History of Middle Tennessee*, 127. French Lick was a large salt lick at the site of Fort Nashborough. In 1784, Nashborough's name was changed to Nashville, local leaders preferring the French suffix to the English.

22. J. G. M. Ramsey, *The Annals of Tennessee to the End of the Eighteenth Century*, 483, 597.

23. From about 1795 to 1800, Col. Benjamin J. Joslin, a pioneer Indian fighter, occupied Dunham's Station on a lease or rental basis. "Old B. J." may have used the station as a base for his mail-carrying operations to Natchez (Clayton, *History of Davidson County*, 75; Herschel Gower, "Belle Meade: Queen of Tennessee Plantations," 205).

24. Sherrill Jane Kilgore, BHAPTA, 10.

25. DCD, bk. G:192.

26. Ibid., bk. L:354. Following Giles Harding, Jr.'s, death in 1843, his family sold the nine-hundred-acre plantaton to Maj. Daniel Graham, a native North Carolinian, who became a good friend of John Harding's son, William Giles (DCD, bk. 7:308). According to A. E. McClanahan, a subsequent owner of the property, the Giles Harding house burned about 1905 (Albert Ganier notebook, copy, collection of the author).

27. Clayton, *History of Davidson County*, 412; Robert Gray, *The McGavock Family*, 19; Mount Olivet Cemetery Records.

28. HFR collection of Mrs. James Balch; Henry Glassie, "The Types of the Southern Mountain Cabin," 345.

29. DCCM, Oct. 1796, bk. B:362, bk. C:1.

30. Clayton, *History of Davidson County*, 322; DCD, bk. I:492. In the Dillahunty-McFadden graveyard, which was located in a field between present-day Nichol Lane and West Tyne Boulevard in Nashville, Dillahunty's tombstone read, "John Dillahunty, Dec. 8, 1728-Feb. 9, 1816; was for 60 years a minister of the gospel, Baptist order." Although there is no evidence of the graveyard today, the author played around it as a child. See also Jeannette Tillotson Acklen, comp., *Tennessee Records, Tombstone Inscriptions and Manuscripts Historical and Biographical*, 169.

31. Clayton, *History of Davidson County*, 412.

32. *Tennessee Clarion*, Jan. 19, 1818; DCCR, July Session, 1806. The purchase of Ben, plus others bought between 1804 and 1818, refutes the claim that all the slaves John Harding left his son William Giles were the result of natural increase (DCRWI, bk. 3 [1805-1811]: 6; DCD, bk. H:53).

33. DCCM, July session, 1806, p. 6; WCCM, 1806, p. 214; DCRWI, bk. 34:105 ; DCCM, July session, 1810, p. 105.

34. William S. Speer, ed. and comp., *Sketches of Prominent Tennesseans*, 3.

35. Clayton, *History of Davidson County*, 425.

36. Ibid. 181.

37. Edith Rucker Whitney, *Pioneers of Davidson County*, 60.

38. *Evening Herald* (Nashville), Jan. 9, 1890.

39. DCCM, Jan. session, 1816, p. 642; July session, 1816, p. 658. The court minutes of that year show that Harding lost ten days of work to jury duty.

40. Clayton, *History of Davidson County*, 425.

41. Guild, *Old Times in Tennessee*, 44-45.

42. *Nashville Banner*, May 11, 1881.

43. DCD, bk. O:145. This deed was not filed until Nov. 28, 1820. David Morris Harding married Fanny Davis, the youngest daughter of John and Dorcas Davis, in 1816. At an early

date, he bought his brother Tom's interest in Oak Hill and ultimately enlarged the farm to nearly one thousand acres (DCD, bk. 9:212).

44. DCD, bk. G:486, 569; bk. I:250, 407, 409, 413. Harding also purchased three land grants in Hickman County between 1808 and 1813: Tennessee Land Grants 698, 4746, and 4750 (bk. A:545, bk. G:41, TSLA); Hickman County (Centerville), Tenn., Deeds, bk. G:213.

45. DCD, bk. L:581, bk. M:356, 364; bk. N:58, 76; bk. Q:455, bk. R:392. The county road connecting these parcels was later named Richland Pike and is today known as Harding Road.

46. *Democratic Clarion and Tennessee Gazette* (Nashville), Mar. 3, 1818.

47. Ibid., Jan. 18, 1818.

48. "Recollections of Memucan Hunt Howard," 56. Benjamin Fooy (1759-1823) came to North America from Holland as a young man. Expelled from Mobile by the Spanish, he lived among the Chickasaw and later became an interpeter in their negotiations with the Spanish. When Spain ceded all of its claims to the United States on the east side of the Mississippi above the 31st parallel, Fooy moved across the river and built a home at Hopefield Point, where he lived the rest of his life (James Roper, "Benjamin Fooy and the Spanish Forts of San Fernando and Campo de la Esperanza," 41-64).

49. "Recollections of Memucan Hunt Howard," 55; Clayton, *History of Davidson County,* 249.

50. JHL, box 1, vol. 2, 1820, inside front cover, TSLA. This collection is a principal source of information about Belle Meade. It includes about five hundred items covering the years 1819-1911: accounts dealing with the raising, feeding, and boarding of horses; plantation operations; and three generations of family and business correspondence. Nine of the sixteen volumes of accounts cover the 1819-30 period when John Harding was master of the plantation.

Chapter 2. From Middletown to McSpadden's Bend

1. JHL, box. 1, vol. 2, 1820.

2. W. G. Harding to William Oliver Harding, Mar. 3, 1875, HFR letters collection of Jack Harding.

3. W. W. Clayton, *History of Davidson County, Tennessee,* 267. John Harding's interest in education preceded Amanda's admission to the Nashville Female Academy. In 1811, Harding was one of three men named by the State Legislature to the Board of Trustees of Robertson Academy (*A Bicentennial Chronicle* [booklet], 118-19).

4. CDEP, box 1, folders 2, 9; JHL, box 1, folder 3, TSLA.

5. Jane H. Thomas, *Old Days In Nashville, Tennessee,* 33-34.

6. Thomas Hutchinson, ed., *Xenophontis De Cyri Institutione,* inscribed with "Wm. G. Harding, C[umberland] College," collection of Mr. and Mrs. Robert Ring, Franklin, Tenn.

7. Clayton, *History of Davidson County,* 419.

8. An 1825 prospectus announced the relocation of the academy from Norwich, Vermont, to Middletown, Connecticut. Because the prospectus indicated no students were from Tennessee, it seems likely that Harding enrolled when the school reopened in Middletown in August 1825 (Walter Hill Crockett, *Vermont, The Green Mountain State,* 531, 535; William A. Ellis, ed. and comp., *Norwich University, 1819-1911: Her History, Her Graduates, Her Roll of Honor* 1:7).

9. *In Memoriam, Gen. William G. Harding* (booklet), 6; List of Cadets of the American Literary, Scientific and Military Academy during the 1820s, HJFR collection of the author.

10. Ellis, *Norwich University* 1:44-45.

11. Ibid., 45-46.

12. Samuel Houston to W. G. Harding, Feb. 6, 1827, HJP, JAHL.

13. Ellis, *Norwich University* 1:51.

14. *In Memoriam, Gen. William G. Harding* (booklet), 20.

15. Charles H. Dickinson to W. G. Harding, Dec. 20, 1826, HJP, box 4, folder 4, TSLA. Cumberland College was renamed the University of Nashville in 1826 (John E. Windrow, ed., *Peabody and Alfred Leland Crabb*, 32-33).

16. Francis McGavock to W. G. Harding, Mar. 10, 1827, HJP, box 3, folder 9, TSLA; DCD, bk. S:787, 789.

17. Albert W. Dunbar to W. G. Harding, Oct. 25, 1827, HJP, box, 4, folder 4, TSLA; Ellis, *Norwich University* 1:20; 2:105. Another former Middletown cadet who transferred to the University of Nashville was Van P. Winder of Winder Plantation, Houma, Louisiana. Winder later studied law in Nashville under Felix Grundy and in 1828 married Grundy's daughter, Martha Ann. Twenty years later, Van and Martha Ann Winder's daughter, Caroline, married John McGavock, a brother of William Giles Harding's wife, Elizabeth McGavock Harding (Winder Campbell, interview with the author; see also Robert Gray, *The McGavock Family*, 23).

18. Ellis, *Norwich University* 2:263.

19. Malcolm D. McLean, ed. and comp., *Papers Concerning Robertson's Colony in Texas* 1:xli-xlvi. Among the other petitioners were Sam Houston, six Robertsons, Daniel A. Dunham, William Harding, John and James Overton, Dr. James Roane, Hugh Roland, and Wilkins Tannehill. See also Ellis, *Norwich University* 2:263.

20. George D. Norris to W. H. Jackson, Dec. 1, 1888, WHJP. Horatio Seymour (1810-86) twice served as governor of New York. In the 1868 Democratic Convention in New York, he was nominated as a candidate for president of the United States. In that election, Seymour was defeated by U. S. Grant. Charles D. Drake (1811-92) studied law in his hometown of Cincinnati after graduating from "the Academy" in 1827. Drake later moved to St. Louis, where he became a prominent attorney. He served as U. S. senator from Missouri from 1867 until 1870, resigning to accept the appointment as chief justice of the U. S. Court of Claims, an office he held until 1889. Andrew B. Huntington (1805-51) moved from Connecticut to Baltimore after graduating from "the Academy" in 1827. He was in the mercantile business there (Ellis, *Norwich University* 2:103-4, 146, 215-16).

21. Clayton, *History of Davidson County*, 419.

22. Ellis, *Norwich University* 1:16.

23. JHL, box 2, vol. 7, TSLA.

24. Washington J. Bennett to W. G. Harding, Aug. 5, 1828, HJP, box 4, folder 2, TSLA.

25. R. T. Rodgers to W. G. Harding, Oct. 27, 1828, HJP, box 5, folder 7, TSLA.

26. Ellis, *Norwich University* 1:65.

27. William S. Speer, ed. and comp., *Sketches of Prominent Tennesseans*, 1; JHL, box 2, vol. 8, TSLA.

28. JHL, box 1, vols. 1, 4, TSLA.

29. William H. Bumpous, interview with the author.

30. JHL, box 1, vols. 2, 3, 4, TSLA.

31. Robert E. Corlew, *A History of Dickson County*, 60.

32. Sherrill Jane Kilgore, BHAPTA, 34.

33. Roberta Seawell Brandau, ed., *History of Homes and Gardens of Tennessee*, 128.

34. Carrie Eliza Ewing to Mary Harding Ragland, HFR letters collection of Mr. and Mrs. William A. Perkins, Jr.

35. John Hervey, *Racing in America, 1665-1865* 1:233-35; 2:61, 67.

36. Imported Thoroughbreds such as Boaster are often identified as being imported by the abbreviation *imp.* appearing before their names in print, e.g., "imp. Boaster."

37. JHL, vol. 1, 1819, pp. 3, 34, TSLA. William Carroll was governor of Tennessee (1821-27; 1829-35). Ralph E. W. Earl was a portrait painter who lived at the Hermitage for many years and was known for his fondness for painting Andrew Jackson. Felix Grundy was a noted criminal lawyer, a member of the Tennessee House of Representatives, a United States senator, and attorney general during President Van Buren's administration. Sam Houston was governor of Tennessee (1827-29) before gaining international fame as hero of San Jacinto, president of the Republic of Texas, United States senator, and governor of Texas.

38. James Douglas Anderson, *Making the American Thoroughbred*, 57.

39. Ibid., 63; Roger Mortimer, *The History of the Derby Stakes*, 33.

40. *Nashville Clarion*, June 13, 1821.

41. Anderson, *Making the American Thoroughbred*, 63; *Nashville Gazette*, Mar. 21, 1823; JHL, box 1, vol. 7, TSLA.

42. Anderson, *Making the American Thoroughbred*, 63.

43. JHL, box 1, vol. 7, TSLA; *Nashville Republican*, Feb. 21, 1835.

44. Anderson, *Making the American Thoroughbred*, 39-40.

45. Bluford E. Edwards, interview with the author; *Daily American* (Nashville), Apr. 24, 1880.

46. *Nashville Banner*, Aug. 8, 1920; *Nashville American*, Mar. 12, 1899.

47. JHL, box 2, vols. 7, 8, TSLA.

48. DCD, bk. I:250, bk N:76, bk. Q:504, bk. Y:391.

49. DCD, bk. O:356, 367; bk. Q:193, 269, 515; bk. R:267, 290, 393, 395, 458, 616; bk. S:81, bk. Y:426, bk. 1:612, bk. 6:365; Middle Tennessee Land Grants #4842, 8055, 8087, 12431, TSLA. In 1835 John Harding was sufficiently interested in the Sams Creek area, where he owned 650 acres, to become a trustee of the congregation of Christians who formed that year to worship at Sams Creek Meeting House. That fall, Harding and two other trustees bought two acres of land for the congregation.

50. Clayton, *History of Davidson County*, 204.

51. John Wooldridge, ed., *History of Nashville, Tennessee*, 102.

52. John Harding's account book, page designated "Number 2 wt. of bails[sic] of cotton delivered to Josiah Nichol," account book page designated "number of bails maid [sic] for Moses Norvell," and "Cotton Receipts," listed in the back of the account book, JHL, box 1, vol. 6, TSLA.

53. DCMR, bk. 1:95.

54. DCD, bk. R:395.

55. Leona Taylor Aiken, *Donelson, Tennessee, Its History and Landmarks*, 213. Joseph and Elizabeth Clay may have named their home for the historic Belair Stud fifteen miles west of Annapolis, Md. Clay's most noted stallion, Sir William, was the get of the dam Bellona, by Bellair, a celebrated stallion owned by John Taylor III, son-in-law of Gov. Benjamin Ogle, owner of Belair Stud (Hervey, *Racing In America* 2:7).

56. Bk. S:135.

57. JHL, box 2, vol 7, TSLA.

58. During this period, Harding purchased 250 acres from Felix Grundy on the east side of Mill Creek and two small land grants in the same area. He sold most of this land to Joseph Clay in 1840 (DCD, bk. R:394-95, 458; Middle Tennessee Land Grants #8055 and 8087, TSLA).

59. DCD, bk. N:486, bk. Q:486.

60. DCMR, bk. 1:117. The Reverend William Hume officiated at the wedding of William Harding and Elizabeth Clopton. Their daughter, Willie Elizabeth, and her husband, David H. McGavock, built Two Rivers in 1859 (DCCM, Oct. Session 1833, p. 136).

61. DCMR, bk. 1:62.

62. DCD, bk. N:506, bk. O:76, bk. R:9. Thomas Harding's house, thought to have been built by William and John B. Hall before 1800, still stands on Kent Road. It is known as the McCampbell-Born house (Eleanor Graham, ed., *Nashville, A Short History and Selected Buildings*, 223).

Chapter 3. Stones River Years

1. William S. Speer, ed. and comp., *Sketches of Prominent Tennesseans*, 1.

2. Andrew Jackson to Captain Alden Partridge, Jan. 12, 1817.

3. At the time of Harding and Partridge's visit to the Hermitage, Andrew Jackson was in the midst of his successful presidential campaign of 1828.

4. Washington J. Bennett to W. G. Harding, Aug. 5, 1828, HJP, box 4, folder 2, TSLA. On Apr. 20, 1829, George Little, a former student at the American Literary, Scientific and Military Academy, wrote William Giles Harding from North Carolina. Little said "Old Parte" had visited him for a few days and that the captain had been "highly delighted with his visit to Nashville" (George Little to W. G. Harding, HJP, box 5, folder 1, TSLA).

5. Obituary of Elder N. A. McNairy, W. A. Provine Papers, box 12, folder 7, TSLA.

6. Miscellaneous files, microfilm #678, folder 10, reel 5, TSLA.

7. Speer, *Sketches of Prominent Tennesseans*, 1.

8. The Bible, in which family records were carefully recorded through 1913, is owned by the Nashville Chapter, APTA.

9. Mary Selena Harding's Bible, collection of the Nashville Chapter, APTA; Mount Olivet Cemetery records. W. G. and Mary Selena Harding named their first son John Harding, Jr., even though the baby was named for his grandfather, John Harding, and not his father.

10. *Nashville Herald*, May 16, 1832.

11. Jane Thomas, *Old Days in Nashville*, 125.

12. DCCR, roll 1611, p. 137, TSLA; DCRWI, bk. 10, 1832-1836, part 1, 301-3.

13. HFR letters collection of Mrs. C. William Green.

14. Mary Selena Harding's Bible; Mrs. F. A. Butler, *Mrs. D. H. M'Gavock: Life-Sketch and Thoughts*, 22.

15. DCD, bk. V:394, 396.

16. *Nashville Banner*, Dec. 15, 1904; *Republican Banner* (Nashville), July 10, 1858.

17. Mary Selena Harding's Bible.

18. DCD, bk. V:546. James Priestley, the president of Cumberland College, lived in his McSpadden's Bend home, Monte Bello, until his death in 1821 (John E. Windrow, ed., *Peabody and Alfred Leland Crabb*, 30-31).

19. Butler, *Mrs. D. H. M'Gavock*, 22; Samuel Cole Williams, *Beginnings of West Tennessee*, 188.

20. James D. Davis, *Early History of Memphis; Also the Old Times Papers*, 242. The Reverend Mr. Owen was an affectionate father to Willie, who did not learn that he was her stepfather until many years later.

21. Mt. Olivet Cemetery records. Joseph W. Clay remarried twice following Elizabeth's death. His second wife was Bethenia Walker, William Giles's first cousin (DCMR, bk. 1:503).

22. Mary Selena Harding's Bible.

23. *Nashville Banner and Nashville Whig*, March 28, 1836.

24. Dr. Boyd McNairy to the Hon. Henry Clay, Aug. 24, 1836, HJP, box 5, folder 3, TSLA.

25. *Nashville Republican*, Aug. 16, 1836.

26. *Sacred to the Memory of Mrs. Mary Selena Harding, Consort of Mr. William Giles Harding, and daughter of Nathaniel A. McNairy, Esq.* (booklet).

27. Mount Olivet Cemetery records; James Challen to Brother (Alexander) Campbell, Feb. 29, 1860.

28. *In Memoriam, Gen. William G. Harding* (booklet), 21-23.

29. WGHL, 1838-39, box 2, vol. 10, TSLA.

30. Richard B. Morris, ed., *Encyclopedia of American History* (New York: Harper & Brothers, 1953), 178.

31. WGHL, 1838-39, box 2, vol. 10, TSLA.

32. W. G. Harding to Messrs. Boyd McNairy and Ephraim H. Foster, Apr. 13, 1838, HJP, box 3, folder 5, TSLA.

33. Jacob McGavock Dickinson, "Stories and Reminiscences of Jacob M. Dickinson," Dec. 1926, 6-7.

34. Boyd McNairy and Ephraim H. Foster to Messrs. George C. Childress and W. G. Harding, Apr. 12-13, 1838, HJP, box 5, folder 3, TSLA. General Armstrong, Nashville postmaster and long-time friend of Andrew Jackson, was the unsuccessful Democratic candidate for governor in 1837. Washington Barrow was editor of the *Nashville Republican* during the mid-1830s.

35. W. G. Harding to Messrs. Boyd McNairy and Ephraim H. Foster, Apr. 13, 1838, HJP, box 3, folder 5, TSLA; Robert Armstrong and Washington Barrow to W. G. Harding, Apr. 14, 1838, HJP, box 4, folder 1, TSLA.

36. Dickinson, "Stories and Reminiscences of Jacob M. Dickinson," Dec. 1926.

37. *Republican Banner*, Oct. 29, 1841; San Antonio Express, June 9, 1938.

38. R. Henderson Shuffler, "Signing of Texas' Declaration of Independence: Myth and Record," 328-29.

39. *Nashville American*, June 13, 1909. The incident Jackson referred to was his celebrated duel with Charles Dickinson on May 30, 1806, at Harrison's Mill in Logan County, Kentucky.

40. James Douglas Anderson, *Making the American Thoroughbred*, 92, 121.

41. *Republican Banner*, Oct. 24, 1838.

42. Anderson, *Making the American Thoroughbred*, 190.

43. *Nashville Banner*, Aug. 8, 1920.

Chapter 4. John Harding: Land and Spirit

1. W. W. Clayton, *History of Davidson County, Tennessee*, 412.

2. J. M. Powell, *History of the Franklin, Tennessee, Church of Christ*, 5, 7.

3. WCD, bk. O:390-91, bk. U:362, Register's Office. Franklin's Indigo Street is now named Fourth Avenue. Accordingly, the church is now named the Fourth Avenue Church of Christ.

4. *National Banner and Nashville Daily Advertiser,* Oct. 28, 1833.

5. William H. Carter, "The Master of Belle Meade," 728.

6. *Republican Banner* (Nashville), Jan. 27, 1840; (Tennessee) *Senate Journal,* 1839, 633, TSLA.

7. DCD, bk. 2:550-51. During the thirty-two years that he managed his Richland Creek plantation, John Harding sold parcels of it only twice, once in 1818 and again in 1834. Both sales were probably made to accommodate friends and neighbors (DCD, bk. N:475, bk. X:129). After William Giles assumed responsibility for Belle Meade, John Harding occasionally sold parts of the plantation to former neighbors.

8. *Biographical and Historical Memoirs of Northeast Arkansas,* 484-85.

9. Ibid., 531.

10. William S. Speer, ed. and comp., *Sketches of Prominent Tennesseans,* 3.

11. Ibid.

12. DCD, bk. 2:605; John P. Campbell, comp., *Nashville Business Directory,* 99.

13. Speer, *Sketches of Prominent Tennesseans,* 4.

14. Document, WHJP, box 1, folder 24.

15. Davidson County, Tenn., Census Records, 1860, Microfilm records, p. 203, TSLA.

16. *Nashville Whig,* June 6, 1843.

17. Mary Harding Ragland, interview with John Hilboldt.

18. Giles Harding Page and Henrietta Wilkes Page to "Dear Children," Nov. 9, 1845, Page Family Records.

19. Washington Cooper's diary, microfilm account #100, TSLA. Although William Giles's portrait was neither signed nor dated, Cooper mentioned it in his diary.

20. Giles Harding Page and Henrietta Wilkes Page to "Dear Children," Nov. 9, 1845, Page Family Records.

21. H. W. Poynor to W. G. Harding, Jan. 16, 1851, HJP, box 5, folder 6, TSLA.

22. John H. McGavock to W. G. Harding, Feb. 1, 1852, HJP, box. 5, folder 3, TSLA.

23. Josephine Grider Jacobs, "Couple Finds Adventure at Sans Souci." The wedding cake at the McGavock-Moore reception was a replica of the new state capitol in Nashville. Georgia Moore baked the cake in honor of her fiancé.

24. Josephine Grider Jacobs, "Sans Souci Enjoys Happier Times as War Ends." In 1991, Mrs. John McGavock Grider, Jr., and her brother-in-law, George Grider, both of Memphis, owned a portion of the plantation once owned by the Griders' great-grandfather, John H. McGavock.

25. Clayton, *History of Davidson County,* 429.

26. *Nashville True Whig,* Oct. 6, 1855.

27. DCD, bk. 16:353, bk. 17:471.

28. Samuel D. Smith, ed., *Woodlawn Mansion, Nashville, Tennessee: History, Architecture, and Archaeology,* 11, 16.

29. James Challen to Brother (Alexander) Campbell, Feb. 29, 1860.

Chapter 5. A New Role

1. *Republican Banner* (Nashville), Feb. 20, 1839.

2. John Harding to W. A. Ellis, Jan. 9, 1911, HFR, Papers.

3. WGHL, 1838-39, box 2, vol. 10, TSLA.

4. Ibid.

5. *National Banner and Nashville Daily Advertiser*, Apr. 20, 1833.

6. One Belle Meade rock quarry was on the west side of Richland Creek on the present-day Belle Meade Country Club golf course. A second quarry was near the present-day residence at 609 Belle Meade Blvd. The third is thought to have been between present-day Jackson Blvd. and Sutherland Ave., northwest of Belle Meade Blvd.

7. Mt. Olivet Cemetery Records.

8. HMP, box 4, folder 4.

9. Sam Houston to W. G. Harding, July 17, 1841, HJP, small collection, folder 3, TSLA.

10. *Republican Banner* (Nashville), May 28, June 27, 1839.

11. Sam Houston to W. G. Harding, July 17, 1841, HJP, small collection, folder 3, TSLA.

12. *Nashville Union*, May 21, 1844.

13. WGHL, "Farm Proceeds," box 2, vol. 11, TSLA.

14. Ibid.

15. Ibid.

16. *In Memoriam, Gen. William G. Harding* (booklet), 23.

17. WGHL, box 2, vol. 11, TSLA.

18. Robert Gray, *The McGavock Family*, 8.

19. Reid Smith, *Majestic Middle Tennessee*, 74.

20. Wilena Roberts Bejack and Lillian Johnson Gardiner, comps. and publishers, *Williamson County, Tennessee Marriage Records 1800-1850*, 115.

21. *Nashville Banner*, Dec. 15, 1884.

22. The portraits are in the collection of Mr. and Mrs. John H. Zink III. Mrs. Zink is a great-great-great-granddaughter of William Giles and Elizabeth McGavock Harding.

23. Emma W. Bragg, *Scrapbook: Some Family Reminiscences of a Native Nashville Septuagenarian* (booklet), 1, 3-4.

24. Ibid. Ann married John Richardson, a slave who subsequently purchased his freedom and became a barber at Nashville's Commercial Hotel.

25. DCCM, Jan. session, 1843, pp. 92, 409; Jan. session, 1844, p. 172; Jan. session, 1845, p. 20.

26. WGHL, box 2, vol. 15, TSLA.

27. William Claiborne to W. G. Harding, Mar. 18, 1842, HJP, small collection, folder 2, TSLA.

28. Sherrill Jane Kilgore, BHAPTA, 51-52.

29. Ibid.

30. Mary Selena Harding's Bible.

31. *Rural Sun* (Nashville), Oct. 3, 1872.

32. John Wooldridge, *History of Nashville, Tennessee*, 322.

33. Survey of a route for macadamized road from John Harding's to beyond the Harpeth River, Mar. 30, 1838, HJFR collection of the author.

34. Wooldridge, *History of Nashville*, 322.

35. *Nashville Union*, June 12, 1845.

36. P. 454. The painting of Gen. Andrew Jackson is in the collection of John Keith Maddin, Jr. Maddin is a great-great-grandson of William G. and Elizabeth McGavock Harding.

37. *Nashville Whig*, May 16, 1843.

38. Nicholas Perkins to the Secretary of War, Mar. 29, 1807, Records of the War Department, p. 116, National Archives.

39. Gray, *The McGavock Family*, 7. Randal McGavock died Sept. 27, 1844.

40. Last Will and Testament of Randal McGavock, WCM, bk. 8:108.

41. DCD, bk. 8:93. Southfield was a field south of Nashville's Broad Street that was famous as a mustering ground. There, four thousand Tennessee Militia were reviewed by Andrew Jackson and General Lafayette on the latter's 1825 visit.

42. DCD, bk. 4:504, bk. 5:110.

43. Ibid., bk. 11:56.

44. Ibid., bk. 9:70.

45. Ibid., bk. 10:90.

46. Ibid., bk. 12:185, bk. 14:625-26.

47. Joseph J. B. Southall was married to Elizabeth Harding's sister, Mary McGavock Southall. In 1846, William Giles agreed to convey his seven-hundred-acre plantation below the mouth of Stones River in McSpadden's Bend, along with thirty-one slaves who lived there, his crops, stock, and other personal chattels to his father for John Harding's Mississippi County, Ark. plantation with its "slaves, stock, crop, and other personal chattels, implements and effects thereon." The undated indenture either never went into effect or was rescinded (DCD, bk. 9:81).

48. Stephen Cantrell to W. G. Harding, Jan. 23, 1845, HP, box 4, folder 3, TSLA; Jefferson County, Ark., Deeds, bk. D:215.

49. *Nashville Union*, Dec. 8, 1846.

50. Mary Selena Harding's Bible.

51. Gray, *The McGavock Family*, 23.

52. Mary Selena Harding's Bible.

53. Ibid., 680.

54. Jeannette Tillotson Acklen, comp., *Tennessee Records, Tombstone Inscriptions and Manuscripts Historical and Biographical*, 79.

55. Jimmie Lou Sparkman Claxton, *Eighty-Eight Years With Sarah Polk*, 132; Andrew B. Ewing to Dr. Hugh McGavock Ewing, June 5, 1849, Andrew B. Ewing Family Letters.

56. James P. Thomas, *From Tennessee Slave to St. Louis Entrepreneur: The Autobiography of James Thoms*, ed. Loren Schweninger, 78.

57. This encounter may have occurred during an Eastern trip General Harding took with his family in the summer of 1850. See chapter 7.

58. Ibid. The runaway slave was probably Will, who escaped from Harding in 1844 (*Nashville Union*, Sept. 2, 1844).

59. Thomas, *From Tennessee Slave to St. Louis Entrepreneur*, 78.

60. Frank L. Owsley, "The Fundamental Cause of the Civil War: Egocentric Sectionalism," 245.

61. Thelma Jennings, "Tennessee and the Nashville Convention of 1850," 70-82.

62. Ibid.

Chapter 6. Alpha to Omega

1. James Douglas Anderson, *Making the American Thoroughbred*, 57.

2. Ibid., 121.

3. Ibid., 140.

4. Ibid., 142; *Republican Banner* (Nashville), Oct. 12, 1839.

5. Jacob McGavock Dickinson, "Stories and Reminiscences of Jacob M. Dickinson," Jan. 1927, 12.

6. *Spirit of the Times* (New York), Oct. 16, 1841.

7. Ibid., June 12, 1841 The *Spirit of the Times* correspondent said, "There is no place so hard to win stakes as at Nashville. It must be the American Doncaster."

8. Ibid., July 31, 1841.

9. Ibid., Oct. 16, 1841.

10. HJP, box 6, folder 3, TSLA.

11. R. R. Rice to W. G. Harding, Jan. 10, 1845, HJP, box 5, folder 7, TSLA.

12. John Lamar to W. G. Harding, Apr. 18, 1843, HJP, box 5, folder 1, TSLA; Roger Mortimer, *The History of the Derby Stakes*, 95-99. Priam was owned by Leonard P. Cheatham. Apparently, he moved the stallion to Belle Meade from his own stud in Robertson's Bend for part of the 1843 season.

13. Joseph T. Harrison to W. G. Harding, HJP, box 4, folder 7, TSLA.

14. The 1843 English Derby was worth about twenty thousand dollars (John Hervey, *Racing in America, 1665-1865* 2:169).

15. *Spirit of the Times*, Oct. 28, 1843.

16. Anderson, *Making the American Thoroughbred*, ix, x.

17. Alexander MacKay-Smith, *The Race Horses of America, 1832-1872: Portraits and Other Paintings by Edward Troye*, 79, 80, 145-46.

18. *Nashville Union*, Jan. 27, 1844.

19. Agreement between Henry W. Poynor and W. G. Harding, Mar. 1, 1844, HEJP, box 5, folder 1.

20. HJP, box 6, folder 1, TSLA.

21. *Nashville Union*, Jan. 9, 1845.

22. HJP, box 6, folder 1, TSLA.

23. Hervey, *Racing In America* 2:144-145.

24. Anderson, *Making the American Thoroughbred*, 69. A statue of Priam by Meme, presumably the one Harding acquired about 1848, is in the collection of Mrs. Elliston Williams. Mrs. Williams is a great-great granddaughter of William G. and Elizabeth McGavock Harding.

25. *Nashville Union*, June 20, 1844.

26. *Spirit of the Times*, March 3, 1849.

27. Ibid., July 22, 1848.

28. DCD., bk. 1:320.

29. *Spirit of the Times*, July 22, 1848.

30. Ibid.

31. Ibid., July 1, 15, 1848.

32. Ibid., Oct. 2, 1848.

33. Ibid., Oct. 7, 1848. Harding also sent two mares and a sorrel gelding to Memphis that fall for the racing season there (HJP, box 6, folder 3, TSLA).

34. *Nashville Daily Union,* May 17, 1849.

35. *Union and American* (Nashville), Oct. 7, 1854.

36. Agreement executed by W. G. Harding, President of the Walnut Association, J. C. and D. T. McGavock, dated Oct. 15, 1851, HJP, box 6, folder 7, TSLA; D. T. McGavock to Messrs. Southall and others, Oct. 4, 1851, HJP, box 5, folder 3, TSLA.

37. "Walnut Grove Race Track," an undated newspaper article, collection of Margaret Lindsley Warden.

38. *Spirit of the Times,* Dec. 6, 1856.

39. *Union and American,* July 9, 1856.

40. *National Sporting Library Newsletter,* no. 15, Dec. 1982.

41. *Union and American,* May 6, 1855.

42. Flyer advertising that Childe Harold would spend his second season (1857) at General Harding's stables, Nashville Chapter, APTA.

43. *Republican Banner,* Oct. 17, 1856.

44. Julep cups for Harding's victories at the 1856 Maury County, Crab Orchard, Kentucky, and Danville, Kentucky, fairs are in the collection at Belle Meade.

45. *Republican Banner,* May 8 and Oct. 16, 1857. In 1857 the Tennessee State Fair was located where Nashville's Centennial Park was later built. The grounds consisted of about forty acres "enclosed by a high and substantial fence." That year, the board reconstructed the amphitheater, roofed over the seats, and added new stables. To accommodate visitors, Nashville & Northwestern trains ran between the depot on Church Street and the fairgrounds on a regular schedule, leaving the station on every hour and leaving the fairgrounds on the half hour (*Spirit of the Times,* Sept. 5, 1857).

46. Hervey, *Racing in America* 2:116, 247.

47. Margaret Lindsley Warden, *The Belle Meade Plantation* (booklet), 32.

48. *Union and American,* Feb. 15, 1866.

49. Warden, *The Belle Meade Plantation* (booklet), 33, 35.

50. *Spirit of the Times,* June 5, 1858.

51. Ibid., Oct. 9, 1858.

52. *Republican Banner,* Oct. 17, 19, 20, 1860.

53. Ibid., Oct. 10, 1860.

Chapter 7. A Spacious and Elegant Home

1. Mary Selena Harding's Bible.

2. H. W. Poynor to W. G. Harding, Apr. 14, 1850, HJP, box 5, folder 6, TSLA.

3. Mrs. F. A. Butler, *Mrs. D. H. M'Gavock: Life-Sketch and Thoughts,* 27-29.

4. Dr. Andrew B. Ewing to Hugh McGavock Ewing, June 25, 1850, Andrew B. Ewing Family Letters. "The Misses Bass" were the daughters of John M. and Mary Malvina Grundy Bass. One of the daughters, Ann Margaret Bass, married General Harding's first cousin, Thomas J. Harding, the following spring.

5. W. G. Harding to William O. Harding, Sept. 3, 1875, HFR collection of Jack Harding.

6. *Nashville Union,* Sept. 4, 1850. The *Daily American* of Aug. 20, 1850, mentioned that someone named David was with the Harding party at Cape May. He may have been Harding's nephew, David H. McGavock. If so, David and Willie were on their wedding trip.

7. In the antebellum years, Southerners traveling in the North often encountered the breakdown of what Frank Owsley ("The Fundamental Cause of the Civil War: Egocentric

Sectionalism") called the comity of sections: abusive language and vilification from people who found slavery and the Southern way of life objectionable.

8. *Nashville Union*, Sept. 4, 1850. The *Philadelphia Public Ledger* version of the fight was that McGavock had peremptorily ordered a bootblack to take his bags to his room. When the man said he was blacking a gentleman's boots and did not have time to do so, McGavock seized him and, after a few blows were exchanged, hit the Negro with a wine bottle, "terribly mutilating the poor fellow's head and face" (*Daily American*, Aug. 21, 1850).

9. *Nashville Union*, Sept. 4, 1850.

10. John Harding, Jr., entered Harvard in the fall of 1850 (W. W. Clayton, *History of Davidson County, Tennessee*, 429).

11. William A. Ellis, ed. and comp., *Norwich University, 1819-1911: Her History, Her Graduates, Her Roll of Honor* 1:66. Wesleyan University, established by the Methodist Church in 1833, occupied the old academy campus at the time of Harding's New England visit.

12. In New York City, the Harding party stayed at Lovejoy's Hotel (E. G. Eastman to Daniel Dodge, June 24, 1850, HJP, box 5, TSLA).

13. Report by Henry A. Judd of his visit to the Belle Meade Mansion on Dec. 13, 1968, APTA, Nashville Chapter.

14. *Nashville Banner*, July 30, 1883.

15. Sherrill Jane Kilgore, BHAPTA, 59.

16. Ronald W. Miller, "Initial Report on the Belle Meade Parlors," Attachment E, p. 2, APTA, Nashville Chapter.

17. Agreement between APTA and Leatherwood, Inc. July 2, 1987, APTA, Nashville Chapter.

18. Carol Rifkind, *A Field Guide to American Architecture*, 39.

19. Miller, "Initial Report," Attachment E, p.1, APTA, Nashville Chapter; Kilgore, BHAPTA, 60.

20. The 1987 mantels were designed by William W. Howell, architect, A.I.A., Helmey and Howell, Architects, Nashville, Tenn.; Kilgore, BHAPTA, 60.

21. *Union and American* (Nashville), Oct. 7, 1854.

22. *Nashville Banner*, July 30, 1883.

23. Ibid.

24. James Patrick, *Architecture in Tennessee, 1768-1897*, 154.

25. Agnes Addison Gilchrist, *William Strickland: Architect and Engineer, 1788-1854*, 19.

26. Patrick, *Architecture in Tennessee*, 136.

27. Notes on the Belle Meade Plantation attached to an obituary notice for Mrs. Hill McAlister, APTA, Nashville Chapter.

28. Mrs. James K. Polk declined an invitation to the housewarming. This was not unexpected; Mrs. Polk declined most invitations she received following her husband's death (Jimmie Lou Sparkman Claxton, *Eighty-Eight Years With Sarah Polk*, 144).

29. Undated, unsigned document, HMP, box 4, folder 4.

30. Ibid.

31. Ibid. The Hardings are not known to have made wine from their grapes.

32. *Nashville Tennessean Magazine*, Mar. 30, 1947.

33. *Union and American*, Oct. 7, 1854.

34. Herschel Gower, *Pen and Sword: The Life and Journals of Randal W. McGavock*, 367; *Union and American*, Apr. 18, 1858.

35. *Republican Banner and Nashville Whig*, July 10, 1858.

36. *Daily American*, Oct. 16, 1887.

37. Jacob M. Dickinson, "Stories and Reminiscences of Jacob M. Dickinson," Mar. 1927, 23.

38. Harry J. Seiforth, "A Miniature History of Belle Meade."

39. DCD, bk. 335:101. When Jacob McGavock Dickinson bought Belle Meade and four hundred acres in !906, the deed provided him with all rights to the waters of the Red House Spring, including pipes, pumps, and pumping station. The spring was later used by Mr. and Mrs. Leslie Cheek as a source of water for their home, Cheekwood.

Chapter 8. Life in the Fifties

1. Henry W. Poynor to W. G. Harding, Jan. 17, 1852, HJP, box 5, folder 6, TSLA.

2. Mary Selena Harding's Bible.

3. Elizabeth Harding to John McGavock, May 23, 1856, HFP, box 1, folder 11.

4. Bay de Menang to Honorable John Culbertson, Aug. 24, 1856, HJP, small collection, folder 5, TSLA.

5. Mary Selena Harding's Bible.

6. "In Memory of Miss Josephine Southall," APTA, Nashville Chapter; Andrew B. Ewing to Hugh McGavock Ewing, Feb. 4, 1856, Andrew B. Ewing Family Letters.

7. Elizabeth McGavock Harding to W. G. Harding, June 16, 1862, HJP, JAHL.

8. Mary Selena Harding's Bible, obituary pasted on inside cover; Andrew B. Ewing to Hugh McGavock Ewing, Dec. 17, 1851, Andrew B. Ewing Family Letters.

9. Ellen Snell Coleman, "The Harding House" (pamphlet).

10. *Tribune and Sun* (Jackson, Tenn.), Jan. 24, 1879; William S. Speer, ed. and comp., *Sketches of Prominent Tennesseans*, 449.

11. Eunice F. Jackson to Dr. Alexander Jackson, Nov. 9, 1851; Dr. Alexander Jackson to Eunice F. Jackson, Feb. 9, 1852, both in the JFR collection of Eunice H. Ridley. Dr. Jackson was interested in bringing railroads to West Tennessee, while General Harding was a proponent of both railroads and turnpikes for Middle Tennessee.

12. W. W. Clayton, *History of Davidson County, Tennessee*, 419.

13. *Union and American* (Nashville), Apr. 19, 1854.

14. *In Memoriam, Gen. William G. Harding* (booklet), 2.

15. Ibid.

16. *Republican Banner* (Nashville), Jan. 5, 1853.

17. John H. McGavock to W. G. Harding, Feb. 27, 1853, HJP, box 3, vol. 2, TSLA.

18. *Union and American*, July 8, Aug. 4, 1855.

19. Andrew Johnson, *The Papers of Andrew Johnson* 2:357-58.

20. Ibid., vol. 4, 1860-1861, p. 344.

21. David Herbert Donald, *Charles Sumner and the Coming of the Civil War*, 272; *In Memoriam, Gen. William G. Harding* (booklet), 15.

22. 1850 and 1860 Slave Census, 11th Civil District, Davidson County, Tennessee, TSLA.

23. DCD, bk. 14:661, bk. 15:71, 167, 173, 327; bk. 18:215-216.

24. Ibid., bk. 27:398-99, bk. 29:339.

25. Joseph H. Reall, "Belle Mead," 57. In his article Reall said that General Harding bought only one slave and sold only one slave during his lifetime.

26. *Union and American*, Dec. 28, 1856.

27. *Republican Banner,* Jan. 11, 12, 1860. Henry Hardin was owned by David H. McGavock. After emancipation, Hardin spelled his last name as Harding.

28. Kenneth McKellar, *Tennessee Senators as Seen by One of Their Successors,* 405.

29. Herschel Gower, *Pen and Sword: The Life and Journals of Randal W. McGavock,* 367.

30. Ibid., 487, 506.

31. Ibid., 398.

32. *Republican Banner,* Dec. 20, 1856.

33. William Hague to the Reverend Isaac Hague, Apr. 26, 1852, WHL. It is likely that Hague supervised the construction of many of Belle Meade's slave-built stone walls.

34. Ibid., June 2, 1856.

35. William Hague to "Dear Relations," Dec. 18, 1859, WHL.

36. *Union and American,* Nov. 20, 1860.

37. William Hague to "Dear Relations," Apr. 14, 1860; Louis and James C. McNall to Gen. W. H. Jackson, Feb. 13, 1873, HJP, small collection, folder 5, TSLA.

38. *Daily Nashville Patriot,* May 8, 1858.

39. Julep cup #0124, APTA, Nashville Chapter; *Daily Nashville Patriot,* May 21, 1859; *Premiums and Regulations for the Third Annual Spring Fair of the Davidson County Agricultural and Mechanical Association* (booklet), collection of the author.

40. *Union and American,* Oct. 16, 1859. Mark R. Cockrill was a wealthy Davidson County farmer who owned thousands of acres in Cockrill's Bend. In 1851 he was awarded a bronze medal at the London World Fair for having grown the finest wool in the world.

41. Matthew F. Maury to George Hobson, Nov. 23, 1859; George Hobson to Matthew F. Maury, Nov. 29, 1859; Matthew F. Maury to John R. Clay, Dec. 19, 1859, all in the HJP, JAHL.

42. Matthew F. Maury to W. G. Harding, Sept. 27, 1860, HJP, JAHL.

43. Ibid., Dec. 20, 1860.

44. Ibid.

Chapter 9. War Arrives

1. Stanley J. Folmsbee, Robert E. Corlew, and Enoch L. Mitchell, *Tennessee: A Short History,* 317.

2. "A Testimonial to Gen. William G. Harding, Friend and Patron, The Earliest, Truest and Best of the Harding Light Artillery, by Him Organized and Equipped for the Confederate Service, Jan. 12 1861," a printed broadside, HJFR collection of Mr. and Mrs. John H. Zink III.

3. DCD, bk. 31:506.

4. Folmsbee, Corlew, and Mitchell, *Tennessee: A Short History,* 318.

5. Alfred L. Crabb, *Nashville: Personality of a City,* 117-18.

6. Dr. Alexander Jackson to Isham G. Harris, May 16, 1861, IGHP.

7. William Hague to "Dear Relations," Apr. 14, 1861, WHL.

8. Folmsbee, Corlew, and Mitchell, *Tennessee: A Short History,* 320.

9. Dr. Alexander Jackson to Isham G. Harris, May 16, 1861, IGHP.

10. *Osceola (Ark.) Times,* Sept. 19, 1985.

11. Folmsbee, Corlew, and Mitchell, *Tennessee: A Short History,* 320.

12. *Nashville Daily Union,* Apr. 15, 1862; Andrew Johnson, *The Papers of Andrew Johnson* 5:368n.

13. W. R. Garrett and A. V. Goodpasture, *History of Tennessee, Its People and Its Institutions*, 204.

14. John Fitch, *Annals of the Army of the Cumberland*, 604.

15. *Nashville Daily Union*, Aug. 22, 1863.

16. Telegram, F. K. Zollicoffer and W. G. Harding to A. Anderson, Apr. 27, 1861, MFBT.

17. MFBT.

18. Unsigned letter from Mag Harding to Mrs. Julia L. Watson, May 22, 1861, HFR collection of Mrs. James Balch.

19. Folmsbee, Corlew, and Mitchell, *Tennessee: A Short History*, 322.

20. Order #122, signed by Neill S. Brown, W. G. Harding, and J. E. Bailey, June 7, 1861, MFBT.

21. W. G. Harding to N. C. Kellogg, June 14, 1861, MFBT. A percussion cap is a paper or metal container holding an explosive charge; Stanley F. Horn, ed., *Tennessee's War: 1861-1865, Described by Participants*, 21.

22. William A. Ellis, ed. and comp., *Norwich University, 1819-1911: Her History, Her Graduates, Her Roll of Honor*, 127.

23. William S. Speer, *Sketches of Prominent Tennesseans*, 447.

24. Order, Daniel S. Donelson to Conductor of Railroad, July 5, 1861, WHJP, box 3, folder 17.

25. J. E. Bailey and W. G. Harding to Gov. Isham G. Harris, Aug. 10, 1861, MFBT.

26. Telegram, Neill S. Brown and W. G. Harding to Gen. Leonidas Polk, Aug. 17, 1861, MFBT.

27. Garrett and Goodpasture, *History of Tennessee*, 204.

28. Military and Financial Board to Capt. W. R. Hunt, Sept. 23, 1861, MFBT.

29. "Statements of Receipts and Expenditures of the MFBT," Oct. 1, 1861, in *War of the Rebellion: A Compilation of the Official Records of the Union and Confederate Armies*, series 2, vol. 52, part 2, 162-63.

30. James K. Polk Blackburn, *Terry's Texas Rangers, Reminiscences of J. K. P. Blackburn*, 8, 9, 41-42.

31. Ibid., 9-11.

32. T. L. Ritter to W. G. Harding, Jan. 7, 1862, HJP, box 5, folder 11, TSLA.

33. Byrd Douglas, *Steamboatin' on the Cumberland*, 111-12.

34. "Receipts and Expenditures of the MFBT," Jan. 18, 1862, HJP, box 6, folder 9, TSLA.

35. Herschel Gower, *Pen and Sword: The Life and Journals of Randal W. McGavock*, 585, 597.

36. Ibid., 597-601.

37. *Great Panic*, 16.

38. Horn, *Tennessee's War*, 68-69.

39. James A. Hoobler, "The Civil War Diary of Louisa Brown Pearl," 319.

40. John Harding, Jr., to W. A. Ellis, Jan. 9, 1911, HFR Papers.

41. General Order No. 13, Headquarters Department of the Ohio, Feb. 26, 1862, statement of Major General Buell in review of the evidence before the military commission appointed by the War Department in Nov. 1862, TSLA.

42. Johnson, *The Papers of Andrew Johnson*, 5:xxxv.

43. *Cincinnati Commercial*, Mar. 19, 1862.

44. *Nashville American*, Nov. 10, 1906.

45. Johnson, *The Papers of Andrew Johnson* 5:261, 265; Henry Lee Swint, "Travellers' Rest," 131.

46. Johnson, *The Papers of Andrew Johnson* 5:319.

47. Jacob McGavock Dickinson, "Stories and Reminiscences of Jacob M. Dickinson," Jan. 1927, 13. Harding, Overton, and John D. Winston reported to Governor Harris on the condition of the prison in 1861. Their report included comment on improved sanitation as well as the prison's financial condition (Johnson, *The Papers of Andrew Johnson,* 4:344n).

48. Johnson, *The Papers of Andrew Johnson* 5:289, 295.

49. Dickinson, "Stories and Reminiscences of Jacob M. Dickinson," Jan. 1927, 12.

50. Johnson, *The Papers of Andrew Johnson* 5:304.

51. *Nashville Daily Union*, Apr. 20, 1862.

52. Elizabeth Harding to W. G. Harding, Apr. 27, 1862, HJP, box 3, folder 2, TSLA.

53. Gower, *Pen and Sword*, 618-19.

54. J. E. Bailey to W. G. Harding, May 28, 1862, HJP, small collection, folder 1, TSLA.

55. Randal M. Ewing to W. G. Harding, May 18, 1862, HJP, small collection, folder 2, TSLA.

56. *Nashville Daily Union*, May 6, 24, 1862.

57. Johnson, *The Papers of Andrew Johnson* 5:366, 366n.

58. *Nashville Daily Union*, May 24, 1862.

Chapter 10. Imprisonment

1. Elizabeth Harding to W. G. Harding, May 15, 1862, HJP, JAHL.

2. W. E. Million to W. G. Harding, Apr. 15, 1862, HJP, box 5, folder 2, TSLA.

3. Selene Harding to W. G. Harding, May 8, 1862, HJP, box 3, folder 4, TSLA.

4. Letter, Selene Harding to W. G. Harding., May 11, 26, 1862, HJP, JAHL; Eugene T. Peterson, *Mackinac Island: Its History in Pictures*, 33.

5. Mary E. Franks to W. G. Harding, Aug. 12, 1863, HJP, small collection, folder 2, TSLA.

6. Elizabeth Harding to W. G. Harding, May 26, 1862, HJP, JAHL.

7. Ibid., May 15, 18, 21, 1862; William Hague to W. G. Harding, May 18, 1862; *Nashville Daily Union*, May 9, 1862.

8. Elizabeth Harding to W. G. Harding, May 31, 1862, HJP, JAHL.

9. Ibid., June 8, 1862.

10. Randal M. Southall to W. G. Harding, June 5, 1862, HJP, TSLA.

11. Thomas Eakin to W. G. Harding, May 5, 1862, HJP, TSLA.

12. J. A. Beasley to W. G. Harding, May 28, 1862, HJP, small collection, folder 1, TSLA.

13. Elizabeth Harding to W. G. Harding, May 6, 1862, HJP, JAHL.

14. Ibid., May 11, 1862.

15. Ibid.

16. Herschel Gower, *Pen and Sword: The Life and Journals of Randal W. McGavock*, 638.

17. Randal M. Southall to W. G. Harding, May 23, 1862, HJP, JAHL.

18. Randal W. McGavock to W. G. Harding, June 5, 1862, HJP, folder 5, TSLA.

19. J. E. Bailey to W. G. Harding, May 28, 1862, HJP, small collection, folder 1, TSLA.

20. McGavock to Harding, June 5, 1862.

21. Elizabeth Harding to W. G. Harding, June 8, 1862, HJP, JAHL.

22. Mary Southall to W. G. Harding, June 20, 1862, HJP, JAHL.

23. Elizabeth Harding to W. G. Harding, June 24, 1862, HJP, JAHL.

24. Ibid.

25. Louise Hamilton to W. G. Harding, June 26, 1862, small collection, folder 3, TSLA.

26. Elizabeth Harding to W. G. Harding, July 4, 1862, HJP, JAHL.

27. Ibid., July 12, 1862.

28. Mag Harding to W. G. Harding, July 22, 1862, HJP, JAHL.

29. Ibid.

30. Elizabeth Harding to W. G. Harding, July 24, 1862, HJP, JAHL.

31. Ibid.

32. Ibid.

33. Mary Southall to W. G. Harding, July 30, 1862, JHP, JAHL.

34. Ibid., Aug. 14, 1862.

35. Randal M. Ewing to W. G. Harding, Aug. 17, 1862, JHP, JAHL.

36. Elizabeth Harding to Andrew Johnson, Sept. 14, 1862, AJP, v-615.5, microfilm 081177.

37. Randal M. Ewing to W. G. Harding, Aug. 17, 1862, HJP, JAHL.

38. Susanna Carter to W. G. Harding, Aug. 25, 1862, HJP, JAHL.

39. Randal M. Ewing to W. G. Harding, Aug. 17, 1862, HJP, JAHL.

40. Susanna Carter to W. G. Harding, Aug. 25, 1862, HJP, JAHL.

41. Elizabeth Harding to Andrew Johnson, Aug. 27, 1862, AJP, series 1, p. 2.

42. Susanna Carter to W. G. Harding, Aug. 25, 1862, HJP, JAHL.

43. Jo C. Guild, *Old Times in Tennessee with Historical, Personal and Political Scraps and Sketches*, 361-62.

44. Ibid., 362-65.

45. *Three Rivers Reporter*, Aug. 30, 1862.

46. *Nashville Daily Union*, June 28, 1862.

47. Jo C. Guild to Baily Peyton, June 20, 1862, and to Robert A. Bennett, June 20, 1862, AJP, series 1, p. 4.

48. Andrew Johnson, *The Papers of Andrew Johnson* 5:587; 6:14.

49. Randal M. Ewing to W. G. Harding, Aug. 28, 1862, HJP, JAHL.

50. Ibid.

51. Elizabeth Harding to Andrew Johnson, Sept. 14, 1862, AJP, v-615.5 microfilm 081177.

52. Ibid.

53. Ibid. Mrs. Harding's "family" of 150 is thought to have included herself and her two daughters, Selene and Mary; her sister, Mary McGavock Southall; William Hague; James and Amanda Beasley and their five children; Rachael Noris, the free mulatto; and 137 slaves.

54. Ibid.

55. Ibid.

56. Johnson, *The Papers of Andrew Johnson* 5:xxxv.

57. W. G. Harding to Elizabeth Harding, Sept. 24, 1862, HJP, JAHL.

58. Johnson, *The Papers of Andrew Johnson* 6:14.

59. Washington Barrow to W. G. Harding, Feb. 22, 1863, HJP, small collection, folder 1, TSLA. After spending two months at Fort Johnson, where he lost twenty pounds and "suffered a great deal," Barrow was paroled to St. Louis, where he reported twice a week to the Provost Marshal. The following February, he was identified as one who wanted to be exchanged south.

In March 1863, Barrow was among 350 Southern prisoners exchanged at City Point, Virginia, for a number of Northern soldiers who had been imprisoned in the South (*The War of the Rebellion: A Compilation of the Official Records of the Union and Confederate Armies*, series 2, 5:302; 3:805).

60. Johnson, *The Papers of Andrew Johnson* 6:14n.

61. William S. Speer, ed. and comp., *Sketches of Prominent Tennesseans*, 2.

Chapter 11. The Long Ordeal

1. Randal M. Ewing to W. G. Harding, August 26, 1862, HJP, JAHL.

2. Mary Selena Harding's Bible.

3. Herschel Gower, *Pen and Sword: The Life and Journals of Randal W. McGavock*, 672.

4. National Archives: Civil War Claim 833/218.

5. National Archives: Nashville Board of Claims, claims 12 and 303.

6. "Another Atrocious Murder by Turchin Men in Nashville, Tenn.," unsigned statement dated October 3, 1862, Whitefoord Cole Collection, Felix Grundy Papers, TSLA.

7. Carrie Eliza Ewing to Mary Harding Ragland, undated, HFR letters collection of Mr. and Mrs. William A. Perkins, Jr.

8. W. G. Harding to Gen. William S. Rosecrans, undated, HJP, small collection, folder 3, TSLA.

9. Andrew Johnson, *The Papers of Andrew Johnson* 5:625.

10. Ibid. 6:98-99.

11. Walter T. Durham, *Nashville, The Occupied City*, 170.

12. Johnson, *The Papers of Andrew Johnson* 6:99.

13. National Archives: W. G. Harding to W. S. Rosecrans, December 17, 1862.

14. John Berrien Lindsley, ed., *The Military Annals of Tennessee, Confederate*, 1st series, 637-38.

15. Ellen Snell Coleman, "The Harding House" (pamphlet), 1-2.

16. Ibid., 2.

17. Ibid., 2-3. The medallion is in the collection of Ellen Amy Harding's granddaughter, Ellen Snell Coleman.

18. Washington Barrow to W. G. Harding, February 22, 1863, HJP, small collection, folder 1, TSLA.

19. DCD, bk. 36:10.

20. John Ellerson Brown, "Belle Meade Plantation: Tale of a Northern Trooper in the Civil War."

21. Ibid. The stallion may have been Childe Harold, who came to Belle Meade in 1856 and was the sire of Codicil, a bay colt foaled in 1863 out of Eureka, a Belle Meade mare. See Sanders D. Bruce, *The American Stud Book* 1:402.

22. Brown, "Belle Meade Plantation."

23. Ibid.

24. Ibid.

25. Ibid.

26. Ibid. Because she disapproved of Ida's marrying a Yankee, Selene Harding took a trip to New Orleans so Ida would not ask her to be in the wedding (Louise Elliston to Josephine ("Joe") Elliston, Dec. 16, 1865, Elliston Family Records).

27. National Archives: Journals of the Nashville Board of Claims. Capt. E. B. Kirk, U. S. A, reported that General Harding took the oath of allegiance in 1863 (supplemental report dated September 3, 1874, Civil War Claim 218/833). In 1885, Harding received $11,624.79 as settlement for his Civil War claim of $33,825.75 for supplies Federal soldiers appropriated from Belle Meade (National Archives: Civil War Claims 218/833 and 218/1141).

28. National Archives: Microfilm records, roll 118, RPM.

29. National Archives: Journals of the Nashville Board of Claims; Civil War Claims 218/833 and 218/1141.

30. National Archives: Journals of the Nashville Board of Claims.

31. Lucie M. Harris to "Dear Cousin Oliver," May 31, 1863, HFP, box 2, folder 10.

32. Elizabeth Harding to W. G. Harding, May 11, 1862, HJP, JAHL.

33. Police Report of Operations of Spies, Smugglers, Traitors, etc., 1863.

34. Ibid.

35. Gower, *Pen and Sword*, 675.

36. *Nashville Daily Union*, August 22, 1863.

37. W. G. Harding to Agent, Adams Express Co., July 1, 1863, HJP, box 1, folder 11, TSLA.

38. IRS Memorandum, 1863, box 6, folder 15, HJP, TSLA.

39. *Nashville Daily Union*, August 22, 1863.

40. Ibid.

41. Lucie M. Harris to Mag McGavock, September 20, 1863, HFP, box 2, folder 10, TSLA.

42. Ibid.

43. *Nashville Daily Union*, September 19, 1863.

44. Johnson, *The Papers of Andrew Johnson* 6:409; National Archives: Microfilm records, copy 345, roll 118, RPM.

45. The safeguard or protectorate, signed by Capt. J. B. Stubbs, Assistant Quartermaster, U. S. A., supposedly offered protection for Harding's property (National Archives: Microfilm records, copy 345, roll 118, RPM.

46. *Nashville Dispatch*, January 19, 1864.

Chapter 12. Surrender, Loss, and Endurance

1. Walter T. Durham, *Reluctant Partners: Nashville and the Union*, 128; *Nashville Daily Union*, February 9, 1864.

2. Sister Aloysius Mackin, O. P., ed., "Wartime Scenes from Convent Windows, St. Cecilia 1861 through 1865," 414-15.

3. Ibid.

4. Lucie M. Harris to Mag McGavock, June 6, 1864, HFP, box 2, folder 10. Contrabands were black slaves who escaped during the Civil War or were brought within the Union lines.

5. Frank Moore, *Speeches of Andrew Johnson, President of the United States, With a Biographical Introduction*, xxxvii-xli; Durham, *Reluctant Partners*, 191.

6. Durham, *Reluctant Partners*, 198.

7. *Nashville Daily Times and True Union*, November 19, 1864.

8. Stanley F. Horn, ed., *Tennessee's War: 1861-1865, Described by Participants*, 319.

9. WCRW, bk. 8:108; Robert Gray, *The McGavock Family*, 23-24.

10. Virginia McDaniel Bowman, *Historic Williamson County; Old Homes and Sites*, 64.

11. Horn, *Tennessee's War*, 311.

12. Bowman, *Historic Williamson County*, 62-63.

13. Mrs. W. G. Harding to Mary Harding, November 29, 1864, HEJP, box 1, folder 3, TSLA.

14. William T. Alderson, ed., "The Civil War Reminiscences of John Johnston, 1861-1865," 80.

15. *Nashville Daily Times and True Union*, December 8, 1864.

16. James Dinkins, *1861 to 1865, By an "Old Johnnie": Personal Recollections and Experiences in the Confederate Army*, 243-44.

17. Ibid., 240, 244-45.

18. Ibid., 246-47; Gen. George H. Thomas, "Report by Maj. Gen. George H. Thomas," 1:417.

19. Dinkins, *1861 to 1865, Personal Recollections and Experiences*, 247.

20. *Nashville Tennessean*, January 10, 1943.

21. Mrs. W. G. Harding to William G. LeDuc, dated "Tuesday," WHJP, box 1, folder 24.

22. William G. LeDuc to Mrs. Jackson, April 6, 1903, WHJP, box 2, folder 5. When he wrote this letter, LeDuc was unaware that Selene Jackson died in 1892.

23. *Nashville Daily Times and True Union*, January 9, 1865.

24. National Archives: Microfilm records, copy 345, roll 118, RPM.

25. Mrs W. G. Harding to Col. John G. Parkhurst, January 27, 1865, HJP, small collection, folder 3, TSLA.

26. William G. LeDuc, *Recollections of a Civil War Quartermaster: The Autobiography of William G. LeDuc*, 139-41.

27. *Encyclopedia of American History*, 245.

28. W. R. Garrett and A. V. Goodpasture, *History of Tennessee, Its People and Its Institutions*, 232-34.

Chapter 13. The Old Order Changes

1. Jean Haslip, *Crown of Mexico: Maximilian and His Empress Carlota*, 324-26, 328.

2. Mary Selena Harding's Bible. Except for increasing deafness, John Harding was in excellent heath until near the end of his long life. In the summer of 1862, he still rode his horse around Belle Meade (Susanna Carter to W. G. Harding, Aug. 25, 1862, HJP, JAHL).

3. William S. Speer, ed. and comp., *Sketches of Prominent Tennesseans*, 3; W. W. Clayton, *History of Davidson County, Tennessee*, 412.

4. DCD, bk. 34:353.

5. DCRWI, bk. 20, roll 435, pp. 131-35.

6. Henry Lee Swint, ed., "Reports from Educational Agents of the Freedmen's Bureau in Tennessee, 1865-1870," 54.

7. Ibid., 55.

8. "Contract with laborers at Belle Meade, 1879," HJP, box 2, folder 14, TSLA.

9. *Union and American*, Jan. 15, 1871.

10. John Hope Franklin, *Reconstruction After the Civil War*, 151.

11. Harding's taxes were required by a Federal income tax law passed in 1862. The law expired at the end of 1871 and was not successfully revived until after the passage of the

sixteenth amendment to the Constitution in 1913. See United States Bureau of the Census, *Historical Statistics of the United States: Colonial Times to 1970*, 1093.

12. HJP, box 6, folders 7, 15, TSLA.

13. Josephine ("Joe") Elliston to Mary ("Maria") Cage, March 17, 1866 and Elizabeth Boddie Elliston to Joe Elliston, March 18, 1866, Elliston Family Records.

14. *Nashville American*, Mar. 21, 1896.

15. Dr. Alexander Jackson to Eunice F. Jackson, Oct. 27, 1866, JFR collection of Eunice H. Ridley.

16. W. G. Harding to W. H. Jackson, Dec. 17, 1866, WHJP, box 1, folder 24.

17. Henry C. Shapard to W. H. Jackson, Mar. 2, 1867, HEJP, box 1, folder 11. In June 1866, Jackson heard from F. H. McNairy, who was then in New Orleans. Although McNairy said that his intentions were "to live in this city for the present, as my old town is becoming too much Yankee for me," it seems likely that he was the man who was courting Selene in 1867 (F. H. McNairy to W. H. Jackson, June 4, 1866, WHJP, box 2, folder 7).

18. Henry C. Shapard to W. H. Jackson, Apr. 8, 1867, HEJP, box 1, folder 11. Draughts was a game played by two players on a board exactly like a chessboard (Dr. Larry Freeman, ed., *Yesterday's Games*, 91).

19. HJP, box 5, folder 7, TSLA.

20. *Republican Banner*, Aug. 8, 1867.

21. *Nashville Union and Dispatch*, Aug. 10, 1867.

22. Katherine M. Jones, *Heroines of Dixie: Confederate Women Tell Their Story of the War*, 1955), 155-65.

23. *In Memoriam. Gen. William G. Harding* (booklet), 21.

24. *Evening Herald* (Nashville), Apr. 28, 1889.

25. J. H. Martin to W. H. Jackson, June 17, 1867, WHJP, box 2, folder 7.

26. Dr. Alexander Jackson to W. H. Jackson, Apr. 4, 1867, JFR collection of Eunice H. Ridley.

27. Dr. Alexander Jackson to Eunice F. Jackson, Mar. 14, 1868, JFR collection of Eunice H. Ridley.

28. *Daily Press and Times* (Nashville), May 6, 9, 13, 1868.

29. Henry C. Shapard to W. H. Jackson, July 16, 1868, HEJP, box 1, folder 11.

30. Margaret Lindsley Warden, "Fabulous Belle Meade: Part II, The Blooming."

31. Archival records of the U.S. Military Academy, West Point, New York.

32. *Evening Herald*, Apr. 28, 1889.

33. J. Cooper McKee to W. H. Jackson, Oct. 16, 1887, WHJP, box 2, folder 7.

34. *Thirty-fifth Annual Reunion of the Association of the Graduates of the United States Military Academy at West Point, New York, June 14, 1904* (booklet), 33.

35. Clement A. Evans, *Confederate Military History* 8:316; Speer, *Sketches of Prominent Tennesseans*, 446.

36. Theodore Roosevelt, *Hunting Adventures in the West*, 363-64.

37. W. H. Jackson resigned his commission as a U. S. Army officer on May 16, 1861. W. H. Jackson to President Andrew Johnson, sometime in 1865, WHJP, box 2, folder 3.

38. Speer, *Sketches of Prominent Tennesseans*, 447.

39. Ibid.

40. Dr. Alexander Jackson to W. H. Jackson, May 30, 1861, WHJP, box 2, folder 26.

41. John Berrien Lindsley, ed., *The Military Annals of Tennessee, Confederate*, 809.

42. "The Battle of Columbus, Kentucky," 210.

43. Dr. Alexander Jackson to Eunice F. Jackson, Nov. 12, 1861, WHJP, box 2, folder 26.

44. Lindsley, *The Military Annals of Tennessee*, 809; Speer, *Sketches of Prominent Tennesseans*, 447. The bullet was never removed from Billy Jackson's side.

45. *Nashville Banner*, Apr. 25, 1932. In 1869 President Grant appointed Deloach postmaster of Memphis. Sometime later, when General Grant met Gen. W. H. Jackson for the first time, he reminded Jackson of the incident.

46. "Tales of an Old Mississippi Town," p. 1sct; Speer, *Sketches of Prominent Tennesseans*, 447.

47. Speer, *Sketches of Prominent Tennesseans*, 447.

48. *War of the Rebellion: A Compilation of the Official Records of the Union and Confederate Armies*, series 1, vol. 45, part 1, p. 467.

49. Stanley F. Horn, *The Army of Tennessee*, 217; Joseph E. Johnston, *Narrative of Military Operations*, 190.

50. Communication from Gen. S. D. Lee to Hon. James Seddon, C. S. A., Secretary of War, Dec. 9, 1863, WHJP, box 2, folder 6.

51. Speer, *Sketches of Prominent Tennesseans*, 448; Communication from S. D. Lee to Hon. James Seddon, Dec. 9, 1863, WHJP, box 2, folder 6.

52. Johnston, *Narrative of Military Operations*, 319, 349.

53. Speer, *Sketches of Prominent Tennesseans*, 448.

54. *War of the Rebellion*, series 1, part 1, vol. 45, pp. 1228, 1260-61.

55. Stanley F. Horn, *Tennessee's War: 1861-1865, Described by Participants*, 323.

56. B. L. Ridley, *Battles and Sketches of the Army of Tennessee*, 448.

57. William Tecumseh Sherman, *Personal Memoirs of Gen. W. T. Sherman* 1:363. What reason Davis gave Johnston for not promoting Jackson is unknown. In 1885, General Johnston wrote Marcus J. Wright of the War Office in Washington to remind him that Jackson had operated as a division commander for two years during the Civil War and should have been promoted (Joseph Johnston to Marcus J. Wright, Apr. 24, 1885, WHJP, box 2, folder 4).

58. William T. Alderson, ed., "The Civil War Reminiscences of John Johnston, 1861-1865," 173; *War of the Rebellion*, series 2, 3:542.

59. W. R. Garrett and A. V. Goodpasture, *History of Tennessee, Its People and Its Institutions*, 232-34; Certificate of parole #1382, WHJP, box 3, folder 16.

60. W. H. Jackson to President Andrew Johnson, 1865, WHJP, box 2, folder 3. President Johnson never pardoned General Jackson.

61. Sherman, *Personal Memoirs* 1:365-66.

62. Eunice F. Jackson to Dr. Alexander Jackson, Jan. 14, 1852, JFR collection of Eunice H. Ridley; C. H. Williams to Col. J. G. Totten, Mar. 5, 1852, National Archives, Washington, D. C.

63. *Union and American*, Dec. 16, 1868.

64. Speer, *Sketches of Prominent Tennesseans*, pp. 449-50.

65. Ellsworth Elliot, Jr., *West Point in the Confederacy*, 362.

Chapter 14. The Hardings and the Jacksons

1. *Republican Banner*, May 5, 1869.

2. *In Memoriam, Mrs. Selene Harding Jackson* (booklet), 15.

3. Mary Selena Harding's Bible.

4. 1870 Census, 11th Civil District of Davidson County, Roll 1521, p. 382, TSLA.

5. Ibid.; E. Merton Coulter, *The South During Reconstruction, 1865-1877*, 49, 77.

6. 1870 Census, Agricultural Schedule, 11th Civil District of Davidson County, pp. 3-4, microfilm, TSLA. In addition to wartime losses of stock, Harding was plagued by thievery during the postwar years. In 1866, three horses and seventeen head of fine cattle were stolen from Belle Meade (*Union and American*, Feb. 8, 1866; *Nashville Daily Press and Times*, Feb. 1, 1866).

7. DCD, bk. 39:716, bk. 42:194, 433.

8. *Republican Banner* Jan. 17, 1871; DCD, bk. 42:328, bk. 43:89.

9. *Republican Banner*, Mar. 10, 1872.

10. Ibid., Jan. 17, 1871.

11. W. W. Clayton, *History of Davidson County, Tennessee*, 425.

12. Coulter, *The South During Reconstruction*, 85.

13. *Republican Banner*, July 2, 1871.

14. Mary Selena Harding's Bible.

15. Harding-Jackson household to "Whom It May Concern," Mar. 15, 1871, JFR collection of Eunice H. Ridley.

16. W. G. Harding to Randal M. Ewing, July 18, 1871, HJP, small collection, folder 9, TSLA.

17. Tennessee Agricultural and Mechanical Assosiation stock certificate, WHJP, box 1, folder 12.

18. William S. Speer, ed. and comp., *Sketches of Prominent Tennesseans*, 450.

19. Hearn Watts to the president of the Agricultural Congress, Sept. 28, 1871, HJP, box 5, folder 11; box 6, folder 8, TSLA.

20. Edward William West, "A Visitor to Belle Meade in 1874," 62-63.

21. Charles B. Parmer, *For Gold and Glory*, 115.

22. J. B. Killebrew, *Recollections of My Life: An Anthology by J. B. Killebrew* 2:124; Speer, *Sketches of Prominent Tennesseans*, 450. Governor Brown also named Jackson financial agent for the Bureau of Agriculture.

23. Frances Leigh Williams, *Matthew Fontaine Maury: Scientist of the Sea*, 442, 456, 473; Matthew F. Maury to W. H. Jackson, Mar. 26, 1872, HJP, JAHL.

24. Speer, *Sketches of Prominent Tennesseans*, p. 450.

25. *Republican Banner*, Dec. 10, 1871.

26. *Rural Sun*, Oct. 3, 1872.

27. HJP, box 6, folder 7, TSLA.

28. *Rural Sun*, Apr. 17 and June 5, 1873.

29. Dr. Alexander Jackson to Eunice F. Jackson, June 23, 1873, JFR collection of Eunice H. Ridley; *Rural Sun*, July 3, 1873.

30. HJP, box 6, folder 13, TSLA; *Rural Sun*, Sept. 25, 1873.

31. *Rural Sun*, Sept. 18, 1873; HJP, box 6, folders 6, 8, TSLA.

32. One of those children, Sophie, died Mar. 27, 1874 (Elmwood Cemetery Records). A few months earlier, General Harding's sister, Amanda McGavock, died on Oct. 24, 1873, at the age of 66. In her will, Mrs. McGavock left all the land inherited from her father, John Harding, to her grandson, William B. Cheatham (*Union and American*, Oct. 25, 1873; DCRWI, bk. 23, roll 437, pp. 363-64).

33. Howell E. Jackson to Eunice F. Jackson, Dec. 10, 1873, JFR collection of Eunice H. Ridley.

34. Ibid., Mar. 2, 1874, HJP, small collection, TSLA.

35. Ibid., Mar. 12, and Apr. 6, 1874; Mary Jackson to Howell E. Jackson, Apr. 22, 1874, HEJP, box 1, folder 6.

36. *Republican Banner,* May 1, 1874.

37. Speer, *Sketches of Prominent Tennesseans,* 425.

38. Mary Harding to Howell E. Jackson, Feb. 24, 1874, HEJP, box 1, folder 7.

39. Terry Calvani, "The Early Legal Career of Howell Jackson," 43-45.

40. Nathan Green to Dr. Alexander Jackson, Mar. 7, 1856, HJP, small collection, folder 8, TSLA.

41. After graduating from Cumberland, Howell wanted to go into farming. His father, Dr. Jackson, convinced him to practice law instead (Speer, *Sketches of Prominent Tennesseans,* 425).

42. Calvani, "The Early Legal Career of Howell Jackson," 46-47.

43. Ibid., 48-49. Although records of Howell's whereabouts during the war are sketchy, it is known that he and his family moved several times after leaving Memphis in 1862. In Nov. 1863, they were living in LaGrange, Ga.

44. National Archives: Howell E. Jackson to President Andrew Johnson, June 18, Dec. 7, 1865. As late as Dec. 31, 1863, Howell acknowledged receipt of property from the Confederate Quartermaster's Office (Receipt signed by Howell E. Jackson).

45. National Archives: Amnesty petition No. 3370.

46. Howell's postwar law partner was Bedford M. Estes, a prewar friend (Calvani, "The Early Legal Career of Howell Jackson," 53, 54, 56, 59).

47. Mary Jackson to Howell E. Jackson, Mar. 24, 1875, HJP, small collection, box 1, folder 7, TSLA.

48. "Order of Business," National Agricultural Congress, Atlanta, May 13-16, 1874, HJP, box 6, folder 8, TSLA.

49. Speer, *Sketches of Prominent Tennesseans,* 450. Killebrew felt that Jackson took undeserved credit for being the father of the Bureau of Agriculture and for having its report published (Killebrew, *Recollections* 2:124-25).

50. Mary Selena Harding's Bible; W. H. Jackson to W. G. Harding, Sept. 15, 1874, WHJP, box 2, folder 3.

51. Mary Jackson to Howell E. Jackson, Mar. 21, 1875, HEJP, box 1, folder 7.

52. Billy Jackson to Howell E. Jackson, Mar. 20, 1875, HEJP, box 1, folder 17. Howell Jackson, Jr., and Billy Jackson were also in Memphis staying with their Molloy grandparents.

53. Mary Jackson to Howell E. Jackson, Apr. 7, 1875, HJP, small collection, TSLA; Calvani, "The Early Legal Career of Howell Jackson," 63.

54. Howell E. Jackson to Mary Jackson, Apr. 3, 22, 1875, HEJP, box 1, folder 5.

55. Selene Jackson to Mary Jackson, Sept. 24, 1875, HEJP, box 1, folder 17.

56. Ibid.

57. Ibid.

58. W. H. Jackson to G. M. Morrow, Sept. 20, 1875, reprinted in *Daily American,* Sept. 24, 1875.

59. Mary Jackson to Howell E. Jackson, June 24, 1876, HEJP, box 1, folder 7.

60. Mary Selena Harding's Bible.

61. *Rural Sun,* Feb. 8,1877.

62. Ibid., Mar. 1, 1877.

63. Ibid., Feb. 28, 1878.

64. *Republican Banner,* July 25, 1862.

65. *Tribune and Sun*, Jan. 24, 1879.

66. W. H. Jackson to Selene Jackson, Oct. 19, 1879, HJP, small collection, folder 4, TSLA.

67. *Daily American*, Oct. 4, 1879.

68. W. H. Jackson to Selene Jackson, Oct. 19, 1879, HJP, small collection, folder 4, TSLA. On Sept. 1, 1879, Mary Harding Jackson gave birth to her second child, Louise Jackson, at Belle Meade. Mary and the baby remained there until that fall (Howell E. Jackson to Mary Jackson, Sept. 23, 1879, HJP, small collection, folder 2, TSLA).

69. W. H. Jackson to Selene Jackson, Oct. 19, 1879, HJP, small collection, folder 4, TSLA.

70. Ibid., Dec. 7, 8, 1879.

71. 1879 Belle Meade Account Book, HJP, box 2, vol. 14, TSLA.

72. W. H. Jackson to Selene Jackson, Dec. 15, 1879, HJP, small collection, folder 4, TSLA.

73. W. H. Jackson to his daughter, Eunice Jackson, Dec. 29, 1879, HJP, small collection, folder 4, TSLA.

Chapter 15. Home of the Racehorse

1. *Union and American*, Apr. 29, 1869.

2. Ibid., Aug. 8, 1867.

3. *Republican Banner*, Aug. 8, 1867.

4. HJP, box 5, folder 7, TSLA.

5. *Nashville Daily Press and Times*, May 6, 1868.

6. *Nashville Gazette*, May 9, 1868.

7. *Republican Banner*, Oct. 17, 20, and 24, 1868.

8. *Union and American*, Apr. 29, 30, 1869.

9. Ibid., Apr. 29, 1869.

10. Alexander MacKay-Smith, *The Race Horses of America 1832-1872: Portraits and Other Paintings by Edward Troye*, 320. Harding purchased Vandal as a proven sire several months earlier for twenty-five hundred dollars. The horse was nineteen but had ranked second on the stallion list in 1862, and Harding felt the price was reasonable.

11. *Turf, Field and Farm*, Jan. 1, 1870. Troye's painting of Jack Malone is in the collection of Mr. and Mrs. Donald U. Bathrick, Jr.

12. Ibid., September 28, 1888.

13. W. G. Harding to the editor, *Turf, Field and Farm*, undated, WHJP, box 2, folder 3.

14. W. W. Clayton, *History of Davidson County, Tennessee*, 420.

15. W. G. Harding to Col. A. R. Wynne, Mar. 30, 1870, George Winchester Wynne Collection, box 12, folder 10, TSLA.

16. *Public Ledger*, May 1, 1871.

17. *Union and American*, May 7, 1871.

18. *Republican Banner*, June 20, 1871.

19. John Hervey, *Racing In America 1665-1865* 2:148.

20. *Republican Banner*, Apr. 18, 1872.

21. *Union and American*, May 12, 1872.

22. Margaret Lindsley Warden, *The Belle Meade Plantation* (booklet), 33.

23. *Nashville Banner,* Apr. 7, 1929; *Republican Banner,* June 29, 1872.

24. *Rural Sun,* Oct. 10, 1872.

25. *Republican Banner,* May 18, 1872.

26. Ibid., May 20, 1873.

27. *Rural Sun,* May 22, 1873.

28. *Republican Banner,* May 20, 1873.

29. *Nashville American,* May 23, 1898.

30. Dr. Alexander Jackson to Eunice F. Jackson, Sept. 23, 1873, JFR collection of Eunice H. Ridley.

31. *Republican Banner,* Sept. 28, 1873.

32. *Union and American,* Sept. 28, 1873.

33. Jacob McGavock Dickinson, "Stories and Reminiscences of Jacob M. Dickinson," Dec. 1926, 7.

34. *Union and American,* May 5, 1874.

35. Ibid., Apr. 28, 1875.

36. Sanders D. Bruce, "Bramble," in *The Horse-Breeders' Guide and Hand Book,* 24.

37. *Union and American,* May 4, 1875; *Courier-Journal* June, 23, 1874.

38. *Union and American,* May 4, 1875.

39. Ibid., Apr. 16, 1875.

40. Mary Jackson to Howell E. Jackson, May 12, 1875, HEJP, box 1, folder 7.

41. Ibid., May 15, 1875.

42. Ibid., May 18, 1875.

43. Ibid.

44. Kentucky Derby race results, scales book transcript.

45. *Republican Banner,* May 21, 1875.

46. Ibid., May 23, 1875.

47. W. H. Jackson to Howell E. Jackson, June 18, 1875, HJP, box 3, folder 7, TSLA.

48. William S. Speer, ed. and comp., *Sketches of Prominent Tennesseans,* 3.

49. Mary Jackson to Howell E. Jackson, May 23, 1875, HEJP, box 1, folder 7.

50. *Spirit of the Times,* Oct. 5, 1878.

51. *Daily American,* May 1, 1877; Warden, *The Belle Meade Plantation* (booklet), 33, 35.

52. *Daily American,* Apr. 30, 1876.

53. Howell E. Jackson to Mary Jackson, Sept. 19, 1876, HJP, TSLA.

54. *Daily American,* May 1, 1877.

55. *Thoroughbred Record,* Oct. 22, 1934.

56. *Spirit of the Times,* Oct. 5, 1878.

57. May 1882 Louisville Jockey Club program, collection of the author.

58. *Spirit of the Times,* Jan. 10, 1878.

59. *Daily American,* Apr. 30, 1878; Joseph H. Reall, "Belle Mead," 59.

60. *Daily American,* Apr. 30, 1878.

61. Minutes of the May 31, 1878, Stockholders' Meeting, Blooming Grove Hunting and Fishing Club.

62. *Thoroughbred Record,* January 12, 1935.

63. *Spirit of the Times,* Oct. 5, 1878. Henry Stull's oil portrait of Bramble hangs in the front hall at Belle Meade.

64. *Nashville Banner,* Apr. 14, 1929; Bruce, *The Horse-Breeders' Guide and Hand Book,* 24.

65. *Rural Sun,* Dec. 19, 1878; Bruce, *The Horse-Breeders' Guide and Hand Book,* 164.

66. *Rural Sun,* Jan. 23, 1879.

67. *Daily American,* Apr. 29, 1879.

68. Cash account of William Giles Harding for 1879, HJP, box 3, folder 8, TSLA.

69. *Daily American,* Apr. 29, 1879.

70. Ibid.

71. *Nashville Banner,* Apr. 14, 1929.

72. W. H. Jackson to Howell E. Jackson, June 3, 1879, HJP, box 3, folder 8, TSLA.

73. Ibid.

74. Ibid., June 18, 1879.

75. Bruce, *The Horse-Breeders' Guide and Hand Book,* 24.

76. W. H. Jackson, interview by a *Denver Tribune* correspondent, reprinted in the *Nashville American,* Oct. 4, 1879.

77. *Nashville Banner,* Apr. 14, 1929.

Chapter 16. Family and Friends

1. W. H. Jackson to Selene Jackson, Feb. 15, 29, Mar. 9, 1880, HJP, small collection, folder 4, TSLA.

2. Ibid., Jan. 26, 1880.

3. Ibid., Feb. 10, 1880.

4. Ibid., Feb. 29, 1880.

5. *In Memoriam, Mrs. Selene Harding Jackson* (booklet), 9; HMP, box 3, folder 2.

6. Joseph E. Johnston to W. H. Jackson, Apr. 10, May 11, 1880, WHJP, box 2, folder 4; W. H. Jackson to Selene Jackson, May 17, 1880, transcribed copy in the HJFR collection of the author.

7. *Daily American,* May 19, 1880; Howell E. Jackson to Mary Jackson, May 21, 1880, HMP, box 1, folder 6.

8. Document, HFR collection of Mrs. James Balch.

9. William Waller, ed., *Nashville in the 1890s,* 154.

10. *Daily American,* July 17, 1881.

11. Ibid., Nov. 2, 1881. General Jackson could not vote because he had never been pardoned by the Federal government.

12. Selene Jackson to Eunice F. Jackson, Nov. 26, 1882, JFR collection of Eunice H. Ridley. During the 1884-85 school year, the Jackson children, including Bessie Jackson, attended Miss Lucy Chambliss's school (*Nashville Banner,* June 5, 1885).

13. Selene Jackson to Eunice F. Jackson, Jan. 7, 1883, JFR collection of Eunice H. Ridley. General Harding's mill, located a short distance upstream from the old Harding cabin, was finished in Jan. 1883.

14. Ibid.

15. Robert F. Jackson to Eunice F. Jackson, Feb. 7, 1883, JFR collection of Eunice H. Ridley.

16. Selene Jackson to Eunice F. Jackson, Apr. 15, 1883, JFR collection of Eunice H. Ridley. The Tealey place, a mile beyond Belle Meade on the Richland Turnpike, was formerly owned by F. W. Tealey, who died in 1881 (*Daily American,* Mar. 30, 1881).

17. Selene Jackson to Eunice F. Jackson, Apr. 15, 1883, JFR collection of Eunice H. Ridley; Selene Jackson to Ellen McGavock Ewing, Aug. 15, 1883, HJP, small collection, folder 9, TSLA.

18. Selene Jackson to Eunice F. Jackson, Apr. 22, 1883, JFR collection of Eunice H. Ridley.

19. Ibid., Apr. 15, 1883, JFR collection of Eunice H. Ridley.

20. Ibid., Aug. 16, 1883, JFR collection of Eunice H. Ridley.

21. Ibid., Apr. 15, May 8, 1883, JFR collection of Eunice H. Ridley.

22. The double parlors were restored in 1988 by APTA's Nashville Chapter. At that time the folding doors, which had been removed early in the 20th century, were rebuilt and the walls and ceiling repainted using the 1883 color scheme.

23. Selene Jackson to Ellen McGavock Ewing, Aug. 15, 1883, HJP, small collection, folder 9, TSLA.

24. Selene Jackson to Eunice F. Jackson, Oct. 1, 1883, JFR collection of Eunice H. Ridley. In Louisville, the Jacksons may have visited either Dr. David Wendel Yandell, a prominent physician, or Dr. Yandell's brother, Lunsford Yandell, M.D. David Yandell's wife, the former Fanny Crutcher, was a Nashvillian. Lunsford's wife, the former Louise Elliston, was a sister of Selene's close friend, Josephine Elliston Farrell. General Jackson had known Dr. David Yandell when they served together under Gen. Joseph E. Johnston during the Mississippi campaign of 1863 (Nancy Disher Baird, *David Wendel Yandell, Physician of Old Louisville*, 26, 51, 62).

25. DCRWI, bk. 30:412.

26. DCD, bk. 82:189, bk. 118:159.

27. Ibid., bk. 118:159.

28. Selene Jackson to Eunice F. Jackson, Jan. 7, 1883, JFR collection of Eunice H. Ridley.

29. William S. Speer, ed. and comp., *Sketches of Prominent Tennesseans*, 453.

30. *Daily American*, May 15, June 17, 1884.

31. Speer, *Sketches of Prominent Tennesseans*, 453.

32. Among those present were Josh Compton, J. H. Keeble, James C. Napier, Mrs. Elias W. Napier, and Mrs. H. T. Noel, all of Davidson County, and the Reverend Dr. G. W. Bryant of Washington, D.C. (*Nashville Union*, July 24, 1885).

33. *Daily American*, Sept. 26, 1884.

34. Ibid.; Resolution of Thanks to Gen. W. G. Harding and family, Gen. W. H. Jackson and family, and Sen. Howell E. Jackson and family, APTA, Nashville Chapter; Testimonial, HJFR collection of Mr. and Mrs. John H. Zink III.

35. *Nashville American*, July 9, 1899.

36. *Nashville Union*, Apr. 15, 1885.

37. *Daily American*, Oct. 19, 1884.

38. *Nashville Banner*, Oct. 28, 1886.

39. Stephen D. Lee to W. H. Jackson, Feb. 7, 1885, Stephen D. Lee Presidential Papers. Lee was president of Mississippi Agricultural and Mechanical, a predecessor of Mississippi State University.

40. Bess White Cochran, *The First One Hundred Years . . . the History of the Nashville YMCA, 1875-1975*, 15.

41. Speer, *Sketches of Prominent Tennesseans*, 5.

42. *In Memoriam, Gen. William G. Harding* (booklet), 22.

43. *Nashville Union*, May 16, 1885.

44. Kathleen Minnix, "'That Memorable Meeting': Sam Jones and the Nashville Revival of 1885," 159.

45. *Nashville Banner*, Jan. 1, 1886.

46. Ashworth Bros. to Gen. W. H. Jackson, Jan. 16, 1886, WHJP, box 1, folder 8.

47. *Nashville American,* May 18, 1902.

48. Ibid.

49. Ibid.

50. *Nashville Banner,* Mar. 26, 1886.

51. Roberta Seawell Brandau, ed., *History of Homes and Gardens of Tennessee,* 128-29; Edmund Morris, *The Rise of Theodore Roosevelt,* 383-84.

52. HJP, box 3, folder 8, TSLA; W. R. Garrett and A. V. Goodpasture, *History of Tennessee, Its People and Its Institutions,* 268.

53. *Suburban News* (Nashville), Feb. 28, 1974; HMP, box 1, folder 1 and box 2, folder 3.

54. Charles Dudley Warner's diary. When Eunice Jackson joined McKendree Methodist Church in 1883 at age 12, her father said that she had a purer Christian character than anyone her age he had ever seen (W. H. Jackson to Eunice F. Jackson, Sept. 9, 1883, collection of Eunice H. Ridley).

55. Charles Dudley Warner's diary. Mrs. Jackson was also affected by Sam Jones, the revivalist who converted General Harding in 1885. During his revivals, Jones attacked social ills, such as gambling and saloons. His sermons on drinking probably helped shape her ideas in favor of prohibition.

56. Ibid.

57. Ibid.; Margaret Lindsley Warden, "Fabulous Belle Meade: Part II, The Blooming."

Chapter 17. Palmy Days

1. *Nashville Banner,* Apr. 14, 1929.

2. *Daily American,* Mar. 11, 1880.

3. *Nashville Banner,* Apr. 7, 1929.

4. Ibid., Apr. 24, 1880.

5. Ibid., Feb. 22, 1925.

6. Sanders D. Bruce, *The Thoroughbred Horse: His Origin, How to Breed and How to Select Him,* 208.

7. William S. Speer, ed. and comp., *Sketches of Prominent Tennesseans,* 452.

8. Baron Favoret de Kerbreck to W. H. Jackson, Apr. 26, 1881, WHJP, box 2, folder 5.

9. *Spirit of the Times,* Jan. 21, 1881.

10. *Daily American,* May 1, 1881.

11. Jacob McGavock Dickinson, "Stories and Reminiscences of Jacob M. Dickinson," Apr. 1927, 35.

12. *Daily American,* May 1, 1881.

13. Ibid.

14. Howell E. Jackson to Mary Jackson, May 4, 1881, HEJP, box 1, folder 4.

15. *Daily American,* Oct. 24, 1886.

16. Salvator (John L. Hervey), "Bramble: Part IV."

17. *Daily American* Apr. 29, 1882. Arthur P. Gorman served as United States senator from Maryland from 1881 until 1899, and from 1903 until 1906 (*Lamb's Biographical Dictionary of the United States,* 3:337).

18. Mrs. James K. Polk to Howell E. Jackson, Apr. 12, 1882, HJP, small collection, folder 5, TSLA.

19. *Daily American,* Apr. 30, 1882; Randall S. Baron and Philip Von Borries, *The Official Kentucky Derby Quiz Book,* 13.

20. *Daily American*, Apr. 30, May 1, 1882.

21. Margaret Lindsley Warden, *The Belle Meade Plantation* (booklet), 9.

22. Joseph H. Reall, "Belle Mead," 52.

23. Ibid. The internal fences at Belle Meade in 1883 were made of posts, planks, and rails.

24. Ibid. Reall learned about Belle Meade from Henry W. Grady at the Atlanta Exposition in 1882. Grady, who had an enthusiasm for everything pertaining to the South's interests, had been greatly impressed with Belle Meade when he visited there in July 1881.

25. *Daily American*, June 6, 1882.

26. *Frank Leslie's Illustrated Newspaper*, June 3, 1882.

27. HJP, box 3, folder 8, TSLA. Perry & Lester, Livestock Traders, were located at the Union Stock Yards, 21 North Cherry Street (*Nashville City Directory*, [1886], 476).

28. Selene Jackson to Eunice B. Jackson, Apr. 15, 22, 1883, HJP, TSLA.

29. *In Memoriam, Gen. William G. Harding* (booklet), 20.

30. *Daily American*, Apr. 25, 29, 1883; *Nashville Banner*, Apr. 27-28, 1883.

31. Warden, *The Belle Meade Plantation* (booklet), 36.

32. *Daily American*, May 1, 1884.

33. *Nashville Banner*, May 3, 1884.

34. Reall, "Belle Mead," 54.

35. *Daily American*, June 7, 1884. In the article, the writer said that "lunch was served in the dining room, an annex reached through an open porch."

36. *Nashville Banner*, Nov. 27, 1882; *Daily American*, Apr. 24, 1880.

37. W. H. Jackson to Howell E. Jackson, Jan. 20, 1885, HJP, box 3, folder 8, TSLA.

38. Margaret Lindsley Warden, "Fabulous Belle Meade: Part II, The Blooming."

39. *Turf, Filed and Farm*, Jan. 16, 1885.

40. *Nashville Banner*, Oct. 21, 1884, Apr. 30, 1885, *Daily American*, May 1, 1885.

41. *Turf, Field and Farm*, Dec. 1885.

42. *Daily American*, Mar. 28, 1886.

43. Ibid., Apr. 28, 1886. Jackson bought Plenipo from C. H. Gillock, vice-president of the Nashville Blood Horse Association, on April 23, 1886 (*Daily American*, Apr. 24, 1886).

44. Speer, *Sketches of Prominent Tennesseans*, 451. Plenipo stood at Belle Meade through the 1889 season.

45. *Daily American*, Apr. 28, 1886; William H. P. Robertson, *The History of Thoroughbred Racing in America*, 143.

46. *Daily American*, Sept. 24, 1886.

47. Ibid., Oct. 25, 1886 (reprinted from *Spirit of the Times*).

48. Robertson, *History of Thoroughbred Racing*, 128.

49. *Daily American*, Oct. 25, 1886.

50. Ibid., Oct. 24, 1886.

51. Will Grimsley, "Yas, Suh! Dat Iroquois Was Some Hoss!"

52. Turf, Field and Farm, Dec. 1886.

53. A storm in April 1886 caused the Cumberland River to flood, covering the lower end of the track and coming within a few feet of the stands (*Nashville Banner*, Apr. 3, 1886). A few years earlier, stables were washed away, fencing was destroyed, and stands suffered damage (*Turf, Field and Farm*, April 9, 1886).

54. *Daily American*, Oct. 25, 1886.

55. *Spirit of the Times*, Apr. 27, 1889.

56. *Daily American*, Dec. 16, 1886.

57. Warden, *The Belle Meade Plantation* (booklet), 31.

58. *Daily American*, Dec. 16, 1886; *St. Louis Daily Globe-Democrat*, Dec. 25, 1886; *Chattanooga Times*, Dec. 18, 1886.

59. *In Memoriam, Gen. William G. Harding* (booklet), 8, 18.

60. Jacob McGavock Dickinson, "Stories and Reminiscences of Jacob M. Dickinson," Dec. 1926, 6.

61. *Daily American*, Dec. 18, 1886; *In Memoriam, Gen. William G. Harding* (booklet), 26-27.

62. *Spirit of the Times*, Feb. 13, 1887.

63. Anson and Fanny Nelson, *Memorials of Sarah Childress Polk*, 207, 212.

64. "A Morning At Belle Meade," undated newspaper article (April 1887), collection of the author.

65. *Daily American*, Oct. 16, 1887.

66. Ibid.

67. Ibid., May 1, 1887.

68. Ibid. Like Capt. James Franklin's Kennesaw, the Fairvue Stud was located in Sumner County and had been owned since 1882 by Charles Reed of New York (Margaret Lindsley Warden, *The Saga of Fairvue, 1832-1977* [booklet], 9).

69. Robertson, *History of Thoroughbred Racing*, 198.

70. *Daily American*, Apr. 28, 1888.

71. Charles McClung McGhee to W. H. Jackson, June 28, 1888, Charles McClung McGhee Papers.

72. "Winning Sires of 1888," in *The American Thoroughbred Stallion Register*, 399.

73. Special dispatch to the *Daily American*, Sept. 4, 1888, reprinted in the *Nashville American*, Apr. 17, 1910. A painting by L. Maurer of Proctor Knott winning the 1888 Futurity Stakes is in the collection of the National Museum of Racing, Saratoga Springs, N.Y.

74. *Spirit of the Times*, May 2, 1889.

75. *Evening Herald*, May 3, 1889.

76. Baron and Von Borries, *The Official Kentucky Derby Quiz Book*, 78.

77. Robert Nash, "A Race Horse and a Race Track: The Story of the Kentucky Derby and Churchill Downs, 1875-1948" (unpublished thesis), 21-22; *Spirit of the Times*, May 18, 1889.

Chapter 18. New South, Old South

1. W. H. Jackson to T. F. Bayard, May 14, 1887, GCC.

2. Howell E. Jackson to His Excellency, the President of the United States, July 28, 1887; President Grover Cleveland to Howell E. Jackson, Aug. 2, 1887, GCC.

3. *Daily American*, Sept. 6, 23, 1887.

4. Ibid., Oct. 16, 1887.

5. W. H. Jackson to B. G. Wood, Oct. 10, 1887, Walton Papers, general correspondence, 1848-1906, small collection, folder 3, TSLA.

6. *Daily American*, Oct. 16, 1887.

7. Ibid.

8. *Nashville Banner Magazine*, Oct. 24, 1937.

9. *Daily American*, Oct. 16, 1887.

10. *Nashville Banner Magazine*, Oct. 24, 1937.

11. *Daily American*, Oct. 17, 1887.

12. Ibid.

13. Ibid.

14. *Cincinnati Commercial Gazette,* Feb. 14, 1893.

15. *Daily American,* Oct. 17, 1887.

16. Ibid.

17. Ibid., Oct. 18, 1887.

18. *Nashville Tennessean,* Jan. 10, 1943.

19. Mary Harding Ragland, interview with John Hilboldt; "Mrs. Caldwell Makes Plea for Preservation of Historic Buildings," undated Nashville newspaper article.

20. The photograph of Mrs. Grover Cleveland given to Mannie Baxter is in the JFR collection of Eunice H. Ridley.

21. *Daily American,* Oct. 16, 17, 1887.

22. W. H. Jackson to Col. Daniel S. Lamont, Oct. 25, 1887; Dr. Charles F. Smith to W. H. Jackson, Oct. 22, 1887, GCC.

23. Supplement to *Harper's Weekly,* Oct. 29, 1887.

24. Nellie was a nickname for Miss Ellen Fall Malone. Her father, Judge Thomas H. Malone, was Dean of the Vanderbilt Law School from 1874 until 1904.

25. Thomas H. Malone to Mrs. Thomas H. Malone, Apr. 25, 1889, Thomas H. Malone Letters. Because of his impending yearling sale in New York, General Jackson could not conveniently leave the country at that time.

26. Ibid.

27. Ibid.

28. Thomas H. Malone to Mrs. Thomas H. Malone, May 1, 1889, Thomas H. Malone Letters.

29. Alexander Jackson family Bible.

30. *Daily American,* Nov. 8, 1889.

31. Ibid.

32. Thomas H. Malone, *Little Rachel's Debut* (booklet), 7-8.

33. Ibid., 8-9.

34. Ibid., 9-12.

35. Ibid., 13-15.

36. Ibid., 16-18.

37. *Evening Herald,* Apr. 28, 1889.

38. Margaret Lindsley Warden, "Fabulous Belle Meade: Part III, The Breaking." Although Ms. Warden did not name the male caller in her article, she identified him as James H. Kirkland in her personal notes. Despite never liking so-called society, Kirkland enjoyed associations with cultivated people and often visited Belle Meade during his bachelor days at Vanderbilt (Edwin Mims, *Chancellor Kirkland of Vanderbilt,* 90).

39. Selene Jackson to Eunice F. Jackson, Nov. 25, 1889, JFR, Letters.

40. *In Memoriam, Mrs. Selene Harding Jackson* (booklet), 24.

41. W. H. Jackson to Selene Jackson, Feb. 29, 1880, JFR, Letters. William Harding Jackson attended Montgomery Bell Academy, 1890-92.

Chapter 19. Tennessee Day

1. TMT 934, p. 2.

2. W. H. Jackson to William Easton, Apr. 22, 1889, TMT 934, exhibit #3, p. 101.

3. TMT 934, Easton's deposition, pp. 91-92. The Belle Meade Stud was identified on stationery as the Belle Meade Blood Horse Department during the years that W. H. Jackson, Howell E. Jackson, and John Harding, Jr., owned it.

4. Ibid., 93.

5. *Nashville Banner*, Feb. 8, 1889.

6. TMT 934, exhibit 3, p. 101.

7. TMT 934, pp. 4, 11.

8. Ibid, exhibit A, p. 103.

9. John S. Ogilvie, *History of the Great Flood in Johnstown, Pa.*, 51, 53, 77; TMT 934, p. 4.

10. TMT, p. 5.

11. Ibid., 5-7.

12. Ibid., 7, 105.

13. Ibid., 66-67.

14. Margaret Lindsley Warden, "Fabulous Belle Meade: Part II, The Blooming."

15. TMT 934, pp. 7, 106.

16. Ibid., 60.

17. Ibid., 8, 330-31.

18. Ibid., 61-62.

19. Ibid., 8, 62.

20. Ibid., 65.

21. *Spirit of the Times*, June 22, 1889. Black dialect was not easily transliterated. The correspondent likely took liberties with Bob Green's grammar and pronunciation, imitating the popular local colorist writers.

22. Ibid.

23. *Daily American*, May 1, 1881.

24. *Spirit of the Times*, June 22, 1889.

25. TMT 934, p. 64.

26. Ibid., 9, 102-3.

27. Ibid., 106.

28. *Daily American*, Apr. 25, 1890; Apr. 28, 1891.

29. TMT 934, pp. 11-12.

30. Ibid., 326-34.

31. *Daily American*, Apr. 28, 1891.

32. TMT 934, p. 2.

Chapter 20. Cracks in the Foundation

1. *Daily American*, Apr. 26, June 14, 1890.

2. Ibid, June 14, 1890.

3. Margaret Lindsley Warden, *The Belle Meade Plantation* (booklet), 43.

4. *Complete Dispersal Sale: Belle Meade Stud* (unpaged sale catalog, booklet).

5. WHJP, box 3, folder 21. The West Meade Farm consisted of nearly three thousand acres.

6. Howell E. Jackson to W. H. Jackson, Jan. 7, 1891, HJP, small collection, folder 2, TSLA.

7. *Nashville American,* July 9, 1899.

8. *Memphis Weekly Commercial,* Apr. 23, 1891.

9. *Nashville Tennessean and Nashville American,* Feb. 6, 1916.

10. Tremont arrived at Belle Meade on Oct. 6, 1891 (*Nashville Banner* Oct. 6, 1891); unpublished reminiscences of Henry "Speedy" Green, copy in the collection of the author; *Nashville American,* June 17, 1900.

11. *Daily American,* Apr. 19, 21, 1892.

12. *Nashville Tennessean and Nashville American,* Feb. 6, 1916.

13. *Turf, Field and Farm,* Aug. 21, 1891.

14. Warden, *The Belle Meade Plantation* (booklet), 38-39; *Evening Herald,* Dec. 1, 1891.

15. *Spirit of the Times,* Apr. 23, 1892.

16. Ibid., June 25, 1892.

17. *Turf, Field and Farm,* Nov. 25, 1892.

18. Warden, *The Belle Meade Plantation* (booklet), 43. Gleneig stood for two seasons at Belle Meade.

19. Sherrill Jane Kilgore, BHAPTA, 67.

20. Warden, *The Belle Meade Plantation* (booklet), 26. The first known picture of the carriage house/stable appeared in *Art Work of Nashville,* published in Chicago by the W. H. Parrish Publishing Co. in 1894.

21. *Nashville American,* Nov. 7, 1897.

22. Warden, *The Belle Meade Plantation* (booklet), p. 43.

23. J. Fairfax-Blakeborough, *Sykes of Sledmere: The Record of a Sporting Family and Famous Stud,* 153, 156, 187.

24. *Daily American,* Apr. 9, 1893.

25. *Nashville Banner,* June 20, 1893. Yearling sale catalogs were available each spring upon request to Gen. W. H. Jackson, Nashville.

26. WHJP, box 1, folder 17.

27. *Nashville Tennessean and Nashville American,* Feb. 6, 1916.

28. *Spirit of the Times,* June 2, 1894.

29. *New York Sunday Mercury,* 1895. Uncle Bob unsuccessfully bid for Tallulah at the 1890 Belle Meade auction of brood mares. At the 1891 yearling sale, he successfully bid eight hundred dollars for Chattanooga, a bay colt by Luke Blackburn.

30. Ibid. St. Blaise won the English Derby in 1883 and was America's leading sire in 1890. Charles Reed bought him for one hundred thousand dollars in 1891 and brought him to stand at his Fairvue Stud (Margaret Lindsley Warden, *The Saga of Fairvue, 1832-1977* [booklet], 18).

31. Ibid.

32. Ibid.

33. Charles Morton, *My Sixty Years of the Turf,* 131.

34. Option to W. H. Jackson signed by Richard Croker, Jan. 16, 1895, copy, WHJP, box 6, folder 5.

35. *Nashville American,* May 26, 1895.

36. *Spirit of the Times,* Apr. 27, 1895. No record has been found of the prices at the Chicago sale.

37. Ibid., July 13, 1895.

38. *Nashville American,* Oct. 2, 1895.

39. *Spirit of the Times,* June 27, 1896.

40. Harry J. Seiforth, "A Miniature History of Belle Meade."

41. *Nashville American*, Dec. 17, 1896.

42. *Nashville Banner*, June 22, 1897.

43. *Spirit of the Times*, June 26, 1897.

44. W. H. Jackson to Mrs. George S. Richardson of Lowell, Mass., collection of John L. Heflin, Jr. U.S.M.S. stood for U. S. Maritime Service.

45. *Nashville American*, Nov. 7, 1897.

46. Ibid., Sept. 15, 1895. Enquirer's grave is in the back yard of a private residence at 404 Leake Ave., less than half a mile from the Belle Meade mansion.

47. Ibid., Aug. 27, 1897. The statue has been moved several times. For many years it faced Leake Ave. near the log cabin. It now stands northeast of the stable near Parmer Ave.

48. Herman Justi, ed., *Official History of the Tennessee Centennial Exposition*, 406.

49. *Complete Dispersal Sale*, (unpaged sale catalog, booklet).

50. *Nashville American*, Nov. 7, 1897.

51. *Nashville Banner*, Dec. 15, 1904.

52. Walter Stokes, Jr., "Hillsboro Pike and Something Personal," 83.

53. *Nashville Banner*, Dec. 15, 1904.

54. *Nashville American*, Mar. 22, 1898.

55. *Spirit of the Times*, May 28, July 2, 1898.

56. *Nashville Ameican*, Oct. 13-15, 1898.

57. Margaret Lindsley Warden, "Fabulous Belle Meade: Part II, The Blooming" and "Part III, The Breaking."

58. *Nashville American*, Sept. 12, 1899.

59. William Waller, ed., *Nashville in the 1890s*, 163; *Nashville Banner*, June 9, 1900.

60. WHJP, box 3, folder 4.

61. *Spirit of the Times*, June 17, 1899.

62. *Nashville American*, June 21, 1899.

63. *Nashville Banner*, Sept. 18, 1899.

64. *Nashville Tennessean and Nashville American*, Feb. 6, 1916. The inkwells are on display at the Belle Meade Mansion.

65. *Nashville Banner*, June 7, 1900.

66. *Nashville American*, June 17, 1900.

67. *Nashville Tennessean and Nashville American*, Feb. 6, 1916.

68. *Nashville American*, Sept. 28, 1900.

69. *Complete Dispersal Sale*, (unpaged sale catalog, booklet).

70. *Nashville Banner*, Sept. 18, 1899.

71. Ibid., June 12, 1901.

72. *Complete Dispersal Sale*, (unpaged sale catalog, booklet).

73. *Nashville Banner*, June 18, 1901.

Chapter 21. The Last Hurrah

1. Francis Nichols, an 1855 graduate of the U. S. Military Academy, lost an arm and a foot in the Confederacy's cause. He was governor of Louisiana from 1878 to 1880 and from 1888 to 1892. *(Lamb's Biographical Dictionary of the United States* 6:5).

2. *Daily American*, Oct. 9, 1891.

3. Selene Jackson to Eunice F. Jackson, Nov. 9, 1891, JFR, Letters.

4. *Nashville Banner*, Jan. 17, 1969.

5. Ibid.

6. Walter Stokes, Jr., "Hillsboro Pike and Something Personal," 82-83. General Jackson was not eligible to vote, never having been pardoned by the U.S. Government.

7. Mrs. John Marshall to Eliza Marshall Ewing, Jan. 25, 1892, Andrew B. Ewing Family Letters.

8. Selene Jackson to Eunice F. Jackson, Feb. 16, 1892, JFR, Letters; Mrs. John Marshall to Eliza Marshall Ewing, Jan. 25, 1892, Andrew B. Ewing Family Letters.

9. Selene Jackson to Eunice Jackson, Feb. 28, 1892, JFR, Letters.

10. Ibid., June 15, 22, 1892.

11. *Daily American*, Mar. 12, 1892.

12. *Nashville Democrat*, Oct. 25, 1888.

13. *Minutes of the . . . United Confederate Veterans* 1:6.

14. *In Memoriam, Mrs. Selene Harding Jackson* (booklet), 23.

15. Selene Harding Curd to Charles P. Curd, Aug. 3, 1892, HFR collection of Mrs. James Balch.

16. Howell E. Jackson to W. H. Jackson, July 5, 1892, HEJP, box 1, folder 5.

17. *Daily American*, July 27, 1892.

18. Terry Calvani, "The Early Legal Career of Howell Jackson," 40.

19. *Daily American*, Oct. 3, 1892.

20. Selene Jackson to Eunice F. Jackson, Nov. 17, 1892, JFR, Letters. Howell E. Jackson's granddaughter, Ellen Buckner Wills of Nashville, always felt that General Jackson enlarged his dining room so that it would be larger than the one at West Meade.

21. Selene Jackson to Eunice F. Jackson, Nov. 17, 1892, JFR, Letters.

22. *In Memoriam, Mrs. Selene Harding Jackson* (booklet), 18.

23. Ibid., 28.

24. W. H. Jackson to Eunice F. Jackson, Dec. 12, 1892, JFR, Letters.

25. *In Memoriam, Mrs. Selene Harding Jackson* (booklet), 26. Susanna Carter probably died later in the decade, although the exact date of her death is unknown.

26. Ibid., 21.

27. *Nashville Banner*, Dec. 14, 1892.

28. Mannie Baxter Jackson to Eunice F. Jackson, Dec. 31, 1892, JFR, Letters.

29. *Daily American*, Jan. 14, 1893.

30. Margaret Lindsley Warden, "Fabulous Belle Meade: Part II, The Blooming"; J. B. Killebrew, *Recollections of My Life: An Anthology by J. B. Killebrew* 2:210.

31. *Nashville Banner*, Aug. 18, 1893.

32. "Gen. William H. Jackson," 176.

33. Ibid.; Account of expenses, Sept. 23, 1895, HMP, box 1, folder 1. In the obituary for Howell E. Jackson, Jr., printed in the *Nashville Banner* on Jan. 13, 1947, a reporter wrote that General Jackson financed his part of the project partially with funds he received when Richard Croker purchased his interest in the Belle Meade Stud.

34. *Chattanooga Times*, Mar. 19, 1903.

35. Kenneth McKellar, *Tennessee Senators as Seen by One of Their Successors*, 412.

36. President Benjamin Harrison to Howell E. Jackson, Feb. 4, 1893, HMP, box 8.

37. Howell E. Jackson, Jr., to Mrs. Howell E. Jackson, Feb. 20, 1893, transcribed copy, HJFR collection of the author.

38. Mattie H. Maddux to Mrs. Howell E. Jackson, Apr. 26, 1893, HFR letters collection of Mr. and Mrs. William A. Perkins, Jr.

39. William Howard Taft to Howell E. Jackson, Feb. 2, 1893, HFR letters collection of Mr. and Mrs. William A. Perkins, Jr.

40. *Nashville Banner*, Feb. 28, 1893.

41. Charles M. McGhee to Howell E. Jackson, Mar. 8, 1893, HFR letters collection of Mr. and Mrs. William A. Perkins, Jr.

42. Howell E. Jackson to Mary Harding Jackson, Aug. 11, 1893, APTA, Nashville Chapter.

43. Howell E. Jackson to President Grover Cleveland, Jan. 24, 1894, GCC.

44. Mannie B. Jackson to Eunice F. Jackson, Mar. 7, 1894, JFR, Letters.

45. William Waller, ed., *Nashville in the 1890s*, 5.

46. Ibid., 100-101.

47. "Minutes of the Fourth Annual Meeting and Reunion of the United Confederate Veterans," in *Minutes of the . . . United Confederate Veterans* 1:13.

48. Mannie B. Jackson to Eunice F. Jackson, Mar. 7, 1894, JFR, Letters. Mannie was the wife of Robert Fenner Jackson, Gen. W. H. Jackson's younger half brother. Albert Marks's father, Albert S. Marks of Winchester, was governor of Tennessee from 1879 until 1881.

49. Undated, typewritten reminiscences of Henry ("Speedy") Green, collection of the author.

50. *Nashville Banner*, June 21, 1894.

51. Howell E. Jackson to William H. Taft, Nov. 16, 1894, WHTC, section 3.

52. Howell E. Jackson to Jacob McGavock Dickinson, Oct. 28, 1894, JMDP, box 22, folder 9.

53. Howell E. Jackson to Jacob McGavock Dickinson, Oct. 28, 1894; to Richard Olney, Nov. 2, 1894, both in the JMDP, box 22, folder 9; and to William H. Taft, Nov. 16, 1894, WHTC, section 3.

54. Mrs. Howell E. Jackson to Grover Cleveland, Aug. 10, 1895, GCC.

55. DCD, bk. 194:616.

56. *National Encyclopedia of American Biography* 3:244-45.

57. *Nashville American*, June 9, 1895.

58. Ibid., Aug. 13, 1895; *Nashville Banner*, Aug. 12, 1895.

59. Justice and Mrs. Jackson had insisted on Elizabeth's trip to break up a romance with Charlie Buntin.

60. W. H. Taft to Mrs. Howell E. Jackson, Aug. 10, 1895, transcribed copy, HJFR collection of the author.

61. *Cincinnati Commercial Gazette*, Aug. 18, 1895.

62. "Leading Citizen Series—Gen W. H. Jackson," unidentified Nashville newspaper, 1895, collection of the author.

63. *Nashville American*, Dec. 11, 1896. General Jackson was thought to own "something over $100,000 of bonds and over $300,000 in stock."

64. DCD, bk. 255:317, bk. 260:438.

65. Waller, *Nashville in the 1890s*, 103-4.

66. Herman Justi, ed., *Official History of the Tennessee Centennial Exposition*, 482; *Daily American*, June 20, 1894.

67. Justi, *Official History*, 30-31.

68. Ibid., 33.

69. *Nashville Tennessean*, Mar. 15, 1925.

70. *Tennessean*, Aug. 28, 1988.

71. Justi, *Official History of the Tennessee Centennial,* 133.

72. Ibid., 230, 235, 246, 247, 481.

73. Ibid., 156, 275, 281, 283, 308, 470.

74. Killebrew, *Recollections* 2:281-82.

75. *Nashville American,* Nov. 25, 1897.

76. Warden, "Fabulous Belle Meade: Part III, The Breaking."

77. *Nashville Banner,* May 19, 1896.

78. Warden, "Fabulous Belle Meade: Part II, The Blooming."

79. Ibid., "Part III, The Breaking."

80. *Nashville American,* Feb. 17, 1897.

81. Anne W. Magruder, interview with the author.

82. Undated, typewritten reminiscences of Henry ("Speedy") Green, collection of the author.

83. *Nashville American,* May 8, 1898.

84. Ibid., Oct. 19, 1898.

85. *A Sermon, In Memoriam Eunice Jackson Marks* (booklet), 16-17.

86. The Catholic Center: John Marks Handly to the Reverend John B. Morris, May 28, 1899.

87. The Catholic Center: Diocese of Nashville Baptismal Certificates.

88. Ibid., Jan. 7, 1900. Edwards Sinclair survived the shooting.

89. Martha Lindsey, interview with the author.

90. Davidson County Chancery Court Minute Book no. 61, p. 441.

91. The Catholic Center: Diocese of Nashville Baptismal Certificates.

92. Mary Harding Ragland, interview with the author.

93. *A Sermon, In Memoriam Eunice Jackson Marks* (booklet), 16-17.

94. DCRWI, bk. 36:8.

95. Margaret Early Wyatt, interview with the author.

96. Mrs. Andrew B. Benedict, Jr., interview with the author.

97. William Waller, ed., *Nashville, 1900-1910,* 271.

98. Jeannette Acklen Noel, interview with the author.

99. Arthur Singleton, interview with the author.

100. DCCM, bk. 7:392.

101. DCRWI, bk. 36:8.

102. The Catholic Center: Selene Jackson Elliston to the Right Reverend Bishop Byrne, Thursday [date not known], and Bishop Byrne to John J. Vertrees, Apr. 20, 1903.

103. DCD, bk. 260:438; *Nashville American,* Nov. 27, 28, 1901.

104. Waller, *Nashville, 1900 to 1910,* 279.

105. *Nashville American,* Dec. 29, 1901.

Chapter 22. End of an Era

1. *Nashville American,* Mar. 16, 1902.

2. *Nashville Banner,* June 17, 1902.

3. *Spirit of the Times,* June 21, 1902.

4. *Nashville American,* June 15, 1902.

5. Ibid., June 16, 1902.

6. *Nashville Banner,* June 17, 1902.

7. *Nashville American,* June 27, 1902.

8. *Nashville Banner,* Sept. 2-3, 1902.

9. *Complete Dispersal Sale,* (unpaged sale catalog, booklet).

10. *Nashville American,* Oct. 30, 1902.

11. Ibid. The sires Longstreet, imp. Madison, and imp. Tithonus were sold at the Oct. 1902 dispersal sale.

12. *Nashville Banner,* Dec. 15, 1904.

13. Jeannette Acklen Noel, interview with the author.

14. " 'Jack' and 'Fitz,'" 272-73.

15. *Nashville Tennessean,* Jan. 10, 1943.

16. *Nashville Daily News,* Mar. 31, 1903.

17. *Nashville American,* Mar. 31, 1903.

18. *Nashville Banner,* Apr. 1, 1903.

19. Ibid., Nov. 17, 1906.

20. *Nashville American,* July 20, 1903.

21. *Nashville Daily News,* July 20, 1903.

22. Robert H. Cartmell Papers, 1849-1915, 20:81.

23. *Nashville American,* Nov. 25, 1903; *Nashville Banner,* Oct. 22, 1903.

24. Family notes in collection of the author. Hill McAlister, who married Mary Jackson's daughter Louise on November 27, 1901, later became governor of Tennessee (1933-37), following in the footsteps of his grandfather, Aaron Brown, who was governor of Tennessee from 1845 to 1847.

25. *Nashville Banner,* Oct. 14-15, 1903. William McGavock of Williamson County, who frequently visited the Belle Meade Stud, said that Inspector B would have sold at a higher price had buyers not noticed a mole the size of a small marble. McGavock also said that Huron's sale price was depressed by an enlarged ankle, the result of catching his foot under a stall door while a suckling.

26. *Nashville American,* Nov. 24-25, 1903.

27. Ellen Marshall to Eliza M. Ewing, Nov. 28, 1903, Andrew B. Ewing Family Letters.

28. Margaret Lindsley Warden, "Fabulous Belle Meade: Part III, The Breaking." William B. Cheatham later "drifted west" where he worked in Arizona at $1.50 a day. In 1909, through the help of Jacob McGavock Dickinson, Will got a job as one of the inspectors at the Culebra Cut on the Panama Canal project. There, Dickinson said Will made "a fine record" (Jacob McGavock Dickinson to "My Three Sons," May 5, 1909, JMDP, box 16, folder 13).

29. *Nashville Banner,* Nov. 17, 1906.

30. Ibid.

31. Robert C. Brien to Master W. H. Jackson, July 14, 1904, WHJP, box 1, folder 19.

32. *Nashville American,* Oct. 16, 1904.

33. Ibid., Oct. 13, 1904.

34. Ibid., Nov. 16, 1904.

35. Ibid., Nov. 18, 1904.

36. Warden, "Fabulous Belle Meade: Part III, The Breaking." Trilby Elliston Williams of Nashville, a granddaughter of Selene Jackson Elliston, told the author on Mar. 8, 1990, that the Elliston family inherited or acquired some of the Jackson silver, including a tray, pitcher, and goblets that General Jackson gave Selene as an anniversary present. According to Ellen Buckner Wills of Nashville, William Harding Jackson's son also received some of the silver.

37. *Nashville American,* Nov. 18, 19, 1904.

38. Ibid., Nov. 23, 1904.

39. *Nashville Banner,* Feb. 15, 1904.

40. Ibid., Dec. 15, 1904.

41. *Nashville American,* Nov. 23, 1904.

42. *Nashville Banner,* Apr. 30, 1906. When Acklen visited the park on May 20, he found several "good-sized" deer herds, the fences in uniformly good condition, and only a portion of "the wire work on the rock walls" torn away (*Nashville Banner,* May 21, 1904).

43. Jeannette Acklen Noel, interview with the author.

44. *Nashville Banner,* Dec. 27, 1904; Feb. 22, 1925.

45. William Waller, ed., *Nashville, 1900 to 1910,* 20.

46. DCD, bk. 70:437.

47. DCD, bk. 69:113, bk. 307:551-57, bk. 310:73.

48. Jacob McGavock Dickinson, "Stories and Reminiscences of Jacob M. Dickinson," July 1924, 23.

49. Oscar Cromwell Tidwell, Jr., *Belle Meade Park,* 13-14.

50. *Nashville Banner,* Sept. 22, 1906.

51. Tidwell, *Belle Meade Park,* 13.

Epilogue

1. Ellen Wemyss, "Recollections Concerning the History of the Association for the Preservation of Tennessee Antiquities," an audio-taped speech; APTA Minutes, Board of Directors Meeting, bk. 1, Oct. 7, 1952.

2. *Nashville Banner,* Nov. 28, 1952.

3. APTA Minutes, bk. 1, Jan. 23, 1953; *Public Acts of the State of Tennessee Seventy-eighth General Assembly* (booklet).

4. Larry Wallerstein and Greg Anderson, in telephone interviews with the author.

5. *Nashville Banner,* Sept. 29, 1971.

6. Trilby Elliston Williams, interview with the author.

7. *Nashville Banner,* Apr. 22, 1909.

8. Unpublished family notes in the collection of the author.

9. Will of Selene Jackson Elliston, HEJP, box 2, folder 17.

10. *Nashville Tennessean,* Oct. 8, 1913; Mount Olivet Cemetery records.

11. *Nashville Banner,* Sept. 22, 1906.

12. *Nashville Banner,* Nov. 17, 1906; *Nashville American,* Nov. 12, 1906; Mrs. Milton M. Reece, interview with the author. Bob Green was so well known and respected in the Thoroughbred world that the *Spirit of the Times* reported his death on Nov. 26, 1906. The servants' cemetery was located on the hillside near the present-day intersection of Harding Place and Windsor Drive.

13. *Nashville Banner,* May 22, 1908. The Dickinsons built the upstairs bathroom above the office at Belle Meade in anticipation of Taft's 1908 visit. Family members always understood that Taft became stuck in the bathtub during his visit.

14. *Tennessee Bar Journal,* May 1908, 25.

15. JMDP, box 16, folder 13; Jacob McGavock Dickinson III, interview with the author. J. Overton Dickinson died in 1910.

16. *Nashville Banner*, Oct. 20, 1909.

17. Undated clipping, *Nashville American*, Luke Lea Papers.

18. Oscar Cromwell Tidwell, Jr., *Belle Meade Park*, 24-25. The Leakes' daughter, Dorothy, later married William Jackson Elliston, the only child of Selene Jackson and William Robert Elliston.

19. Ibid., 15.

20. Ibid., 15-16.

21. John Joseph Ellis, "Belle Meade: Evolution of an Aesthetic, 1905-1938," (unpublished thesis), 7.

22. Tidwell, *Belle Meade Park*, 17.

23. DCD, bk. 409:52-53.

24. Ibid., bk. 805:181.

25. Tidwell, *Belle Meade Park*, 18, 94.

26. Ibid., 21; Morgan B. Reynolds, *Seventy Years of the Belle Meade Country Club, 1901-1971*, unpaged.

27. Spring Hill Cemetery Records.

28. *Nashville Tennessean and Nashville American*, May 18, 1916; Tidwell, *Belle Meade Park*, 25.

29. Architectural drawings of Belle Meade, the residence of Mr. and Mrs. Meredith Caldwell, measured and drawn by Donald Miller, 1947-48, Nashville Chapter, APTA.

30. 1917 and 1919 catalogs of the Belle Meade yearling sales at Saratoga, New York, collection of the author.

31. Tidwell, *Belle Meade Park*, 25-26.

32. Ibid., 27.

33. Ibid., 56.

34. Melinda Sneed Brink, interview with the author, Nashville, Feb. 1989.

35. A *Bicentennial Chronicle* (booklet), 114-15.

36. Undated Nashville newspaper quoting Martha Gaines, a granddaughter of William Jackson.

37. In 1937, the Nashville Park Board designated all the portions of Percy Warner Park west and south of Old Hickory Blvd. as Edwin Warner Park in memory of a brother of Percy Warner. Following Percy's death in 1927, Edwin became a member of the park board and eventually its chairman. He was a driving force in the acquisition of the remainder of the park's 2,665 acres between 1927 and 1930.

38. The Steeplechase bell, made by the C. S. Bell Co. of Hillsboro, Ohio, during the nineteenth century, was given to the non-profit organization in 1951 by Jacob McGavock Dickinson, Jr., who inherited it from his father, Judge Jacob McGavock Dickinson. The senior Dickinson had been given the bell by Frank McGavock Ewing, who had been given it by Mary Harding Jackson. The bell had been owned by Gen. W. G. Harding, Mary's father, and had been at Belle Meade for an unknown period. See Margeret Lindsley Warden, "Belle Meade's Bell"; F. M. Ewing to Judge R. E. Saunders, Saundersville, Tenn., Oct. 28, 1918, JMDP.

39. *Nashville Banner*, Oct. 27, 1913; Last Will and Testament of Mary Harding Jackson, HMP, box 2, folder 13.

40. *Nashville Tennessean*, Mar. 15, 1944; Ivar Lou Duncan, "West Meade: Bequest From Past to Present," *Suburban News* (Nashville), Feb. 28, 1974.

41. Margaret Lindsley Warden, *The Belle Meade Plantation* (booklet), last page.

42. *Hall of Fame, National Museum of Racing, Inc.* (booklet), 8, May 15, 1889.

Bibliography

Articles

Alderson, William T., ed. "Civil War Reminiscences of John Johnston, 1861-1865." *Tennessee Historical Quarterly* 14 (1955): 142-75.

"The Battle of Columbus, Ky." *Confederate Veteran* 5 (Jan. 1897): 210.

Bell, Wayne H., Dr. "A History of Vine Street Christian Church." In *Seven Early Churches of Nashville.* Nashville: Elder's Bookstore, 1972.

Blakeborough, John Fairfax. *Sykes of Sledmere: The Record of a Sporting Family and Famous Stud.* London: Philip Allan & Co., 1929.

"British Mercantile Claims, 1775-1803." *Virginia Genealogist* 7, no. 2 (1963): 73.

Brown, John Ellerson. "Belle Meade Plantation: Tale of a Northern Trooper in the Civil War." *Los Angeles Times*, February 23, 1908.

Burrow, Suzanne, Fred G. Hawkins, and Joe P. Distretti. "The Old Island Road." *Tennessee Conservation Magazine*, November-December 1985, 17-18.

Calvani, Terry. "The Early Legal Career of Howell Jackson." *Vanderbilt Law Review* 30 (January 1977): 39-72.

Carter, William H. "The Master of Belle Meade." *Outlook*, July 27, 1912, 725-26, 728-30.

Coleman, Ellen Snell. "The Harding House." Rutherford County Historical Society Publication no. 23 (Summer 1984).

Dickinson, Jacob McGavock. "Stories and Reminiscences of Jacob M. Dickinson." *Outdoor America:* July 1924; December 1926; January, March, April 1927.

Duncan, Ivar Lou. "West Meade: Bequest from Past to Present." *Suburban News* (Nashville), February 28, 1974.

"Gen. William H. Jackson." *Confederate Veteran* 2 (June 1894):176-77.

Glassie, Henry. "The Types of Southern Mountain Cabin." In Jan Harold Brunvard, *The Study of American Folklore.* New York: W. W. Norton, 1968.

Gower, Herschel. "Belle Meade." *Tennessee Historical Quarterly* 22 (1963): 203-22.

Grimsley, Will. "Yas, Suh! Dat Iroquois Was Some Hoss!" *Nashville Tennessean*, 1944, day and month unknown. Collection of the author.

Hoobler, James A. "The Civil War Diary of Louisa Brown Pearl." *Tennessee Historical Quarterly* 38 (1979): 308-21.

"'Jack' and 'Fitz.'" *Confederate Veteran* 11 (June 1903): 272-73.

Jacobs, Josephine Grider. "Couple Finds Adventure at Sans Souci." *Osceola (Ark.) Times*, September 12, 1985.

————. "John McGavock's Death Mars Life in Paradise." *Osceola (Ark.) Times*, September 19, 1985.

Jennings, Thelma. "Tennessee and the Nashville Conventions of 1850." *Tennessee Historical Quarterly* 30 (1971): 70-82.

Kegley, Mary. "The Big Fort." *Journal of the Roanoke Historical Society* 10 (1978): 6-30.

Mackin, Sister Aloysius, O. P., ed. "Wartime Scenes from Convent Windows, St. Cecilia 1861 through 1865." *Tennessee Historical Quarterly* 39 (1980): 401-22.

Minnix, Kathleen. "'That Memorable Meeting': Sam Jones and the Nashville Revival of 1885." *Tennessee Historical Quarterly* 48 (1989): 151-61.

Owsley, Frank L. "The Fundamental Cause of the Civil War: Egocentric Sectionalism." In *A Vanderbilt Miscellany, 1919-1944*. Ed. Richmond Croom Beatty. Nashville: Vanderbilt Univ. Press, 1944.

Reall, Joseph H. "Belle Mead." *Agricultural Review and Journal*, January 1883, 48-61.

"Recollections of Memucan Hunt Howard." *American Historical Magazine* 7 (January 1902), 55-68.

Roper, James. "Benjamin Fooy and the Spanish Forts of San Fernando and Campo de la Esperanza." *West Tennessee Historical Society Papers* 36 (October 1982): 41-64.

Salvador (John L. Hervey). "Bramble: Part IV." *Thoroughbred Record*, Jan. 19, 1935.

Seiforth, Harry J. "A Miniature History of Belle Meade." *New Orleans Picayune*. Reprinted in the *Nashville American*, Oct. 20, 1902.

Shuffler, R. Henderson. "Signing of Texas' Declaration of Independence: Myth and Record." *Southwestern Historical Quarterly* 65 (January 1962): 327-29.

Smith, Samuel D. "Fort Southwest Point, A New View." *Tennessee Conservationist* 51, no.6 (1985): 4-5.

Stokes, Walter, Jr. "Hillsboro Pike and Something Personal." *Tennessee Historical Quarterly* 24 (1965): 70-84.

Swint, Henry Lee. "Travellers' Rest." *Tennessee Historical Quarterly* 26 (1967): 119-36.

_____, ed. "Reports from Educational Agents of the Freedmen's Bureau in Tennessee, 1865-1870." *Tennessee Historical Quarterly* 1 (1942): 51-80.

"Tales of an Old Mississippi Town." *Southern Living,* April 1990, pp. 1sct-2sct.

Thomas, George H., Maj. Gen. "Report by Major General George H. Thomas." In *Supplemental Report of the Joint Committee on the Conduct of the War, in Two Volumes.* Washington, D.C.: Government Printing Office, 1866.

"Walnut Grove Track." An undated newspaper article, collection of Margaret L. Warden, Nashville.

Warden, Margaret Lindsley. "Belle Meade's Bell." *Nashville Tennessean Magazine,* May 6, 1951.

_____. "Fabulous Belle Meade: Part I, The Building." *Nashville Tennessean Magazine,* April 30, 1950.

_____. "Fabulous Belle Meade: Part II, The Blooming." *Nashville Tennessean Magazine,* May 7, 1950.

_____. "Fabulous Belle Meade: Part III, The Breaking." *Nashville Tennessean Magazine,* May 14, 1950.

West, Edward William. "A Visitor to Belle Meade in 1874." *Tennessee Historical Magazine.* Series 2, vol. 1 (Oct. 1930): 62-63.

Artifacts

Artifacts. Collection of Association for the Preservation of Tennessee Antiquities, Nashville Chapter.

Medallion. Collection of Ellen Snell Coleman, Nashville.

Statue of Priam. Collection of Mrs. Elliston Williams, Nashville.

Stirrup Cup. Collection of Stuart Ragland, Jr., M.D., Gallows Bay, St. Croix.

Books

Acklen, Jeannette Tillotson, comp. *Tennessee Records, Tombstone Inscriptions and Manuscripts Historical and Biographical.* Nashville: Cullom & Ghertner Co., 1933.

Aiken, Leona Taylor. *Donelson, Tennessee; Its History and Landmarks.* Nashville and Kingsport, Tenn.: Kingsport Press, 1968.

_____. *The McGavocks of Two Rivers.* Kingsport: East Tennessee Printing Co., 1975.

The American Thoroughbred Stallion Register. Lexington, Ky.: Compiled by Treacy and Walker, 1921.

Anderson, James Douglas. *Making the American Thoroughbred.* Nashville: Grainger Williams, 1946.

Art Work of Nashville. 1894. Reprint. Nashville: Tennessee Historical Society.

Baird, Nancy Disher. *David Wendel Yandell: Physician of Old Louisville.* Lexington: Univ. of Kentucky Press, 1978.

Baron, Randall S., and Philip Von Borries. *The Official Kentucky Derby Quiz Book.* Louisville: Devyn Press, 1986.

Bartlett, Genevieve Wilson. *Forefathers and Descendants of Willard & Genevieve Wilson Bartlett and of Allied Families.* Portland, Maine: Anthoenson Press, 1952.

Bejach, Wilena Roberts and Lillian Johnson Gardiner, compilers and publishers. *Williamson County, Tennessee Marriage Records 1800-1850.* Memphis: 1957.

Biographical and Historical Memoirs of Northeast Arkansas. Chicago: Goodspeed Publishing Co., 1889.

Blackburn, James K. Polk. *Terry's Texas Rangers; Reminiscences of J. K. P. Blackburn.* 1919. Reprint. Austin, Tex.: Ranger Press, 1979.

Bowman, Virginia McDaniel. *Historic Williamson County; Old Homes and Sites.* Nashville: Blue & Gray Press, 1971.

Brandau, Roberta Seawell, ed. *History of Homes and Gardens of Tennessee.* Nashville: The Garden Study Club of Nashville, 1936.

Bruce, Sanders D. *The American Stud Book.* Vol. 1. New York: Turf, Field and Farm, 1884.

_____. *The Horse-Breeders' Guide and Hand Book.* New York: Turf, Field and Farm, 1883. Revised in 1892 as *The Breeders' Hand Book and Guide.*

_____. *The Thoroughbred Horse: His Origin, How to Breed and How to Select Him. With the Horse-Breeders' Guide. . . .* New York: Turf, Field and Farm, 1892.

Butler, Mrs. F. A. *Mrs. D. H. M'Gavock: Life-Sketch and Thoughts.* Nashville: Publishing House of the Methodist Episcopal Church, South, n.d.

Campbell, John. *Nashville Business Directory.* Nashville: Smith, Camp & Co., 1857.

Claxton, Jimmie Lou Sparkman. *Eighty-Eight Years With Sarah Polk.* New York: Vantage Press, 1972.

Clayton, W. W. *History of Davidson County, Tennessee.* Philadelphia: J. W. Lewis & Co., 1880.

Clements, Paul. *A Past Remembered.* Nashville: Clearview Press, 1987.

Cochran, Bess White. *The First One Hundred Years: Being a More or Less Lighthearted Look at the History of the Nashville YMCA, 1875-1975.* Nashville: Metropolitan Board of the YMCA, 1975.

Corlew, Robert E. *A History of Dickson County.* Nashville: Tennessee Historical Commission and the Dickson County Historical Society, 1956.

Coulter, E. Merton. *The South During Reconstruction, 1865-1877.* Baton Rouge: Louisiana State Univ. Press, 1947.

Crabb, Alfred L. *Nashville: Personality of a City.* Indianapolis: Bobbs-Merrill, 1960.

Crockett, David. *The Autobiography of David Crockett.* New York: Charles Scribner's Sons, 1923.

Crockett, Walter Hill. *Vermont, The Green Mountain State.* New York: Century History Co., 1923.

Davis, James D. *Early History of Memphis; also the Old Times Papers.* Memphis: Hite, Crumpton and Kelly, 1873.

Davis, Joel, comp. *Nashville City Directory.* Nashville: Marshall and Bruce, 1886.

Dinkins, James. *1861 to 1865, by an "Old Johnnie": Personal Recollections and Experiences in the Confederate Army.* 1897. Dayton, Ohio: Morningside Bookshop, 1975.

Donald, David Herbert. *Charles Sumner and the Coming of the Civil War.* New York: Alfred A. Knopf, 1960.

Douglas, Byrd. *Steamboatin' on the Cumberland.* Nashville: Tennessee Book Co., 1961.

Doyle, Don H. *Nashville in the New South.* Knoxville: Univ. of Tennessee Press, 1985.

Durham, Walter T. *Nashville: The Occupied City.* Nashville: Tennessee Historical Society, 1985.

———. *Reluctant Partners: Nashville and the Union.* Nashville: Tennessee Historical Society, 1987.

Elliot, Ellsworth, Jr. *West Point in the Confederacy.* New York: G. A. Baker & Co., 1941.

Ellis, Franklin. *History of Fayette County, Pennsylvania.* Philadelphia: L. H. Everts & Co., 1882.

Ellis, William A., ed. and comp. *Norwich University, 1819-1911: Her History, Her Graduates, Her Roll of Honor.* Montpelier, Vt.: Capital City Press, 1911.

Fitch, John. *Annals of the Army of the Cumberland.* Philadelphia: J. B. Lippincott, 1864.

Folmsbee, Stanley J., Robert E. Corlew, and Enoch L. Mitchell. *Tennessee: A Short History.* Knoxville: Univ. of Tennessee Press, 1969.

Franklin, John Hope. *Reconstruction After the Civil War.* Chicago: Univ. of Chicago Press, 1961.

Freeman, Dr. Larry., ed. *Yesterday's Games.* Watkins Glen, N.Y.: Century House, 1970.

Garrett, W. R., and A. V. Goodpasture. *History of Tennessee, Its People and Its Institutions.* Nashville: Brandon Printing Co., 1900.

Gilchrist, Agnes Addison. *William Strickland: Architect and Engineer, 1788-1854.* New York: Da Capo Press, 1969.

Gower, Herschel. *Pen and Sword: The Life and Journals of Randal W. McGavock.* Nashville: Tennessee Historical Commission, 1959.

Graham, Eleanor. *Nashville: A Short History and Selected Buildings.* Nashville: Historical Commission of Metropolitan Nashville-Davidson County, 1974.

Gray, Robert. *The McGavock Family.* Richmond, Va.: William Ellis Jones, 1903.

The Great Panic. Nashville: Johnson & Whiting. 1862.

Guild, Jo C. *Old Times in Tennessee with Historical, Personal and Political Scraps and Sketches.* Nashville: Tavel, Eastman & Howell, 1878.

Haslip, Jean. *Crown of Mexico: Maximilian and His Empress Carlota.* New York: Holt, Rinehart,and Winston, 1972.

Hervey, John. *Racing in America, 1665-1865.* 2 vols. New York: Jockey Club, 1944.

Horn, Stanley F. *The Army of Tennessee.* Norman: Univ. of Oklahoma Press, 1952.

———, ed. *Tennessee's War: 1861-1865, Described by Participants.* Nashville: Tennessee Civil War Centennial Commission, 1965.

Hutchinson, Thomas, ed. *Xenophontis De Cyri Institutione*. Philadelphia: William Poyntell, 1806.

Johnson, Andrew. *The Papers of Andrew Johnson*. 8 Vols. Edited by Leroy P. Graf and Ralph W. Haskins. Knoxville: Univ. of Tennessee Press, 1967-   .

————. *Speeches of Andrew Johnson, President of the United States; with a Biographical Introduction by Frank Moore*. Boston: Little, Brown, 1866.

Johnston, Joseph E. *Narrative of Military Operations*. New York: D. Appleton & Co., 1874.

Jones, Katherine M. *Heroines of Dixie: Confederate Women Tell Their Story of the War*. Westport, Conn.: Greenwood Press, 1955.

Justi, Herman, ed. *Official History of the Tennessee Centennial Exposition*. Nashville: Brandon Printing Co., 1898.

Killebrew, J. B. *Recollections of My Life: An Anthology by J. B. Killebrew*. 2 vols. Nashville: n.p., 1896-98. TSLA microfilm.

Lamb's Biographical Dictionary of the United States. Boston: James L. Lamb Co., 1900.

LeDuc, William G. *Recollections of a Civil War Quartermaster: The Autobiography of William G. LeDuc*. St. Paul: The North Central Publishing Co., 1963.

Lindsley, John Berrien, ed. *Military Annals of Tennessee, Confederate*. 1st series. Nashville: J. M. Lindsley & Co., 1886.

MacKay-Smith, Alexander. *The Race Horses of America, 1832-1872: Portraits and Other Paintings by Edward Troye*. Saratoga Springs, N.Y.: National Museum of Racing, 1981.

McKellar, Kenneth. *Tennessee Senators as Seen by One of their Successors*. Kingsport, Tenn.: Southern Publishers, 1942.

McLean, Malcolm D., ed. and comp. *Papers Concerning Robertson's Colony in Texas*. 2 vols. Fort Worth: Texas Christian Univ. Press, 1976.

Mims, Edwin. *Chancellor Kirkland of Vanderbilt*. Nashville: Vanderbilt Univ. Press, 1940.

Minutes of the . . . United Confederate Veterans. Vol. 1. 1889-92, 1894-97. New Orleans: n.p., 1907.

Moore, Josiah S., ed. *Annals of Henrico County*. Richmond, Va.: Williams Printing Co., 1904.

Morris, Edmund. *The Rise of Theodore Roosevelt*. New York: Ballantine Books, 1979.

Morris, Richard B., ed. *Encyclopedia of American History*. New York: Harper & Brothers, 1953.

Mortimer, Roger. *The History of the Derby Stakes*. London: Michael Joseph, 1973.

Morton, Charles. *My Sixty Years of the Turf*. London: Hutchinson & Co., Ltd., 1930.

National Encyclopedia of American Biography. New York: James T. White & Co., 1900.

Nelson, Anson, and Fanny Nelson. *Memorials of Sarah Childress Polk*. New York: A. D. F. Randolph & Co., 1892.

Ogilvie, John S. *History of the Great Flood in Johnstown, Pa*. New York: J. S. Ogilvie, 1889.

Parmer, Charles B. *For Gold and Glory*. New York: Carrick and Evans, 1939.

Patrick, James. *Architecture in Tennessee, 1768-1897*. Knoxville: Univ. of Tennessee Press, 1981.

Peterson, Eugene T. *Mackinac Island: Its History in Pictures*. Mackinac Island, Mich.: Mackinac Island State Park Commission, 1973.

Powell, J. M. *History of the Franklin, Tennessee, Church of Christ*. Franklin: n.p., 1953.

Putnam, A. W. *History of Middle Tennessee*. 1859. Reprint. Knoxville: Univ. of Tennessee Press, 1971.

Ramsey, J. G. M. *The Annals of Tennessee to the End of the Eighteenth Century*. Charleston, S.C.: Walker & James, 1853.

Reynolds, Morgan B. *Seventy Years of the Belle Meade Country Club, 1901-1971*. Nashville: McQuiddy Printing Co., 1971.

Ridley, B. L. *Battles and Sketches of the Army of Tennessee*. Mexico, Mo.: Missouri Printing Co., 1906.

Rifkind, Carol. *A Field Guide to American Architecture*. New York: New American Library, 1980.

Robertson, William H. P. *The History of Thoroughbred Racing in America*. New York: Bonanza Books, 1964.

Roosevelt, Theodore. *Hunting Adventures in the West*. New York: G. P. Putnam's Sons, 1927.

Sherman, William Tecumseh. *Personal Memoirs of Gen. W. T. Sherman*. 4th ed. 2 vols. New York: Charles L. Webster, 1891.

Smith, Reid. *Majestic Middle Tennessee*. Prattville, Ala.: Paddle Wheel Publications, 1975.

Smith, Samuel D., ed. *Woodlawn Mansion, Nashville, Tennessee: History, Architecture and Archaeology.* Nashville: Northern Telecom, 1985.

Speer, William S., ed. and comp. *Sketches of Prominent Tennesseans.* Nashville: Albert B. Tavel, 1888.

Thomas, George S. Reports in *Joint Committee on the Conduct of the War.* 2 vols. Washington, D.C.: Government Printing Office, 1866.

Thomas, James P. *From Tennessee Slave to St. Louis Entrepreneur: The Autobiography of James Thomas.* Edited by Loren Schweninger. Columbia: Univ. of Missouri Press, 1984.

Thomas, Jane. *Old Days in Nashville.* Nashville: Publishing House of the Methodist Episcopal Church, South, 1897.

Tidwell, Oscar Cromwell, Jr. *Belle Meade Park.* Nashville: n.p., 1983.

United States Bureau of the Census. *Historical Statistics of the United States: Colonial Times to 1970.* Bicentennial Edition, Part 2. Washington, D.C.: Government Printing Office, 1975.

Veech, James. *The Monongahela of Old or Historic Sketches of Southwest Pennsylvania to the Year 1800.* Pittsburgh: Mrs. E. V. Blaine, 1892.

Waller, William, ed. *Nashville in the 1890s.* Nashville: Vanderbilt Univ. Press, 1970.

————, ed. *Nashville, 1900 to 1910.* Nashville: Vanderbilt Univ. Press, 1972.

War of the Rebellion: A Compilation of the Official Records of the Union and Confederate Armies. Series 1, vol. 45; Series 2, vol. 52; Series 4, vols. 3, 5. Washington, D.C.: Government Printing Office, 1894 and 1898.

Whitney, Edith Rucker. *Pioneers of Davidson County.* Baltimore: Genealogical Publishing Co., 1981.

Williams, Frances Leigh. *Matthew Fontaine Maury: Scientist of the Sea.* New Brunswick, N.J.: Rutgers Univ. Press, 1963.

Williams, Samuel Cole. *Beginnings of West Tennessee.* Johnson City, Tenn.: Watauga Press, 1930.

Wooldridge, John, ed. *History of Nashville, Tennessee.* 1890. Reprint. Nashville: Publishing House of the Methodist Episcopal Church, South, 1890.

Booklets and Pamphlets

A Bicentennial Chronicle. Nashville: Metropolitan Nashville-Davidson County Public Schools, 1976.

Bragg, Emma W. *Scrapbook: Some Family Reminiscences of a Native Nashville Septuagenarian*. Nashville: E. W. Bragg, 1985.

Complete Dispersal Sale: Belle Meade Stud (unpaged sale catalog). Cleveland, Ohio: Winn & Judson, 1902. Collection of the author.

Cornwell, Ilene. *Footsteps Along the Harpeth*. Nashville: Williams Printing Co., 1976.

In Memoriam, Gen. William G. Harding. Nashville: Southern Methodist Publishing House, 1886.

In Memoriam, Mrs. Selene Harding Jackson. Nashville: n.p., 1892.

Malone, Thomas H. *Little Rachel's Debut*. Nashville: n.p., 1906.

Metropolitan Historical Markers. Nashville: Historical Commission of Metropolitan Nashville-Davidson County, 1973.

National Museum of Racing, Inc. *The Hall of Fame*. Saratoga Springs, N.Y.: National Museum of Racing, n.d.

Premiums and Regulations for the Third Annual Spring Fair of the Davidson County Agricultural and Mechanical Association. Nashville: L. P. Williams & Co., 1858.

Public Acts of the State of Tennessee Seventy-eighth General Assembly. Nashville: Rich Printing Co., 1953.

Sacred to the Memory of Mrs. Selena Harding, Consort of Mr. William Giles Harding, and Daughter of Nathaniel A. McNairy, Esq. N.p., n.d. Collection of the author.

A Sermon, In Memoriam Eunice Jackson Marks. Nashville: n.p., 1902.

Smith, Samuel D. and Stephen T. Rogers. *Historical Information Concerning the Fort Blount-Williamsburg Site, Jackson County, Tennessee*. Nashville: Tennessee Department of Conservation, Division of Archaeology, 1989.

Thirty-fifth Annual Reunion of the Association of the Graduates of the United States Military Academy at West Point, New York, June 14, 1904. Saginaw, Mich.: Seeman and Peters, 1904.

Warden, Margaret Lindsley. *The Belle Meade Plantation*. Nashville: Marshall and Bruce, 1979.

_____. *The Saga of Fairvue, 1832-1977*. Nashville: n.p., 1972.

Interviews and Speeches

Anderson, Greg. Telephone interview with the author. Nashville. June 23, 1987.

Benedict, Mrs. Andrew B., Jr. Interview with the author. Nashville. December 13, 1988.

Brink, Melinda Sneed. Interview with the author. Nashville. February 1989.

Bumpous, William H. Interview with the author. Nashville. March 14, 1989.

Dickinson, Jacob McGavock III. Interview with the author. Nashville. 1988.

Edwards, Bluford E. Interview with the author. Nashville. May 13, 1987.

Lindsey, Martha. Interview with the author. Nashville. October 13, 1984.

Magruder, Anne. Interview with the author. Nashville. November 26, 1986.

Noel, Jeannette Acklen. Interview with the author. Nashville. November 2, 1984.

Ragland, Mary Harding. Interview with the author. Nashville. July 23, 1984.

————. Interview with John Hilboldt. Richmond, Va. January 27, 1980.

Reece, Mrs. Milton M. Interview with the author. Nashville. June 14, 1987.

Singleton, Arthur. Interview with the author. Nashville. January 8, 1985.

Wallerstein, Larry. Telephone interview with the author. Los Angeles, Calif. June 23, 1987.

Wemyss, Ellen. Speech, "Recollections Concerning the History of the Association for the Preservation of Tennessee Antiquities," taped at the annual meeting of APTA. Nashville. May 19, 1981.

Williams, Trilby Elliston. Interviews with the author. Nashville. July 1988; March 8, 1990.

Wills, Ellen Buckner. Interview with the author. Nashville. 1987.

Wyatt, Margaret Early. Interview with the author. Franklin, Tenn. August 19, 1985.

Newspapers

Chattanooga Times
Cincinnati Commercial

Cincinnati Commercial Gazette
Courier-Journal (Louisville)
Daily American (Nashville)
Daily Nashville Patriot
Daily Press and Times (Nashville)
Daily Sun (Jackson, Tenn.)
Democratic Clarion and Tennessee Gazette (Nashville)
Denver Tribune
Evening Herald (Nashville)
Frank Leslie's Illustrated Newspaper (New York City)
Harper's Weekly (New York City)
Los Angeles Times
Memphis Weekly Commercial
Nashville American
Nashville Banner
Nashville Clarion
Nashville Daily News
Nashville Daily Press & Times
Nashville Daily Times and True Union
Nashville Daily Union
Nashville Democrat
Nashville Dispatch
Nashville Gazette
Nashville Herald
Nashville Republican
Nashville Republican Banner and Nashville Whig
Nashville Suburban News
Nashville Tennessean
Nashville Tennessean and Nashville American
Nashville True Whig
Nashville Union
Nashville Union and Dispatch
Nashville Whig
National Banner and Nashville Daily Advertiser
National Banner and Nashville Whig
New Orleans Picayune
New York Herald
New York Sunday Mercury

Osceola (Ark.) Times
Public Ledger (Memphis)
Republican Banner (Nashville)
Richmond Enquirer
Rural Sun (Nashville)
St. Louis Daily Globe-Democrat
San Antonio Express
Spirit of the Times (New York)
Tennessean (Nashville)
Tennessee Clarion (Nashville)
Thoroughbred Record
Three Rivers Reporter (Three Rivers, Mich.)
Tribune and Sun (Jackson, Tenn.)
Union and American (Nashville)

Unpublished Material

(Abbreviations in this section are keyed to the list preceding Notes.)

APTA, Nashville Chapter:
Agreement between APTA and Leatherwood, Inc., July 2, 1987.
Hinshaw, Jane. "Archaeological Investigations at Belle Meade Historic Site," 1982.
Judd, Henry A. Report of his Visit to the Belle Meade Mansion on December 13, 1968.
Miller, Ronald W. "Initial Report on the Belle Meade Parlors," March 30, 1987.
Minutes and Records.
Notes on the Belle Meade Plantation attached to an obituary notice for Mrs. Hill McAlister.
Blooming Grove (Pa.) Hunting & Fishing Club. Stockholders' Meeting Minutes, May 31, 1878. Archives, Blooming Grove, Pa.
Buckner and Wills Families. An unpublished ancestry book. Collection of the author.
Cartmell, Robert H. Papers, 1849-1915. TSLA.
The Catholic Center, Nashville:
Diocese of Nashville Baptismal Certificates. The Records of St. Mary's Church.
Letter. Bishop Byrne to John J. Vertrees, Apr. 20, 1903.

Letter. Selene Jackson Elliston to the Right Reverend Bishop Byrne, Thursday (date not known).

Letter. John Marks Handly to the Reverend John B. Morris, May 28, 1899.

Challen, James. Letter to Brother (Alexander) Campbell, Feb. 29, 1860. Archives, Disciples of Christ Historical Society, Nashville.

Cleveland, Grover. Collection. Manuscript Division. Library of Congress, Washington, D.C.

Cooper, Washington. Diary. Microfilm records. TSLA.

Davidson County, Tennessee, Records:

Census Records 1860, 1870. TSLA.

Chancery Court Minutes.

Court Minutes.

Deeds.

Marriage Record Books 1, 2. TSLA (remainder at the Davidson County Courthouse, Nashville).

Wills and Inventories.

Dickinson, Jacob McGavock. Papers. TSLA.

Ellis, John Joseph. "Belle Meade: Evolution of an Aesthetic, 1905-1938." Master's thesis, Vanderbilt University, 1983.

Elliston Family Records:

Letters. Collection of Col. Norman Farrell, Alexandria, Va.

The Records of St. Mary's Catholic Church. The Catholic Center, Nashville.

Elmwood Cemetery Records, Memphis.

Ewing, Andrew B. Family letters. Collection of Andrew B. Ewing, Jr., Nashville, and Elizabeth Ewing Stanford, Arlington, Va.

Ewing, Randal Milton. "The McGavock Family," May 28, 1896. Copy, collection of the author.

Fayette County Deeds. Fayette County Courthouse, Uniontown, Pa.

Frazier, Mary Warner. Unpublished notes. Copy, collection of the author.

Ganier, Albert Frazier. Papers. TSLA.

General Order No. 13, Headquarters Department of the Ohio, February 26, 1862. Statement of Major General Buell in review of the evidence before the Military Commission appointed by the War Department in November 1862. TSLA.

Goochland County, Virginia, Records, including Records of Deeds, Wills, etc. Goochland County Courthouse. Goochland, Va.

Green, Henry. Reminiscences of Henry ("Speedy") Green. Collection of the author.

Grundy, Felix. Papers. The Whitefoord Cole Collection. TSLA.

Hague, William. Letters. Nashville Room, Ben West Public Library, Nashville.

Harding Family Records (HFR):

Bible. Collection of E. P. Horn, Nashville.

Bible owned by Mary Selena Harding. Collection of APTA, Nashville Chapter.

Letters. Collection of Mrs. C. William Green, Nashville.

Letters. Collection of Jack Harding, Jackson, Miss.

Letters. Collection of Mrs. William A. Perkins, Jr., Charlottesville, Va.

Papers. University Archives. Norwich University, Northfield, Vt.

Records. Collection of Mrs. James Balch, Murfreesboro, Tenn.

Records. Collection of Mrs. Grady Leach, Jr., Gadsden, Ala.

Harding-Jackson Family Papers and Records (HJP, HJFR):

Ledger. John Harding's (JHL). SHC, TSLA.

Ledger. William Giles Harding's (WGHL). SHC, TSLA.

Papers. Harding-Jackson. JAHL.

Papers. Harding-Jackson. SHC, TSLA.

Papers. William H. Jackson. TSLA.

Records. Collection of APTA, Nashville Chapter.

Records. Collection of the author.

Records. Collection of Mrs. Ellen Buckner Wills, Nashville.

Records. Collection of Mr. and Mrs. John H. Zink III, Baltimore.

Harris, Isham G. Papers. TSLA.

Hayes Family Papers. TSLA.

Hickman County, Tennessee, Deeds. TSLA.

Humphreys County, Tennessee, Deeds. TSLA.

Jackson, Alexander, Dr., Family Records (JFR):

Bible. Collection of Emmie Jackson McDonald, Nashville.

Letters. Collection of Eunice Holderness Ridley, Nashville.

Jackson, Andrew. Letter to Captain Alden Partridge, Jan. 12, 1817. Huntington Library, San Marino, Calif.

Jackson, Howell E. Papers (HEJP). TSLA.

Jefferson County, Arkansas, Deeds. Jefferson County Courthouse. Pine Bluff.

Johnson, Andrew. Papers. Presidential Series. Library of Congress, Washington, D.C.

Johnson Family Papers. Collection of Edna A. Raiter, Raleigh, N.C.

Kentucky Derby race results for 1875, taken from the original scales book, Churchill Downs, Inc., Louisville, Ky.

Kilgore, Sherrill Jane. "Brief History of the Association for the Preservation of Tennessee Antiquities and its Belle Meade Historic Site." Master's thesis, Middle Tennessee State University, 1981, Murfreesboro.

Lea, Luke. Papers. TSLA.

Lee, Stephen D. Presidential Papers. Mississippi State University Archives, Mississippi State, Miss.

McAlister, Hill. Papers. TSLA.

McGhee, Charles McClung. Papers. McClung Historical Collection. Knox County Public Library, Knoxville, Tenn.

Malone, Thomas H. Letters. Collection of Anne W. Magruder, Nashville.

Microfilm records. Miscellaneous files. TSLA.

Middle Tennessee Land Grants #4842, 8055, 8087, 10491, 10492, 12431, and 18708. TSLA.

Military and Financial Board of Tennessee. Letters and telegrams. Dillard Jacobs collection. TSLA.

Mount Olivet Cemetery Records. Nashville.

Nash, Robert. "A Race Horse and a Race Track, The Story of the Kentucky Derby and Churchill Downs, 1875-1948." Master's thesis, University of Louisville, 1948.

National Archives:

Amnesty Petition No. 3370 from Howell E. Jackson. Records of the Provost Marshal (RPM).

Civil War Claims #218/833 and 281/1141. Records Group 92, ROQG.

Journals of the Nashville (William Driver) Board of Claims. Entry 949, Document File March 1863-October 29, 1864, ROQG.

Letter. W. G. Harding to W. S. Rosecrans, Dec. 17, 1862. Microfilm records, copy 345, roll 118, RPM.

Letter. Nicholas Perkins to Secretary of War, Mar. 29, 1807. War Department. Office of the Secretary of War.

Letter. C. H. Williams to Col. J. G. Totten, Mar. 5, 1852.

Letter and telegram. Gen. S. D. Lee to Gen. S. Cooper. CMR.

Letters. Howell E. Jackson to President Andrew Johnson. RPM.

Microfilm records, roll 118, RPM.

Miscellaneous Claims Nashville Board, G-H Document File 1861-1869, Claims #12, 303.

Receipt. Signed by Howell E. Jackson, acknowledging receipt of property from the Quartermaster's Office. Civilian and Business Records of the Confederacy.

Record Group 92. ROQG.

North Carolina Land Grants. TSLA.

Page Family Records. Collection of Thomas E. Page, Lebanon, Tenn.

Police Report of Operations of Spies, Smugglers, Traitors, etc., occurring within the lines of the Union Army of the Cumberland, 1863. Army War College, Historical Section. Washington, D.C.

Provine, W. A. Papers. TSLA.

Public Acts of the State of Tennessee, Thirty-third General Assembly, April 1861. TSLA.

Senate Journal (Tennessee) 1839. TSLA.

Shute Family Records. Collection of Mrs. Grady W. Leach, Jr., Gadsden, Ala.

Spring Hill Cemetery Records. Nashville.

Taft, William Howard. Collection, section 3. University of Tennessee Library, Knoxville, Tenn.

Tennessee Land Grants #698, 4746, and 4750. TSLA.

Tennessee State Building Commission Minutes for the Tennessee State Capitol. TSLA.

Transcript Middle Tennessee (TMT), 1892 Tennessee Supreme Court Case, Adams Express Company, appellant, vs W. H. Jackson, H. E. Jackson, and John Harding, Jr., appellees, in the Supreme Court of Tennessee from the Circuit Court of Davidson County.

Transcript #934, including exhibits.

Walton Papers. TSLA.

Warner, Charles Dudley. Diary. The Watkinson Library, Trinity College, Hartford, Conn.

West Tennessee Land Grants. TSLA.

Williamson County, Tennessee, Records (Franklin):

Court Minutes. Clerk and Master's Office, Courthouse.

Deeds. Register's Office, Administrative Office Complex.

Wills. Clerk and Master's Office.
Wynne, George Winchester. Collection. TSLA.

Index

Acklen, Adelicia (Mrs. Joseph A. S.)
  (*see also* Cheatham, Adelicia), 99, 138
Acklen, Jeannette, 272, 276, 278
Acklen, Joseph A. S., 99
Acklen, Joseph H., Col., 278, 284
Adams, Adam G., 119
Adams Express Company, 226, 227, 228,
  229, 230, 231
Adams, John, Gen., 126
Adams, John Quincy, President, 15
Adams, Sue Howell (Mrs. Adam G.), 119
Albion (pen name) (*see also* Hubbard,
  J. R.), 171
Alcock, Theodore, 167, 198
Alexander, A. J., Col., 180
Allison, W. H., 283
American Horse Exchange, 242, 248
American Literary, Scientific and
  Military Academy, 14, 15, 16, 17, 66,
  67, 70, 313 n.8
American party. *See* Know-Nothing party
American Turf Register, 55
Anderson, Greg, 288
Anderson, James Douglas, vii, 55, 196,
  264
Andrew, James (bishop of Georgia), 192
Armistead, W. S. H., 292, 293
Armstrong, Robert, Gen., 33, 307 n.34
Army (*see also* U.S. Army units): of the
  Cumberland, 117, 119; of the Depart-
  ment of Alabama, Mississippi, and
  East Louisiana, 145; Grand Army
  of the Republic, 261; of Northern
  Virginia, 130, 132; Provisional Army
  of Tennessee, 87, 88, 125, 130; of
  Tennessee, 125, 130, 143, 144, 145,
  182, 285
Association for the Preservation of
  Tennessee Antiquities (APTA), 286;
  Nashville Chapter, 27, 287, 288, 296
Association for the Preservation of
  Virginia Antiquities (APVA), 287
Auction pools, 173
Avent, Frank, 284

Avent, J. M., 284
Averill, William W., Lt., 141

Bailey, James E., 85, 87, 88, 90, 94, 98
Baker, Elizabeth. *See* Harding, Elizabeth
  Baker
Bancroft, George, 210, 223
Banks: American National, 260; Bank of
  Tennessee, 36, 48; Chase National,
  211; First National, 246; Fourth Na-
  tional, 179; Nashville Trust Com-
  pany, 275; Safe Deposit Trust and
  Banking Company, 190; Union Bank
  and Trust Company, 274, 275; Union
  Bank of Tennessee, 48
Barbour, Edmund D., 152
Barksdale, Emma, 253, 256
Barnes, Pike, 212
Barnes, T. W., 164
Barrow, Washington, 33, 91, 92, 93, 94,
  95, 96, 97, 104, 105, 108, 112, 318
  n.59
Barrow, Willie, 25
Bass, Felicia (daughter of John M. Bass),
  99
Bass, John M., 38, 48, 110
Bass, William, Dr., 110, 111
Battle, Joel A., Gen., 30
Battle of New Orleans, 9
Battles. *See* Civil War
Baxby, Howard, 245
Baxter, Miranda ("Mannie") Louise (*see
  also* Jackson, Miranda Baxter), 219,
  220
Baxter, Nathaniel ("Nat"), Jr., 220, 261,
  284
Bayard, Thomas F., 199, 201, 214, 223
Beasley, Ben, 193
Beasley, James A., 85, 96, 97, 103
Bell, Jane Erwin Yeatman (Mrs. John),
  121
Bell, Montgomery, 20, 21, 41, 55, 59
Belle Meade: City of, 289, 296; Com-
  pany, 292, 293, 295; Country

Belle Meade: (*continued*)
  Club, 295; Distillery, 204; Land
  Company, 285, 286, 292; Park, 295,
  296; Sunday School and Sick Society,
  275; Tobacco Factory, 204
Belle Meade Plantation: archaeological
  dig at, 19; deer hunts at, 72, 74, 162,
  187, 194; deer park, 28, 71, 72, 74,
  97, 128, 133, 135, 139, 149, 189, 200,
  201, 205, 210, 243, 246, 284; estate
  sale of, 283; named Belle Meade, 12;
  operated as partnership, 190; picnics
  at, 72, 123, 186; pigeon shoot at, 268;
  property damage to, 65, 106, 111, 116,
  117, 130, 131, 149, 158, 201, 324 n.6;
  quarries at, 43, 69, 258, 309 n.6;
  railroad station and siding at, 159, 216,
  228, 229, 243, 290; road completed
  by, 50; sales of, 284, 285, 292;
  threatened with confiscation, 124-25;
  under Union Army protection, 112-13,
  124-25; value of in 1870, 149; vehicles
  at, 46, 136, 218, 253, 272, 292;
  animals: asses, 116; buffalo, 71, 72, 93,
  106, 116, 119; bulls, 35, 46, 164, 283;
  cashmere goats, 80, 107, 116, 119, 120,
  139; cattle (beef), 35, 45-46, 149, 201;
  cattle (dairy), 149, 182, 190, 203-4,
  237, 247, 283; deer, 28, 71, 72, 106,
  116, 119, 175, 177, 210, 217, 255, 283,
  284; elk, 71, 116, 246, 284; fowl, 104,
  106, 243; foxhounds, 192, 221, 222,
  223, 243, 248; hogs, 59, 149, 161,
  164, 167; horses (*see* Thoroughbreds);
  mules, 45, 59, 80, 103, 106, 116, 149,
  253, 283; sheep, 45, 80, 104, 126,
  149, 164, 200; Shetland ponies, 226,
  227, 247, 250, 280, 281, 282; water-
  oxen, 72;
  farm: acreage of, 173, 182, 236, 273,
  279, 287, 292; award given to, 81;
  cattle sale at, 203; cemeteries at, 52,
  290, 293, 341 n.12; contract wage
  system, 134, 135, 149; crimes at, 59,
  79, 193; crops, 19, 24, 77, 97, 104,
  107, 120, 149, 183, 200; dairy, 182,
  189, 190, 237, 280; divided into
  Belle Meade and West Meade, 236;
  equipment on, 19, 49, 189, 190,

  200, 201, 281; expenses relating to, 45;
  flowers grown at, 71; garden, 71, 117;
  given to daughters, 186; grape arbor,
  71; High Pasture, 37, 113, 221, 222;
  hog killing at, 161; indebtedness of,
  280; manager, 255; meadows, 222; mill
  woods, 162; mortgaged, 264, 273;
  orchard, 71; pillaged, 106, 107;
  praised, 197, 200, 204; products from,
  19, 23, 44, 45, 59, 107, 120; purchases
  for, 19; shade trees on, 149, 159;
  sources of income for, 19, 23, 122;
  timber on, 117, 122; tracts on, 133,
  186, 292; 1882 yield of, 200;
  mansion: additions to, 48-49, 68-70;
  anthemions, 70; apartments, 267;
  architectural style, 68; balcony, 69;
  baseboards, 69; brick, 49, 68;
  breezeway, 48; chandeliers, 185;
  chimneys, 68; Christmas at, 161, 183;
  columns, 69, 70; as Confederate
  headquarters, 126; cornices, 69, 185;
  curtains, 216; damage to, 67; dancing
  at, 124; date of construction, 11;
  decorations at, 252; deed to, 287;
  described, 185; designer of, 70; doors,
  68, 185; draperies in, 185; entablature,
  69; exterior, 68; fire at, 67; floors, 69;
  food and drink served in, 11, 84, 216,
  267; foundation, 11, 68; funerals at,
  43, 52, 133, 209, 263, 289; furniture,
  62, 136, 152, 196, 216, 278, 283;
  galleries, 136, 185, 252; governesses at,
  183; graining in, 185; hospitality at,
  89, 201, 250, 285; inscription, 70;
  lighting, 69; mantels, 69; meals at,
  152, 171, 216, 267; moulding, 185;
  paint colors, 69, 185; parties and
  receptions at, 80, 84, 136, 220, 221,
  252, 268, 273; plumbing in, 184;
  porches, 69, 70, 255, 288, 331 n.35;
  porte cochere, 255, 288; portico, 68;
  portraits and photographs hanging in,
  50, 58, 98, 152, 177-79, 196, 201,
  288, 327 n.63; purchases for, 11; renovations of, 45, 184, 255, 287, 288;
  roof, 48, 68; rooms, 48, 49, 68, 69,
  161, 179, 184, 185, 196, 210, 215, 216,
  252, 331 n.25; rugs, 185, 216, 252;

sales of, 287, 295; shutters, 127; stairways, 68; structure attached to, 68; studies of, 68; telephone at, 254; transom, 69; trim, 69; veranda, 216; wallpaper, 185; weddings at, 51; woodwork, 185;

outbuildings and structures: amphitheater, 174, 201; blacksmith shop, 8, 19; bridges, 158; carriage house/stable, 239, 288, 292; carriageway, 215, 252; cisterns, 68, 126, 252; cow barn, 189, 237; dairy houses, 20, 189, 190, 237, 288; fences (stone), 107, 135, 158, 200, 253, 341 n.42; fences (wood), 21, 71, 117, 331 n.23; front gate, 215; garden house, 49; gardener's house, 20; gatekeeper's house, 295; greenhouse, 49, 71; gristmill, 13, 43, 103, 183, 328 n.13; gun club, 268; irrigation system, 74, 236, 239; kitchen house, 48, 49, 184, 252; mill dam and race, 13, 19; monument to Enquirer, 245, 185, 336 n.46, 47; plantation bell, 44, 134, 296, 342 n.38; pump house, 74, 285; racetrack (private), 127, 128, 183, 196, 247; Red House Spring, 74, 175, 186, 252, 285, 292; reservoir, 74, 239, 285; sale barn, 174, 201; sawmill, 19; slave (servant) quarters, 19, 44, 79, 193; smokehouse, 20, 71, 288; springhouses, 20, 74, 128, 186; stalls, 242; storeroom, 20; vault (mausoleum), 43, 71, 133, 209; water gaps, 158;

slaves/servants/workers: conscription of slaves, 103; drunken behavior, 183; families living on plantation, 148; farm manager, 85, 96; fidelity of slaves, 94, 99, 104, 108, 120; gatekeeper, 295; grooms, 205, 229, 230, 232, 239; interest in education, 134; milkers, 237; number of workers, 173, 182; slave census, 78; slave contributions, 117; slave escapes, 10, 53; slaves anticipate emancipation, 132; slaves robbed, 107; stock manager, 84; Swiss gardener, 20, 71; workday routines, 44;

stud: accidents at, 177; auctioneers at, 164, 173, 174, 177, 198, 206, 210, 233, 243, 249, 276, 280; auction sale at, 247; barbecues at, 163, 164, 177, 189, 250, 290; beginning, 20, 55; Blood Horse Department, 225, 232, 334 n.3; boarding horses and ponies at, 21, 23, 58; as center for small stock raisers, 243; clients, 21, 23; consignment sale, 243; as country's oldest breeding farm, 251; demise announced, 282; dispersal sales, 235, 281, 282; dissatisfied partners in, 237; division of, 186; fees at, 46, 58, 59, 238, 242; paddocks, 173, 236, 245; pastures, 21; praised, 62, 198, 206, 210, 237, 238, 239, 276; private sale at, 248; racing silks, 170, 297; records of, 286; reduction sales at, 249, 250, 276; reputation, 57, 61, 64, 147, 168, 180, 208, 238; revived, 295; sale catalogs of, 226, 227, 243; stallions appraised, 206; Thoroughbreds buried at: 249, 336 n.46; trainer at, 248; yearling sales, 163-206 passim, 211, 225-50 passim, 274

Belmont, August II, 242, 272
Bennett, Washington J., 17
Big Harpeth River. *See under* Rivers and Streams
Black, Sam, 167, 207
Blackford, Charles, 263
Blooming Grove Hunting and Fishing Club, 175
Boone and Crockett Club, 194
Bosley, Beal, 25, 59
Bosley, Charlie, 57, 133
Bosley, Elizabeth (*see also* Harding, Elizabeth Bosley), 25
Bosley, Margery Shute (Mrs. Beal), 25
Bosley's Sulphur Spring, 103
Bowling Green, Kentucky, 88, 92
Bragg, Braxton, Gen., 111
Bransford, Johnson, 292
Bransford, William S., 292
Brewer, David J., Associate Justice, 263
Brien, Robert C., 255, 281
Briggs Infirmary, 253, 254
Briggs, William T., Dr., 159, 253

Brink, Melinda Sneed, 295
Brown, Aaron V., Gov., 54
Brown, Campbell, 159
Brown, Elizabeth ("Myssie"). *See* Hogg, Myssie Brown
Brown, John ("Jack"), 112, 113, 115, 116
Brown, John C., Gov., 152, 153, 157
Brown, Milton, 156
Brown, Neill S., Gov., 77, 85, 87, 88, 89, 96, 98, 110
Brown, S. S., 224
Brownlow, William G. ("Parson"), 52
Bruce, Ben, 168, 173, 175
Bruce, H. B., 174
Bruce, Sanders D., Col., 166, 168, 171, 174, 175, 177, 197, 210
Bryant, Sam, 206
Buchanan, James, President, 152
Buckner, Elizabeth Jackson (Mrs. Matthew G.) (*see also* Jackson, Elizabeth), vii, 296
Buckner, Henry Bruce, 119
Buckner, Mary Harding, 270
Buckner, Sadie Gardner (Mrs. Henry Bruce), 119
Buell, Don Carlos, Gen., 130
Buell, George B., Gen., 177
Buford, Abraham ("Abe"), Gen., 164, 166, 179, 285
Buntin, Dan, 283
Bureau of Refugees, Freedmen and Abandoned Lands, 133, 134, 140
Burnham, Asa, 177
Burns, Frank, 22, 197
Burr, Aaron, 50
Buttorff, Henry W., 264
Byrne, Thomas S. (bishop of Nashville), 271, 273, 285

Caldwell, Ellen Thomas (Mrs. Meredith), 287, 295
Caldwell, James E., 285
Caldwell, May Winston (Mrs. James E.), 219
Caldwell, Meredith, 287, 295
Calhoun, John C., Vice-President, 15
Calhoun's Jewelry Store, 162
Campbell, Alexander, Rev., 31, 36, 41
Camp Chase, 90

Cape May, New Jersey, 66, 75
Carey, Sam, 245
Carlota Colony, 132
Carnegie, Andrew, 226
Carroll, Charles, 15
Carroll, William, Gov., 21, 37, 46, 52
Carter, "Big" Ike, 48, 128
Carter, Joe, 128, 161, 219, 229, 278
Carter, Joel W., 246
Carter, Samuel, J., 59
Carter, Susanna: background, 46, 48; as Christian, 257; as cook, 84, 177; correspondence of, 104; death, 337 n.25; as "dialect" story teller, 254; enslavement of, 46; family of, 48; features, 48; as friend, 257; hides silver, 92; as housekeeper, 136; illness of, 223; marriage, 48; as mother, 128; views on emancipation, 195
Cassatt, A. J., 203
Cathcart, Robert, 177
Catron, John, Associate Justice, 52
Cave, R. Lin, Elder, 190, 208, 263
Challen, James, 41
Chalmers, James Ronald, Gen., 126, 127, 130, 136
Chambliss, Lucy, 183
Cheatham, Adelicia (*see also* Acklen, Adelicia), 200
Cheatham, Amanda McGavock (Mrs. Archer) (*see also* McGavock, Amanda), 158, 288
Cheatham, Archer, 111, 133, 169, 288
Cheatham, Benjamin Franklin ("Frank"), Gen., 136, 164, 199
Cheatham, Leonard P., 56, 311 n.12
Cheatham, Richard B., Mayor, 89, 140, 169
Cheatham, William ("Will" or "Bill") B., 207, 229, 232, 253, 281, 324 n.32, 340 n.28
Chickering, C. B., 160
Chickering, John, 46
Childress, George W.,32, 33, 34, 90,
Childress, James W., 96, 199
Churches: Baptist, 32, 45; Belle Meade Methodist, 287; Broad Street Tabernacle, 190; Church of the Advent, 267; Cumberland Presbyterian, 261;

Episcopal, 45; First Christian, 41; First Presbyterian, 27, 70; Franklin, Tennessee, Church of Christ, 36; Harding Pike, 290; McKendree Methodist, 169, 190, 254, 265, 278, 279; Nashville Christian, 38, 146, 148; Nashville Church of the Disciples of Christ, 45; Nashville Presbyterian (*see* First Presbyterian); Providence Baptist, 50; Richland Creek Baptist, 6, 10; St. Mary's Catholic, 269, 275; Two Rivers Baptist, 34; Vine Street Christian, 190, 290, 296

Civil War: anticipated, 81; battles: Belmont, 142, Fort Donelson, 90, Fort Henry, 90, Franklin, 125, 126, Gettysburg, 122, Holly Springs, 111, 143, Mill Springs, 89, Nashville, 92, 127, 136, 144, 175, 185, 285, Shiloh, 142, Stones River, 111, 115, Thompson's Station, 143; Campaigns: Atlanta, 144, Meridian, 143, Tennessee, 144, Vicksburg, 111, 122, 143; capture of Murfreesboro during, 100; effects on Belle Meade, 130-31; and Tennessee's secession, 86

Claiborne, William, 48

Clark, Meriwether Lewis, Col., 168, 175, 200

Clay, Elizabeth Harding (Mrs. Joseph W.) (*see also* Harding, Elizabeth Virginia), 27, 28, 31

Clay, Henry (son of Elizabeth and Joseph W.), 27, 28

Clay, Henry, Hon., 30

Clay, Henry M., 57

Clay, John Randolph, 81

Clay, Joseph W.: as bank director, 48; as cattle breeder, 35; as cotton planter, 25; as father, 27; as jockey club member, 57; as land owner, 24; marriage, 24; as racehorse owner, 24, 56, 57; as shareholder, 32

Cleburne, Patrick R., Gen., 126

Clement, Frank G., Gov., 287

Cleveland, Frances Folsom (Mrs. Grover), 215-19, 260

Cleveland, Grover, President, 190, 194, 213, 214, 215, 216, 217, 218, 223, 258, 260

Clopton, Elizabeth (*see also* Harding, Elizabeth Clopton), 25

Clopton, John, 28

Coburn, John, Col., 143

Cockrill, Benjamin Franklin, Col., 164, 171, 192

Cockrill, Mark R., 58. 81, 86, 111, 124, 133, 136, 315 n.40

Cockrill, Mark S., 192

Cockrill's Spring, 6, 100

Coffee, John, Gen., 8, 50

Cole, Anna Russell (Mrs. Edmund W.), 254

Cole, Edmund W., 254

Colleges. *See* Schools

Collier, William C., 265

Colquitt, Alfred H., 152

Colyar, A. S., Col., 219

Combs, Leslie, 226

Compton, Henry W., 123, 253

Compton, Joshua ("Josh"), 253

Confederate: House of Representatives, 91; military units (*see also* Army): Artillery Corps of Tennessee, 142, Harding Light Artillery (Freeman-Huggins Battery), 83, Tennessee Infantry Regiment, Tenth, 90, Tennessee Infantry Regiment, Forty-ninth, 90, Tennessee Infantry Regiment, Forty-second, 90, Terry's Texas Rangers, 88, 89

Cooper, Washington B., 40, 288

Cooper, Mrs. William F., 119

Cooper, William F., 119

Corrigan, Edward ("Big Ed"), 206, 211

Craig, Andrew, 36

Craighead, David, 37

Craighead, Thomas B., 37

Crittenden, George B., Col., 142

Crockett, David ("Davy"), 36, 150

Croker, Richard, 241-46

Crowell, John, Col., 58

Cummins, W. J., 283

Curd, Charles P., 182

Curd, Charles P. III, 27

Curd, Selene ("Lena") Harding (Mrs. Charles P.) (*see also* Harding, Selene McNairy), 182

Currey, Brownlee O., 297

Currin, David M., 156

Dana, John W., Gov., 81
Daniel (carriage driver), 126
Darden, George W., 171
Davidson County: Chancery Court, 270;
    Circuit Court, 48, 233; Committee on
    Vigilance and Safety, 140; Courthouse,
    44, 77; Court minutes, 8; Farmers'
    Club, 150, 151, 165
Davidson, John R., 16
Davidson, Samuel B., 78
Davis, Dorcas (Mrs. John), 302 n.43
Davis, Jefferson, President, CSA, 87, 92,
    143, 144, 145
Davis, John, 302 n.43
Davis, Joseph, 144
DeCoumout, Vicomtes, 206
Deer Park. *See under* Belle Meade
    Plantation
DeGraffenried, Matthew F., Gen., 144
DeGrove, Quincy C., 140
De La Chere, Capt., 197
De Lattre, Henry, 62
De la Motte Rouge, Vicomtes, 206
DeLoache, Josiah, 142, 143, 323 n.45
Demoss, Abram, 50
Demoville, Annie, 289
Demoville, Mary Felix, 268, 289, 269,
    271
Dennis, Elias S., Gen., 145
Dickinson, Anne McGavock (Mrs.
    Henry), 285
Dickinson, Charles, 34, 307 n.39
Dickinson, Charles H., 15
Dickinson, Helen Grimble Trenholm
    (Mrs. Overton), 290, 292
Dickinson, Helen Trenholm (daughter),
    292
Dickinson, Jacob McGavock, 56, 62, 72,
    198, 209, 260, 262, 285, 290, 292,
    314 n.39
Dickinson, John Overton, 285, 286, 290,
    292
Dickinson, Martha Overton (Mrs. Jacob
    McGavock), 290
Dickson, Caroline T., 262
Dillahunty, John, 6, 302 n.30
Dingley, Nelson, 204
Dinkins, James, Capt., 126, 127, 136
Disciples Movement, 31, 41, 45

Dodge, John Wood, 81, 184
Donelson, Andrew Jackson, 26
Donelson, John, Col., 5
Donnelly, Isabel, 4
Donnelly, James, 3, 4
Donnelly, John, 4
Donnelly, Martha. *See* Harding, Martha
    Donnelly
Dorris, Duncan R., 184
Douglas, Byrd, 86
Douglas, Richard, Dr., 279
Drake, Charles D., 16, 304 n.20
Driver, William, 117
Dudley, Anne Dallas (Mrs. Guilford),
    287
Dudley, Guilford, 287
Dudley, W. L., 264
Dunbar, Albert W., 16
Dunbar, William, 16
Duncan, Thomas, 48
Dunham, Daniel, 5
Dunham, Daniel A., 5, 6, 22, 23
Dunham, Mrs. Daniel, 5
Dunham's Station, 5, 6, 8, 302 n.23
Dwyer, Mike, 177, 225
Dwyer, Phil J., 174, 175, 177, 225, 244

Eakin, Mrs. William, 121
Eakin, Nannie, 117, 121
Eakin, Thomas, 97
Eakin, William, 121
Eakin, Willie, 117, 121
Earl, Ralph E. W., 21, 305 n.37
Easton, William, 206, 225, 226, 227,
    228, 229, 231, 232, 233, 243, 249,
    276
Eaton, John, 46
Edgefield, Tennessee, 91, 140
Edwards, Mark Fletcher, 22
Edwards, Mrs. Walker, 283
Ehret, F. A., Yearling Sale, 239
Ellett, Henry T. Judge, 157, 219
Elliott, Collins D., 183
Elliott, J. A. R., 268
Elliott, Joseph, Maj., 173
Elliott, Lizzie, 183
Ellis, Florence Wynne (Mrs. Osborne),
    242, 243
Elliston, Bettie (servant), 275

Elliston, Josephine ("Joe") (*see also* Farrell, Josephine Elliston), 100, 138
Elliston, Selene Jackson (*see also* Jackson, Selene): death, 290; described, 267; divorce, 270; estate sale purchases by, 283, 340 n.36; executes wills, 273, 289; family relationships, 289; at fox hunt, 269; as hostess, 268; illnesses, 289, 290; mortgages Belle Meade, 264, 273; obtains injunction at estate sale, 283; ownership interest in Belle Meade, 280, 284; religious experiences, 270, 273; in seclusion, 271; trips, 267, 289
Elliston, William ("Billy") Jackson, 268, 270, 271, 290, 342 n.18
Elliston, William R., 100
Elliston, William ("Billy") Robert, 265, 267, 269, 270, 272, 289
Emancipation Proclamation, 120
Emery, Sam, 225
Enterprise Cornet Band. See Harding Light Artillery Band
Estes, Bedford M., 157, 325 n.46
Evans, Robert, Capt., 8
Ewing, Carrie Eliza, 20, 271
Ewing, Mary Ellen McGavock (Mrs. Randal Milton), 103, 107
Ewing, Randal Milton, 103, 104
Ewing, Sallie B., 183

Fairs: Davidson County Agricultural and Mechanical Association, 81; Davidson County Spring, 63; Maury County, 63, 64; Southern Exposition, 185; Tennessee Agricultural and Horticultural Society Stock, 34; Tennessee State, 62, 63, 81, 312 n.45
Fall, Phillip S., Rev., 146
Fall, Willie Evans, 271
Falmouth, Lord, 176
Fanning, Tolbert, 45
Farms. See Plantations
Farrell, Josephine ("Joe") Elliston (*see also* Elliston, Josephine), 257
Fasig-Tipton Company, 274, 276, 280
Ferneley, John, 59
Fish, Stuyvesant, 285
Flagg, Lysander, 182
Fletcher's Lick, 5, 11

Fogg, Francis, 52
Fooy, Benjamin, Judge, 11, 302 n.48
Forrest, Nathan Bedford, Gen., 90, 91, 100, 139, 144, 145, 157, 183
Forts: Chiswell, 4; Craig, 141; Johnson, 108; McHenry, 15; Mackinac, 93, 95, 96, 97, 103, 104, 108; Nashborough, 5, 302 n.21; Riley, 141; Union, 84; Warren, 90, 94, 98
Foster, Ephraim H., Senator, 32, 33
Fox, Peter, 174, 177, 197
Franklin, A. C., 169, 197, 199
Franklin, Isaac, 20,
Franklin, James, 169, 197, 199
Franklin, Tennessee, 128
Franks, Edward A., 96
French Lick, 5, 302 n.21
Fuller, Melville W., Chief Justice, 263

Gaines, Edmund Pendleton, Gen., 50
Gardner, Edwin S., 242, 276, 280
Gardner, Edwin, S., Jr., 242
Gardner, Margaret McClung (Mrs. Robert H.), 121
Gardner, Matthew ("Matt") M., 203
Gardner, Robert H., 121
Garland, Landon C., Chancellor, 218, 219
Gerhardy, H. J., 248
Gillock, C. H., 207, 208, 247, 249
Gordon, John, 3
Gordon, John B., Gen., 261
Gorham, Arthur P., Senator, 199, 330 n.17
Gould, George, 275
Grady, Henry W., 182, 331 n.24
Graham, Daniel, Maj., 50, 54, 97, 110, 112, 302 n.26
Graham, J. W., 228
Granbury, Hiram B., Gen., 126
Grant, Ulysses S., Gen., 142, 143, 245
Gray, William (blacksmith), 19
Green, Henry ("Speedy"), 261
Green, Robert ("Uncle Bob"): buys Thoroughbreds, 242, 335 n.29; corrals deer, 217, 219; death, 290; dialect of, 334 n.21; at dispersal sales, 235; as faithful servant, 97, 231, 279; given horse, 281; hides silver, 92; as hostler,

Green, Robert (continued)
171; introduced to President Cleveland,
216, 217; as pallbearer, 133, 209, 257;
portrait made, 177; as property of
Mary Selena Harding, 26; requests
burial at Belle Meade, 282, 341 n.12;
as resident, 148; shot, 106, 108; sightseeing in New York, 232; "Tennessee
Day" experiences, 229, 230, 231; at
yearling sales, 177, 198, 205, 210, 211,
231, 234, 239, 242
Groton, Connecticut, 117, 119
Grundy, Felix, 21, 23, 37, 46, 305 n.37
Guild, Josephus Conn, 63, 92, 93, 94,
95, 96, 97, 104, 105, 106, 108, 112

Haggin, James Ben Allen, 206, 225,
226, 274
Hague, William, 80, 84, 85, 102, 104,
106
Hailsham, Lord (Lord Chancellor of
England) (see also Hogg, Quintin), 268
Hale, Mrs. E. A., 283
Hamilton, Ida (see also Thruston, Ida
Hamilton), 99, 115
Hamilton, Louise (Mrs. James M.), 99
Hampton, Wade II, Col., 62, 63
Hancock, Winfield Scott, Gen., 245
Handly, John Marks, 269
Harahan, J. T., 285
Hardeman, Thomas, 36
Hardin, Henry, 79, 195, 209, 315 n.27
Harding, Amanda P. (see also McGavock,
Amanda Harding), 6, 13
Harding, Amidia ("Amy") Morris, 1
Harding, Ann Margaret Bass (Mrs.
Thomas J.), 312 n.4
Harding Cemetery. See under Belle
Meade Plantation, farm
Harding, Charlotte Davis (Mrs. Giles,
Jr.), 6, 293
Harding, David Morris ("Morris"), 3, 8,
9, 27, 72, 110, 302 n.43
Harding, Elizabeth ("Betsy") Baker (Mrs.
George), 13, 301 n.10
Harding, Elizabeth Clopton (Mrs.
William) (see also Owen, Elizabeth
Clopton), 27
Harding, Elizabeth Irwin McGavock

(Mrs. William G.) (see also McGavock, Elizabeth Irwin), admired, 127;
concern for family, 90, 125; death,
139; disdain for Unionists, 119; efforts
to visit husband, 99, 100; eulogized,
139; gives birth, 49, 51, 52, 65, 75;
heroism of, 113, 115; hospitality of, 75,
76, 88; as hostess, 80, 123, 127;
illnesses, 65, 75, 136; inheritance, 51;
as musician, 46; pleas for help, 107,
129, 130; praised, 89, 126; preg-
nancies, 49; as prize winner, 81; refuses
to sign oath, 102; relationship with
slaves, 115; threatened, 104, 129; trips,
66, 75, 138; views on dancing, 124;
wartime ordeals, 102-7
Harding, Elizabeth Virginia (see also
Clay, Elizabeth Harding), 6, 13, 24
Harding, Elizabeth W. Bosley (Mrs.
Thomas), 8, 59
Harding, Ellen Amy, 112
Harding, Fannie Davis (Mrs. David
Morris), 110, 302 n.43
Harding, George, 13, 66, 301 n.10
Harding, Giles, 1, 2, 3, 4, 6, 8, 112
Harding, Giles, Jr., 3, 10, 23, 50, 76,
293, 301
Harding, Giles Scales, 76, 111, 112
Harding, Henry. See Hardin, Henry
Harding, James Donnelly, 4, 9
Harding, John
    early years: bartering activities, 19, 23;
begins Belle Meade Stud, 20, 55;
builds clientele for plantation products,
19, 21, 23; builds new home, 11; builds
outbuildings, 13, 19, 20; character, 8;
children born to, 6; as cotton factor,
24; at Dunham Station, 5, 6; education, 1; friendships, 16, 36; interest in
Texas, 16; and jockey club, 23; land
purchases by, 5, 10, 23, 24, 25, 37;
marriage, 4; moves to Tennessee, 2; as
owner of Oak Hill, 3; as overseer, 3;
performs public service, 9, 13; relationship with son, 14, 19; sells slaves,
11; as serious horseman, 34; as stud
manager, 20, 21, 22, 23; trip to
Natchez, 11;

middle years: argument with Childress, 32, 33; as Arkansas planter, 32, 35, 37, 40, 310 n.47; baptized, 36; business involvements, 36; church commitment, 36, 38; death of grandson, 39; education commitments, 13, 303 n.3; family relationships, 38; health of, 38, 40; as host, 36; land transactions, 37, 308 n.7; ledger (accounts) of, 303 n.50, 305 n.52; relinquishes responsibility for Belle Meade, 35; relationships with slaves, 38, 39; temperament, 38; trips, 33, 37, 40;

declining years: in Arkansas, 40, 41; bequests, 133; cared for by Elizabeth, 139; as Davidson County's largest landowner, 41; death, 133; demonstrates Christian faith, 42; family relationships, 41, 85; gifts made, 41, 112; health, 321 n.2; home invaded, 111; portrait of, 40, 288; puzzlement over son's imprisonment, 99; sells land, 41; visits Belle Meade, 97; wife's death, 40

Harding, John, Jr.: assessed, 111; assumes responsibility for plantation at Stones River, 41; birth, 27; brings lawsuit, 233; builds new home, 82; and the burning of Bellevue, 122; entertained, 80; at family weddings, 158, 182; given Bellevue, 133; at Harvard, 67; as horse breeder, 179; indebtedness, 199; marries, 41, 80; moves to Belle Meade, 35; named for grandfather, 306 n.9; ownership in Belle Meade Stud, 186, 225; sells stud interest, 235; threatened by Union soldiers, 102, 122; trips, 66, 166; at yearling sale, 203

Harding Light Artillery. See Confederate Military Units; Harding Light Artillery Band; Militia Units

Harding Light Artillery Band, 189

Harding, Louise Stephenson, 75

Harding, Margaret ("Mag") Murphy Owen (Mrs. John, Jr.), 80, 82, 86, 100, 182

Harding, Marion Roberts (Mrs. William M.), 51

Harding, Martha Donnelly (Mrs. Giles), 3, 8, 9

Harding, Mary Blackman (Mrs. Giles Scales), 76

Harding, Mary Elizabeth (*see also* Jackson, Mary Harding): birth, 65; marriage, 154; takes private lessons, 97; at St. Cecilia, 123, 126; visits with relatives, 97

Harding, Mary Selena McNairy (Mrs. William G.) (*see also* McNairy, Mary Selena), 27, 28, 30, 31, 43, 190

Harding, Nathaniel Adams McNairy, 27, 28

Harding, Nathaniel McNairy, 28, 35, 39, 40, 49

Harding, Peter Perkins, 4, 9

Harding, Rachel (*see also* Overton, Rachel Harding), 25

Harding, Sarah LaForce (Mrs. William), 1, 301 n.4

Harding, Sarah Susan, 52

Harding, Selene ("Lena") (*see also* Jackson, Selene Harding): as an attractive young woman, 89, 127, 136, 138; birth, 51; at boarding school, 120, 121; encounters with soldiers, 102, 107, 127, 128; engagement, 140; entertains beaus, 138, 139; girlfriends, 115, 319 n.26; as heroine, 128; as hostess, 136; marriage, 146; returns from Philadelphia, 124; takes private lessons, 97; trips, 166; on vacation, 119; visits with relatives, 97, 138

Harding, Selene ("Lena") McNairy (*see also* Curd, Selene Harding), 158, 160

Harding, Sophia ("Sophie"), 41, 158

Harding, Sophia ("Sophie") Merritt (Mrs. John, Jr.), 41

Harding, Susannah ("Susan") Shute (Mrs. John) (*see also* Shute, Susannah): birth, 4; buried, 43; character of, 38; death, 40, 49; at Dunham Station, 6, 8; family relationships, 25, 39; as hostess, 36; marriage, 4; as mother, 6; portrait of 40, 288; pride in son, 15, 19

Harding, Thomas (brother of Giles), 2, 3, 4, 9, 301 n.12

Harding, Thomas (brother of John), 8, 24, 25, 27, 32, 38, 59, 303 n.43, 306 n.62

Harding, Thomas J. Dr. (nephew of John), 312 n.4

Harding, Tom (manservant), 209

Harding, William (grandfather of John Harding), 1

Harding, William (brother of John), 8, 24, 25, 27, 65

Harding, William Giles

early years: at American Literary, Scientific and Military Academy, 14-17; attitude toward Christianity, 31; birth, 6; and Childress affair, 32, 33; commissions portrait, 31; as cotton planter, 28; courting days, 17; at Cumberland College, 13; experiences "Yankee parsimoniousness," 15; family relationships, 27, 35; as flatboat owner, 31; friendship with Andrew Jackson, 9, 17, 34; land purchases by, 28; at law school, 17; marriage, 26; militia responsibilities, 30, 43; at "Old Field" School, 13; returns from school, 17, 19; at Stones River, 27, 28, 34, 35; trips 13, 14, 30;

middle years: accounts (ledgers) of, 43, 45, 59; Arkansas interests, 51, 310 n.47; assumes responsibility for Belle Meade, 35; and Cape May affair, 66, 67; as creditor, 44, 48; criticism of, 77, 85; as debtor, 48; as employer, 20; as flatboat owner, 45; friendships, 44, 50, 76, 79, 80; hospitality of, 76, 78, 79, 80; illnesses, 52; interest in raising exotic animals, 81; land transactions, 51, 83; marriage, 46; morality of, 56; personal expenses, 45; and politics, 50, 52, 77; portraits of, 40, 46, 288, 308 n.19; as progressive farmer, 49, 200; as public servant, 78, 79, 317 n.47; as public speaker, 77, 81; as railroad advocate, 76, 77, 314 n.11; relationship with free blacks, 52, 53, 79, with slaves, 79, 314 n.25; religious interests, 45; remodels Belle Meade, 48-49; and Richland Turnpike, 50; sectional

feelings, 53; and theft, 59; as supporter of Texas, 44; trips, 45, 53, 66, 67, 75, 76, 95; wealth, 54;

Civil War years: ambushed, 129; arrested, 92; assessed, 111; considers parole, 106; and conspiracy charges, 123; contributions to the Confederacy, 83, 85, 86, 87, 91, 92; criticism of, 94, 117, 119, 122, 124, 125, 129; despairs of release, 107; files war damage claim, 116, 320 n.27; hospitality of, 88, 89; imprisonment, 93, 94, 96, 104; indicted for treason, 120; innovative ideas, 89, 110; as Military Board member, 85, 86, 87, 88, 89. 117, 120; morality of, 113; parole terms, 109; protected by slaves, 93; rebuked by Governor Johnson, 120; released on bond, 108; retrieves stolen stallion, 113; secessionist feelings, 83, 105; takes amnesty oath, 123; takes oath of allegiance, 116; threatened with banishment, 130; as Vigilance Committee member, 85; wealth, 119;

postwar years: advocates farmers' magazine, 153; compensates W. H. Jackson, 186; controversial views, 150; as convention delegate, 153; death, 208; dependence on Selene, 183; divides Belle Meade among heirs, 186; eulogized, 208, 209; exonerated, 140; and Freedmen's Bureau, 134; funeral of, 209; gifts made by, 175; as host, 136, 138, 152, 167, 171, 187; health, 159, 174, 183, 186, 195, 205, 206; implements contract wage system, 134, 135; income, 136; indebtedness, 170, 199; inherits Belle Meade, 133; land transactions, 149; manages farm, 161, 173, 181; pays taxes, 136; as public speaker, 150, 151, 165; receives annuity, 186; recognition of, 189; relationships with workers, 135, 243; religious conversion, 190; self-doubts, 181; solicits son-in-law's help, 146; trips,138, 158, 166;

Thoroughbred affairs: attends Memphis races, 166; as breeder, 34, 46, 57, 58,

62, 163, 165, 170, 176; commissions horse portraits, 58, 62, 164, 167, 179; inaugurates auction system of selling Thoroughbreds, 163; as innovator, 165; as jockey club activist, 34, 55, 57, 62, 174; opposes professionalism in racing, 170; as purse winner, 34, 57, 61, 62, 163, 166, 167, 170; as racehorse owner, 34, 35, 55, 56, 57, 61, 63, 64, 166, 167, 168, 169; as race official, 34, 35, 56, 62, 163; retires from racing, 170; as stallion keeper, 136; as stake underwriter, 171; as supporter of longer races, 165; as trophy winner, 62, 63, 64, 81, 163; at yearling sales, 163, 164, 166, 168, 171, 174, 175, 177, 198, 205, 206

Harding, William Giles, Jr., 30, 31
Harding, William Giles III, 100, 229, 239
Harding, William M., 51, 52
Harding, William Randal, 75
Harding, Willie Elizabeth (*see also* McGavock, Willie Elizabeth Harding), 27, 28, 65
Harpeth Ridge (Big Hill or Nine Mile Hill) 6, 50
Harris, Chloe (cook), 148
Harris, Isham G., Gov., 78, 83, 85, 86, 87, 88, 89, 100, 142
Harris, Jeremiah George, Commodore, 119, 204
Harris, Lucinda ("Lucie") M. Harris, 117, 119, 121, 138
Harris, Lucinda McGavock (Mrs. Jeremiah George), 119
Harris, Phyllis (child), 148
Harris, Reuben (night watchman), 148, 275
Harris, Richard (laborer), 148
Harris, Richard, Jr. (laborer), 148
Harrison, Benjamin, President, 258
Harrison, Joseph T., 57
Hawkins, Alvin, Gov., 199
Heiman, Adolphus, 43, 70, 90
Henderson, G. W., Dr., 127
Hermann (German valet), 210
Heron, Susan L., 295
Hervey, John L. (*see also* Salvator), 176

Hicks, Edward ("Ed"), 222
Hidalgo (pen name for Thomas B. Merry), 250
Historic Natchez Foundation, 70
Hoar, George F., Senator, 258
Hodgson, Telfair, 293
Hoey, John, Col., 226, 227, 232
Hogg, Douglas, Lord, 268
Hogg, Elizabeth ("Myssie") Brown (Lady Douglas) (*see also* Marjoribanks, Elizabeth Brown), 268
Hogg, Quintin (*see also* Hailsham, Lord), 268
Hoggatt, Philip, Col., 22
Homes (*see also* Plantations): Acklen Hall, 284; Belair, 24; Belle Meade (*see* Belle Meade Plantation); Belmont, 138; Braeburn, 295; Burlington Place, 267; Fatherland, 91; Honeywood, 222; Lockland, 281; Mount Vernon, 15; Polk Place, 84, 199; Southside Villa, 262; Spring Place, 27; Two Rivers, 25; Walter Place, 143; West Meade (*see* main entry)
Hood, Ida E., 295
Hood, John Bell, Gen., 125, 126, 144
Hoover, Elizabeth ("Cousin Lizzie"), 136, 138, 146, 151, 160, 177, 186, 223, 252, 253, 255
Horn, C. B., 293
Horses. *See* Thoroughbreds
Hotels: Columbia House, 66; Duncan, 267; Indian Queen, 15; LaPierre, 121; Maxwell House, 173, 210, 214, 219, 260, 265; Michigan House, 95; Mission House, 96, 104; St. Charles, 33; St. Cloud, 92, 119; Tulane, 289
Houston, Sam, 15, 21, 23, 44, 46, 48, 50, 304 n.19, 305 n.37
Howard, Memucan Hunt, 10, 11
Howell, E. P., 182
Hubbard, J. R. (*see also* Albion), 176
Huddleston, Howell, 112, 149
Hume, William, Rev., 23, 24, 26, 27
Humphreys, West H., 77
Hunt's Point, New York, 228, 230, 232, 233
Huntington, A. B., 16, 304 n.20
Hurricane Springs, Tennessee, 151, 153

Indians: Apache, 84, 278; Cherokee, 9;
    Chickasaw, 9; Chippewa, 105; Choc-
    taw, 9; Kiowa, 141; Ottawa, 105;
    Seminole, 30, 43
Itúrbide, Agustín (President of Mexico),
    16
Itúrbide, Agustín Jerome, 16

Jackson, Alexander ("Alex"), Dr., 76,
    79, 84, 85, 138, 142, 146, 153, 154,
    156, 159, 160, 164, 258
Jackson, Andrew, Gen.: in Battle of New
    Orleans, 8, 9, 26; at Carnton, 46; as
    cotton planter, 24; Dickinson affair
    recalled, 34; death, 50; judicial
    appointment by, 52; as mentor, 26;
    passes Dunham's Station, 9; portrait
    of, 50, 309 n.36; as turfman, 20;
    visited by W. G. Harding, 26, 34
Jackson, Annie Davis ("D") Richardson
    (Mrs. William Harding) (*see also*
    Stevenson, Annie Davis), 271, 279,
    280, 281, 282, 283, 289
Jackson Building, 257, 258, 297
Jackson, Elizabeth ("Bessie") (*see also*
    Buckner, Elizabeth Jackson), 159, 219,
    328 n.12, 338 n.59
Jackson, Eunice Fenner (Mrs. Alex-
    ander), 76, 151, 154
Jackson, Eunice (*see also* Marks, Eunice
    Jackson): admired, 161; attends *bal
    poudre*, 253; birth, 151; callers, 223;
    childhood activities, 186; Colorado
    stay, 160, 161, 162; as hostess, 252; as
    household manager, 257; illnesses,
    253, 254; introduced to President
    Cleveland, 216; marriage, 261; as
    student, 183; as Sunday School
    teacher, 194, 275, 330 n.54; trips,
    220, 255; welcomed into society, 221
Jackson, Harding Alexander, 296
Jackson, Henry, 157
Jackson, Howell E.
    personal life: buys property, 183; death,
    263; death of first wife, 154; descrip-
    tion, 156; dinner at the White House,
    260; education, 79, 156; eulogized,
    263; as fox hunter, 221, 222; as host,
    187, 210, 214, 215, 216, 218; indebted-

ness, 204; marriages of, 154, 156;
    moves to Davidson County, 183; as
    opponent of secession, 156; pardoned,
    157; as partner in Jackson Building,
    258; portrait of, 283; as railroad
    advocate, 214; residences of during
    war, 325 n.43; sibling relationships,
    204, 236, 237, 255, 257; as Southern
    Whig, 156; terminal illness, 258, 260;
    tours battlefield, 185; trips, 185, 186,
    260, 262; visits Belle Meade, 79;
    professional life: action as U.S. Senator,
    199; appointed to Federal Court, 194;
    appointed to U.S. Supreme Court,
    258; dinner in honor of, 260; election
    to U.S. Senate, 182; envies pastoral
    life, 158, 169, 325 n.41; last public
    act, 262; law practice of, 154, 156,
    157; legal opinions, 255, 262; as
    presiding judge for Sixth Circuit
    Court, 255; as Receiver for the
    Western District of Tennessee, 156,
    325 n.44; retires from bench, 262;
    Thoroughbred/agricultural activities:
    borrows money, 179, 211; brings suit
    against Adams Express Company, 233;
    buys share of Enquirer, 179; as cattle
    owner, 201; as poor manager, 181;
    leaves breeding business, 235; manages
    dairy, 190; ownership in Belle Meade
    Stud, 186, 211, 225; at yearling sales,
    199, 200, 203
Jackson, Howell E., Jr., 157, 169, 258,
    290
Jackson, Howell E. III, 297
Jackson, Dorothy Patterson (Mrs. Howell
    E. III), 297
Jackson, Louise (*see also* McAlister,
    Louise Jackson), 262, 326 n.68
Jackson, Mary ("Mamie") Eleanor (*see
    also* also Crosby, Mary Eleanor
    Jackson), 157
Jackson, Mary Elizabeth (infant), 148
Jackson, Mary Harding (Mrs. Howell E.)
    (*see also* Harding, Mary Elizabeth):
    character, 296; children born to, 159;
    considers buying Belle Meade, 280;
    death, 296; dinner at the White

House, 260; estate sale purchases, 283; family visits, 169, 270; as hostess, 218, 252; idiosyncrasies, 40; inherits part of Belle Meade, 186; lack of social aspirations, 260; moves to Davidson County, 183; as owner of West Meade, 236; pays off mortgage, 296; restores Tealey Place, 184; sells "High Pasture," 293; sibling relationships, 184, 237; trips, 185, 186

Jackson, Miranda ("Mannie") Baxter (*see also* Baxter, Miranda), 257, 338 n.48

Jackson, Rachel Donelson (Mrs. Andrew), 26, 71

Jackson, Robert Fenner, 183, 220

Jackson, Selene (*see also* Elliston, Selene Jackson): birth, 159; childhood experiences of 160,161, 183, 186; described, 224; education, 183, 224; family relationships, 256; marriage, 265, 267

Jackson, Selene ("Lena") Harding (Mrs. William Hicks) (*see also* Harding, Selene): advises husband, 257; asthma attacks, 148, 159, 184; attends weddings, 158, 253; children born to, 148, 151, 157, 159; Christian experiences, 194, 254, 256, 257; convalescence in Colorado, 160, 161, 181; as counsellor, 223; death, 257; envies city life, 183; expresses love for Belle Meade, 181; final illness, 255, 256; as hostess, 177, 186, 211, 216, 220, 252, 254; interview with, 215; as nurse, 183, 187, 254; ownership of Belle Meade, 186; portrait of, 283; praised by husband, 161, 257; relationships with servants, 256, 257, with sister, 184; remodels Belle Meade, 184, 185, 255

Jackson, Sophia ("Sophie") (daughter), 157, 324 n.32

Jackson, Sophia ("Sophie") Molloy (Mrs. Howell E.), 154

Jackson, Tennessee, 142, 154

Jackson, William ("Billy") H., 157, 158, 262

Jackson, William Harding: ambitions, 279; assumes responsibility for Belle Meade, 274; birth, 157; builds private racetrack, 247; childhood experiences, 160, 161, 181, 183, 185, 186, 192; christened, 169; death, 279; described, 267; education, 183, 224, 333 n.41, 247; as executor, 272; as groomsman, 239; as host, 245; introduced to President Cleveland, 216; marriage, 265; mortgages Belle Meade, 264, 273; as racehorse owner, 248, 276; as sportsman, 248, 268, 269; as stud manager, 248; trips, 248, 279

Jackson, William ("Billy") Harding, Jr., 271, 279, 282, 289

Jackson, William Hicks, Gen.

civic/professional activities: as advocate of inexpensive transportation, 153, 214; announces construction of office building, 257, 337 n.33; assists police investigation, 193; as bank president, 190; Bureau of Agriculture activities, 152; as commander in sham battle, 219; Grange activities, 154; Nashville Gas Light Company, 264; Nashville Street Railroad Company, 261, 264; and National Agricultural Congress, 151, 152, 153; as parade marshal, 218; and *Rural Sun*, 152, 153; shuns public office, 182; and Tennessee Agricultural and Mechanical Association, 151, 153; Tennessee Centennial Celebration responsibilities, 244, 264, 265, 273; and Tennesee Farmers' Association, 153; and Tennessee Stockbreeders Association, 159; and United Confederate Veterans, 254, 261;

family/personal life: the "Baxter note" affair, 261; as best man, 285; boyhood, 146; bust of, 264; conveys Belle Meade to his children, 264; courts Selene, 138; death, 278; as debtor, 204, 211, 212, 239; as defense lawyer, 160; description of 140-41, 207, 267; discusses rental property, 160, 181; eulogized, 278; as father, 162, 181, 254; feelings of toward the North, 187; frustrations, 204, 212, 267; gives financial aid to married daughters, 276; as host, 185,

Jackson, William Hicks, Gen. *(continued)*
187, 194, 199, 204, 210, 215, 216, 217,
220, 241, 244, 250, 257, 268, 273;
hunting activities, 161, 183, 192, 248,
253, 269; illnesses, 153, 160, 181, 253;
life style of, 267; marriage, 146, 148;
political activities, 156, 182, 253, 255,
328 n.11; portraits of, 283, 297;
praised, 204, 276; praises wife, 161,
257; reflections on Civil War's out-
come, 204; relationship with brother,
181, 204, 236, 255, 257, with workers,
187, 253; religious experiences, 190-92,
192, 254; as respected citizen, 223,
245; tours battlefield, 185; trips, 79,
139, 140, 158, 160, 176, 190, 215, 232,
238, 239, 242, 244, 245, 255, 257,
274; victimized by son-in-law, 275;
waning energies, 244, 263; writes will,
272;

farming activities: as cattleman, 201;
manages Belle Meade as partnership,
190; manages dairy, 190; as progressive
farmer, 74, 200; responsibilities at
Belle Meade, 159, 161, 173, 179;

military experiences: on active duty with
U.S. Army, 84, 141; appointed Captain, 87; in battle, 142, 143, 144; fails
to capture U.S. Grant, 142; kills
grizzly bear, 141; kills buffalo, 141;
never pardoned, 323 n.60; offends Jefferson Davis, 144; promotion denied,
143, 145, 323 n.57; promotions, 142,
143; saves officer's life, 141; succeeds
Forrest in command, 145; at U.S.
Military Academy, 79, 141; wounded,
142, 323 n.44;

Thoroughbred activities: announces a
new racetrack, 208; becomes less
active, 248, 274; borrows money, 179,
211; brings suit against Adams Express
Company, 233; builds carriage house/
stable, 239; buys out other stud interests, 235, 237; compensated for
services, 186; decides to sell yearlings
in New York, 226; declines offer for
Iroquois, 239; expresses satisfaction
over foals, 205; leases West Meade

pasture, 247; makes Iroquois's hooves
into inkwells, 249; as partial owner of
Belle Meade Stud, 186; praises Proctor
Knott, 211; repurchases Croker's stud
interest, 246; retires, 274; sells stud
interest to Croker, 241; sends horses to
Louisville races, 169; visits Colorado
stockbreeders, 160; at yearling sales,
164, 199, 201, 203, 242
Jackson, William (sign maker), 296
Jefferson County, Arkansas, Court, 51
Jennings, Obediah, Rev., 31, 42
Jennings, Thomas, Dr., 121
Jennings, Mrs. Thomas, 121
Jockey Clubs: Ashland, 57; Brooklyn,
176; Coney Island, 211; Franklin,
Tennessee, 35, 56; Highland Park,
282; Huntsville, Alabama, 57;
Louisville, 168, 169, 170, 174, 200;
Nashville, 23, 56, 57, 62, 170;
Nashville Blood Horse Association,
64, 164, 167, 168, 171, 173, 174, 208;
Walnut Association, 62
Johns, John, 51
Johnson, A. W., 77
Johnson, Andrew: as governor, 77, 78,
92, 94-96, 98-100, 102, 103, 106, 107,
109, 110, 120-122, 124, 125; as presi-
dent, 145, 156
Johnson, W. H., Col., 168, 169, 171,
179, 198
Johnson, William R., Col., 22, 62
Johnson's Island, 90, 98
Johnston, Albert Sidney, Gen., 88,
89
Johnston, Joseph E., Gen., 130, 143,
144, 145, 182
Johnston, Matthew Locke, 8, 9
Johnstown flood, 227, 232
Jonah ("Grandma"), 48
Jones, Sam, Rev., 190, 192
Jones, Uriah (overseer), 45
Jones, William (overseer), 45
Jordan, Lee Roy, 207
Jordan, Thomas, Gen., 139
Joslin, Benjamin J., 302 n.23
Joslin, John M., 149
Joslin, Lewis, 78
Judd, Henry A., 67

Keeling, Leonard, 28
Keene, James R., 177, 203, 250
Kelley, D. C., Rev., 181, 190, 209, 257, 279
Kerbreck, Favorot de, Baron, 197
Kercheval, Thomas A., Mayor, 214, 218
Kerrigan, Thomas, 193
Kidd, P. C., Capt., 173, 174, 177, 198, 206
Killebrew, J. B., 153, 157, 257, 265
Kirkland, James H., Chancellor, 223, 333 n.38
Kirkman, Catherine ("Kate") Thompson (Mrs. Van Leer), 265
Kirkman, Hugh, 34, 70
Kirkman, John, 34
Kittredge, Herbert S., 177, 196
Know-Nothing party, 77, 78

LaForce, René, Dr., 301 n.4
LaForce, Sarah (Mrs. René), 301 n.4
Lamar, John, 57
Lamont, Daniel S., Col., 215, 216
Laurel Furnace, 19
Lea, John M., 86
Lea, Luke, Col., 292, 293, 296
Leake, Bessie Lea (Mrs. James O.), 292, 293, 342 n.18
Leake, Esther, 292
Leake, James O., 292
LeDuc, William G., Bvt. Brig. Gen., 129
Lee, Betsy (child), 148
Lee, Betsy (house servant) 148
Lee, Fitzhugh, Gen., 279
Lee, Julius (carriage driver), 148
Lee, Monroe (child), 148
Lee, Robert E., Gen., 132
Lee, Stephen D., Gen., 143, 146, 185, 190, 285
Leigh, Eugene, 238, 244, 247
Letcher, John, Gov., 86
Le Vert, Octavia, 138
Lewis, Eugene C., Maj., 264
Linares, José María, President of Bolivia, 81
Lincoln, Abraham, President, 84, 85, 86, 120, 122, 123
Lincoln, Robert Todd, 245

Lind, Jenny, 46
Lindsley, Dr. Van S., 136
Lindsley, Goodloe, 285
Lipscomb, Mary D. Cheatham (Mrs. Thomas H.), 288
Livingstone, George A., 295
Longstreet, James, Maj., 142
Lorillard, George, 198
Lorillard, Pierre, 168, 198, 199, 207
Loring, John B. (Commissioner of Agriculture), 199
Lurton, Horace H., Judge, 265

Mabry, Joseph A., Gen., 164
McAlister, Hill, Gov., 280, 340 n.24
McAlister, Louise (Mrs. Hill) (*see also* Jackson, Louise), 70, 290, 296
McCall, Addie Timberlake (Mrs. John Ethridge), 283
McGavock, Amanda. *See* Cheatham, Amanda McGavock
McGavock, Amanda Harding (Mrs. Francis) (*see also* Harding, Amanda P.), 10, 15, 24, 41, 85, 133, 324 n.32
McGavock, Caroline Winder (Mrs. John), 125, 126, 138, 304 n.17
McGavock, David H., 15, 48, 65, 96, 102, 111, 123, 133, 158
McGavock, David T., Dr., 59, 62
McGavock, Elizabeth Harding, 52
McGavock, Elizabeth Irwin (*see also* Harding, Elizabeth McGavock), 46
McGavock, Felix Grundy, 99
McGavock, Francis ("Frank"), 10, 15, 41, 50, 85, 111
McGavock, Frank Owen, 158
McGavock, Georgia Moore (Mrs. John H.), 41
McGavock, Harriet Young, 125
McGavock, Jacob, 38, 51, 79
McGavock, James, Jr., 2
McGavock, James Randal, 52, 125
McGavock, John, 125, 126, 138, 304 n.17
McGavock, John H., 15, 40, 41, 77, 85
McGavock, Louisa Chenault (Mrs. James Randal), 52, 125
McGavock, Lula Spence (Mrs. Frank Owen), 158

McGavock, Mary Manoah Bostick (Mrs. Felix Grundy), 99
McGavock, Randal, 46, 51, 66, 258
McGavock, Randal W., 77, 79, 80, 90, 94, 98, 120
McGavock, Sarah ("Sallie") Rodgers (Mrs. Randal), 46, 71, 76, 139
McGavock, Seraphine (Mrs. Randal W.), 79
McGavock, William, 38, 340 n.25
McGavock, Willie Elizabeth Harding (Mrs. David H.) (*see also* Harding, Willie Elizabeth), 48, 158
McGavock, Winder, 125
McGhee, Charles McClung, 211, 264
McKee, J. Cooper, 141
McKendree Methodist Church. *See* Churches
Mackey, John, 244
Mackinac Island, 98, 99
McKinley, William, President, 265
McNairy, Boyd, Dr., 30, 32, 33
McNairy, F. H., Maj., 138, 140, 322 n.17
McNairy, Francis ("Frank"), 32, 33
McNairy, John, Judge, 26
McNairy, Kitty Hobson (Mrs. Nathaniel), 26
McNairy, Mary Selena (*see also* Harding, Mary Selena McNairy), 17, 26
McNairy, Nathaniel, 26, 43
McNeilly, James H., Rev., 263
McSpadden's Bend (Pennington Bend), 23, 25, 27, 34, 41, 51, 82
Maddin, Elizabeth Buckner (Mrs. John Keith), 287
Maddin, Mary Belle Keith (Mrs. Percy D.), 252
Magruder, Ellen ("Nellie") Malone (Mrs. William) (*see also* Malone, Ellen), 252, 267
Magruder, William, 267
Mallory, Steven R. (Secretary of the Navy, CSA), 89
Malone, Ellen ("Nellie") (*see also* Magruder, Ellen Malone) 220, 221
Malone, Ellen Fall (Mrs. Thomas H.), 220

Malone, Thomas H., Judge, 203, 220, 221, 263, 333 n.24
Manakin Town, Virginia, 301 n.4
Marmaduke, John S., Gen., 152
Marjoribanks, Archibald J., 268
Marjoribanks, Elizabeth ("Myssie") Brown, (Mrs. Archibald), 268
Marks, Albert D., 261, 262, 267, 268, 271, 272, 274, 275, 280, 285, 290
Marks, Albert D., Jr., 267-70
Marks, Albert S., Gov., 214
Marks, Eunice Jackson (Mrs. Albert D.) (*see also* Jackson, Eunice), bequests, 271; death, 270; death of son, 268; on honeymoon, 262; as hostess, 268; illness, 270; mortgages Belle Meade, 264; religious experiences, 268, 269, 270; sibling relationships, 289
Marshall, Ben, 59
Marshall, Ellen McClung (Mrs. John), 281
Martin, Ellen Wills (Mrs. William Swift III), 288
Martin, Johnny (jockey), 104
Matthews, Stanley (provost marshal), 92, 93
Maury, Dabney H., Gen, 143
Maury, Matthew Fontaine, Commodore, 80-83, 132, 152
Maximilian (Emperor of Mexico), 132
Maxwell, James, 10, 23
Meigs, Return J., 92
Memphis, 28, 87, 88, 154, 156
Mero District, 4
Merritt, Sophia. *See* Harding, Sophia
Mexican War, 215, 218
Meyer, Henry R., Maj., 92
Middletown, Connecticut, 14, 67
Miles (carriage driver), 100, 102
Military and Financial Board of Tennessee, 85-89, 98, 120
Militia units: Blues and Guards, 50; Cantrell Guards, 189; Capt. Mullen's Militia Company, 4; Harding Light Artillery, 187, 189, 209; Hermitage Guards, 189; Nashville Blues, 50; Porter Rifles, 189; Stanton Guard, 104, 108; Tennessee Brigade of Volunteers, 30
Miller, Ronald W., 69

Million, W. E., 96
Mississippi County, Arkansas, 37
Mississippi Territory, 51
Molloy, Sophia ("Sophie") (*see also* Jackson, Sophia Molloy), 156
Moore, Georgia, (*see also* McGavock, Georgia Moore), 308 n.23
Moore, T. B., Capt., 166, 173
Morgan, Carey E., Rev., 290, 296
Morgan, John Hunt, Gen., 99, 145
Morgan, Marshall, 246, 247
Morgan, Samuel D., 87
Morgan, Thomas ("Tom"), 253
Morris, John B., Rev., 270, 271, 275, 289
Mt. Olivet Cemetery, 183, 289
Mulherrin, James, Sr., 24
Murfreesboro, 113, 144, 158

Napier, James Carroll, 195
Napier, Richard C., 19
Napier, William C., 195
Narragansett, Rhode Island, 282
Nashville: as beleaguered city, 121; Board of Claims, 116, 117; Centennial Exposition Building, 181; as convention site, 54; as cotton port, 24; descriptions of, 2, 124; fortifications at, 103; Gas Light Company, 264; Golf and Country Club, 293, 295; Industrial Exposition, 198; looting of, 90; Masonic Lodge, 70; as racehorse center, 57; secessionist sentiment in, 85, 86; sectional feelings in, 53; Street Railway Company, 261, 264, 293; as Tennessee's largest city, 54; threatened by Confederates, 100; YMCA, 190
Natchez, Mississippi, 5, 11, 14
National Agricultural Congress, 150, 152, 153, 157, 159
National Horseracing Museum (New Market, England), 59
National Museum of Racing, 59, 297
Newman, John, Dr., 23
New Orleans, 14, 33, 48, 59
New Town. *See* West Nashville
Nichols, John, 23, 32
Nichol, Josiah, 24, 305 n.52

Nichol, Julia Margaret Lytle (Mrs. William), 100
Nichol, William, 37
Nichols, Francis T., Gov., 252, 336 n.1
Nichols, Hattie, 252
Nichols, Sam (groom), 242, 243
Nicholson, Hunter, 153
Noris, Rachael (free mulatto), 39
Norris, George, 16
Norris (slave), 38, 39
Northwestern Mutual Life Insurance Company, 264, 273

Oakdale Hunting Club, 248
Ogden, John, 134
Olney, Richard (U.S. Attorney General), 262
Olsen, Susan, 288
Opryland U.S.A., 25
Overton, James, Dr., 76, 93
Overton, Jesse M., 253, 285
Overton, John, Col., 25, 86, 92, 96, 111, 140, 164
Overton, John, Judge, 23, 46, 292
Overton, Rachel Harding (Mrs. John) (*see also* Harding, Rachel), 92
Owen, Elizabeth Clopton (Mrs. Francis A.) (*see also* Harding, Elizabeth Clopton), 28, 65
Owen, Francis ("Frank") A., Rev., 28, 65, 80, 307 n.20
Owen, Margaret ("Mag") Murphy. *See* Harding, Margaret Murphy Owen
Owen, Martha Shute (Mrs. William E.), 136
Owen, Robert, 31

Page, Giles Harding, 8, 40, 78, 83
Page, Henrietta Mariah Wilkes (Mrs. Giles Harding), 40
Page, James M., 149
Page, Robert Thomas, 3, 8
Page, Robert Thomas, Jr., 8
Page, Sallie Ann Harding (Mrs. Robert Thomas), 8
Page, Thomas Nelson, 254
Pagette, Ned, 133
Palmer, Joseph B., Gen., 219
Parkhurst, John G., Col., 129, 130

Parks, C. C., 166
Parks, George, 290
Parks, Mrs. Hamilton, 283
Parks, R. H., 166
Parmer, Walter O., 280, 282, 283, 293, 295, 296
Partridge, Alden, Capt., 14, 17, 19, 26, 306 n.4
Patterson, Robert, Gen., 50
Payne, Reuben, 235
Pennington, John W., 51
Perkins, Nicholas ("Bigbee"), 36, 50
Perkins, Thomas Harden, 14, 36
Peters Colony, 80
Peyton, Balie, 58, 164
Philadelphia, 14, 117, 121, 124
Pierce, D. C., 228, 232
Pierce, Frankie, Dr., 224
Pillow, Gideon J., Gen., 54, 87, 142
Plantations (*see also* Studs): Belair, 28, 35, 305 n.55; Bellevue, 41, 122; Belle Meade (*see under* Belle Meade Plantation); Carnton, 46, 71, 125, 126, 128, 144; Cliff Lawn (*see also under* Studs), 85, 133, 158; Devon Farm (*see also* Oak Hill), 3; Diamond Grove, 57; Dunbarton, 16; Fairvue (*see also under* Studs), 20; The Hermitage, 34, 71; Lynnwood, 203; Millwood, 62; Oak Hill, 3; Oaklands, 62; Richland Grange Farm, 203; Riverside, 97, 125; Rosemont, 51, 75, 98; Sans Souci, 41, 85; Tealey Place, 183, 184, 194, 328 n.16; Travellers' Rest, 185; Two Rivers, 48, 65; Walnut Grove, 139; Winder, 304 n.17
Plum Point Bend, Arkansas, 37
Polk, James K., President, 15, 36, 46, 50, 52, 210, 313 n.28
Polk, Leonidas, Gen., 87, 88, 142, 143
Polk, Marshall, 173
Polk, Sarah Childress (Mrs. James K.), 84, 210, 215, 218, 313 n.28
Porter, A. J., Capt., 182
Porter, Felicia Grundy, 117, 119
Porter, James D., Gov., 173, 203
Porterfield, John, 97
Poynor, Henry W., 40, 58, 75
Price, George, Dr., 183, 224

Priestley, James, Dr., 13, 28, 306 n.18
Proclamation of Amnesty and Reconstruction, 122
Pryor, John, 139

Quarles, William A., Gen., 128

Races (*see also* Stakes): English Derby, 21, 57, 59, 199, 207, 249, 296, 311 n.14; Iroquois Memorial Steeplechase, 296; Kentucky Derby, 169, 170, 206, 212, 244; Kentucky handicap, 219; Proprietor's Purse, 56, 61
Racetracks: Burns's Stable and Race Track, 22; Gallatin, 22; Jerome Park, 175; Monmouth Park, 197; Nashville, 22, 35, 57, 58, 59, 61, 167, 168, 208, 311 n.7, 331 n.53; Oakley, 244; Sheepshead Bay, 244; Walnut Grove, 59, 61, 62; West Side Park, 208, 212, 218, 219, 264
Railroads: Louisville & Nashville (L&N), 214, 227, 272; Midland, 214; Nashville & Chattanooga, 77, 91, 144, 168; Nashville & Northwestern, 133, 164; Nashville Chattanooga & St. Louis (NC&StL), 215, 229, 272; Pennsylvania Central, 227, 229; Tennessee and Alabama, 91, 128
Railroad Stations: Nashville and Chattanooga Depot, 189; North College Street Depot, 169; Union Station, 271, 272, 276
Reall, Joseph H., 200
Reed, Charles, 197, 200, 226, 229, 232, 241, 243
Reed, Ann Jane (Mrs. Charles), 200
Reform Movement. *See* Disciples Movement
Richland Turnpike Company, 275
Richards, A. Keene, 174
Richardson, Ann McGavock (Mrs. John), 48, 309 n.24
Richardson, Annie Davis (*see also* Jackson, Annie Davis; Stevenson, Annie Davis), 265
Richardson, Henrietta, 271
Richardson, James B., 280, 281, 282, 283, 284, 286

Richardson, John, 309 n.24
Richardson, Sally Evans (Mrs. James B.), 271, 283
Ritter, T. L., 88, 89
Rivers and streams: Cumberland River, 2, 4, 25, 31, 86, 89, 102, 122, 229; Flat Creek, 6, 23; Fletcher's Creek, 83; Harpeth River, 2, 3, 4, 9, 46, 50, 125, 144; Little Harpeth River, 3; McCrory's Creek, 25; Mansker's Creek, 5; Mill Creek, 23, 24, 51; Richland Creek, 5, 6, 10, 11, 23-27, 74, 109, 128, 189, 193, 236, 271; Sam's Creek, 23; Stones River, 25, 26, 111; Tennessee River, 86, 125; Whites Creek, 23
Roads: Avery's Trace, 2; Belle Meade Blvd., 292, 296; Briley Parkway, 25; Charlotte Turnpike, 100, 127, 133, 293; Chickering Road, 296; Great Wagon Road, 2; Harding Road, 303 n.45; Harding Turnpike (see also Richland Turnpike), 127, 128, 149, 209, 246, 272, 273, 292; Hillsboro Turnpike, 127, 222, 253; Island Road, 2; Jackson Blvd., 292; Lebanon Turnpike, 24, 32, 100; Lower Franklin Turnpike, 186, 292; Murfreesboro Turnpike, 34, 98; Natchez Road, 5, 8, 9, 55; Nolensville Road, 282; Old Natchez Road (see Natchez Road); Richland Turnpike, 50, 74, 133, 160, 303 n.45; Three Notched Road, 2; Wilson Turnpike, 144
Roberts, Marion. See Harding, Marion Roberts
Robertson, Anna B., 136
Robertson, Felix, Dr., 37
Rodes, J. B., 170
Roosevelt, Theodore, 141, 194, 223
Rosecrans, William S., Gen., 110, 111, 113, 116, 119
Rural Sun Publishing Company, 152, 153

Salvator (pen name) (see also Hervey, John L.), 176
Sanford, Mabel Reynolds (Mrs. Samuel R.), 283
Sappington, Robert B., Dr., 21
Saratoga Springs, New York, 59, 248, 295

Schofield, John M., Gen., 125
Schools: American Literary, Scientific and Military Academy, 14-18; Belmont College, 295; Belmont Collegiate and Preparatory School, 295; Catholic University, 269; College of New Jersey (Princeton), 14; Culver Military Academy, 290; Cumberland College, 13, 14, 19; Cumberland Law School, 79, 156; Fisk University, 194; Harvard College, 14, 67, 289; Howard School, 11; Litchfield Law School, 17; Madame Masse's French School, 117, 121; Mississippi Agricultural and Mechanical College, 190, 329 n.39; Nashville Female Academy, 13, 65, 117, 303 n.3; "Old Field" School, 13; Parmer School, 296; Price's School for Young Ladies (Nashville College for Young Ladies), 183, 224; Richland Creek Meeting House, 13; Robertson Academy, 303 n.3; St. Cecilia Academy, 117, 123, 124, 126; St. Mark's School, 289; Transylvania College, 297; United States Military Academy, 14, 26, 79, 141, 146, 278; University of Nashville, 15, 16, 51, 70; University of North Carolina, vii, 41; University of Virginia, 156; Vanderbilt University, 194, 196, 199, 218, 223; Virginia Military Institute, 152; Ward Seminary, 194; Washington University, 182; Webb school, 224, 247; West Tennessee College, 156
Scott, Thomas, 283
Seaton, Bruce, 248
Seddon, James (Secretary of War, CSA), 143
Seymour, Horatio, 16, 304 n.20
Shapard, Henry, 138, 139, 140
Sheepshead Bay, Long Island, 245, 280
Shepherd, David, 295
Sherman, William T., Gen., 145, 146, 245
Shute, Elizabeth Waller (Mrs. Philip), 4, 301 n.17
Shute, John, 10
Shute, Philip, 111
Shute, Philip ("Phil"), 4, 301 n.17

Shute, Susannah ("Susan") (*see also* Harding, Susannah Shute), 4
Shute, William, 301 n.17
Sinclair, Edwards, 269, 270, 272, 282
Singleton, Richard, Col., 34, 55
Singleton, Zack Boyd, 272
Smith, Charles F., Dr., 219
Smith, R. T., 290
Smith, Susan McGavock (Mrs. William Henry), 133
Smith, William C., Capt., 264
Southall, Henry, 90
Southall, Joseph J. B., 51, 75, 310 n.47
Southall, Josephine, 75
Southall, Mary McGavock (Mrs. Joseph J. B.): at Belle Meade, 75, 90, 98, 139; death, 109, 111; and family deaths, 75; illnesses, 75, 98, 102, 106; sells property, 51; visits Rosemont, 99
Southall, Randal McGavock, 70, 90, 97, 98, 109
Southern Historical Collection, vii
Southwest Point, Tennessee, 2
Speer, William S., 50
Spence, David, 158
Spence, Lula. *See* McGavock, Lula Spence
Spence, Sally (Mrs. David), 158
Spring Hill Cemetery, 293
Stakes (*see also* Races): Alabama, 57; Belle Meade, 171; Champion, 197; Clark, 170; Criterion, 55; Doncaster St. Leger, 207; Fall City, 170; Futurity, 211, 225, 231; Galt House, 96; Grand Union Hotel, 197; Great America Stallion, 176, 197; Great Challenge, 197; Great Champion, 249; Great Eclipse, 249; Hawthorne, 248; Kentucky, 174; Kentucky St. Leger, 197; Lassie, 238; Long Island St. Leger, 197; Maxwell House, 176; Peyton, 57, 58; Prince of Wales, 199, 249; St. Leger, 199, 249; San Francisco, 173; Saratoga, 174; Tidal, 197; Two Thousand Sweepstakes, 212; United States Hotel, 197; Withers, 175; Young America #1, 174; Young America #2, 174
Standish, Francis, Sir, 21

Stanton, Edwin M., Secretary of War, 95
Starke, Peter B., Gen., 139
Stevenson, Adlai E., 257
Stevenson, Annie Davis (*see also* Jackson, Annie Davis ["D"]), 289
Stevenson, Maxwell, 289
Stevenson, Vernon K., 77, 197
Stevens Sanitorium, 290
Stewart, Alexander P., Gen., 126
Stockton, Robert F., Commodore, 82
Stokes, William B., Col., 107
Strahl, Otho F., Gen., 126
Stuart, James Ewell B. ("Jeb"), Gen., 145
Strickland, William, 70
Studs: Avondale, 242, 276; Belle Meade (*see under* Belle Meade Plantation); Bull Run, 297; Cliff Lawn (*see also under* Plantations) 207, 226, 229, 232; Edenwold, 282, 289, 295; Elmendorf, 203, 225, 238; Fairvue (*see also under* Plantations) 200, 203, 211, 226, 229, 232, 243, 332 n.68; Fannymede, 238; Glen Flora Farm,166; Kennesaw, 199, 211; La Belle, 237; McGrathiana, 200, 225; Rancho del Paso, 225, 226, 274; Rancosas, 207; Runnymede, 203; Shepherd's Bush, 235; Sledmere, 241, 245; Woodburn, 171, 203, 238
Stull, Henry, 179,196, 283
Sumner, Charles, 78, 79, 80
Swigert, Daniel, 175, 199, 225, 226, 227, 229
Sykes, Tatton, Sir, 241, 245

Taft, William Howard, 260, 262, 263, 290
Tammany Hall, 241
Tarbot, Lord, 187
Tattersalls' Sale Repository, 233, 239, 241
Taylor, Richard, Gen., 130, 145
Taylor, Robert Love, Gov., 218
Tealey, F. W., 328 n.16
Temple, L. M., 77
Tennessee: Agricultural & Mechanical Association, 151, 153; Bar Association, 290; Bureau of Agriculture, Statistics, and Mines, 152, 157, 257; Centennial Celebration, 244, 245, 246, 252, 265, 273; Centennial Exposition Company,

264, 265; Day, 226, 231, 234; Farmers'
Association, 153, 182; General As-
sembly, 78, 88, 141; Grange, 154;
Historical Commission, 296; Historical
Society, 10, 210, 264; State Capitol,
70; State Legislature, 76, 83, 85; State
Museum, 288; State Prison, 93, 284;
Stockbreeders Association, 159; Su-
preme Court, 52, 158, 233
Terry, F. B., Col., 88
Thomas, George H., Gen., 106, 127,
129, 175
Thomas, Henry K., 53
Thomas, James, 52, 53
Thomas, Jane, 27
Thomas, John W., Maj., 215, 264, 265
Thompson, Jacob, 152
Thornton, George, 187
Thoroughbreds (including those
twentieth-century descendants of Belle
Meade sires mentioned in the text);
    colts: Allandorf, 63; Alpha, 34, 55;
Bancroft, 210; Ben Ali, 206; Ben
Brush, 244; Bill Bruce, 170; Bramble,
168, 171, 173, 174, 175, 176,177, 180,
198; Camargo, 168, 169, 170; Canon-
ero II, 196; Carry Back, 196; Chivalry,
64; Come to Taw, 212; Corsair, 64;
Dancer's Image, 196; Economy, 205;
Editor, 205; Egmont, 219; Endurance,
236; Enlister, 170; Falsetto, 179;
Forward Pass, 196; Frogtown, 166;
George Kinney, 203, 297; Glidelin,
199; G. W. Johnson, 249; Helmet,
164; Hindoo, 199; Inspector B, 205,
236; Invictus, 248; Iroquois, 199;
Irritable, 249; Jack Malone, 63; Joe
Blackburn, 198, 199; Johnstown, 196;
Julius Sax, 249; Iron Liege, 196;
Labrador, 64; Lamar, 61; Louden, 64;
Loyalty, 63; Luke Blackburn, 197, 198,
199, 201, 204; McCreery, 170; Majestic
Prince, 196; Man O'War, 284; Milam,
174; Needles, 196; Never Say Die, 196,
207; Nijinsky II, 196; Northern
Dancer, 196; Pacolet, 20; The Parader,
250; Red Banner, 238, 249; Riva
Ridge, 196; Roberto, 196; Searcher,
170; Secretariat, 196; Skirmisher, 163,

164; Spendthrift, 175; Spokane, 211;
Sunday Silence, 196; Tammany, 241,
249; Trifle, 201; Truxton, 20; Vagabond, 170; Ventilator, 168, 169, 170;
Volcano, 169; Voltigeur, 168, 169, 170;
Warfield, 176; White Frost, 249;
    fillies: Addie, 249; Arab, 22; Bangle,
249; Belle Meade, 64; Belle of the
Meade, 173, 174; Beta, 34, 55, 56,
57; Bonita, 249; Bonnie Wood, 176;
Bounding Doe, 168, 169; Burlesque,
177; Caroline, 64; Corsett, 61; Dewdrop, 207; Espionage, 236; Eucre, 167;
Flaxinalla, 57; Gamma, 34, 55, 56,
57, 58, 61; Haydee, 238; Hermitage,
139; Indian Fairy, 249; Iroquois Belle,
249; Kathleen, 203; Leila, 35; Loyalty,
64; Maggie Hunter, 164; Peytona, 58;
Pique, 174; Planchette, 168; Priora, 61;
Sarah Bladen, 35; Swift, 206; Telie
Doe, 206; Tullahoma, 241; Vandalite,
166, 176; Vocalist, 168;
    geldings: Proctor Knott, 211, 212, 225,
231, 238, 282, 297, 332 n.73;
    mares: Augusta III, 280; Beta, 61;
Blondin, 176; Bribery, 231; Bric-a-
Brac, 205; Bude Light, 61; Corsett, 61;
Delta, 61, 63, 64, 97; Democracy, 246;
Diamond, 61; Equity, 34; Florestine,
34, 61; Gamma, 61, 103, 196; Gem,
64, 170; Giantess, 58; Gloriana, 63;
Immortelle, 246; Isabella, 57; Ivy Leaf,
168; Juliet, 34, 55; Kate King, 61;
Lida, 179; Linnet, 61; Little Trick, 81;
Madam Reel, 247; Mariposa, 250;
Martica, 205; Miss Peyton, 63; Mollie
Jackson, 166; Nannie Killam, 34, 61;
Nevada, 197; Nubia, 177; Seabird, 61;
Terbera, 248; Tinnet, 61; Trade Wind,
247; Tule Blackburn, 247; Velvet, 61;
Vesperlight, 166; Volante, 61; Wanda,
250; Woodbine, 200;
    sires: Albion, 63, 117; American
Eclipse, 63, 117; Anvil, 57; Autocrat,
57; Bagdad, 21, 22; Bertrand, 57; Bill
Cheatham, 163; Blalock, 57; Boaster,
21, 55; Bonnie Scotland, 22, 166-80
passim, 196-208 passim, 231, 281, 283,

Thoroughbreds (*continued*)
284, 296; Bramble, 199, 200, 203,
205, 206, 217, 235, 238, 244; Brown
Dick, 136, 163, 164, 167; Chanticleer,
55; Childe Harold, 63, 64, 97, 117,
163, 170; Clarendon, 239, 242, 249,
296; Clodium, 55; Commodore, 176;
The Commoner, 250, 276, 280, 283;
Dandie Dinmont, 247; Eagle, 21, 55;
Eclipse, 57; Enquirer, 170, 179, 180,
197, 198, 200, 201, 203, 205, 206,
208, 217, 219, 231, 235, 236, 238,
245, 296; Epsilon, 58, 59, 61, 62, 63,
117, 208; Fellowcraft, 203; George
Elliott, 63; Glencoe, 58, 117; Gleneig,
239; Great Tom, 176, 177, 179, 180,
197, 198, 200, 203, 205, 206, 210,
217, 235, 238, 243; Hampton, 246;
Hanover, 276; Harry Hill, 57; Highlander, 139, 163, 164; Huron, 249,
250, 276, 280, 340 n.25; Inspector B, 235, 238, 242, 249, 250,
276, 280, 340 n.25; Iroquois, 205,
207, 208, 210, 217, 231, 238-50
passim, 296, 297; Jack Malone, 63,
163, 164, 165, 231, 235; John Morgan,
171, 174, 179, 208; Jolly Roger, 55;
Kosciusko, 34, 55; Leamington, 179,
180, 199; Leviathan, 34, 35, 55;
Lexington, 63, 164, 166, 176, 179,
180, 197, 203; Longstreet, 242, 249,
250; Loyalist, 238, 242, 249, 250,
276, 280; Loyalty, 103, 163; Luke
Blackburn, 205, 206, 210, 211, 217,
218, 235, 238, 242, 243, 249, 250,
281, 282, 296, 297; Luzborough, 35;
Madison, 246, 250; Melsare, 55;
Merman, 55; Messina, 21; Mont d'Or,
250; Pacific, 34, 55, 61; Pacolet, 22;
Philip, 57; Picton, 57; Plenipo, 206,
210, 331 n.43; Priam, 57, 58, 59, 61,
63, 64, 117, 208, 231, 297; St. Blaise,
239, 243, 335 n.30; St. Simon, 246;
Silver-Eye, 55; Sir Archy, 22; Sir
Archy, Jr., 22; Sir Richard Tonson,
55; Sovereign, 171; Sterling, 55, 282;
Sythian, 64; Tithonus, 246, 249, 250;
Tremont, 238, 242, 247, 249, 335
n.10; Vandal, 164, 165, 166, 169, 170,
208, 231, 297, 326 n.10; Virginian, 57;
stallions: Torpedo, 167; Wagner, 56, 61;
other horses: Bob Taylor, 281;
Chappaqua, 249
Thruston, Gates P., Col., 116
Thruston, Ida Hamilton (Mrs. Gates P.)
(*see also* Hamilton, Ida), 116
Toombs, Robert L., 92
Torbet, Granville, 77
Totten, A. W. O., 156
Treviranus, Stewart, 179
Troye, Edward, 35, 46, 58, 164, 167, 283
Turney, Peter, Gov., 257
Turnpikes. *See* Roads
Tweed, William M. ("Boss"), 241

Ugly Club, 187, 329, n.32
Uncle Bob. *See* Green, Robert
Underwood, Noah, 77
United Cashmere Company, 139
United Confederate Veterans, 254, 261,
265
United Daughters of the Confederacy,
279
U.S. Army units: Army Cavalry School,
141; Indiana Infantry, Tenth, 92;
Michigan Light Artillery, DeGrice's,
109; Michigan Volunteers, Eleventh,
109; Pennsylvania Volunteer Cavalry,
Fifteenth, 112; Regiment of Mounted
Rifles, 84, 141; Tennessee Cavalry,
Tenth, 122; Tennessee Infantry, Tenth,
93
United States Government: Office of
Archaeology and Historic Preservation,
68; Senate, 182, 194; Sixth Circuit
Federal Court, 194; Supreme Court,
52, 218, 262
United States Military Academy. *See*
schools

Van Dorn, Earl, Gen., 111, 143
Vanleer, Anthony Wayne, 19
Vanleer, Bernard, 19
Van Ness, Louisa Looney (Mrs. Allen),
287
Vaughan, Johnson, 133
Vaughn's Gap, 50, 222

Vaulx, Alex (carriage driver), 148
Vaulx, Hamit (dining room servant), 148
Vaulx, Jacob (laborer), 148
Vaulx, Milly (child), 148
Vaulxhall Gardens, 44
Vernon, Harrison ("Bud"), vii
Vertrees, John J., 273
Voss, Margaret Price (Mrs. Ronald L.), 297

Wade, Henry, 21
Walker, Bethenia, 307 n.21
Wall, Moses, 269, 272
Wallerstein, Larry, 288
Warden, Margaret Lindsley, 196
Warner, Charles Dudley, 194, 223
Warner, Edwin, 283
Warner Parks, 293, 296, 342 n.37
Warner, Percy, 247, 293
Washington, George, President, 15
Washington Peace Conference, 84
Watkins Hall, 254
Watkins, William, 110
Watson, Thomas, Col., 58
Watts, Hearn (U.S. Commissioner of Agriculture), 150
Webster, William J., 203
Welling, J. C., 285
Wells, Thomas, 48
West, Edward William, 152
West End Park (Acklen Park), 284
West Meade, 40, 190, 194, 216, 218, 221, 236, 247, 255, 261, 263, 293, 296, 297, 334 n.5
West Meade Farms, 297
West Nashville (New Town), 214

West Point. *See under* Schools, United States Military Academy
White, George W., 171
Williams, Gladys (Mrs. John M.), 253
Williams, John H., 72
Williams, Willoughby, 133
Williamson, R. N., 77
Williamson, Robert, 139
Wills, Irene Jackson (Mrs. Ridley II), 288
Wilson, James H., Gen., 144
Winchester, James, Gen., 242
Winder, Martha Ann Grundy (Mrs. Van P.), 304 n.17
Winder, Van P., 304 n.17
Winston, Charles K., Dr., 97
Wood, C. H., Capt., 95, 96, 98
Woodard and Shanklin Yearling Sale, 244
Woods, Joseph, 23
Woods, Robert, 23
Worley, Frank, 175
Wormer, Grover S., Capt., 104, 105, 108
Worth, Jackson, Gov., 151
Wortham, E. A., 297
Wyatt, Faye Hocutt (Mrs. Joe B.), 295
Wyatt, Joe B., Chancellor, 295
Wynne, Alfred R., Col., 57, 165

Yeatman, Thomas, 23
Young, G. Chapman, 212
Young, Milton, 197, 199, 225, 226, 227, 280

Zollicoffer, Felix, Gen., 86, 90
Zolnay, George, 264